D1599484

Infinity Beckoned

Outward Odyssey
A People's History of Spaceflight

Series editor
Colin Burgess

Infinity
Beckoned

Adventuring Through the Inner Solar System, 1969–1989

Jay Gallentine

Foreword by Bobak Ferdowsi

UNIVERSITY OF NEBRASKA PRESS • LINCOLN AND LONDON

© 2016 by Jay Gallentine
Foreword © 2016 by the Board of Regents
of the University of Nebraska

Library of Congress
Cataloging-in-Publication Data
Gallentine, Jay.
Infinity beckoned: adventuring through the
inner solar system, 1969–1989 / Jay Gallentine;
foreword by Bobak Ferdowsi.
pages   cm.—(Outward odyssey:
a people's history of spaceflight)
Includes bibliographical references and index.
ISBN 978-0-8032-3446-8 (cloth: alkaline paper)
ISBN 978-0-8032-8515-6 (epub)
ISBN 978-0-8032-8516-3 (mobi)
ISBN 978-0-8032-8517-0 (pdf)
1. Space probes—History—20th century.
2. Artificial satellites—History—20th century.
3. Inner planets—Exploration—History—
20th century. 4. Moon—Exploration—
History—20th century. 5. Outer space—
Exploration—History—20th century.
6. Astronautics—Biography. 7. Astronautics—
History—20th century. I. Title.
TL795.3.G355 2016
629.43'54—dc23
2015008519

Set in Adobe Garamond Pro by L. Auten.

Dedicated to the people of Crimea.

May this help to communicate what you
and your lands have given toward Earth's
understanding of the solar system.

Большое спасибо!

In the eyes of the world they have no names or faces.
Not many people know who they are.

Erect an obelisk and inscribe their names in gold, so that they will
live on in the minds of their successors for centuries to come.

We pay tribute to them, value them,
and care about their personal safety.

—Soviet premier Nikita Khrushchev

Contents

Illustrations

Foreword

If I have seen further it is by standing on the shoulders of giants.

—Isaac Newton

When *Curiosity* landed on August 5, 2012, I celebrated one of the most meaningful moments in my life. Looking around the control room, I saw the faces of men and women I had spent the last nine years with, helping to design, build, test, and operate a spacecraft to the surface of Mars. I cried tears of joy, not just because of the hard work I had put in, but because I knew that all of us had done it together. The accomplishment of landing a one-ton rover on the surface of another planet took thousands of people, long hours, and many personal sacrifices. There's a singularity of focus that comes with such a challenge, but that doesn't mean there aren't moments of disagreement or personalities that don't mesh. Nevertheless, in that moment, in the control room, watching the telemetry tell us we had a happy rover on the surface of Mars, we were a perfect family, rover and all. Exploring the cosmos, after all, isn't just a robotic endeavor—it is ultimately the people who make it happen.

Jay Gallentine's *Infinity Beckoned* tells the story of how the world went from peering from the surface of our planet to sending robotic explorers to the surface of planets like Venus and Mars. More refreshingly, it tells the story of the people behind the missions—the people who made the giants happen, that missions like Cassini and Curiosity stand on today.

It's a fascinating insight into the kind of people who have the willpower and patience to spend decades of their lives turning a dream of understanding the cosmos into a mission that can answer those questions. It's something we can all learn from: these incredible accomplishments take people and personalities who have a vision, but more importantly, have the strength of character and tenacity to turn that into a reality.

Infinity Beckoned gets into the experiences of these men and women who send robotic proxies to explore the solar system. The story delves into their lives and the stories surrounding their adventures. It describes the challenges they face personally and professionally, the woes of failures and the highs of achieving their goals.

As someone who has been inspired by these missions and the people who toil to make them a reality, I was fascinated to realize the parallels between the pioneers and our Mars rover. What was especially intriguing to me was to read about the Soviet space program—and the people behind it. As a student of history, I know a little about the Soviet robotic exploration program—the many setbacks and incredible accomplishments—but it was fascinating to read about the people behind the projects for the first time, to see the tremendous hurdles they had to overcome—different from ours. Often pressed by their government to perform firsts in space exploration, with short deadlines and resources lagging those of their American counterparts, sometimes with reluctant and corrupt industry partners, these men and women came up with innovative solutions that are impossible for me not to admire, particularly as an engineer.

I was also fascinated by the parallels to my experience with team members on Curiosity. Like the folks in *Infinity Beckoned*, the space bug bit members of the Curiosity team at different times in their lives. For me, it was the moment I saw the Mars Pathfinder mission in the summer of 1997. While I had always loved science fiction, the realization that we were driving cars on Mars meant that the future had already arrived, and I wanted to be a part of it. Eventually I'd get to work with the men and women who made that happen. Our brilliant and fearless leader during entry, descent, and landing, Dr. Adam Steltzner, often talks about seeing the night sky while driving home one night and realizing that it was not the same as before— the question of *why* led him to a career in space exploration.

The flip side of that token, of course, is the sacrifices to make these missions happen. The missed events or dinners with friends due to testing, sometimes the working through the holidays to ensure the spacecraft or rover has an eye on it, can be difficult for relationships. I won't purport to speak for everyone and say that it's worth it, but I will say that few things in life result in a more satisfying experience. If you haven't seen the footage from the *Curiosity* landing, it's fear and tension for most of it, then the raw emotion of sheer joy and tears and happiness at the end. It's the realization that the difficult work, long hours, and sacrifices were not in vain. It's about being part of something so much bigger than yourself. I see the same in this book, and I hope that everyone gets to have that experience in life.

Throughout the book, Jay manages to chronologically tell the story of the origins of the robotic space program while infusing that timeline with the origin stories of the people behind these undertakings. For many it's a love of space coupled with a moment when they happened to be captured by their respective national programs. Many have an innate curiosity about the universe, attempting to answer the fundamental question of whether we are alone—to provide a context for our world in the solar system. As the story progresses we see the growth and expansion of robotic exploration in parallel with the evolution of the engineers' and scientists' lives, their roles in these missions intertwined with professional and personal challenges. Even as this exploration reaches a fervor in the late 1970s and early 1980s, we see these men and women check off their bucket lists for space, most of them always wishing to keep asking questions and exploring, never satisfied. Even after these missions were long over, these people were still poring over results, trying to answer the questions asked by an ambitious space program.

Today, missions to our neighboring planets continue to ask many of the same questions, sometimes taking a step back from the zealousness of the 1970s to address fundamentals, taking cautious steps into the darkness of space and the darkness of knowledge science has yet to answer. With missions to Mars, orbiters and rovers alike went back to fundamentals— not the question of life directly, but questions about the history of Mars: whether there was once (or is) water on the surface, whether the ingredients life requires were there. These are in large part a continuation of the Viking research experiments that this book covers in detail—while also trying to conclusively answer the same question, step-by-step.

I remember watching the original *Cosmos* series, hearing stories of explorers and scientists throughout history into the early days of cosmic exploration (to be fair, I hope this is still in the early days of what one day people will look back on as the foundation for a species moving beyond a single planet). Carl Sagan was a spokesperson for a way of thinking about our humanity and our species: that Pale Blue Dot. I remember rewatching *Cosmos* during *Curiosity*'s eight-and-a-half month cruise to Mars, and as the episodes came to an end, being sad that Carl would not be there to witness our rover's landing. I think it would have made him happy.

Reading through *Infinity Beckoned*, I'm reminded of the personal and professional connections to the men and women who helped paved the way. The stories in this book tell not only of the projects and programs that led us to send proxies off of our planet and on to others but also of the people who through their dedication and patience and hard work made it happen—and what it took for them to persevere through challenges and adversity. These are stories from around the world and, in some cases, even from the same hallways and buildings that I work in today. There was a moment as I read this book when I realized I and many others are part of a larger family of people who were bitten by the same curiousness about the world, about doing things greater than ourselves. Reading this book was a chance for me to learn more about the giants on whose shoulders we stand, and I hope that everyone finds a piece of themselves in these pioneers.

Bobak Ferdowsi

Acknowledgments

Contemplating who to thank on this book was almost as intimidating as writing the book itself. So many people have made such innumerable and invaluable contributions along the way. My dear, dear wife, Anne, is perhaps the most patient and understanding person I will ever know. Who else could put up with so many dinnertime conversations about space probes? Anne, I cherish you with all my heart and simply could not have done this without your love and support. To my wonderful sons Matt and Ben, your ongoing encouragement was of limitless value. You guys make me the proudest dad this side of the asteroid belt and I thank you both so very much.

Colin Burgess served a dual role of editor and counselor—offering advice and guidance and subtle nudges during those many times I needed it. Thank you, Colin! I am also blessed with the greatest publisher in the known solar system, the University of Nebraska Press, with Rob Taylor keeping watch on the project and assisting me with tons of questions. You're the best!

Even the most grand and regal thank-you that I could extend to Alexander Dzhuly is simply not enough. This lifelong resident of Simferopol spent years educating me on the beautiful Crimean Peninsula. He unearthed everything from 1970s car maps to railroad timetables and information about bus fares to period photographs of the towns and provided endless rich detail about the region, its history, and its present state. From him I learned the topography, the culture, the people. He was always very patient and understanding with the language barrier and explained the tiniest of trivia with broad descriptions and photographs or video. Alexander, you are a true ambassador for your homeland and I am deeply in debt to your generosity.

A cascade of appreciative gestures to Philip Corneille—fellow of the Royal Astronomical Society and the British Interplanetary Society, seasoned space writer, and all-around great guy. Philip reviewed early drafts, asked constructive questions, and continually prodded me to settle for nothing less than the best, most interesting, and rare photographs I could possibly trowel up. He was a constant sounding board.

I am highly appreciative of all those who sat for interviews and told me their amazing stories. Roald Sagdeev set aside three valuable days of his own time to discuss his remarkable life. Pat Straat and I held many week-end conversations about Viking. Alexander Basilevsky and Viktor Kerzhanovich seemed to never tire of my "What was it like?" kinds of questions. Gil Levin and Jerry Hubbard and Klaus Biemann and Fritz Woeller and Don Hearth all maintained running dialogues while their respective sections took shape. Frank Borman and Chris Kraft gracefully fielded repeat inquiries about a Soviet flight that took only a week out of their lives but months out of mine.

Many participants were also very generous in examining their personal photographic collections to provide never-before-seen imagery. Hans-Peter Biemann, in particular, sifted through the hundreds of photographs he snapped during the Viking surface operations and filled several requests, with the assistance of his father, Klaus. JPL's Bob Preston dug through his Vega files and sent one wonderful shot after another. Nikolay Babakin provided many images of his own father, Georgiy. Izrail Rozentsveyg kindly sent many pictures I would have only dreamed existed. He also put up with my struggling Russian and repeated translations to ensure that I had faithfully described his experiences.

I am indebted to Joy Margheim for professionally copyediting this work. The role of an editor should never go unrecognized. Terry Sunday's encyclopedic knowledge of aerospace history and diligent fact-checking have been immensely valuable in improving the accuracy of this work. Much appreciated, Terry!

A deep bow to Ralph Gibson, photo librarian at RIA Novosti's UK Bureau in London. Ralph was of great assistance in finding rare images and graciously put up with all my "Have you got any more . . . ?" kinds of questions. Tamara von Schmidt-Pauli provided critical assistance in translating select documents from their original Russian.

Kudos to biophysical chemist Eric Peterson for helping me to understand mass spectrometry and gas chromatography and peroxides and perchlorates and so many other bits of chemistry on which so many important questions hinge. Oodles of gratitude to Daniel Kojiro and his associates at Ames Lab for connecting me with members of the Gas Exchange experiment from Viking. Daniel, you're helping to keep history alive!

I greatly appreciate the assistance of Sven Grahn for educating me about radio in general and space radio in particular. Don Mitchell provided indispensable information about Soviet planetary exploration. In addition, he is to be credited with preserving and enhancing so many amazing photographs taken by Soviet spacecraft that might otherwise be rotting on forgotten reels of magnetic tape. Fellow space history writers Brian Harvey, Asif Siddiqi, and Paolo Ulivi are also to be credited with helping me endure the seemingly endless fact-checking. Francis French netted some thoughts from Al Worden about Lunokhod. Thanks to Michael Carroll for such motivational enthusiasm and his contribution of amazing paintings.

No list of acknowledgments would be complete without mentioning the cherished Ms. Kay Griffith, who likely has no real idea of her lasting impact. Ms. Griffith, not only did you artfully demonstrate how humor and the teaching of high school chemistry could go hand-in-hand, but you instilled a certain fearlessness in me that engendered confidence when plodding through the multitudinous scientific papers and other minutiae that go with the territory of this subject. I can still warmly recall your hilarious lectures on oxidation-reduction reactions and, of course, The Atom Hotel. Without you I wouldn't have the word "precipitate." My twenty-five-year-old notebook still rests proudly on a shelf where I can get to it at a moment's notice. The outcome of your efforts is interwoven all through the following pages, and to you I extend *the* most sincere of thanks.

Introduction

Listen, and you might hear them. Or you might not.

Either way they're out there: drumbeats. With low lumbering tones, they sound in a fashion that is barely discernable from the ever-present murmurs of earthly background noise. Although very faint the beats are immensely powerful, and only certain individuals hear them. For those tuned in, they are a beacon. An undercurrent of rhythm. A call to arms—urgently shaking people out of bed in the morning, tugging, sending hands lunging for coffee, whiplashing them out the door to seek what they cannot help but. The incessant tempo energetically propels these individuals through adversity and frustration and the sweet nectar of success and cannot be turned off and simply will not let them rest for long.

The drums have always been out there, quietly summoning, but picked up strength around the time World War II ended and these newfangled things called *rockets* gradually took to the skies. Of course it's not rockets per se that were so new or fangled at that time; the concept arced back through millennia of pesky technological maturation. Over two thousand years ago, curious Greek handymen filled hollow balls with water and lit fires underneath. Steam would blow out through little nozzles on the balls' midsections and spin them round. Outcome: plaything. Hundreds of years later, Chinese soldiers employed tiny gunpowder rockets against the Mongols. By today's standards they were more firework than arsenal; Wisconsin residents get stronger stuff in a Happy Meal. But China's "flaming arrows" represented another stepping-stone laid down upon evolutionary waters. Rockets, in concept and in practice, are very old indeed.

That which emerged in the late 1940s, then, was an idea hitting puberty: rockets able to carry things of substance to great heights and over long distances. In particular, the German war machine sired a four-story cylinder of hell called the v-2. Launched from divergent sites in northwestern Europe, each carried an elephant's weight of explosives to the atmosphere's jagged edge at three thousand miles an hour . . . crossing two hundred linear miles to flatten a London city block. Extraordinary, unparalleled, and biblically terrible all at once.

Regardless, Germany lost and their v-2s fell into plundering hands from the Soviet Union and America. Engineers who understood what they were looking at recognized a v-2 as the gateway drug it really was. This rocket could literally get them high—beyond the atmosphere and up into that which had long ago been christened *space*. And the pieces clicked: *that's* where those primal, beckoning beats emanated from. All that apparent nothingness up there is exactly what'd been yanking people from their sleep. *Nothing* must be *some*thing. Upon their grasping this, the drumbeats only grew enticingly louder, because rockets functioned as a method to reach the source.

Every goal changed over time. In the late forties, it was all about reaching as high as possible into that mysteriously discomfiting transitional region of the upper atmosphere where blue skies went to ink. This area could now be examined scientifically, using a former weapon of war to lift experiments instead of explosives. As the 1950s drew to a close, Earth's two superpowers gleaned the rich PR value of orbiting radios and cameras and science-fair gadgets. Wheels of progress began turning more quickly. Things started flying at the moon: past it, into it, around the back of it.

Governmental crosshairs subsequently refocused onto the neighboring planets. Understand that something of a natural property line bisects our solar system into two distinct regions. An "inner" territory harbors Mercury, Venus, our own Earth and moon, plus Mars and its moons. Past those lies a mostly benign ring of asteroids; it's the divisor. Many feel this "belt" of cosmic debris represents the mortal remains of some wannabe planet that long ago tried very hard to join the club, yet never managed. And then, worlds beyond the belt signify "outer" planets: the enormous, gassy-glassy marbles of Jupiter and Saturn, plus Uranus and Neptune. They are numbingly far away in distance and time and mentality combined.

Nearness aside, even inner planets proved elusive to early 1960s knowhow. Mars picked up a nickname: the "Great Galactic Ghoul," because spaceships never seemed to get there in one piece. Ever-more-giant rockets blew up, electronics crapped out, instruments failed. *Sooo* many lessons still to be learned, and all the while, these planets seemed to be winning. They unfairly devoured numerous precursor missions having goals no more ambitious than the rudimentary metering of vital signs during a short fly-by; the slow creep of technology permitted little else. Just *go*. Prove out some design element. Snap a picture. Learn enough to send more elaborate gear the next time around.

Further complicating this effort was the simple problem of not really understanding what lay out there in the first place. Nobody knew, for example, whether their moon-landing craft would alight upon a hard, rocky surface—or collapse into layers of thick dust. How about Mars: did it really have canals, as some had insisted? Was Mercury radioactive? And that she-devil Venus . . . were her clouds hiding lush tropical oases, or brutally hot netherworlds? Elementary school facts we nowadays take for granted remained pure conjecture at the time.

By the mid-1960s, much of this dirt-under-the-nails groundwork was down and well tracked. Rockets and probes finally did manage to start going the distance—flying-by a target to rewrite science books. Perhaps it's obvious, but none of these space jugs ever carried any people. They were unmanned—modest boxes of wires remotely puppeteered by earth-bound explorers. Regardless, nothing had yet to *visit a surface*. Driving past France's Louvre art museum is fundamentally different from going inside. Who wouldn't want a ground view? To maybe dig around a little?

Followers of the beat slowly improved on methods and workmanship, compiling arsenals of the needed gadgets and goodies to delve ever deeper. Engineers and scientists learned to build on their skill-sets, applying lessons from the past to what sat on tomorrow's drafting boards. And as the 1970s appeared on the horizon—delivering forth new generations . . . and budgetary crunches . . . and unfortunately disco, the locus of exploration began shifting. No longer would ventures to Venus, or Mars or the moon, revolve around boring fly-bys or coarse atmospheric measurements, or average-quality photographs from tens of thousands of miles away. Instead, mission architects thought more in terms of making port. Fly-bys could give way to *stations*: on-the-scene robotic habitats capable of supporting extensive scientific research. Deconstructing the atmosphere. Analyzing soil. Testing for life. Returning samples. Making any of that happen would require bleeding-edge electronics, metalwork, automation, remote control. And plenty of good ol' sweat.

Those manic beats are the siren song of space exploration, a rhythm that demands endless hours of labor in pursuit of machines never before created, flown, operated, ambulated, or driven—which are then sent off to worlds millions of miles away to probe the unprobed, roam the uncharted, and discover the new.

The people who do this work are not like others. Some heard the beats as a sort of professional accident—experiencing them only in adulthood, because an intriguing work-related tangent caught their fancy or after the boss-man assigned a particular task. Others got into it because they had mechanical minds and excelled at problem solving, and the field held a certain allure.

However they came, an unquenchable thirst set in—partly because the very last details will never be known. We haven't come remotely close to knowing everything about Earth, and for heaven's sake, we *live* here. The thrill of the hunt keeps everyone going. And entropy reigns. No matter how many uncharted byways are explored, or facts are bagged, the end of the road will never materialize. Some people wonder why we keep sending thermometers to Mars. Don't they already know the temperature out there? Yeah, but people know the temperature in Singapore, too: ninety degrees (oh, and humid). What about next week's forecast? Yup, ninety degrees and humid. But at some point Mother Nature will send a curveball of a cold front through there and, by golly, everyone will want to know what the hell's going on. Mars is in stasis no more than Earth is.

And so—armed with improved equipment and a fierce desire to understand, with ancestral pathways delicately laid—these gutsy adventurers embarked on a new quest to uncover the most closely guarded secrets of our inner solar system. It was work without precedent. No advice from wizened retirees who'd seen it all before. No user manuals. No "best practices." Yet persist they did, failing as often as they succeeded, and always pushing the boundaries forward.

Who were these faceless people who selflessly worked for us all? What exactly did they do? And *how*?

A good place to start is with Gil.

1. Beach Brainstorm

Good ideas are common. What's uncommon are people
who'll work hard enough to bring them about.

—Ashleigh Brilliant

Way back in 1951 Gilbert Levin was out for a morning drive.

Sunny, cheerful weather. Nearly perfect. At the wheel of a state-issue Jeep, the agile twenty-seven-year-old adroitly crawled his way along Santa Monica's famous beachfront, gazing around at everything before him. This was his job.

"A very nice one," he pointed out.

Santa Monica beaches offered much in the way of visual amusements. He watched people, appraised the endlessly restyling beach sands, embraced the busy soundtrack of surf and life. From the breezy air he caught whiffs of tanning oils and food vendors and garbage and seawater. Especially the water. Briny, outdoorsy, fishy. The water was why he'd come.

Every hundred yards or so Levin would brake and hop from the Jeep, ambling his rail-thin self on down by the water's edge to carefully fill one miniature, sterilized bottle with a sample of liquid prized by Southern California bathers. The bottle received a handwritten label and went into a case with others to wait patiently for the next sample to join their group—from down the beach another hundred yards or so.

Levin did this most every week. And that day, after yet another morning of said activity, he swung the Jeep around and trucked over to the California State Health Department's laboratory. There the bottles went into the hands of trained biologists who tested each sample in order to quantitatively establish how dirty the water was. Specifically, everyone felt most concerned about microbes of *E. coli*—that is, human feces. Were they swarming, or sparse? Test outcomes were used by Health Department officials to judge whether the water currently seemed unpolluted enough to swim in. "Based on the results, we established quarantine limits," explained Gil Levin. "At that time, this was very important because raw sewage from Los Angeles was being spilled out onto the beach." Citizens expected regular reports on water quality, and in this fashion the Health Department gave it to them. If, in 1951, you ever had to abort a Santa Monica beach outing due to signs proclaiming QUARANTINED, UNSAFE FOR SWIMMING, well . . . you can thank Gil Levin.

He liked the job—except for one bothersome problem, which hadn't fully coalesced inside Levin's active brain until that very morning: "We don't get the results of our tests for about a week," he grumbled. "So when we establish a boundary, it's based on *last week's* water quality, not the *current* water quality." So what good was any of this, then? People weren't swimming in last week's water. And that bothered Gilbert Levin very much. Having been fascinated with sanitary engineering since high school, not to mention having made it the focus of his college years, Levin was prone to get excitable about such trivialities. He pondered the issue more and more, this dilemma of testing time. How to speed things up? How to produce a more relevant water forecast?

Nice jobs don't always last. Within a year Levin moved back to the Washington DC area where he'd grown up and took a new job in public health engineering. Now he faced the greater responsibility of ensuring a safe and clean municipal water supply. No longer did his position involve sunny drives and leisurely collections of water from public beaches, yet Gil Levin was not a fellow who dismissed unresolved problems. It wasn't in his nature. So, despite the three thousand miles of Santa Monica separation, this troublesome matter of delayed water-quality results came surging back to command his attention.

He reconsidered the overall process. In a lab, techs had combined Levin's beach-water samples with something called a nutrient, consisting of vitamins and sugar and amino acids. Think of it as a growth stimulant, available by mail order in huge bags of ready-mix powder. For use it had to be sterilized. Any bacteria in the water ate this stuff—generating carbon dioxide in the process—and at some point they'd start giving off bubbles. So

1. Here's Gil Levin from his 1941 Forest Park High School yearbook, Woodbridge, Virginia. Home of the Bruins! Courtesy Gil Levin.

the California techs had to sit around for days upon end waiting to see if any little toots started forming in the dosed water samples. The greater the levels of bacteria, the greater the frothing.

"Evidence of their metabolism," clarified Gil Levin.

But to him it all seemed so darn slow and archaic. The quandary got him to thinking about a course he'd recently taken. In those days, postwar America occupied much of its time fretting about the potentiality of nuclear war with the Soviets. Endless articles jabbered about preparing for war, living through atomic bombings, surviving the fallout. And Levin's class had explored the handling of public radiation exposure.

"I got to know something about isotopes," he mentioned.

One day his frustrations over the water-testing method fused with his knowledge of isotopes to generate an idea that maybe you could somehow "mark" or "tag" the nutrient with low-level radioactivity. If it worked the way he thought it would, carbon dioxide gas coming off the water sample would be ever-so-slightly radioactive, and therefore a whole lot easier to detect because even your basic el cheapo Geiger counter measured radiation in unbelievably small quantities. So, wouldn't that dramatically speed up the testing process?

Levin called around to nearby chemical supply houses and amusingly discovered that he could order up lightly radioactive carbon-14 glucose. "It's a sugar that almost everything eats—from microorganisms to people," he indicated. "There are many companies that make that." And the prospect of doing what he proposed now seemed ridiculously easy. Just take a pinch of the nuked-up glucose—"That's all it takes," he assured—and stir it into the regular nutrient. Then park a Geiger counter over the sample, run the test as usual, and wait no more.

After piecing it all together, Levin mentioned the idea to his boss, who remarked, "Gee, that's not a bad idea." He really adored the concept. He liked it so much that he suggested Levin arrange a meeting with the dean of the medical school at Georgetown University (Levin's boss happened to know him). The two hit it off and in short order the dean presented Levin to the head of the school's Biochemistry Department, Walter Hess, who listened intently to the young charge before him and also pronounced the idea to be a sound one.

"Why don't you write a proposal?" came Hess's suggestion.

Levin went blank. "What's a proposal?"

Hess explained. If some governmental body were to show interest in this concept, Levin might obtain funding in order to conduct a smattering of research. But first the government had to be sold on the idea, and that's where a proposal came in. Think of it as a detailed sales pitch, in writing.

Today Levin chuckles at his erstwhile naïveté. "I didn't even know what it was," he snickered. The men drafted up some paperwork and forwarded everything to the Atomic Energy Commission, which promptly sat on it. For a *year*. As Levin explained, "We had asked for the magnificent sum of sixty thousand dollars and they just couldn't make up their minds." Hess got so fed up with delays that he finally collected Levin and the two of them marched down the Washington Mall into the AEC's temporary offices and cornered the guy reviewing their work. It was a completely unannounced ambush.

"Look," spat Hess. "We're gonna cut mustard here. Either you're gonna fund this thing or we're pulling out."

The AEC guy thought a minute and offered, "Well, tell you what I'll do. I'll give you six thousand dollars."

Levin felt ecstatic. "We took it!"

Others shared in the enthusiasm. From the weekly schedule, his boss carved out a day for Levin to spend at Georgetown in the biochem lab. There, the ex–beach worker set up a rudimentary shop and hired a man to assist in conducting the first experiments.

"It was remarkable," cheered Levin, on these early tests. "They were immediately successful!"

Other people his age had been into cars, or sports, but not Gilbert Levin. How rare is that—an undistracted young man, wholly consumed by the selfless task of providing clean water to the general population?

Every Friday his labors would recommence on the new water-testing scheme. And the more time he spent refining its particulars, the more his positive outlook ballooned. "I felt, here was a method that could solve some major public health problems. Prevent epidemics." He could help a lot of people. He liked how that sounded.

But clean water was only the beginning.

Little did Gil Levin know that one day in the hazy future his radioactive brainstorm would signal the presence of life on Mars.

2. What If . . .

. . . you could, tomorrow morning, make water clean in the world?
You would have done, in one fell swoop, the best thing you
could have done for improving human health.

—American ecologist William C. Clark, in a speech

After refining the experiment as best he could, Gil Levin managed to publish a few low-key articles about using radioactive cuisine in testing water
quality. The effort garnered little attention; he couldn't seem to coax any
city councils, boards of directors, or other stagnant legislative bodies into
implementing the process. "The threat of atomic radiation was so great at
that time that none of the states would readily accept it. Nor would the U.S.
Public Health Service." Levin didn't try very hard to disguise his irritation.
"They wouldn't use it when the amount of radioactivity used was far less
than you experience in an X-ray, and was less than the amount the Atomic
Energy Commission, at that time, said you could *drink*!" Gee, didn't anyone like good ideas? About the best he could get were halfhearted promises from a few states to maybe try the method—if some unthinkably dire
emergency arose in which they were in a complete pants-down situation.

"This really frustrated me."

Occasionally, however, preparation meets opportunity, and that's exactly
what happened in the trailing weeks of 1958. Levin's wife, Karen, wrote for
Newsweek magazine and that year the couple attended a Christmas party
thrown by the periodical's Washington Bureau chief—who also invited
somebody named Keith Glennan. By sheer coincidence Glennan just happened to be in charge of a new government entity called NASA.

Over martinis, Levin and Glennan small-talked their way through current events that included, for whatever reason, the topic of flying saucers. NASA's head honcho appeared social enough, so at one point Levin impulsively set down his martini and half-jokingly blurted, "Is NASA ever going to look for life on Mars?"

Glennan didn't seem the least bit fazed. "Strange you should ask that," he replied. "I've just hired an MD to set up a biology division, to do that."

Levin came right back with, "Well, I have an idea of how it might be done!"

Glennan seemed genuinely intrigued. "Well," came the response, "why don't you go down and see this guy, his name is Dr. Clark Randt, and I'll tell him you're gonna call."

"Great!"

What prompted Levin to ask was the sudden realization that his experiment wasn't so much about testing water quality as it was about hunting bacteria. And by doing so, he was essentially detecting the presence of life.

Jeepers—that's thorny business. As humans we seem to intrinsically know when things are alive, or not, but how is life even defined? How do you put a ruler on it? Objectively speaking, an entity judged to be "alive" has demonstrated the ability to consume, excrete, reproduce, and evolve. Leave any one of those out and you're in solid gray territory. (The first three criteria, for example, are met by *fire*.) Part of consumption is metabolism, or the process of converting food into energy. And metabolism is precisely what Gilbert Levin's magic idea happened to detect.

Of all the possibilities when trying to unmask a living system, why keep an eye on this one? Why not just set out a dish of food? Well, all known forms of life have to, in some fashion, process what's been ingested. A typical house cat isn't perpetually eating, or depositing another gift in its litter box, or even shedding—but it *is* constantly expending energy on activities like digestion or movement or growth or healing. So are we; it's involuntary. Go take a long nap and you're still metabolizing all the way through it. Metabolism indicates that an exchange of energy is taking place. One that affects an entire organism: its temperatures fluctuate; gases are released. And at a chemical level, what's transpiring is nearly identical among all known species. This *continual* and *never-ending* course of action can therefore be monitored much more easily than, say, waiting around for kitty to scarf up more Tender Vittles.

Presently Levin met up with Randt, who liked what he heard and requested a proposal. Slightly more savvy about such things, Levin produced one and less than a year later found himself the recipient of NASA seed money for the purposes of developing a Martian life-finding experiment. He wasn't even first through the gate: some biology professor at the University of Rochester was already cashing NASA checks to help hatch a bug-detector called "Wolf Trap." Perhaps that guy's first-over-the-moat stature had made the process easier for all who followed.

By this time, Gilbert Levin had amicably divorced himself from public health employment and instead cofounded a small environmental consulting firm in Washington DC. The offices of Resources Research lay within a rectangular brick two-story on northwest Taylor Street, just upstairs from a plumbing company. Four small offices complemented a quadruplet of long lab benches. "The space had recently been renovated, featuring grass wallpaper and built-in lobby furniture," according to Levin. He certainly wasn't able to devote himself full time to the NASA gig—it took up maybe 15 percent of any typical workweek—but had received enough funding to employ a couple of full-time assistants. They cataloged any design or procedural enhancements as memoed by Levin, typed everything up, and generally tried to keep pace with his effervescent imagination and new ideas that came in spontaneous, fully automatic bursts.

"There were no real deliverables," explained Levin of the arrangement. "It was just scientific research, and support of space biology research by NASA, with the ultimate intention of looking for life on Mars. So all I produced were reports!"

Every potential variable got attention: wet soils, dry soils, frozen soils. Frozen *and* dry. Pure germ cultures, mixed cultures, dormant cultures. They wanted simply to try everything. "We didn't know what the heck might be on Mars," he reminded of the time period. "If anything."

One issue that quickly sprang to mind was this: what happens if the thing lands on Mars, spritzes nutrient on a dirt sample, and radioactive carbon dioxide is given off—*but* it's really because of a chemical reaction? How would they know? "We could be fooled by it," Levin remarked—heightening the danger of blind trust in his own creation.

"But you know," he continued, "every experiment isn't a true experiment unless there's a *control* to demonstrate that you really had achieved what you thought." In this case, Gil Levin's team required a way to distinguish between a chemical process and one that was biological. On the surface that seemed pretty easy: chemicals react, right? But they don't *live*, so what if the Grim Reaper somehow paid a visit? What if they tested once, normally, then killed off any possible bacteria in the testing chamber and ran a second trial? It'd have to be done precisely, without disrupting basic chemical reactions. But the concept made good sense and topped their list of must-haves.

Tests continued, one round after another, while Levin struggled to flesh out every last aspect of how his final machine might realistically operate on the surface of a foreign world. Real operations got them all thinking hard. And that's when the group confessed to a fundamental flaw: without exception, every trial had begun with dirt already in the testing chamber.

Well, wait a second. How's it going to get there in the first place?

"We had no idea whether a spacecraft was going to have a sampling arm on it, or how the sample would be obtained," fretted Levin. One thing he did know was that the sensitive experiment required a laughably miniscule amount of dirt in order to work. "Just a few grains," he proudly advertised. "I'm sure it wasn't a tenth of a gram in total."

What if, he suggested, the machine had two projectiles fastened to its exterior? Like spear-tips, or bullets? Right after landing they fire off, trailing strings coated with a sterile grease. Dirt globs onto the strings. Reel each line into separate testing chambers, and voilà! Samples—one for the "active," they called it, and one for the control.

The group loved it. As Levin elaborated, "We constructed a control which worked the same as the original test. Except what we did was put poison, metabolic antibiotic poison, on the string. So that when the nutrient was put on there—if it were bacteria, there'd be no reaction." Any positive response from the poisoned chamber would definitely indicate chemical-specific behavior. "That was our control." A hallmark of quality experiments is simplicity, and by this point Gil Levin figured his was about as simple as anyone could make it.

The team next scrounged up a brilliant engineer named George Perez, who courageously assumed responsibility for producing the group's design. George organized their concepts and began collaborating with a contract fabrication outfit known as American Machine and Foundry. It lay just south of them in Alexandria, Virginia, and faced a respectable number of hurdles in transforming Levin's reams of paper into three dimensions. Look at just the sample-collection method. Easy to scribble on a Big Chief pad: *bullet shoots out string and reels it in*. Now try making such a device— one that must function perfectly every single time in a complete hands-off configuration, zillions of miles from Earth, with nobody around if it gets hung up. A device that wouldn't break the strings when they were fired. Or overstress the retraction mechanism. Extend that thinking to the rest of the machine: a device with some magic way to puncture glass vials and release the nutrient. A device that wouldn't blow radioactive dust into the Geiger counter and report back false positives. It went on and on.

But engineers hate giving in, and besides, Perez surmised that a flying projectile whipping out string really seemed like the kind of deal that somebody somewhere would've already perfected. So rudimentary as to be almost Neanderthal. "We went back to an 1860 patent for the design," Levin triumphantly reported, after weeks of research. "Used in the whaling industry! When they harpooned something, the rope had to uncoil very rapidly, and this had been developed as a method." New mockup tests showed that the properties of flying string really hadn't changed much in a hundred years. But Mars probably wasn't smooth and groomed and it sure wasn't oceanic. So Perez called for weak spots to be built into the lines—guaranteeing that any snags would break free and return a maximum of dirt to the sampling chambers. Both lines received a coating of sterilized silicone grease and Perez loaded twenty-three feet of it inside each hollow projectile. Every inch deployed smoothly, every time, and at that point the group reckoned they had the sample-collection end of it nailed down tight.

Bit by bit, everything slowly coalesced into a complete, miniature package weighing less than one and a half pounds. During peak operation the current draw measured just a couple of watts and used only two hundred milliwatts at idle. They installed one concept model on a wooden stand, complete with little brass nameplate reading "Gulliver." Into his arms Gilbert Levin hoisted the creation, twisting it around in the light to admire from all angles.

The contraption worked. It was lightweight, consumed a pittance of energy, and employed its own approach to bring in samples. In hundreds upon hundreds of trials the soil-testing regime had proved itself to be absolutely bulletproof. Exclaimed Levin, "The darn thing worked every time!"

The really big thing Gilbert Levin now needed was to pull off a full-up, bona-fide test in front of as many NASA bigwigs as possible. If he dared.

Three and a half miles due north of Washington DC sits the nondescript Upshur Park. It's a modest rectangle of walking paths and basketball courts and on a cold-ass winter's morning in 1961 played host to an entirely different sort of activity. Down at the park's southwestern corner, barely seven minutes by foot from his oddly wallpapered offices, Gil Levin positioned Gulliver on the park's frosty baseball diamond. Two helpers ran wiring back to an auxiliary box holding controls and a data recorder. Nearby, Freeman Quimby and Richard Young hunched their shoulders against the wind, biding time until things got underway. They'd come from NASA's Life Science Division in order to witness how the experiment they'd been funding might operate. Quimby functioned as Levin's sugar daddy, the NASA handler. Young played boss. Both men likely cursed the weather, but Levin's choice of seasons had been deliberate. Mars is particularly cold and dry, so running the test in winter made good sense.

After all was situated, everyone stood back at a healthy radius while Levin confidently flipped switches on the control box. With a *pop* two metallic plumb-bobs catapulted themselves out from Gulliver, arcing low across the diamond, thin lines of chenille whistling along behind. After both lines went taut the plumb-bobs snapped off, thumping onto barren ground. It was supposed to happen that way. Levin kept still with his arms crossed; this needed to be a hands-off demo.

Presently two bitty motors came to life—slowly reeling in the strings and sealing them within identical chambers. A buffet of spiked vitamins and sugar and other nutrients dribbled down over the strings. In short order little pinches of radioactive carbon dioxide ascended from the mixture in one chamber and contacted a small detector plate—in turn monitored by a shockproof Geiger counter positioned directly above. The counter lit up and began tracing its findings onto the data recorder beside Levin. His eyes darted over to readings from the control chamber, which'd been deliberately poisoned. Flat line. He smiled.

That day, all parties felt the test to be an unqualified success. Good news for Young and Quimby: every quarter they had reviewed Levin's activity reports, and every year they'd re-upped his funding. All the effort and moolah had paid off in spades.

Everyone abandoned the park to warm up, Levin utterly thrilled by Gulliver's exultant performance. It could detect almost *anything*. "We would run the string over a plate-glass window in our laboratory," he detailed, "and we would pick up enough microorganisms to get an immediate response!" The group wondered just what Gulliver's minimum threshold might be— how small of a sample could it detect. So for one test they prepared a known population of microbes and diluted it down until only fifty cells remained. *Gotcha!* Then another batch with only ten measly cells in the whole entire sample. *Found 'em!* What if something on Mars exhaled carbon monoxide, or methane, or even poisonous hydrogen cyanide? "It doesn't matter," asserted Levin. "*Any* carbon gas produced from the culture is going to use some of the radioactive carbon. And it will be radioactive."

Mr. Sanitation was beyond ecstatic. "Everything went beautifully with this experiment! It was just so sensitive and easy to use!"

As a small-business owner, Levin regularly felt himself to be the underdog in what had evolved into a multifaceted and surprisingly competitive landscape. By the time of Gulliver's ball-field debut, NASA had about twenty contracts going with all sorts of different entities—every one as focused as Levin on the development of their own life-detection methods. Some were huge corporations or sprawling universities with enough resources to detail an entire team to the effort if required.

Not long after the Upshur Park grand slam, Levin found himself summoned to a meeting with Quimby and Young at NASA Headquarters. From behind a desk, Quimby's supervisor introduced himself: Reynolds. *Doctor* Orr Reynolds, director of Bioscience Programs, thank you very much. The cordial atmosphere quickly dissipated as Levin's handlers informed him that they might very well have to confiscate Gulliver. As in: the instrument, the experiment, the design, the research notes. The whole shebang. Everything might be taken away from him.

All Levin could say was this: "*What??*"

"Yes," the men responded. "You do not have a PhD."

Levin slumped in his chair. After a bit he managed, "*What?*"

"And if this experiment *were* to detect life on Mars," they coldly went on, "we would have to have that scientist go around the world giving lectures on it. And you just aren't qualified."

Again, meekly this time: "What?"

The NASA men folded their hands. "So, we want *you*, we'll give *you* this opportunity, you select a PhD from this list." Levin glanced at a column of names on the paper shoved his way. The men continued. "He will become your co-experimenter. And that way you can stay associated with it."

Levin returned home in a mood. "I was an engineer. Not a scientist," he admitted, well aware of the hungry competition's readiness to devour his small-potatoes operation. "We knew the funding was limited. We knew the opportunity was enormous." As such, what else could he do but acquiesce? He reviewed the options and after several interviews chose to partner with a seasoned biologist at the California Institute of Technology, Norm Horowitz. "He agreed to be my co-experimenter," said Levin, finding the arrangement pointless. "He came once every three months and spent one or two days with me." Horowitz was short and stout and getting on in age. He wore glasses and frumpy clothes and a surly expression. The duo composed an unlikely pairing, forged more from politics than sensibility. They worked well enough together. In the beginning.

"Everything suggested that there was a good possibility of life on Mars," Horowitz later offered of his initial assessment. "The Martian environment appeared to be Earth-like, but a very cold and dry Earth-like environment. An extreme form."

Before long the guy's attitude on Martians—having started out with comments like "a plausible idea"—began to swing as Horowitz focused on new estimates of the planet's atmospheric pressure. They kept dropping. Liquid water couldn't exist at such low pressures, and most biologists categorized water as essential for any life to exist anywhere. Soon Horowitz had changed his tune completely. "There *can't* be any life on Mars," the guy started claiming, to anyone who'd listen. "Because there's no water on Mars. And if there's no water, there can't be life." Levin could never determine what a turncoat like this was doing helping him out. Caltech or not, *PhD* or not, Norm Horowitz failed to impress. And he'd been the top choice! After struggling for a relatively brief period of time, Levin felt the need for corrective action. One day at Resources Research he approached his business partner and said, "I wanna get a PhD."

"You can't do that," insisted the other man. "We can't afford to let you out of the business!" It was partially true; Levin juggled multiple projects and was a core bringer of revenue. The argument flirted with ugliness—escalating into a standoff about what was going to happen around there and what wasn't.

"Finally," remembered Levin, "we agreed that I could work for the company, Resources Research, 75 percent of the time. And I'd have 25 percent time off with appropriate salary reduction. And if I could work a PhD program in on that, okay." Satisfied, both men retreated to neutral corners and resumed business. With his newly freed-up time, Levin approached Johns Hopkins University and worked up a program thick with biochemistry and organic chemistry, plus anything else he could reasonably fit in that would satisfy NASA requirements and lead to Horowitz liberation.

Embarking on a PhD at this point in life for someone like Gil Levin is not exactly recommended. He lived twenty minutes from his Washington DC office and still appeared there every day in order to tackle the stacks of business. Come late afternoon, Levin would head out and grab a McDonald's hamburger to munch during the forty-mile commute up to Johns Hopkins in Baltimore.

"I went through three years of hell." His and Karen's five-year-old son was not exactly going to raise himself, so at the tail end of each long effort Levin would materialize in the family home to shake off that day's tribulations and pitch in however he could on the domestic end of things. Kid goes to bed, do homework, write paper.

Having so much going on is perhaps one of the reasons Gilbert Levin never tuned in to the goings-on of his associate. Not long after familiarizing himself with the particulars of Gulliver, Horowitz came to think that radioactive markers could be applied to life detection in other ways. While Levin attended his classes and worked his daytime projects and raised his boy and somehow managed to continue being a functional husband, Norm Horowitz began sketching out what would ultimately join Gulliver on the bitterly cold surface of Mars.

3. Dead at Birth

We would do some constructive work of trying to figure
out just what the hell it is we're gonna do.

—Don Hearth, describing NASA's approach to
Voyager development

An amazing thing happened in 1989—several, actually. First of all, the
Sega Genesis video game system hit North America. Who didn't get a rise
out of *Golden Axe*? And then a more or less impromptu concert kicked up
on the site of the original Woodstock Music & Art Fair, in celebration of
its twentieth anniversary. Possible crescendo: Pete Rose accepted a lifetime
ban from baseball due to, um, a few gambling-related hang-ups.

The aforementioned deeds may perhaps be categorized as profound, or
electrifying, or some other glitzy superlative. But really, none held a can-
dle to another mote of drama that also transpired that August.

Three billion miles away from video games and rock concerts and baseball, power surges and parking hassles and courtroom drama, a meek little spaceship flew by the planet Neptune. It did so after a twelve-year-long
slalom run arcing back through Uranus, Saturn, and Jupiter. "The Grand
Tour," it's called, for obvious reasons. The ship, known as *Voyager 2*, was,
along with its sister, *Voyager 1*, the valiant product of a feverishly dedicated
group out of Pasadena, California, at a facility known as the Jet Propulsion Laboratory. Essentially it's a wing of NASA.

Over a dozen years before their final planetary encounters, when they
were still under construction, JPL's twin machines hadn't yet been officially named. Instead, they possessed what could be thought of as a working title—a mostly bureaucratic, atrociously unmajestic, fifteen-syllable

string of mediocrity better suited for corporate accounting than planetary flight.

The ships were called "Mariner-Jupiter-Saturn-1977."

Although these creations were headed to parts unexplored, where was the grandeur in that name? The romance? To help rectify such naked injustice, anonymous hands erected a blackboard in one of the JPL common areas. Anyone floating through was invited to heft a chalk piece and scribble out whatever suggestions happened to mind. All kinds of possibilities went up on that board—things like "Pilgrim" and "Nomad," plus a ton of others. During this period some brave soul added "Voyager"—likely knowing full well how it would irritate the crap out of certain people.

"There was a lot of baggage to the Voyager name," remembered John Casani, who served as Grand Tour headmaster during its prelaunch phase. He had *not* been the person writing that name on the board. As Casani explained, "Years before there was another project which I happened to be involved in. It was called Voyager Project, and it was a project that was intended to go to Mars, and it was a very ambitious project." Therein did he employ a tactful choice of words, because JPL and NASA and the hordes of outside Voyager contractors who all bit off more than they could chew weren't merely being *ambitious*. They were foolhardy. Delusional. Gravely optimistic. They bit off things that weren't even there—appallingly outrageous impossibilities like four spacecraft on one massive booster. Controlled entry into a planet's undefined atmosphere. Pillow-soft landings on a totally unseen and unknown surface. What this original Voyager promised to do was, at that time, supreme folly.

In a sober monotone Casani reported the outcome. "Eventually, you know, it didn't survive." He stayed quiet for a moment. Dead projects generally never leave a minty-fresh aftertaste in anyone's mouth—especially of those who spent years laboring over them. In a way, Voyager's demise was shameful.

John Casani's discreet remarks may help in understanding the trepidation of some JPL'ers to christen their Grand Tour younglings after what many had regarded as failure. People tend to shun any association of their children with the infamous, which for example leads to a deficit of babies named Adolf. Yet once all the dust settled, Casani's new machines had inherited the name of a ghost.

This *original* Voyager was essentially birthed in the spring of 1960. Satellites and modest lunar probes had been flying for all of twenty-nine months. Just one year prior the Soviet Union had managed to swing one around our gray moon and send home pictures of its far side, which back then was quite a deal. It had everyone thinking about what might be next. Up and down the NASA corridors, people were starting to think big—like plump, car-sized vessels to orbit Mars and Venus for months on end, releasing landers to set down with expansive instrument packages. Weather reports from Venus. Surface photos. Life-detection experiments. Wouldn't *that* be plucky!

Getting all this fancy hardware out into space required a monstrous rocket booster. On paper NASA had one called "Saturn," conceived for everything from spy satellites to manned flight. And as soon as it went into production, NASA could also use a Saturn for this grandiose next-generation planetary ship. They called the effort "Voyager," and its very first public mention came during an aerospace industry conference that July. Like every planetary program, this one got assigned to the Jet Propulsion Laboratory. It did so as placeholder only, a shapeless cubby for dollars. Voyager's entire formal description occupied half a dozen sentences in the middle of some bland report.

By that time, JPL was operating somewhere between the outer realms of NASA control and the inner fringes of chaos. It had begun life in the 1930s as a side project at Caltech—where a handful of brazen forward thinkers had, among other ventures, strapped rocket engines onto aircraft for the purposes of rapid takeoff. That's where the concept of "jet propulsion" came from, and the name stuck—even though the Lab's eventual role had basically nothing to do with propelling jets. So from its very inception the facility regarded free-form experimentation as its birthright: measures of liberal and unrestricted thinking permeated every wall of JPL's campus.

Then, over in Washington sat the headquarters of America's two-year-old National Aeronautics and Space Administration. The distinguished gentlemen roaming *its* halls were about as far from a bunch of tin-bending yahoos as possible. Most of them had cut teeth at one of seven citadels of buttoned-down aeronautical study around the United States. When NASA took root in the closing months of '58, these facilities collectively became "NASA Field Centers." So Virginia's Langley Research Center was now the NASA Langley Research Center. Same job, bigger sign out front. And at places like these the work had always been disciplined, logical, structured, thorough. Langley guys knew how to run a project! Never would anybody willy-nilly bolt stuff together just to see what happened, which is how Pasadena liked to work. Strictly speaking, headquarters felt the JPL guys—though talented and energetic—were fundamentally a rogue band of undisciplined hippies, patently incapable of orchestrating their way through a dot-to-dot puzzle.

Such cold sentiments were mutual. For Pasadenans, the NASA brass represented a wad of humorless, suit-wearing bureaucrats who needed a fifty-page outline and ten meetings in order to make one decision and couldn't thread the gas cap onto a Plymouth Valiant. This kind of stylistic mismatch was plainly counterproductive. Yet these two opposites were supposed to mate in loving harmony, till death did they part, and rear an interplanetary spacecraft?

One of those suit-wearing fun-suckers at HQ was a bright fellow named Ed Cortright. He played second banana to NASA's director of the Office of Space Sciences. Like many associates, Cortright had migrated in from one of the research centers—Lewis Lab in Cleveland—having spent years immersed in the minutiae of topics like jet engine air intakes. He was a doer: the one inaugurating Voyager at that conference, and now the one in need of some go-getter to ramp it up.

The guy he had in mind was Don Hearth—an associate from the old Lewis days. Cortright liked him for a variety of reasons. Hearth had chops. He was organized and efficient. He put first things first. He didn't let politics get in the way of effective decisions. He always had a very specific reason for implementing what he did. And Hearth operated in a direct, unsugared manner that Cortright appreciated very much.

The only problem was that his star candidate wasn't exactly interested in joining the team. "I had just gotten promoted at where I worked," related Hearth. "So that was the end of that." He was entrenched within the Marquardt Corporation out in Van Nuys, California, producing little rocket motors.

But engineers are nonemotional, patient types and Cortright bided his time until a year later when the schedule took him to Los Angeles. The pair connected once again, where the NASA man learned that Hearth had warmed to his advances. "My wife and I and kids were enjoying southern California, but we were basically Easterners," Hearth elaborated. "So, you know it sort of was appealing to all of us." What might Cortright want him to do?

The employer-in-waiting explained that at NASA HQ, four major divisions controlled the vast bulk of the agency's activities. First came an Office of Manned Space Flight—currently stacked to the gills with a recent mandate to land Americans on the moon. Beyond that, two separate offices focused on advanced research and technological applications. Then there was Cortright's Office of Space Sciences, which broke down its role into half a dozen subdisciplines. They had a section for launch vehicles, one for grants and research contracts, another for budgets, and one dealing with the conduct of biological sciences. This latter group wished to do things like search for life on other planets.

Where Cortright saw Hearth fitting in was one of two remaining areas. He could take a slot in Geophysics and Astronomy. The other opening sat inside Lunar and Planetary Programs. Specifically, Cortright really wanted someone like Hearth to be "Voyager Program Manager." Geophysics didn't sound terribly exciting, so Hearth asked for more on what this other thing might involve. Cortright told him, "It's just in the study phase right now." NASA envisioned Voyager as their advanced planetary lander— more advanced, that was to say, than the puny Mariner probe JPL had only recently begun flying. Mariner seemed promising enough, but it couldn't orbit or land on anything. Only a few weeks earlier the first one to launch had veered off course and unintentionally become fireworks.

So Voyager didn't exist yet. "Okay, fine," dismissed Hearth—understanding that the name stood for more of a proxy concept than tactile hardware. "All it was, was something in the budget." Nobody knew what the darn thing looked like or even how much money it might cost. "They invented numbers to put in the budget," claimed Hearth, of headquarters' actions. "And I'm sure they were inventions. I mean, maybe Ed Cortright wouldn't agree with that, but I bet they were."

Nevertheless, Voyager's prenatal condition appealed to him as a pristine, unspoiled entity that could be taken from start to finish. No baggage, no unswept messes; the proverbial empty white canvas. He told Cortright to sign him up—then went home to inform the family.

"I inherited a paper program," is what he said.

Donald P. Hearth's new boss was not Ed Cortright but a rail-straight, type-A specimen of a human being named Oran Nicks who expected as much exceptionally high-quality output from his associates as he did from himself. "My greatest fear is living in a meaningless manner," he once wrote. Nicks was goal oriented. He came to work for the purpose of working. He wanted A players. He despised sluff-offs, put-offs, goof-offs, and write-offs. With a controlled smile, Hearth introduced himself and explained that he'd been hired as Voyager's program manager. Nicks pursed his lips. "Well, you know Voyager hasn't been established yet," he dissented. "It's still in the study phase." Hearth wondered if he'd said the wrong thing. Nicks continued. "So I'd like you to take the position of chief of advanced programs."

A job change on day one? The new hire stood there processing this other man. "Ed had told me good things about him," remembered Hearth of his new superior. "I didn't have any problem going to work for him." So Hearth replied, "That's fine, okay," and settled into his renamed assignment. Only weeks later came news that *Mariner 2* had safely made it off the pad for Venus. Hearth looked around at all the jubilant faces and silently confessed his lack of empathy. Like a new stepfather, he hadn't been around for Mariner's development. Or growing pains.

"I didn't know much about spacecraft, okay? And I didn't know a thing about JPL," he volunteered. "So I was on a learning curve, fairly steep learning curve, in those first several months." Right away he figured out that virtually every space mission *not* involving astronauts ran through Jet Propulsion. It worked this way because of posturing. Only months after NASA had formed, the Lab's director had sent an impassioned letter to the president's science adviser. In it he recommended that America "accept the concept of JPL as the national space laboratory. If this is not done, then NASA will flounder." Consequently, the Lab had in effect become NASA's sole-source vendor for lunar and planetary work. HQ ordered up what they wanted, and JPL gave it to them.

"I'm in there," detailed Hearth, wearily, of the endless meetings and bone-dry reports, "trying to understand what's going on in the world, and how spacecraft are designed, and, you know, what some of the driving forces are. And then getting a sense of the scientific community that had an interest in lunar and planetary exploration. Particularly planetary." Hearth had noticed how the Lab overtly prioritized Venus and Mars—as if these targets were somehow more prestigious or desirable than Earth's moon. Outer planets weren't even up for consideration.

And by gaw, did JPL seem to have its hands full already. Besides Mariner, the Lab was hammering the kinks out of some disaster-prone lunar ship called Ranger. "It didn't take me long just to hear from the scuttlebutt in the halls and talking to other people that Ranger was having its difficulties." Hearth wondered how anyone was going to explain away five straight failures of the cursed machine. In his opinion, the Lab had clearly overextended its reach—even though Pasadena's finest seemed to adore taking on more projects! Soon Hearth learned that beyond Ranger and Mariner, JPL was also scheduled to develop a lunar soft-landing machine called Surveyor that currently was . . . how else could he describe it? "A project in a horrible mess." What gave? "I *know* that there were concerns in Oran's mind and in Cortright's mind about JPL's ability to handle so much."

At least they were *building* Rangers, he supposed. Whether in a memo, a filing cabinet, or a snippet of lunchtime repartee, Hearth's newborn Voyager remained a blurry blob. After two years JPL hadn't even begun designing its chassis per se; their bulk effort revolved around the development of core technologies like power and navigation. Only in recent months had the Lab formally defined a few high-level attributes of what the Voyager mission and spacecraft would consist of. So already the project wallowed in ambiguities and risked never leaving the confines of a three-ring binder in Hearth's office—let alone planet Earth.

"They didn't want to have anything to do with this great big thing, undefined big thing. They wanted to keep building Mariners," Hearth accused JPL. "This was Bill Pickering right down the line." How could wheels of progress turn in a place like that? "If you weren't a Jack James or a Bud Schurmeier, you had a hell of a time getting any real access to the key talent in the JPL. And they had a lot of talent! Don't get me wrong." Pickering ran the Lab, while the latter men signified two of his star pupils.

Another gathering went on the calendar for that November. On the appointed date, three JPL planners met with Hearth and a colleague of his from HQ named Andrew Edwards. It was a long slog. Over the course of three headache-inducing days, nonstop meetings plodded through basic mission possibilities and objectives. Settled: Voyager would land on Venus or Mars. To do that, the group envisioned an in-orbit mother ship dropping one or more large entry vehicles. (Remember that part about *large.*) Farsight-edly, the men also discussed gouging out alien dirt samples and schlepping them on home for analysis. But everyone there agreed that mission objec-tives had to happen in stages: learn how to navigate past the planet before stepping up to orbiting. Add the landers only after acing everything else.

Now, these may not seem like very large differences. If it's flying by, the ship's already out there, right? What's the big deal with orbiting? Can't it just start looping around? Ah, no. Spacecraft must be precisely *inserted* into orbits: the exact velocity, at just the right time, lined up at the optimal angle. All this demands a highly sophisticated vehicle capable of micro-adjusting its speed and position—either autonomously or via commands from ground control. At the moment JPL's best of breed remained Mari-ner, and all it could do was fly by something. The ship's operational brain resembled a washing machine timer more than it did a computer. Jumping to "Voyager-class" technology, as everyone started calling it, would require major efforts all the way around.

On his tablet of lined paper, Hearth noted the agreed-upon progres-sion. Next, the men addressed a major concern about hardware steriliza-tion. It went like this: at some point in the future, either the United States or those uppity Soviets would succeed at landing on another planet. When that happened, the last thing anyone needed would be contamination of the unmolested landscape upon which they'd just alighted. Therefore, method-ical prelaunch techniques needed to be developed to thoroughly disinfect every part down to the last rivet and screw.

This whole area needed work. After baking one Ranger, JPL had pulled a warped spacecraft from the oven. Hearth fiddled with his pipe, mashing flakes of tobacco into the bowl and relighting them. His hand was sweaty from writing fast, cramped from writing for so long. Maybe this job change hadn't been such a sweet idea after all.

Once the JPL guys left, Hearth assembled his opinions for Oran Nicks. Despite the amount of material covered in their meetings, plus the group's overall harmony, Hearth had come away decidedly unimpressed with Voy-ager's inchworm progress. Specifically, he thought the Lab had been sit-ting on its duff for way too long. "It was clear to me," he later complained, "that JPL had very little interest in a Mars lander." JPL staff never offered up definitive schedules for future activities. They lollygagged. They were seventh graders letting the homework pile up. He felt double-irked that Lab workers had yet to submit the entirety of their Voyager expenses so far. The accountants would freak!

Don Hearth was a man gradually learning that JPL didn't care what NASA wanted. JPL answered only to Caltech. "We couldn't tell them what to do," he carped. "We *could not*." Oran Nicks certainly did not appreciate the slacking, stagnancy, lethargy, delinquency, negligence, or dereliction of duty. Time and again he memoed the Lab regarding yet another incomplete task, the language of his words escalating to the point where everything was YOU SHALL DO THIS, in all caps and with the strongest directives professionally imaginable.

Hearth just shook his head. "That didn't mean diddly in reality."

Immediately reassigning Voyager to some other NASA center seemed obvious. Yet as much as Hearth wanted to grab a phone and fire those Pasadena cud-chewers, his alternatives were zilch. "Where did NASA have to go?" he griped aloud. "Goddard was loaded! And look, Langley didn't have any space!" To Hearth neither would have been a quality fit, anyway. "They were aeronautical types," he intimated of the other two NASA centers. "They were researchers! They weren't project-management types."

With each passing week the alarm bells in Don Hearth's brain grew stronger. "Look, I'm sick and tired of waitin' for you guys," he finally told his JPL contacts. Ever proactive, Hearth rapidly spread two hundred thousand bucks between two private-sector defense contractors for in-depth Voyager design studies. First, they'd provide a check on the pabulum that JPL kept feeding HQ by reviewing the progress made so far. Third-party opinions would also, in Hearth's mind, demonstrate the agency's commitment to outside industries—as NASA depended upon the trail-breaking attitudes inherently present within them. Contractors needed to know that NASA wouldn't run away with all the funding and pay themselves for work. Profit could be found in space. Then the contractors, he reasoned, would likely sink plenty of their own money into the effort. And headquarters would therefore emerge with a much greater understanding of the capabilities present in outside industry. Good things all the way around!

After an exhaustive interval of proposal judging, HQ awarded the contracts to General Electric and Avco. The pair bested eight competitors, including a putzy firm out of Denver named Martin Marietta. The Martin engineers had demonstrated severe testicular fortitude by submitting the highest cost estimate—along with the largest percentage of those costs given over to administrative and executive salaries. *Come again?* Seventeen million *above* the next-cheapest guy did not shine well on any contractor. Additionally, Martin proffered the absolute largest number of estimated project man-hours—nearly two times that of the next-closest firm. No wonder they didn't get chosen.

Despite the GE and Avco involvement, Jet Propulsion blissfully continued its own freewheeling Voyager efforts. Hearth checked their progress and felt less than tickled. Near as he could infer, the JPL'ers were more or less ignoring every issue related to landing craft while focusing almost exclusively on the orbiter. One Lab study went so far as to discuss the particulars of separating an orbiter and lander during flight, while obfuscating nearly every detail of the lander itself.

Said a fatigued Don Hearth, "I was gettin' so damn frustrated that JPL wouldn't look at the entry problem into Mars!"

A world of difference separated Voyager's feather-soft touchdown from that of Ranger—intended only to whomp the moon while shooting pictures on the way in. The difference would be *control*. Think about an airplane headed for the runway. Cruise flight transitions to descent and must occur in a certain fashion. Things transition again on approach: the wings assume a specific shape, with the nose angled just so, as the plane bleeds off most of its velocity. But it can't fly like that at low speed, and so before long the configuration must transition again. As ground contact looms a bunch of wing extensions slide out and the plane goes nose up/gear down. Brake and reverse thrust. Landing must happen *in stages*, and this process would be no different on Mars. Drop from orbit. Enter atmosphere. All right, but then what? How do you decelerate without losing control? Use pop-out wings? A shaped parachute? And then, once near ground, the ship will have to change over to something entirely different—be it dinky rocket motors or shock absorbers or skid plates or maybe all of the above. Such was the minefield JPL didn't want to step in, which maybe helps explain their tendency to sweep it under the rug.

Furthermore, the Martian atmosphere was looking even thinner as of late. An uncharacteristically great photograph had just been taken up at the Mount Wilson Observatory in California. Snapped on a very dry, calm night, its recording of Mars's infrared spectrum carried forth bad news: the planet's surface pressure now appeared to be less than half as much as previously thought. Hearth extended Avco and GE's deadline by a month in order for both parties to address new complications born of "thin air." In private Hearth had already conceded to Oran Nicks that a 1967 Voyager launch was going to be pretty much impossible.

Perhaps *the* factor chafing Hearth most of all was that everyone seemed to be going about this whole process in the supremely wrong order. In essence, one and all were guessing about Mars. *Guessing* about what conditions really were like there, and then planning a very expensive mission based around all these whipped-up assumptions. Hearth couldn't believe it. "I rapidly realized," he began—in something of a huff—"that we didn't know a *damn much* about that planet in terms of its atmosphere. So how do you design a craft to enter an unknown atmosphere?!" It came out rhetorically. Despite having fifty years to mellow about it, the boondoggle still knotted up Hearth. All this time and money for a spacecraft mission based on imbecilic speculation! "Landing on a planet's a hell of a lot tougher than even orbiting it, let alone flying by it, let alone looking at it through a telescope!" he denounced. "Particularly if it's a planet like Mars!"

With each passing day Hearth felt more certain that an intermediate step was called for. Something *between* Mariner and Voyager. Secretly he'd been chatting with people out at Ames Lab—another NASA center lying off the southern edge of San Francisco Bay. Hearth treasured Ames's input, as they'd already compiled reams of research on entry methods. And guess what? Ames didn't like the Voyager approach either.

"Well, look, the next time we have a Mariner go to Mars on a flyby," pitched Hearth to Nicks during yet another sweat-and-coffee meeting, "put a probe on. As part of the payload. And basically send it into the Mars atmosphere." By this he meant an *entry probe*: a small, bucket-sized wad of sensors to measure the air—"in terms of *how* thick it was or how thin it was. *Before* we even tried to design something to go in and land."

Entry probes are never meant for landing or even long-term survival. They're scouts. The idea of one is to whistle down through a planet's atmosphere and characterize the environment. To take readings along the way—temperature, pressure, and wind speed are high on the list. Controlled, "soft" landing is never an expectation, or even part of its design, so at some point the poor thing obliterates itself.

Follow that by having some rudimentary ball clatter down on the surface and send back *its* findings (which early Rangers had also been slated to do, on the moon). Behind the curtain, Hearth prodded Ames into submitting a proposal for every bit of this. It would probably cost one-third as much as Voyager's gargantuan landing machine, currently planned to descend with vigilance under parachutes and steering rockets before magically plopping down upright on legs.

But tension levels around headquarters ratcheted up when Oran Nicks disclosed his hatred for the little stowaway-can idea. Nicks favored sticking with the existing plan. Hearth tried very hard to once again justify his rationale. "Have a sense of where you're goin'!" he advocated. "*Then* go in with a soft lander."

Nicks wouldn't hear of it.

"Don't!" challenged Hearth. "*Don't* do this great big multi-million-dollar thing until we get some direct measurements of the atmosphere!"

"No no no!" bellowed Nicks. He was not interested in arguments, counterarguments, grievances, reluctance, objections, disputes, or stopgap proposals.

After everyone's heart rates descended to normal levels, Hearth had gotten nowhere with his boss. As in, "He and I totally disagreed on what the strategy for exploring Mars ought to be." Ames's proposal? "Didn't get through the system," winced Hearth.

Comprehending Nicks's stark defiance calls for an appreciation of the enormous pressure blowing his way from vocal ranks of planetary scientists. "There was some heat coming in from that direction," Hearth affirmed. "They wanted to land big. Big big." See, up to this point, space scientists hadn't had many opportunities to catch a ride. At best they could claw-kick-bite-throw-a-tantrum for one of six to eight experiment slots on a Mariner—and those things weren't going anywhere near the surface of a planet. Conversely, Voyager meant deliverance: a luxurious quarter ton of payload, set right down on alien topsoil. Who *wouldn't* be clamoring for that kind of gizmo?

Oran Nicks wasn't the only one feeling squeezed by all these college types. Increasingly, Hearth had been attending meetings of the various space science committees in order to bone up on their specific goals. Every time, he came away with the same two conclusions. First, beyond the Caltech walls, JPL had a terrible reputation. "You'd begin to rub elbows with the Jim Van Allens," he reported, "and I heard a lot of that." Second, flying instruments in space was narcotic-like for these guys. They lived for the rush—and once it happened, berserkly needed another fix. How amused Hearth might have been to know that a counterpart in the world's other major space program felt the exact same way.

NASA had to fish or cut bait because sooner or later Voyager's bubble would pop like an infected zit. During a congressional presentation two years before, Ed Cortright had set the expectation of it as a two-ton orbiter— not including "several hundred" pounds' worth of descent probe. At that exact moment JPL was still trying to legitimize its scrawny Ranger, whose own bulk had been restricted to less than 750 pounds. Mariner came off the scale three hundred bills lighter than even that. So . . . NASA straight-facedly intended to shoot something at Mars weighing more than a Buick?

Hearth pulled the corners of his eyelids out and down, exercising them slightly.

"So you know, it became sort of apparent to me that this great big multi-million-dollar thing called Voyager seemed to be somewhat premature."

That summer, two men visited the offices of Gil Levin and Resources Research. Larry introduced himself as having a life-sciences background, while Jim was more into physical science. They'd come from Ames Lab in order to study Gulliver and run the machine through its paces. See, with new Mariners almost ready for Mars fly-bys, and then Voyager on the table, NASA's Bioscience Office felt a need to check in. What were the statuses of the dozen-odd life-detection experiments currently in development with agency funding? How far along were they? How were things looking? Levin knew of the visit in advance, although it came at a hectic time. He and his partner were in the process of selling their company wholesale to a larger firm called Hazleton Labs. Once the deal closed, Levin would assume directorship of a new Life Systems Division and essentially continue his previous activities under the same business name.

While striving to maintain neutrality, Larry and Jim nevertheless appreciated Gulliver's maturity. Frankly, they were blown away. Levin's instrument was "not affected by temperature, radiation, pressure, impact, or vibration," as they documented in the final report. "All requirements are within the state of the art." Both visitors duly noted Gulliver to be one of the very few experiments containing its own provision for sample collection. *Ni-i-ice.* "No major problem areas foreseen." They also commented that during the on-site visit, Gulliver had been "field tested in a flawless manner" and would likely be Mars-worthy with another $400,000 or so sunk into it. "In fact," concluded the men, "this experiment was the farthest along, in terms of hardware development, of all those surveyed."

Larry and Jim made a few other stops before returning to Ames. One of them was up at the University of Rochester to see a man with the slightly imposing name of Wolf Vishniac. Name and butchy goatee notwithstanding, he was a teddy bear of a microbiologist and eagerly demonstrated his aptly named Wolf Trap machine. It had been funded in part by a $4,485 NASA grant and monitored bacterial growth by dunking soil into water. If, over time, variations appeared in the water's overall cloudiness or in its acidity, little somethings had probably been growing in there. Vishniac smiled at his guests through large and dark-rimmed glasses. What did they think?

It was decent enough, though Larry and Jim identified many flaws. Alarmingly, the experiment didn't utilize real-world conditions; dirt on Mars undoubtedly wasn't bobbing around in little tidal pools. If Wolf Trap received too thick of a dirt sample, fluctuations in cloudiness likely wouldn't be noticed. Same problem if the dirt loved water and swelled up too much. Also, many soils are naturally resistant to acidity changes and might not demonstrate any variance at all even if they were loaded with bacteria. Or: the slow *chemical* release of acidic material could signal positive results for life—even though nothing had actually been growing. Fine dust sometimes rose in the water, creating more false positives. The visitors smiled at Vishniac, *Thanks very much*, and proceeded on to the next stop.

As the tree leaves began their seasonal color changes, Larry and Jim turned in their work, which in turn became part of a robust seventy-three-page *Survey of Life-Detection Experiments for Mars*. Three submissions—including Levin's—were deemed advanced enough to fly as early as 1966. Ames also brought up a few key disclaimers. Right on page one they flagged "the large uncertainties existing in knowledge of the Martian atmosphere, particularly surface pressure." The report also shamelessly noted how further development of life-detection projects was being hampered by "lack of a clear definition of the experiment-vehicle interface."

Immediately after Larry and Jim's departure the Gulliver testing resumed. Levin's team packed up and hit the road—traipsing back and forth across North America, consuming gas-oil-tires, their precious machinery wedged in the back of a van. One stop was California's Salton Sea. This meager body of water has more salt dissolved in it, by volume, than the Pacific Ocean. "We got a good response there," announced Gil Levin. Next stop? "We went to Death Valley," he said. "And where people thought there was nothing alive on hot sand, we *immediately* found living microorganisms, at noon, in the hot hundred-degree heat on the top of the sand!" The most surprised person of the bunch seemed to be him. "Not deep under, just even on the top!" In this instrument's capabilities, he found sheer amazement. "And we just built up a heck of a record for that very sensitive system."

North of Death Valley, they drove twelve thousand feet up White Mountain—home to an extinct volcano and a 4,700-year-old tree considered the world's oldest. Bits of the most exposed and windblown rocks went into Gulliver.

Levin couldn't believe it. "We got positive responses!"

Shortly after returning from the trip, Norm Horowitz approached his colleague.

"Gil, guess what?"

Lately Gilbert V. Levin had been feeling upbeat. Not only a trouncingly good visit with Larry and Jim, but every last mote of classwork had been finished. He stood there inside Resources Research as a recently anointed PhD graduate in environmental engineering and *wait*, did Horowitz just say something? Levin tried but couldn't guess the news, offering Horowitz a last laugh.

"He got funded," said Levin, genuinely surprised at the development. Behind everyone's back, Norm Horowitz—while simultaneously insisting that Martian life could never exist—had nonetheless developed his own way of testing for it. He'd become competition. It happened too late for Ames's survey, but his money had begun flowing after submitting proposals to NASA.

What Norm Horowitz created was based on the idea that for life to survive on Mars, it would need some easy way of fortifying itself, as breakfast cereals are not yet shipping there. He reckoned that alien organisms would most likely use the sun in conjunction with atmospheric gases—like plants do with photosynthesis. Horowitz therefore proposed the following: Seal Martian dirt inside a vial. Blow in little puffs of carbon dioxide and carbon monoxide that've been spiked with radioactive markers. After a good hundred hours or so of "incubation" under sunlight, any radiation present in the soil would mean that organisms had metabolized the available carbon gases. *Voilà* . . . life.

It bore the title "Carbon Assimilation."

"An experiment that would work under Martian conditions, and that involved no liquid water," asserted Horowitz. It was a clear dig at the aqueous Gulliver—which, in addition to needing water, also required a tropically warm chamber with which to prevent that water from freezing. *Too many Earth-like dependencies*, charged Horowitz. Mars wasn't that tepid and probably didn't have any water on it!

Levin continued, "Then he told me he was leaving." It felt like Horowitz—the guy who was supposed to be his *partner*, his *mentor*—had hung around only long enough to swipe the idea of radioactive markers in a testing medium. "I thought since it was *my* technology that he was using," said Levin, "I should be a co-experimenter on *his* experiment!"

"But you know," Horowitz insisted before departing, "if there IS any life on Mars, only my experiment can find it." And that was the end of the shotgun marriage.

His cage a bit jiggled, Levin returned to his slightly less cramped work environment. Managerially he excised Horowitz from the Möbius loop of Gulliver correspondence and meetings and scheduling and experimentation. Over there on the shelves sat three versions of its hardware, demonstrating the evolution of life-sensing technology. Perhaps one day, thought Levin, humble Gulliver might even fly to Mars. He'd caught wind of something in the works called Voyager, though none of his contacts knew any more about it.

Don Hearth wasn't sure where to head next. The giant Mars lander had seemingly become JPL's personal touchstone for every stiff neck and muscle cramp. *Increase our budget*, the Lab all but demanded. *Give us more control, and we'll keep workin' on Voyager.* "They just wanted to do more Mariners," scolded Hearth. "And they wanted to fly cameras. And okay, they'd take along some particle detectors, and, you know, look for Van Allen belts and stuff like that to satisfy the scientific community. But frankly JPL's objectives as far as I'm concerned, in those days, was *Whatever we can do to glorify Caltech and JPL*." Hearth ruminated: heck-all, he'd have been the first to get down on his knees in thanks for all the great services provided by Jet Propulsion. The solar system needed that place. But waiting on them might cost his project a full year's delay, meaning a definite no-go for launching even in '69.

Come December, Hearth jogged up two floors in order to join a meeting. He worked inside FOB-6, or Federal Office Building Number 6—spitting distance from the U.S. Capitol, at 400 Maryland Avenue. Its institutionally rectangular white structure could have passed for a Soviet apartment block. Inside, Lunar and Planetary got the fifth floor. Administration roosted up on seven. The whole of NASA HQ occupied a couple of additional nearby buildings as well and by this time employed more than two thousand souls.

That day, Hearth and NASA chief Jim Webb eagerly combed through the just-received Avco and GE studies, as well as whatever material JPL had bothered to release. For their part, General Electric advocated the stacking of two identical landers atop a single orbiting ferry. They envisioned stubby ice-cream-cone-shaped impact capsules that used little thrusters and levers to sit up straight after touchdown. GE also recommended specific Martian landing sites with high scientific potential. Nice touch!

Hearth and Webb moved on to the other submission. Pleasantly, Avco had tackled head-on such trivialities as lander sterility during construction. Excellent! And something called an "aeroshell" would be necessary, they argued—enclosing the lander like a huge piece of UFO-shaped Tupperware. During the entry phase it'd be a heat shield and then provide aerodynamic stability until parachutes took over. Right before impact the chutes would cut away and let Voyager hit the ground. Surrounded by crushable foam, the lander would roll around for a bit, and when it stopped, six triangle-shaped "petals" would open up and right everything. Silently Hearth praised thoughtful engineering. JPL never had this kind of detail!

Despite the hope and promise of these outside contractors, Webb shot down any idea of launching a Voyager in '69. It was just too much, he explained to Hearth—too much money and manpower, too much speculation, with too many assumptions. Too much talking through their hats.

Hearth vacillated, knowing how much tension the administrator carried. Webb's major stress point revolved around a national mandate called Apollo. Two and a half years beforehand, in May '61, President John F. Kennedy had gotten a little paranoid about what his buddies the Soviets were up to in space. As a result, he challenged America to land men on the moon by the end of the decade, and since then, four hundred thousand people had been laboring day and night to figure out how in the hell they were ever going to do such a thing. The challenge increased in relevance after gunshots felled Kennedy only a month prior to this meeting. Apollo was the dead president's legacy. *Nothing* should impede it. And so, Webb continued, everybody needed to hang tight until after its first landing. *Shelve Voyager until 1971*, he said. *Resources would be more available by then.* The reasoning seemed odd because in public Webb always sought balance— valuing planetary flight to the same degree as Kennedy's mandate. Hearth grimaced, collecting his papers. This meeting was at an end.

Resolutely he clung to his belief that amid Mariners and Voyagers they still needed some kind of intermediate step. Months ticked by as Hearth dragged himself from one meeting to another, wearing through endless sets of wingtips as NASA management frittered away 1964 debating the merits of various "precursor" flights and other such in-betweenies. The draining process concluded with a mid-December green light: dual, full-up Voyager flights in '71, plus two more in '73. It was game on: money flowing, with a projected final cost of $1.25 billion. The decision was over his head and out of his hands but Don Hearth was finally in business. He changed shoes and padded off to find just the right contractor.

In late January '65 over a hundred reps from twenty-eight companies all filled the same JPL conference room. Hoarse NASA reps explained that three entities would ultimately be chosen to spend three months preparing Voyager design studies. How these new studies might differ from those already submitted by GE or Avco seemed unclear, but work was work. Mere days after the conference, President Lyndon B. Johnson delivered his proposed space budget for fiscal 1966. The tally came to just over $7 billion, of which $43 million occupied a line bearing the name Voyager. Not a penny of it was meant for the forging of one bolt or the installation of a single wire; forty-three million clams had been allocated to "further define" the Voyager orbiting and landing hardware.

That July, with three contractors and hundreds of people across the country all laboring over Voyager, *Mariner 4* shot past Mars and threw back a curveball. The planet's atmosphere was even thinner than inferred from the Mount Wilson picture—by as much as 80 percent. And the word went forth to line engineers and draftsmen and model makers and technical writers alike: most every preexisting belief about Martian entry and descent would have to be plowed under and resown. For Don Hearth, *Mariner 4* had unquestioningly delivered worthwhile results. "We were learning a little bit more," he smiled, speaking of the flight. "We were beginning to get a better sense of what the atmosphere was like . . . even though we hadn't thrown Don Hearth's probe into the atmosphere yet!"

Engineers recalculated *Mariner 4*'s ultimate impact on Voyager: bloat. A thin atmosphere directly translated into numerous modifications for safely bringing the craft down: beefier descent engines, broader parachutes, thicker shock absorption. With a nudge of a slide rule, not even Apollo's mighty Saturn IB booster offered enough lifting power anymore—and that thing measured 140 feet tall by 22 feet across. Using it on Voyager now meant cutting most of the science experiments. Hearth wondered if the impending changes would push them up to the Saturn V. That was an absolutely colossal machine, over 330 feet high, intended to ferry astronauts and their equipment all the way to the moon and back.

When October rolled around, Don Hearth got the latest shock of his life: Saturn IB production had been canceled outright, leaving no Voyager option beyond the Saturn V. Until the news broke, Hearth had been reserving hope that he could squeeze in a "preliminary" flight around '69 or so. But Saturn V wouldn't sail until '67 at the earliest, and no question, Apollo got first refusal on every one of them (at least, until its first landing). Any precursor Mars mission had to realistically drop from the schedule and in doing so would push the '71 Voyager Mars landing to '73. Maybe they could still fly an orbiter in '71, but it sure wouldn't carry the same excitement of finding out what critters might be trolling around in all that red dirt. A not-unpopular JPL view was that NASA HQ had forced Saturn V onto Voyager in order to further justify the booster's post-Apollo production. True or not, this rumor failed to help soothe relations.

"I didn't wanna have a *damn thing* to do with the Saturn V," roared Hearth. What a total Voyager mismatch; its lifting capacity was nearly *seven times* more than required. With that thing, they'd probably just stack multiple Voyagers on top of each other and send them in one go, on a single rocket. That turned Hearth's project into an all-or-nothing gambit. He knew that one of the leading causes of space probe death was launch failure. With two ships spread across two different boosters, his odds of getting one up doubled—especially if the budget took a pounding. And what *about* those costs? With Saturn V now stirred into the mix, consummating Voyager might easily drain $2 billion. Hearth sighed; Martian flight had turned into a giant tart-up.

Two months after the Saturn V change, more bad news: seventh floor had opted to postpone any 1971 Voyager flight. No orbiters, no nothing. As part of next year's federal budgetary process Jim Webb had gone to Congress requesting, among other dispensations, $150 million with which to transition Voyager from paper to metal. He didn't exactly get laughed out of the room, but already the Bureau of the Budget had been trying to shave nearly a billion in fat off NASA's hips while granting Apollo whatever it needed. In direct support of the manned landing effort, JPL's Surveyor aimed to put dainty three-legged automatons on the lunar surface to examine soil properties and conduct photography. Surveyor kept all of its funding. Not Voyager. The giant Mars project received only $10 million new—life support, really—to string it along until Apollo reached its goal.

The public at large never heard any gory details. In a formal announcement, NASA officials simply explained that Martian orbiters would not be flying until 1973. But as some kind of limp consolation prize, one reworked Mariner *would* embark on a Venus trip in '67. Followed by two Mariners past Mars in '69. And then—mercifully—a somewhat anticlimactic 1973 Voyager trip, piggybacking twin orbiter-lander combos onto a single Saturn V. Identically configured, each Voyager would soft land and perform life-detection experiments. It'd be a great Apollo follow-on, with plenty of money for the job.

All the revised paperwork got signed on January 27, 1967 as part of a package deal establishing parallel offices between NASA HQ and Voyager's designated wet-nurse guardian. As formalized in the docs, this latter facility was *not* GE, or Avco, or even JPL. Overall managerial responsibility for the Voyager Mars program had perplexingly been awarded to the NASA Marshall Space Flight Center in Huntsville, Alabama. Up to this point they'd had absolutely nothing to do with Voyager. Marshall was a rocket town—developing the Saturn V and other boosters. In tandem with another NASA field center, JPL was supposed to cocreate the Voyager lander and report directly to Marshall. The Lab felt mystified: *What the heck?*

Late in the afternoon that very same day, three astronauts were finishing up a launch simulation inside their Apollo spacecraft when fire broke out and suffocated the men. Almost immediately NASA found its entire operation under a weighty congressional microscope. Among other reactions, Jim Webb shoved the just-approved Voyager plan onto ice until he could give it proper attention. Men had died. People wanted answers. Webb needed to route every last calorie into straightening out the chaos.

With Voyager once again in suspended animation, Oran Nicks now advised Don Hearth to pack. A temporary Voyager management office was to be established. Near JPL. So, for the conceivable future, Hearth needed to work out of California.

"Hey!" Hearth groused at him. "How the hell am I gonna do *that*?!"

"Well, you commute!"

Commute between Washington and California?

"You're gonna do it!" commanded Nicks. He did not appreciate protest, bellyaching, dissension, rebellion, refusals, foot-dragging, or alternative suggestions.

A trampled Hearth acquiesced. "Okay, I'll do it." He boarded a plane and flew to Pasadena for some recon. "I had a lot of respect for Oran," he added. "I don't want to say bad things about him."

The trip afforded Hearth an opportunity to hash over these recent events. How come the temporary office? Apparently, Marshall had not yet been ready to assume Voyager's managerial duties. "So somebody came up with the brilliant idea," he explained, "to bring people together in a team from all three organizations under an interim project manager, and we would house everybody *somewhere*." The situational ridiculousness carried through in his tone of voice. "And that somewhere, since JPL was gonna be putting more people into it than either Langley or Marshall, that somewhere would be Pasadena. And the interim project manager would be me." The assignment hadn't been Nicks's idea; it came from seventh floor.

"Wasn't *my* choice."

Hearth rented a bank building and within two months had seventy-seven people humming away inside it. The next six months about killed him. Monday morning he'd fly out nonstop from Dulles Airport and grab a hotel room. Endure the four-day internment. "I'd come back on a red-eye Thursday night and go into the office in Washington Friday morning," he related, laughing over what surely wasn't comic at the time. "Work a full day, go home Friday after work, and try to be a husband and a father." When Hearth first began steering Voyager, it commanded maybe 10 percent of his workload. "Ebbed and flowed," is how he described its relative presence on his to-do lists. "It kind of depended on the budget cycle, and what else was goin' on." After the Pasadena operations began, that shot up to 90 or 100 percent.

The ad-hoc crew forged ahead as best they could, "spending money and doing studies," as Hearth put it. By this time Voyager had existed in various states of consciousness for seven whole years without ever once going three-dimensional. In comparison, New Yorkers opened the Empire State Building less than sixteen months after breaking ground.

With Hearth having solidly lost his can-through-the-air idea, new sketches began appearing for a massive spacecraft to first visit Mars, later Venus, and then reach other planets "in the 1980s," with the possibility of carting along rovers as well. NASA promotional literature advertised that "a spacecraft diameter of up to twenty feet can be accommodated." The glossies went so far as to describe "biological studies" that entailed "searching for growth and metabolic activities." As Voyager matured in capability, "it would also look for fossil life" on these distant worlds.

Hearth despised how immense this stuff was becoming. The Saturn V–based Voyager designs specified over a *ton* of weight for the solar-powered orbiter—now earmarked to utilize a modified engine from the Apollo lunar lander. Voyager would circle a planet for two years while snatching pictures and other measurements. Attached to this colossus would hang a five-thousand-pound, tri-legged landing vessel. Three hundred of those pounds were set aside just for ground experiments—moisture surveys, radiation levels, soil exams, life detection. Three hundred whole pounds of science! Hordes of PhDs were clamoring to get aboard even though no formal invitations had yet been issued.

The *Apollo 1* fire caused even more fallout than the six straight Ranger failures to date. NASA's top hierarchy wound up in front of Congress to justify every planned tiptoe through the inner solar system, no matter how small. Set the scene with a paneled meeting room and wooden swivel chairs. Battered, thirty-year-old desks. Zeppelin microphones on Bakelite bases. Heavy glass ashtrays. Sweaty pitchers of water. Schedules and flip charts and explanations. Much tie fiddling as caustic questions, one after another, washed over the men like sulfur fumes. During one exchange a steamrolling Minnesota representative named Joseph Karth described to the assembled executives how he'd been boning up on Voyager's tribulations. And Representative Karth now wondered aloud why, out of all possible moves on the board, chief responsibility for the biggest planetary ship ever imagined had been transferred to the Marshall Center—a place wholly devoid of spacecraft experience, whose sole product consisted of heavy-lift rockets. *Why*, drilled the representative, *was Voyager taken from a loving parent who'd been rearing it for five or six years already?* Before anyone could answer, Karth raised a dead-serious issue of ethics and conflicting interest. Might the arrangement have been related to the likelihood that, following Apollo, Marshall would run out of things to do?

Senator Margaret Smith jumped in to ask Webb how much Voyager might cost in total. Webb thought it could hit $2.2 billion—excluding NASA salaries, a cool $40 million in facility additions, and another $55 mil to upgrade the radio-tracking network. Attempting to ease the sting, Webb explained that the tracking network could be used for other projects, too. Wouldn't that be nice?

Karth lobbed verbal machetes at Webb and the others, dressing down their pithy excuses for once again running way the hell over budget. NASA seemed to be really good at saying something would cost a hundred million bucks, then coming back six months later with *Oh golly whoops guess what, it'll now cost two hundred million*. No longer could the space agency claim youthfulness and inexperience as some weak rationale for everything— *everything*—costing twice or three times as much as originally submitted.

"We have grown up now," began a fueled Karth. He didn't know what to do with the patently overfed Voyager. Kick it and squeal? "If it is authorized and monies are appropriated by the Congress, I would hope that we will set a different standard by which to gauge ourselves." Karth withdrew. Webb shuffled on home. Three months later he was back in front of Congress again, drab suit wilting under the lights, ordered to choose between

Voyager and something called Apollo Applications. The latter had been created to funnel all the moon-landing know-how into other efforts like space stations and lunar bases. Already NASA had shelled out billions on it.

So what was going to fall, Apollo Applications or Voyager? Jim Webb looked at Senator Spessard Holland and, to the guy's face, actually refused to decide.

"I think it is essential that we do them both," he recommended.

Webb might not have known it, but Joe Karth—genuinely supportive of the space program—had himself been lobbying for Voyager's preservation. Talk about an uphill battle. And Karth's job became exponentially harder when, only a month later, NASA issued a new request for proposals to almost thirty outside contractors. The agency planned to fund a study of manned flights to Venus and Mars.

To the press, "absolutely astounded," is how Karth characterized his reaction. This crap NASA just pulled had instantly recast Voyager as cannon fodder—just a mere sideshow to human planetary flights. "Very bluntly," continued the fuming congressman, "a manned mission to Mars or Venus by 1975 or 1977 is now, and always has been, out of the question. And anyone who persists in this kind of misallocation of resources at this time is going to be stopped."

Karth wasn't kidding; Congress already had too much in its lap. Resuscitating Apollo. The Vietnam War. Race riots.

That September, 1967, Webb and Hearth awoke to the news that Voyager was dead. Its $71.5 million in funding requests had been outright wiped off the board, its line-item budget presence deleted.

Said Hearth, "What was my reaction? One of great relief. Because it was *insane*." No payload had ever been explicitly defined. No formal call for submissions had ever gone forth to any genre of science, be it biology or geology or whatever.

Voyager wasn't the only casualty; lots of programs got fricasseed. One for developing space-based nuclear propulsion took a $27.5 million hit. Apollo Applications developed a $139.2 million hole in its pocket. Only a single program—Human Factors—retained its entire funding base. The absolute lion's share of the dough went to Apollo.

Ed Cortright's boss, Homer Newell, had this to say: "My only hope is

2. Another stroll through the NASA hallways for Don Hearth and his ever-present pipe, 1968. Note the relaxed post-Voyager grin. "I smoked a pipe from my teens until I stopped in the late '90s," he stated. Courtesy Don Hearth.

that we've sold Voyager, and that we're just experiencing a delay because of war and problems on the home front."

Half a decade after signing on, Don Hearth wasn't sure what his future at NASA might hold. He was an engineer with a strong interest in science. "You don't do either engineering or science in Headquarters," he insisted. "Don't kid yourself. And you don't do a lot of management, either."

So what did the job end up being, then?

"Well," he began, with a huge exhale, "what you do is you figure out what the program ought to be. You sell that; you're a marketing type. You sell it through the budgetary system. You defend it before your bosses and the agency. You defend it before the Office of Management and Budget. And you defend it before Congress. And then you're supposed to put the program *together*. Okay?" Hearth's last statement refers to the cumbersome intangible of determining how much everything will cost, assigning var-

ious entities to the subprojects—chassis, propulsion, communications—
and then kick-starting the work.

While your chosen flock designs and builds the spacecraft, its payload
now has to be dealt with. Continued Hearth, "You're responsible for the
solicitation that goes out to the wide world of science. And their proposals
come in, and you make sure they get evaluated by the appropriate scientific
subcommittees, and then you have to work with the project management
center—JPL, Langley, or whoever—on how much can we accommodate
in terms of weight, power, you know, all that kind of stuff. And then you
go through a formal selection process, and you make sure they get properly funded, that there's enough funding for them in the budget, and that
the money gets funneled to them properly." Merely describing the process
tired him out.

"Call that whatever you want to but it's not engineering and it's not
science."

Donald P. Hearth ceased his ridiculous commuting and took a month
off. "I went to Europe with my wife and kind of repaired my marriage and
repaired myself a little bit." After coming back he unexpectedly wound up
with a promotion—taking over Oran Nicks's job as part of a top-end headquarters shuffle. The dead Voyager went into a filing cabinet.

But sometimes death is relative. The program would be reborn—although
not as John Casani's Grand Tour wunderkind. In the meantime, NASA funneled its dwindling appropriations into rebuilding the injured moon program. It took twenty-one months. And then—beginning late in 1968—a
parade of successful missions demonstrated the quality and safety of Apollo's redesigned self. Perhaps America might actually land humans on the
moon before 1970, but . . . would they be the first to bring home lunar samples? Attention now swiveled toward our nearest celestial neighbor and a
complicated duel reaching high climax. Whatever else might happen, for
sure it had ruined one guy's day.

4. Failure to Communicate

Everything gets me edgy!

—Christopher Kraft Jr., NASA director of flight operations

"Get Frank Borman on the phone!" barked Chris Kraft. He didn't have time for this—another bothersome issue on his lengthy list. The order vortexed his secretary into a scramble.

It was mid-July 1969. At the beginning of that month, Charles Philip Arthur George had been crowned the Prince of Wales. And then Rolling Stones guitarist Brian Jones had managed to drown in his own swimming pool at the age of twenty-seven. Quite possibly the last man on Earth to know or care, Chris Kraft worked for NASA at someplace in Houston called the Manned Spacecraft Center. This facility had been carved out from over a thousand acres of Texas swampland for the express purpose of realizing Kennedy's moon goal.

Apollo required some of the most complicated machinery that had ever been devised up to that time. Atop its thirty-six-story Saturn V rocket, three astronauts would occupy a cone-shaped "command module" for nearly the whole trip. It served as kind of an ultimate clubhouse: their bedroom and bathroom and boardroom and wardroom. It wore a thick heat shield for returning to Earth and held parachutes for the concluding splashdown. But lowering the heat shield and parachutes and every last provision down to the moon's surface made absolutely no sense; all that stuff would just have to come back up again, wasting precious fuel and bedeviling an already-tricky procedure. So from lunar orbit two astronauts would climb through the command module's hatch into a second, paper-thin craft known as the "lunar module" and take that down instead. The flyweight thing provided only those essentials necessary for use on the moon (it didn't even have seats) while the command module remained aloft.

Two single-purpose, one-use-only ships in lunar orbit: they'd have to uncouple and recouple with each other, all while circling around and around again a quarter million miles from home. Their orbits would have to be perfect; each rendezvous, flawless. In sum, *way* too much for three over-worked fellows to handle all by themselves while still managing to eat and rest and navigate and take pictures and keep house. And so fairly early on came the realization that getting to the moon was also going to require a slew of experts on the ground to orchestrate all those space-borne proceedings in real time. One particular individual owned a personality that lent itself well to such ventures, and that man was Christopher Columbus Kraft. Junior. He came to work for NASA at its very inception, practically inventing what's now known as Mission Control. By the summer of '69 Kraft served as director of flight operations and, in overly simplistic terms, did virtually everything except fly the spacecraft.

And he would have been in a much better frame of mind that July 12 had the Soviet Union not just launched something at the moon.

It wasn't so much that they'd launched in the first place. "I didn't give a damn *what* the Rush'ns were doin'!" he burst forth, in a Tidewater drawl that would not have been out of place on a beachcombing wino. That country launched incessantly. No, Kraft's frustration had more to do with timing. In only four days he planned to send up *Apollo 11*, intending to put humans on the moon for the very first time. No matter how smooth the operation of their giant rocket or how prepared the astronauts, eventual success would depend largely upon the almost organic interaction between crew in space and team on the ground. Bad things happen on the best day of the week. So this Soviet flight, coming when it did, filled the man with concern. In particular, he started worrying about the quality of ship-to-ground contact.

Spacecraft, whether people are in them or not, communicate using radio. It works the same as it does when calling up a station in the car. Every broadcaster employs unique frequencies, and all their transmitting equipment is calibrated to operate on just those. In the United States, frequencies are allocated by the Federal Communications Commission, which spends part of its time making sure that when WLS in Chicago plays "Honky Tonk

3. At center, Chris Kraft sits in short sleeves, with a headset on. "I was head of mission planning," he explained. "I was head of the flight control organization." Courtesy NASA.

Women" at 890 kilohertz on the AM dial, nobody else in that geographic area is trying to muscle in on the same airwaves.

However, the long, strong arm of the FCC doesn't reach out into space. Kraft's ground team had to decide on a radio frequency to use when talking with the astronauts. Not to complicate things, but they actually had to decide on at least two. One of them is used for "uplink"—that is, the ground talking to the ship. Uplinks also include command-and-control directives for the spacecraft systems. The other frequency is used for "downlink": astronauts talking to the ground, sending biomedical readings, fuel stats, and other information. You want to be able to receive data while transmitting commands at the same time. Then the flight isn't dependent on a single frequency, and both parties can gabber away in simultaneity.

The enemy of any radio signal is noise, and some type of noise is going to exist anywhere you go. If you go in space, well, that has a certain type of noise all its own. *Apollo 11* would chat with Mission Control above two thousand megahertz, which is at a point on the dial where space noise is at its lowest. That seemed like a good choice.

One problem—it was also going to be a good choice for the Soviets. "We were all concerned that they would be communicating *near* or *on* our voice frequencies." Kraft sounded deadly serious. "It could also have disrupted our efforts to send commands." International agreements supposedly quarantined each nation to its own exclusive wedge of the space-radio pie. But Kraft swore up and down that the Reds never stayed inbounds and often used American frequencies. What if he couldn't hear his boys during some critical mission phase? All because of something as mundane as radio crosstalk?

As Kraft festered in his office that hot evening, waiting for his secretary to complete the connection, most people knew only that the Russians called their ship *Luna 15*. But industry periodicals like *Aviation Week* had thinly alluded to Soviet objectives, and Kraft read everything. The *New York Times* had mentioned something about it, too. "I knew they were tryin' to bring back samples from the moon," he claimed. "And that would've been quite a feat, frankly, from an engineering point of view." *Luna 15* apparently didn't have any people on board, but Kraft's trepidation held. The same frequencies could still be in use. "That's dangerous!" he snapped. "And they were *always* messin' up our communications when we were flyin' around the Earth! Which ticked me off also!"

Frank Borman picked up. Sadly, Kraft could've stopped worrying that very instant and avoided troubling his friend. No Luna spacecraft ever used Apollo frequencies; they weren't anywhere close. Radio transmissions were coming and going from *Luna 15* in the hundred-megahertz range—way down at the bottom end of what defines microwaves. The Zenith Space Commander 600 TV remote would've been more likely to interfere.

On the other end of the phone, Borman stood inside his Houston residence, listening to his colleague's stern voice rocketing through the line. "He was edgy," Borman recalled.

Kraft did not object to the depiction. "When yer in operations, and yer goin' to the moon to land the first time? If yer *not* edgy . . . you don't understand the problem!"

And this edginess more than characterized his first question to Borman: "What's the hell's goin' on?!"

Attentively Borman listened as Kraft outlined his anxieties. "Even though it would be unlikely," recollected Borman of the uneasiness, "he didn't want their orbit interfering, or in any way endangering the *Apollo 11* mission."

Kraft doesn't remember everything he said to Borman during the call—only that he asked him to please look into the matter and to do it immediately. "I asked him, through his contacts, to go find out what the hell they were doin'," Kraft brooded. "And tell 'em I was worried about it, and I didn't want them screwin' up our communications!"

Except for one chance encounter at a party, Frank Frederick Borman likely would never have materialized at the forefront of Chris Kraft's brain that day. Until very very recently Borman had been an active-duty astronaut. A little more than six months prior, he'd commanded *Apollo 8*. Breathlessly it flew to the moon and parked three men in lunar orbit on Christmas Eve. The world froze. Today that might come across as nothing, but it represented the very first time people had ever left the gravitational confines of Earth.

Even before *Apollo 8*, Borman had planned to step down and do something else. The only problem there was that his Air Force pension wouldn't be totally vested yet. The man had to kill some time, and to that end he accepted a new position as NASA's liaison to the Richard Nixon White House. "Somebody in NASA told me to do it," justified Borman, in a clipped, matter-of-fact tone that characterized most of his responses. "I wasn't invited. I was in the military. They told me to do it so I went and did it."

So when NASA—or Nixon—faced some interlinking concern, Borman would catch a plane to Washington. From the airport he'd grab a rental car to his office away from the office and bunk at some nearby hotel for the duration. "It'd be a week at a time, sometimes," he said. "It just depended on what was goin' on." The rate of return trips also varied, based on the state of current events. "I was just a temporary person there," he clarified. "I wasn't working in the White House full time."

Not long beforehand, with *Apollo 11* preparations well underway, Borman had gotten to contemplating the most dangerous part of the trip. To him that was liftoff from the moon—what to Joe Citizen might be an anticlimax more than anything. But America's mood would change real quick if the blastoff engine didn't work and two astronauts got stranded up there. After noodling this over for a while Borman got Nixon speechwriter William Safire on the phone and told him, "You want to be thinking of some alternative posture for the president in the event of mishaps." Safire wasn't sure what the guy was telling him. Borman elaborated: "Like what to do for the widows." Clarity in hand, Safire drafted a speech for Nixon to use in the event that astronauts would not be coming home. Such was the role Borman now played.

Then came that chance encounter. White House liaisons are occasionally required to attend Washington dinner parties, and Frank Borman was no exception. During one of them he and his wife happened to bump into Anatoly Dobrynin. Portly and bespectacled and balding, the Soviet ambassador to the United States chatted Susan Borman up about her trip through Western Europe after *Apollo 8*. The entire Borman family had tramped up and down the continent and enjoyed a gay old time.

"Why didn't you go to the Soviet Union?" Dobrynin wondered aloud.

Frank Borman certainly knew the answer. But standing there at his wife's side, he wasn't sure how to diplomatically respond. In a room filled with diplomats! Finally he said, "Well, we weren't invited." There didn't seem to be any way to sugarcoat things.

"Well, now you are!"

Travel to the Soviet Union? No American astronaut had done that; it was one of those abominably far-fetched unmentionables. Yet Borman swears he immediately understood this to be a genuine proposal. "Yes, I thought he was serious." And for the remainder of that dinner, the guy had something new to ponder. "I was excited about it. I thought it would be, you know, an interesting thing to do."

He'd been to the moon, might as well go to Russia!

Once again the family packed up their two sons. "It was a commercial flight," detailed Frank Borman. "It wasn't a military flight or a government flight. We just went over Pan Am by ourselves. We didn't have an American escort." Straight off the plane he totally bungled an attempt to voice a simple Russian greeting and never tried the language again. So everything downstream had gone through an enormous female interpreter the Borman kids called Big Red. In retrospect, there was never any discussion between husband and wife about *not* taking their kids to scope out the communist bloc. "We just thought it'd be wonderful for them, and it was," marveled Borman. "There was no fear at all." He did an interview for Moscow Radio. He made a couple of speeches. He laid carnations at the graves of two Soviet cosmonauts, then laid more at the final resting place of Sergei Korolev, who'd been the undeniable backbone of Russia's entire space program until dying a few years prior.

In total the family stayed nine days and thoroughly loved Russia. They got back on July 10, a Thursday. That Saturday night *Luna 15* launched and Kraft called Borman. A Houston Saturday night is very early Sunday morning in Moscow.

Adjusting his telephone receiver, the *Apollo 8* commander said he knew zilch about the Russian flight. "I had no idea," Borman insisted. He'd never heard of the thing; it certainly hadn't been mentioned by any of the people he visited. Big Red never said *"Luna 15."* So what did Chris Kraft want from him?

"It's goin' to the moon," Kraft warned, "and we wanna know what the orbit is."

Borman didn't say anything just yet. He needed think time.

Apollo 11 was supposed to launch that coming Wednesday. As Borman later gossiped, "I'd been told the previous August that the CIA had heard that the Russians were gonna try to have a manned lunar flyby before the end of 1968." Maybe this was it, happening right now?

Kraft held the phone to his ear, waiting on an answer.

Finally Borman suggested, "Why don't we ask 'em?"

He didn't get a response and spoke up again. "Why don't we ask the Russians?"

"Well, you know 'em so well," Kraft shot back, "see what you can find out!"

Now, today it might seem odd that Kraft didn't call over to the Soviet Union himself, that he leaned on a semiretired astronaut to somehow cough up answers. For such an impossibly structured man as Christopher Kraft, this might indeed seem a questionable way to conduct business. But understanding why the man acted like he did requires context.

Such indirect circuitions wouldn't be necessary only a few years later, when both nations planned a gestural linkup of their respective manned spacecraft in Earth orbit. This Apollo-Soyuz collaboration forced open pathways between Soviet and American space agencies and defused tension. "I got to know a lot of very fine Russian engineers and leaders," Kraft remarked of the later period, as both sides came to appreciate that the other guy was as human as them.

That evening, though, no links existed for Chris Kraft: "In '69, I knew not a *damn thing*!" To him there weren't any individuals behind *Luna 15*; it was just a potential menace launched by some faceless and practically nonhuman entity. He simply *couldn't* pick up the phone and ring the Soviet Union and ask for the guy in charge of *Luna 15*. "I wouldn't have known how to do that," Kraft divulged. "They were just—Russians." And now the mystery ship, whatever it was, had left Earth orbit en route to *Apollo 11*'s destination.

To heck and doggone it all, he knew so little about their space program. For a man who thrived on facts and data, Kraft couldn't fill a thimble with details about *Luna 15*. He didn't know what its intentions were. He didn't know the people behind it. He'd never been to the Soviet Union.

But wait a second—Frank Borman had. And as Chris Kraft pondered this situation, he realized that Borman was his only real in. "He was at the time, yes," confirmed Kraft. "Indeed he was." And that's why the man had called. "I just asked him to find out when the Russians were gonna be around the moon. And that if they were, I would hope that they did not screw up our communication." With that, the call ended. Kraft hung up the phone and stood there for a moment and finally told the corner of his desk, "Well, I've done all I can do."

Borman hung up on his end, still processing the situation. "He was a man that wanted everything gone great," Borman said of his preoccupied colleague. "He didn't wanna leave any detail that might cause a problem."

No matter how bothered Chris Kraft may have been about *Luna 15* at that time, he didn't dwell on it after ending the call. "I had so many other things to worry about, or be concerned about, or *think* about, that you know I just—that was not one of my major concerns at that point." He plowed back into the other gazillion items filling his notes and hours later hopped a plane to Florida and the Kennedy launch complex. Then, with two days until *Apollo 11*'s blastoff, Kraft fled the Sunshine State and returned to Mission Control in Houston. "I was making sure everything was okay with everything I had a responsibility for."

Yet Frank Borman remained troubled, thinking about Kraft's demeanor. The former astronaut genuinely wished he could do something to reduce his friend's edginess. *I'll see if I can help him out.* Borman hadn't been deliberately flippant when suggesting they just ask the Russians. It seemed like an obvious thing to do, but perhaps Kraft was just too distracted, or something, to realize that?

If anybody wasn't helping, it was the Soviets themselves—almost totally mum on their hurtling spaceship. All anybody could get out of them was a vague announcement explaining that *Luna 15* would conduct "further scientific exploration of the moon and the space near the moon." Clear as coal.

Borman needed second and third opinions. Over the next few days, he checked in with White House staffers regarding the delicate subject. He talked to Henry Kissinger. Everyone tried to apply some kind of ruler to Chris Kraft's demeanor. *Does he 100 percent think* Luna 15 *will mess up* Apollo 11? *How much danger does he think they're in?* Or, *Is it more of just a potential for concern? But not too much real concern?* Psychoanalyzing sharks would be easier.

The general consensus was that Borman should try to contact *somebody* behind the Iron Curtain. But gosh . . . who to call? His ear was hot. Teenagers spent less time on the phone. *Apollo 11* would take flight on the sixteenth—punching a devilish countdown timer in Borman's noggin. He had to work faster.

Cogitating over his Russia trip, Frank Borman's memory hopped from one personality to another, reflecting on different people he'd encountered. Of them, who might be able to shed light on the issue? Nobody out-and-out talked moon probes; he'd associated more with cosmonauts and air force jocks. But there had been this one guy . . . one whom Borman had seen at a private reception.

Again he snatched up the telephone and dialed the White House operator. He knew that number well.

"Please put me through to Dr. Keldysh at the Soviet Academy of Sciences."

Dr. Mstislav Keldysh is not a household name. At least, not in most households. But for many years he served as one of the key driving forces behind the Soviet space effort. By 1969 he'd become the academy's president and something of a public face on space science in general. This worked well for a paranoid government that preferred to keep its frontline engineers hidden and therefore supposedly protected. In comparison, the academy was decidedly unrestricted.

Russians consider their Academy of Sciences to be hallowed ground, an institution that clung to principles of scholarship and merit in the face of a Soviet regime that thought almost in the complete opposite direction. Claimed one member, "The academy is the only institution in the country where something similar to democracy exists." It is Russia's oldest scientific institution. Membership was regarded as more significant than a chest full of Lenin Prizes or Hero of Socialist Labor pins. Things like that got doled out with clockwork regularity. But oh, to be an academician! To be a member of this influential scientific institution! Well now, that was something else completely!

Many aren't elected to its roster until they demonstrate a near-lifetime of achievement. Yet Keldysh got in during his twenties after solving a number of aerodynamic brain-busters like flutter—which could literally destroy planes in flight. When Soviet rocketry established the nation as a superpower in the 1950s, Keldysh saw the future loud and clear and deftly wriggled himself onto the ground floor. Very early on he formed a small committee inside the academy, intent on bringing a scientific voice to Soviet space proceedings. He worked closely with academicians and other researchers to identify their top priorities and deliver recommendations to the government. Korolev's Sputnik flights carried experiments—mostly because of Keldysh's grinding insistence that they accomplish something beyond patriotic grandstanding. Later on, when Red probes first went to the moon, Mars, and Venus, Keldysh influenced what they studied and what they carried in order to do so. He shared his vision. Shaped the curve of events. And for a brief part of one evening, he also shared a conversation with Frank Borman.

We should embark on space missions together, suggested the *Apollo 8* commander via Big Red. *Let's end the unnecessary duplication. Think of the message we could send: Here's our world superpowers, joining together in peace to explore.*

4. Mstislav Keldysh, at far left, chatting with Frank Borman during the Borman family's visit to Moscow. Courtesy RIA Novosti.

Keldysh understood the offer but committed to nothing specific. He did remain encouraging, however, and Borman felt sufficiently upbeat about the way they parted. After returning home, Borman reported his new friend's hopeful attitude to Nixon and Kissinger—including Keldysh's agreement that space could indeed serve as an avenue to détente.

But that tense Wednesday, Borman couldn't get him on the line. "It was something like two o'clock in the morning in Moscow," he later said, which typically fell outside even Soviet work hours. Two a.m. Moscow time is the end of another workday in Houston. Borman had been at this for days now. Collaborating with the White House operator, he left a message for Keldysh at the academy, in his own name. *Please*, Borman implored, *could you assure us that* Luna 15 *will not interfere with* Apollo 11? *What are your ship's orbital parameters?* Then he hung up. Nobody knew a donut hole about Keldysh's personality. Was the guy more likely to respond because they'd met? Only time could deliver answers—or continued silence. The Bormans converged at their dinner table; Susan had overheard his end of the conversation. Frank mentioned something about the call but largely forgot about things until his phone rang at six the next morning.

Neither Kraft nor Borman ever met *the* man directly behind *Luna 15*. They never even heard his name until 2009. Borman was correct in thinking that Mstislav Keldysh would know something about the flight, but Keldysh wasn't in charge of it. Someone else was—someone whom Kraft and Borman never got to look in the eye, shake the hand of, and offer congratulations to. Someone who could have taught them about the world of immense pressure Soviet engineers labored in. Someone who would've been proud to introduce his family, take the Americans for a spirited jaunt in his motorcar, and share with them a traditional Russian tea.

The man Kraft and Borman never met was a quiet mechanical genius named Georgiy Nikolayevich Babakin, who loved to dance and drive cars. He had a son named Nikolay who'd given Babakin and wife, Anne, a new granddaughter only one month before *Luna 15* launched. The elder, fifty-something Babakin would never savor public celebration or attend autograph shows and be treated like a celebrity. He was the proverbial gray man, yet one whose efforts made worldwide headlines. Babakin liked it that way. "It was not a problem for him to be a very closed person," recalled Nikolay. "He was very simple man. He did not think about any honors, any medals." And he would also die early, at his peak.

By 1969 Georgiy Babakin oversaw all efforts at a series of inherited offices called the Lavochkin Design Bureau. They sat on the northwestern outskirts of Moscow in Khimki, near the Moscow Canal. Many places in Russia are quite old, but Khimki had formally claimed a spot on the map for only about thirty years. Back at the dawn of spaceflight, the place was a hub for top-secret fighter plane and missile research. Foreign travelers never got anywhere close; nobody went to Khimki on vacation. Today it's home to a pro soccer team and IKEA.

The Lavochkin Bureau created unmanned lunar and planetary spacecraft, which is not what they originally set out to do, and in pursuit of this work the management emphasized simplicity and nauseatingly extensive testing. Babakin never wanted to fly jack diddly unless it had weathered pretty much every challenge they could think up. With those sorts of guiding principles, bureau engineers were steadily eclipsing the results of their harried colleagues who labored to place cosmonauts on the moon. Even as *Luna 15*'s hardware had moved through the Khimki preflight testing bays, cleanup efforts were well underway out in remote Russia for a to-be-manned moon rocket that'd blown itself to smithereenies after launch.

Georgiy Babakin was *not* the individual ringing Frank Borman's home at 6:00 a.m. Babakin spoke no English and would never have been permitted to call any American on the telephone. Everything about his work, including himself, was classified. Instead the calling party was an interpreter, who startled Susan Borman first. "Sue was lying in bed complaining about the telephone ringing," recounted Frank Borman. She associated calls at that hour with bad news.

But this news was good: the interpreter had a basic rundown of *Luna 15*; Borman described him as "a very knowledgeable man." Then someone else got on the line. "I talked to Keldysh's number-two guy," explained Borman. "He spoke English, and Keldysh did not speak English. They said they would give me their trajectory, and they stuck by their word." Not long after came Western Union screeching to a halt outside, racing up the steps with a little yellow rectangle of history addressed to Borman himself. The few unpolished sentences detailed *Luna 15*'s precise flight path, orbital particulars, and specifics of when that orbit would vary. It closed with a noble YOU WILL BE KEPT INFORMED OF FURTHER CHANGES. Take a second and think about this. For the very first time, Soviet flight controllers had willfully and honestly disclosed detailed mission parameters. All because Frank Borman had gone visiting them with nothing more than goodwill in his heart.

And wonder of wonders, only hours later a second magical telegram arrived in Borman's hands. Methodically he breached the envelope and withdrew a slip of paper. The spacecraft was now orbiting the lunar equator, he read, and here are the date and time when that orbit was achieved. The telegram explained that the ship would remain in that orbit for two days. It said that Borman would receive further information when things changed. And at the very bottom it warmly promised, THE ORBIT OF PROBE LUNA 15 DOES NOT INTERSECT THE TRAJECTORY OF APOLLO 11 SPACECRAFT ANNOUNCED BY YOU IN FLIGHT PROGRAM.

His eyes wandered down to the signature. It read KELDYSH. And then Frank Borman did something that may be construed as unusual: nothing. As in, he didn't follow up with Chris Kraft. He didn't call anybody.

"Since it didn't affect *Apollo 11*," Borman rationalized, "I didn't think it made any difference."

The next day, both Borman and Kraft appeared at a press conference where the latter man came off as a bit surprised himself. "He didn't even tell me until this morning," stated the incredulous Kraft about his cohort's tardy disclosure. Questions and answers rang through the air; neither man had any more dirt on the mysterious ship's true purpose. As Borman told reporters, "Your guess is as good as ours at this point." Kraft surmised that *Luna 15* would probably kick out of lunar orbit at *some* point and head back earthward. He would be wrong.

Then he got to see the telegrams. In their brief, clinical structure, Chris Kraft felt integrity beaming over to him from the other side of the globe. "I took them at their word," he indicated. "I knew they probably would have no intent of trying to fool me. And that they were sincere . . . and *recognized* that my concern was a very valid one, and they recognized that they should not interfere with us."

What's interesting, though, is neither telegram mentioned boo about radio frequencies—pledges to avoid certain ones, or promises of silence during key Apollo maneuvers, or anything like that. Rather, the messages went into considerable detail about *Luna's* orbital parameters—a topic that Kraft himself felt to be almost a nonissue: "I had some minor concern about that, but mostly I was concerned about communication." Was the substance of the telegrams enough of an answer, then? "The fact that they said they would not interfere with *Apollo 11* was good enough for me," he claimed. "They knew full well that we did not want them interrupting our communications during any critical time."

Borman and Kraft disclaimed any knowledge of *Luna 15*'s construction, and both say they never spent any time thinking about how it might look. Spacecraft exhibit practical design; in no way are aesthetics involved. And so *Luna 15* itself was every bit as unsexy as its name might suggest. Lavochkin engineers had devised a low, squarish, broad tubular framework and stuffed it with fuel tanks. One stubby landing leg occupied each corner. Four additional tanks rode atop the frame, in a kind of saddlebag arrangement to be jettisoned on the way down. One of Lavochkin's genius moments was canonizing this as a standard landing platform with which to hold various payloads. And here's the super-secret thing that nobody knew: for *Luna 15*, after touchdown a long, tilting pivot arm would augur into the surface using a drill on its end. Then the arm would swing a dirt sample back up, high above the landing platform, and into the mouth of a waiting twenty-inch globe. Directly underneath it sat the absolute minimum for a trip home: fuel tanks, batteries, radio transmitter—plus a singular rocket engine with no backup. In this fashion the low landing platform became a launchpad.

Babakin's ingenious *Luna 15* was indeed now circling the moon, with every intention of landing and returning home with a souvenir. Britain's *Daily Telegraph* weighed in: "While the moonshot is regarded as a last-minute attempt to detract from the American effort, it is not thought the Russians can land and bring back samples. The technical complexities are thought to be too great."

Without question the timing was intentional: a last-ditch, Hail Mary attempt to beat *Apollo 11*. People took years to come clean; Soviet news agencies and key individuals denied *Luna 15*'s true purpose well into the 1990s. That kind of effort never paid great dividends. U.S. intelligence services crawled all over God's green earth trying to expose what the Reds were up to, and usually they got pretty close. A 1971 report to Congress analyzed the mission's flight profile and concluded that it "looked very much like one intended either to take very high resolution pictures of future landing sites, or as a final adjustment before soft landing."

That's great intelligence; Kraft could've used it. Kraft might also have been amused to learn of the reception awaiting *Luna*'s return. Surrounded by aircraft and soldiers, the scorched globe with its priceless innards would be flown from a landing site in Kazakhstan to Vnukovo Airport at the southwestern outskirts of Moscow. There, with much pomp and circumstance and applause and waving, it would ride atop an armored vehicle bedecked in flowers and flags, past mobs of cheering comrades, all the way to the Academy of Sciences.

Apollo 11 was halfway to the moon. Buzz Aldrin keyed his mike. "Hey Charlie, what's the latest on *Luna 15*?"

NASA Mission Control used a procedure whereby only one single person talked to the crew. It was always another astronaut, who rotated through the position known as "capsule communicator," or CAPCOM. This streamlined every verbal exchange, and the crew personally knew whomever they dealt with. On this particular day it was Charlie Duke, who told Aldrin, "Stand by. I'll get the straight story for you." Less than a minute later Duke had an update.

"Latest on *Luna 15*. TASS reported this morning that the spacecraft was placed in orbit close to the lunar surface, and everything seems to be functioning normally on the vehicle. Sir Bernard Lovell said the craft appears to be in an orbit of about 62 nautical miles. Over."

Apollo 11 crew member Mike Collins replied, "Okay. Thank you, Charlie." At the time, TASS functioned as the official news agency of the Soviet Union. And what of Sir Lovell? *Not* a member of TASS. He ran a mammoth space-tracking facility in England called the Jodrell Bank Observatory, which at the time maintained the largest steerable radio dish in the world. Soviet leaders preferred to keep a nice tight lid on their space program. But once things went flying, not much could be done about Jodrell Bank.

So as *Luna 15* circled the moon, Sir Lovell's mighty dish listened in. And with both missions slowly converging, worldwide speculation only ran feral. Was the Soviet machine there to somehow spy on *Apollo 11*? To covertly snap pictures of its landing? Or was it standing by to rescue the Americans in case of trouble? One editorial cartoon depicted a "LUNA 15 SOVIET SALVAGE SHIP" towing home the remains of a crashed Apollo lander.

Lovell sidestepped all hearsay. To his practiced ear, the beeps coming through his equipment sounded distinctly different from those of previous Soviet flights. The ship had launched toward a new moon, which didn't jive for picture taking. And it had taken an entire day longer on its outbound trip than previous Lunas, indicating an attempt to save fuel. None of this added up to any ho-hum reconnaissance orbiter. "If the Russians intend to put *Luna 15* in orbit and just leave it there," he told reporters visiting his redbrick facility, "the whole operation is incomprehensible." After the newsmen went away, Lovell and his aide resumed work as *Apollo 11* crossed the invisible point in space where Earth's gravity is no longer as powerful as that of the moon's. Jodrell Bank's computer room sat on the observatory's first floor, but the radio room was upstairs. Breathless and sweaty, the Englishmen sprinted to keep pace with an evolving soap opera nearly

239,000 miles away. Lovell patently ignored the rampant Western speculation about who was going to do what and when. He unreservedly predicted that the Soviets intended "to land the whole spacecraft, or part of
it, and collect some rock." He would be right.

Another couple days wagged by. *Apollo 11*'s CAPCOM read up more news.
This time astronaut Bruce McCandless took his turn at the radio mike. He
offered a story about how the pope was preparing to watch the lunar landing—in color, no less—and some tidbits on a lunchtime pool party for the
astronauts' families. "In Moscow," he then read aloud, "space engineer Ana-
tol Koritsky was quoted by TASS as saying that *Luna 15* could accomplish
everything that has been done by earlier Luna spacecraft. This was taken
by the press to mean *Luna 15* could investigate the gravitational fields, photograph the moon, and go down to the surface to scoop up a bit for analysis." McCandless had some baseball scores, too. One thing he didn't know
was that *Luna 15*'s original orbit measured far greater than what Babakin
originally wanted. That probably meant something had gone wrong with
the rocket burn to put it there. Jodrell Bank noted increased amounts of
radio traffic between probe and ground and before Sir Lovell knew it the
ship's orbit had dropped.

On the nineteenth of July, with *Apollo 11* finally entering its own lunar
orbit, *Luna 15*'s was again lowered slightly. Next day it was lowered farther
still—about as low as anything *could* go. Lovell camped by the radio. He
didn't know that Babakin wanted the ship on the ground that evening.
It'd happen only an hour or so before the scheduled touchdown of *Apollo
11*'s lunar lander, called *Eagle*.

They fired up *Luna 15*'s descent radar and it didn't make sense. The ship
was supposed to put down in the Sea of Crises—some of the flattest terrain
our moon has to offer. But the bounceback readings varied wildly. Babakin had to make a very tough decision: forget that radar and dive, dive—or
play it safe? His superior felt it prudent to delay the landing. For the next
eighteen hours *Luna 15*'s controllers retested their equipment and collected
new readings, during which time *Eagle* landed on the moon. Soviet culture thinks highly of glory, and the amount that *Luna 15* might have been
expected to deliver had just vaporized.

Eagle and its two crew members loitered on the surface for nearly a day.
An hour prior to their departure, Babakin got permission to go for it. His

little miracle fired its rockets and headed on down. Now it was in the auto-pilot's hands. Ideally the ship would shed the remainder of its momentum and *ploomp* right down, kitten on a pillow. Babakin couldn't wait until the sample came back.

The machine's uppity landing radar failed to accurately measure the distance between itself and pay dirt. This is very tricky going. Not only does the moon lack easy reference points—like sea level—but it possesses a highly uneven field of gravity. *Luna 15*'s radar wasn't measuring, it was guessing. The cumulative altitude error meant that *Luna* thought it was 9,800 feet higher than it actually was.

Jodrell techs glued themselves to the signals racing in from a quarter million miles distant. Fingertips white from pressing hard on the earcups. "It's landing!" one of them shrieked. "It's going down much too fast!"

Lovell squeezed his own headphones: silence. Then Babakin's team heard it: silence. Only five hundred miles from *Apollo 11*'s triumphant landing site, their glory machine had unceremoniously bum-rushed the Sea of Crises going three hundred miles an hour.

Luna 15 had crashed, and Georgiy Babakin was alone with his thoughts.

5. Halt the Work, Destroy All Materials

You mean Moscow is *not* protected?

—Josef Stalin, upon learning after World War II that the
capital had no safeguard against American bombers

The Lavochkin Design Bureau did not, of course, start off on day one building super-duper lunar pooper-scoopers. They used to make fighter planes. A line may perhaps be conceptually hard to draw between World War II aircraft and moon-drilling automatons, but this place somehow managed to connect those incongruent dots.

Just over 240 miles due west of Moscow lies the town of Smolensk. There, in the opening years of the twentieth century, young Semyon Lavochkin's schoolteaching father instructed his son to apply himself regardless of the task. Come 1917, Semyon graduated secondary school with no less than a gold medal, indicating highest marks. Three years later, following service in the Red Army, Lavochkin entered Moscow Higher Technical School. He spent nine years there, emerging with specialized training in aviation engineering. He married his sweetheart, Rosa, and subsequently morphed into a burly, round-faced man who looked a little like he was always trying to hide something in his cheeks. One colleague described him as "a modest person, who always looked worried." Lavochkin pittered about in Moscow at various design bureaus until the airplane-building genius Andrei Tupolev begged him to join the Office of Aviation Industry. That was in 1938, and the Soviet Union faced peril ahead. Some hooligan named Adolf Hitler had just marched a whole load of troops into Austria and threatened to waste any dissenters with his airborne Luftwaffe. Talk like that got the Soviets to reconsider their own air defenses—or what existed of them.

The high points included poor armament, glacial top speeds, and rampant obsolescence. Many biplanes were still in service.

Requests poured forth at the national level, hunting for motivated citizenry able to produce an improved fighting aircraft. Premier Josef Stalin held the doors wi-i-de open to any and all suggestions; his country was at stake. Lavochkin teamed up with two other engineers and submitted a design and, to the men's general surprise, beat out everyone else. Their plane had been chosen to serve. Within a year they were ready to start building their dream machine. Hitler was already building concentration camps. In Khimki, Lavochkin got the keys to a dog-eared secondhand facility called Plant Number 301 and began collecting the brightest minds that could be scrounged up. "It's very important to select talented people," he once lectured. "You need to give them the freedom to discover their capabilities and to adjust to one another."

With that, the community of Experimental Design Bureau Number 301 switched on the dusty lights and flicked away the cobwebs and plunged into the gestation of modern aircraft hardware. The name change was a routine formality, reflecting the prototypical nature of their efforts. And 301 needed to hurry: in late June 1941, German solders crashed through the western Soviet border and began romping over the Carpathian mountain range toward Moscow. They bombed the hell out of everything. As Lavochkin's people frantically cranked out blueprints and prototypes, Soviet pilots were sacrificing themselves in large numbers with antiquated machinery. Lives ticked away on a morbid clock.

Subsequently, Bureau 301 developed at least ten new aircraft that arguably endowed their nation with parity in the wartime skies. In particular the La-5 and La-7 set new standards for handling—predominantly at low altitudes. The things were top-notch dogfighters. And in a world of severe metal shortages, a major chunk of each was fabricated from wood.

"I can build airplanes until the last tree in Siberia falls," boasted Semyon Lavochkin.

In victory's wake the schoolteacher's son became a war hero. Soviet society adored medals, and upon Lavochkin's bureau they came raining down like sleet. He dressed in the uniform of a general, accented by one magnificent gold star identifying him as a Hero of Socialist Labor. What excitement might come next?

5. Semyon Lavochkin pores over materials in his office. About 30 percent of Soviet Russia's entire stock of World War II planes resulted from Lavochkin's designs and influence. Author's collection.

Naturally, the combat aircraft produced by him (and everyone else) were propeller driven. And the downside of propellers is that they can move a plane only so fast. Pure fantasy during the 1920s and still experimental in the 1930s, jet engines had begun to fly only at the end of that decade. And with jets, the future spoke. One German offering flew a good hundred miles an hour quicker than the fastest prop fighter. Nothing could touch it. Jets might someday even be able to crack the sound barrier. So with the Potsdam Declaration behind them, nations on all sides of the globe began pursuing this young daydream of even faster, more agile combat aircraft. In the Soviet Union, various design bureaus mobilized anew.

Lavochkin re-entered a drafting stage—paralleling such fierce (and often underhanded) competitors as Artyom Mikoyan and Mikhail Gurevich with their own MiG line of fighters. Tall and stoop-shouldered, Lavochkin set a torturous pace. He was roughest on himself, habitually worked late, and had a prototype jet ready in July '47. During a round of acceptance trials, the contest seemed like a dead heat between Lavochkin and Mikoyan. Both planes went the same speed. The MiG-15 climbed better yet handled poorly and tended to drop a wing. Lavochkin's La-174 demonstrated quicker acceleration and more agile turning . . . but commonly blew its tires on landing. Neither had benefited from the high-stress environment and taut deadlines.

The winner? Oddly, Stalin chose *both* for production.

Rechristened the La-15, many started rolling out the door and not even dear Semyon could deny their bicuspid-grinding flaws. Engines overheated, cockpit seals failed, air ducts cracked, hydraulics jammed. Tires continued bursting during the crafts' often-violent landings. One pilot making a test run had to bail out when his engine caught fire. What the heck? Well, one of the two factories that Lavochkin used had zero previous jet experience. Both of them lacked any standards of workmanship. Lavochkin prototypes were always hand built with love and devotion in The Man's own shop and accordingly ran so much better. Six weeks after the bailout incident another engine cashed it in during flight and killed its pilot. Another fatal crash that July. Lavochkin planes were starting to make the *Hindenburg* look dependable.

Unfortunately, the July crash took out no mere staff pilot. The luckless stiff happened to be close personal friends with Josef Stalin's son, who immediately ordered a halt to any further La-15 activities. A month later came official word to cease production immediately and entirely. Only 235 had been made. It was the beginning of the end for Semyon Lavochkin's career in the airplane business.

But his world was about to experience its next major twist. Shortly thereafter, Lavochkin received another customer in the form of Soviet air marshal Konstantin Vershinin, who wanted the war legend to build target drones. He wanted what? The air force, Vershinin explained, wished to begin using inexpensive, remote-control aircraft as expendable training targets for pilots. And, um, their MiGs.

Lavochkin had no idea how to make drones. For years he'd chased the idea of engineering a top-quality piloted aircraft. But now the military wanted unmanned throwaways?

He could have done the easy thing and given up. The Soviet Union was entering a period of considerable slack in the aviation industry. So many facilities that had operated full-tilt during the war now struggled to fill their days. The Politburo looked upon airplane manufacturers as abnormally versatile entities who had it all: enormous buildings, transport vehicles, metal shops, assembly lines, and highly skilled technicians. They were optimized for the production of many different types of equipment. They had gobs of tools. So if your planes weren't needed, well, how about making vacuum cleaners? Seriously! Refrigerators, washing machines, tape recorders . . . anything was fair game. One plant assembled turboprop passenger aircraft right alongside toy horses.

If he'd closed up shop, Semyon A. Lavochkin's postwar legacy would have been the creation of rattletrap airplanes that nobody used much. Going out on a low wasn't his style, and the drone had curb appeal. It was fresh energy, in a bold direction—the kind that'd just led him to open a new department of control systems and hire some workaholic named Georgiy Babakin to run it. Nobody had ever tried a drone before? Right up Lavochkin's alley! He said yes.

Scarcely unpacked, Babakin soon challenged the design bureau's fly-and-fix-later paradigm, strongly in force at the time. He saw many of 301's abandoned projects as neglected stepchildren with unlimited potential—merely in need of guidance and nurturing. Babakin attempted to resurrect a few discards, leading to heavy pushback from Lavochkin himself—who argued that any extra energy should go into the drone effort. The *last* thing they needed, came the strongest of warnings, was to deal with half-dead airplanes the ministry would just cancel anyway. Besides, the target drone wasn't turning out to be some weekending, pajama-clad stroll of easy filler work. The bureau had more or less completely underestimated its specialized requirements, including deployment, automation, and tracking. Subcontractors weren't delivering on time. Deadlines kept slipping.

Yet Babakin wouldn't let up on his big-picture views. With escalating emotion and urgency he preached a covenant of thorough component and ground testing no matter the project. To him every foible could be conquered with this approach and, as if to exemplify it, he began reanimating an abandoned high-altitude interceptor plane concept called the 200. It'd been a temperamental rodeo bull of a design that pretty much everyone else wanted to forget.

Right about then the somber-faced Lavochkin might have been asking himself exactly why he kept Babakin around—if not for Comrade Stalin. Recently, the already-paranoid Soviet leader had been apprised of the vulnerability of his own nation. We all like feeling safe, and this predominantly bleak report drove Stalin into a fresh round of nightmares. In particular, the man was fixated on a looping movie in his head: that of American bombers flying unchallenged over Moscow and dropping a nuclear hello right on top of the Bolshoi Theater. One single plane could level the entire capital city. It wasn't that far-fetched, either: in 1952 at least thirty-four incursions were made on Soviet airspace by enemy planes. Close to one a week! Fighter jets managed to destroy three and tag three more, but so many intruders flew much higher and faster than any defensive weapon in Soviet hands. What might they ever do to protect the eight-hundred-year-old city?

Uncle Joe enjoyed working the small hours. He never hesitated to call a meeting at any time of day or night, whenever the inspiration hit. "One opinion," articulated Stalin during another overnight assembly, "has it that we must immediately begin creating a Moscow air defense system, for repelling a massive attack of enemy aircraft, from any direction." In due time his advisors advised him that safeguarding the city was probably going to involve circling it with armaments. They were thinking missiles. A big project, no question, entailing big divisions of labor: ground facilities, troop quarters, fuel. Specialized range finders. Targeting com-

puters. And, with the MiG decision finalized, perhaps Comrade Lavochkin would be free to spearhead development of the missile itself? Number
301 began a ponderous year of research. Ostensibly, the assignment went
their way because of Semyon's increasing reputation as "most adventurous"
of the airplane builders.

Yet another venture that nobody had ever attempted—one absolutely
hinging on the strength of the missile's automated control system. Now
thirty-something and completely expunged from airplane redesign, Georgiy Babakin feverishly worked the project. He got so into it that some jokingly referred to him as "chief designer of surface-to-air missiles" (not a
real position). Habitually he wore suits, often with sweater vests. He was a
team player. He didn't talk down to anyone. He did not breed fear or conflict or any such discord. His peers liked and respected him. "Extremely
gifted with engineering intuition, common sense, and organizational talent," said one. Another had gotten to know Georgiy and his wife, Anne,
and would occasionally take the couple mushroom picking in the forest—a
classic Russian pastime.

Like anyone, Babakin struggled with unexpected errors and flaws and
subtangents and suppliers who never delivered on time. Yet it was he who
ultimately proved that the missile's technology would succeed, and even
architected its distinctive fin pattern. The situation looked positive. Babakin was on a roll. Whenever he got involved, impossible things seemed to
start happening.

They called it Berkut, or "eagle." Forty feet long by two and a half feet
wide. One could take out an aircraft flying as high as sixty thousand feet.
Over *three thousand* flight-ready Berkuts would eventually go live at fifty-
six Moscow sites located along two enormous and purpose-built concentric ring roads. With Red Square marking a center point, the innermost
ring circled Moscow at a radius of thirty miles or thereabouts, with the second one roughly fifty miles out. One estimate suggests that Russia's entire
output of concrete for one whole year went into building the restricted,
military-only roads—with many miles of them laid down by prisoners.

The scale of the roads was on par with nothing. It blew the scale to kingdom come. When U.S. analysts got back their Moscow spy photos, the twin
rings were impossible to miss. What the hell were those naughty Reds up to?

Not knowing that his own life was running short, Stalin had also talked

6. Accompanied by his only son, Nikolay, Georgiy Babakin heads out
for a bike ride in 1948. "He was a *beautiful* father," praised Nikolay.
"I didn't see him as often as I wish." Courtesy Nikolay Babakin.

up another scenario he'd been ruminating over. With Moscow secure, what
might they do to hit the other guy on his own turf? To strike back? To rain
hot nuclear death on the bitter enemies of socialism? Well, that was going
to be tricky. They had such an awfully long distance to go and nothing that
could reach even the closest of American borders. What, *mail* the warhead?

Everyone knew the solution wasn't going to involve bomber planes.
Anymore they just lumbered along slowly; a marmot could shoot them
down. Other options? From the point of view of Stalin's advisors, two distinct methods existed. One would be to create an intercontinental ballistic missile. This would take the form of a huge rocket with sufficient fuel
to reach the West, carrying enough nuclear pain to level the countryside

once it got there. Right off the pad it would need a little twist of the steering wheel—guidance, they called it—to set the thing moving in the correct direction. But that would only happen during the early boost phase; physics would then take over and arc it down to the target. Almost perfect! *Nothing* could take down a rocket screaming over the North Pole at thousands of miles an hour.

As luck would have it, Soviet engineers had already looted Nazi Germany's v-2, just after the Reich fell. By an order of magnitude it was the biggest working rocket of all time—although still too puny to reach the United States. Stalin gestured: What was the other option?

The other way, explained his advisors, would be with something known as a cruise missile. Instead of a rocket bomb, think winged bomb—a scaled-down airplane holding nukes instead of pilots. Theoretically it'd be easier to produce because it behaves the same as a regular plane, flying horizontally at low relative altitudes—versus a rocket's high arc. That kind of flight profile translates into a smaller engine. And with built-in steering over the whole journey, its accuracy jumps. Don't settle for just hitting Washington; target the Pentagon! Stalin nodded thoughtfully. *Not bad.*

On the downside, though, it appeared more vulnerable than a rocket. It would fly more slowly. And at those low altitudes it could probably be intercepted. *Well, Comrade Stalin, what's your preference?*

Uncle Joe thought and thought and finally decided to make . . . both. He also wanted a third layer of supersonic bombers, just to cover the bases.

Already Stalin had a team working the ballistic missile. In charge of it he left a man who'd been on the scene in Germany and escorted back many v-2 parts: Sergei Korolev, whose hallowed grave Frank Borman would one day visit. Ever since the war's end Korolev had been trying to extrude the v-2 into something capable of reaching American shores, and he was getting closer. That left the cruise missile up for grabs. At one point Korolev had chewed on that one as well, but his hands were too small for both projects. They really needed another guy completely.

The natural aspirant to cruise-missile fabrication would be someone from the airplane industry. Someone who felt completely at home in the wind tunnels. Someone who knew airfoils and navigation and metalwork and large-project management. Someone with chops. *Did they have any such candidates?* Stalin asked. *Anyone with a solid heritage of aircraft construction, who maybe wasn't so busy these days?*

Gosh, one name stood out.

From greater Moscow, follow the Leningrad Highway west. It rambles northish—past a harbor, over a canal, and then on up into Khimki proper and the gates of Design Bureau 301. Insiders called it "The Firm." There Semyon Lavochkin maintained a spacious office dominated by one long table. It served as a great place to spread out the problem of the moment, so he kept his personal affairs confined to a small desk way in the rear. Behind him, groaning shelves tilted under the weight of papers.

The geniuses of 301 kicked off their new Burya effort in the wake of a filthy regime change. With Josef Stalin already dead a month, Soviet leadership appeared to be in a worse state of affairs than even the cruise missile. The country embraced no formal system of succession, no vice president or soundly worded documentation to fall back on. It was more a colossal wrestling match, with at least three individuals jockeying for power in a contest that left weapons development surprisingly unaffected.

Fifty-three years old, Lavochkin snapped open the dog-eared missile blueprints that Korolev had bequeathed to him. Accompanying them were notes from Mstislav Keldysh. The academician had already performed reams of theoretical work on the topic and envisioned a swept-wing, sixty-foot-long beast riding twin boosters underneath. The ninety-six-ton arrangement would launch vertically before nosing over low. Oftentimes the saga of Lavochkin's long days could be read in the litter trails on his big table: empty tea glasses, sandwich plates, Borjomi mineral-water bottles, overflowing ashtrays. Why stop to eat when the work can just continue?

Downstream of his office sat the design halls. In these well-lit areas, draftsmen received piles of sketches and concepts and figures and specs and then took positions on the gridiron of jumbo-sized artist easels. Over time they'd transform the miscellany into dimensioned workshop drawings necessary to fabricate Burya's actual hardware. (That name, by the way, means "storm.") Round and round the blueprints went, with a hike from Keldysh to Lavochkin, who'd drop-back pass to the draftsmen, and a toss-back to Lavochkin with a quick lateral to eligible receiver Babakin, who'd run and shoot and then option over to the draftsmen once more. Fumbles? Yeah, all the time.

"I don't know how it was for you," Semyon Lavochkin wearily told a colleague, "but I had it a lot easier during the war."

Flight testing began in August '57—exactly the same time when Sergei Korolev was out in remote Kazakhstan debugging his rocket. The cruise missile team congregated eight hundred miles southeast of Khimki at a barren test range called Kapustin Yar. Lavochkin watched his first missile ignite . . . then immediately conk out. Isolating trouble takes time, during which technicians crawled over grounded Buryas like ants. Twenty days later Korolev successfully demonstrated his own creation. Not a perfect flight, but the major bits worked as advertised. He made it look so easy that TASS publicly announced the USSR's cool new accessory.

Inside of the next two weeks, fatigued Lavochkin techs witnessed a new Burya lift off—then arc right over and hug the ground. Six days later Korolev flew another rocket and got it declared operational. The Presidium of the Communist Party couldn't believe their good fortune in having Sergei Korolev's weapon at hand. In minutes it could reach what took hours with Lavochkin's own offering. Who needed anything else?

After five straight initial failures, Number 301 got a few Buryas airborne— gunning four thousand miles downrange at three times the speed of sound. But Korolev's baby flew higher, faster, farther and even had the potential to carry something all the way into orbit—which it did, with Earth's first man-made satellite on October 4, 1957. Lavochkin couldn't touch an accomplishment like that. Then Korolev flew one of his into the moon. Not long after, another one went around the moon's back side and took pictures. All this on the shoulders of a device meant to carry nuclear bombs. It generated news headlines unlike even the ones Elvis Presley could make.

In February 1960 a directive arrived in the hands of Semyon Lavochkin. Part of it read, "Halt the work, destroy all materials." Burya had gotten the noose. It was operational, finally—one flight went as long as half an hour. But Sergei Korolev had outclassed even himself with the ballistic rocket, now being readied with extra stages for a flight to *Mars*, of all places. And Korolev was even prepping to send *men* into space on top of his rocket. No way in the world was Lavochkin ever going to Mars, or the moon, on a lowly cruise missile with a derisory success rate of 61 percent.

Bureau 301 still had one missile left in the queue—a Berkut sequel referred to as Dal that'd been riding the developmental slow boat. Semyon Lavochkin got a round of Dal changes implemented the same year as Burya's termination, and he would've been instrumental in orchestrating another update two years after that. But instead, on one June day in 1960 he suffered a heart attack and died in the arms of Georgiy Babakin.

Vladimir Chelomey didn't wait around very long. Mere days after Lavochkin expired, Chelomey invited thirty of 301's top engineers for a private assembly. A black dampness still enveloped the bureau. It hurt. Comrade Lavochkin had been appraising their Dal at a missile-testing range in Kazakhstan when chest pains overwhelmed him. Only sixty, the designer hadn't lived to see his final Burya fly. *Perfectly*, no less. His outfit was renamed "Design Bureau Number 301 in Memory of S. A. Lavochkin." Like that helped soothe anything at all. On top of their immense grief, the men still faced many Dal problems and had little time for extraneous get-togethers. What could this individual possibly want?

Chelomey got right to the point. He asked if perhaps some of them might be interested in coming to work for him?

The men looked around at one another. Realistically, this wasn't an invitation. It was more of a notice. See, Chelomey nurtured big plans. In order to realize them he wanted facilities, tools, equipment, raw materials, and as many skilled workers as he could possibly lay his hands on. He wanted everything. And so with great tenacity, Vladimir Chelomey was in the process of collecting design bureaus.

Nobody had ever been so audacious. First to assimilate was Bureau 23, which up to then had focused on hybrid concepts like intercontinental bombing aircraft. Recently they'd migrated into supersonic bombers, leading to research in space planes. All that sounded great to Chelomey, who officially folded them under his wing in October '60 and insensitively changed their name to Branch Number 1.

The Lavochkin team wouldn't capitulate so easily. Chelomey wanted them to drop what they were doing and move offices to his own design bureau, in Reutov. The men frowned. Reutov lay twenty-five miles east, on the complete opposite side of Moscow. Was he serious?

Chelomey pressed. The Lavochkinites hung on, filibustering, claiming a need to persist with the Dal missile shield. Wasn't that more important? The answer came when bureaucrats cancelled Dal and Chelomey instructed

Bureau 301—sorry, make that Branch Number 3—to get in gear with a submarine-launched, antiship missile he'd been picking away at. The heavy announcement struck only weeks before Christmas and no doubt injected a sour taste into everyone's *kutya*.

Although tagged last, Moscow's Plant Number 642 fell into Chelomey's grip and became his Branch Number 2 in March '63. Chelomey redirected *them* from naval missiles into the design of ground support equipment. And with these transitions now complete—with three born-again branches reporting to his every whim—Vladimir Chelomey smiled and got back to work.

Who the heck *was* this guy?

He was a wanna-be. A missileering also-ran. He came from the aviation sector and by the early 1950s had made a small name for himself with special antiship cruise missiles. Chelomey's eureka moment was the addition of little pop-out wings that deployed only after the missile had launched—meaning they could be stored and transported much more easily than before. That singular bit of icing leapfrogged Soviet Russia beyond American sub technology. What a smart guy. The government then handed Chelomey his own design bureau, but he never settled into progressive momentum the way Korolev had. Assignments came and went, and the more time passed, the more disconcerted Chelomey became. He felt qualified for more than what he had going on; better than these small-potatoes projects. Where was that next rung up the ladder going to be?

The man's fortunes really changed when Nikita Khrushchev won the battle for Stalin's succession. Chelomey managed to score an audience with his new premier and sell him on the idea of funding a few pet projects. It went over well; Khrushchev really liked the origami wings. Subsequently, Keldysh phoned Chelomey and told him he'd been assigned a dinky brick building atop an otherwise empty tract of land in Reutov. So Chelomey opened shop there and began production. Like gushing water, money flowed into the growing empire: Antisatellite systems. Ocean reconnaissance. He figured out a way to launch missiles from submarines that were still underwater—another delight altogether.

The main hitch now seemed to be Korolev, who'd lofted Sputnik satellites and flown machines to the moon. He was getting all the glory! Chelomey understood PR like nobody else and stair-stepped his way into space rockets by wooing the ministers with erotic visions of orbiting nuclear bombardiers. Not to mention antiship rockets: they'd fall from space, pop open wings, and snuff out that pesky American aircraft carrier.

Once he had the military pied-pipered into agreement—with Khrushchev's important nod—Chelomey began several initiatives for planetary exploration. He would build exotic new engines. Larger spacecraft. He'd fulfill complicated mission profiles using his new "space planes" to reconnoiter, photograph, or bomb that which became necessary. Today most of this comes across as a gigantic reinvention of the wheel. But Chelomey always slanted his approach so as to make it appear fresh. Look at the term "space planes." Didn't they sound newfangled and agile, compared to dumb old capsules?

So for the next several years—right on into the early 1960s—Vladimir Chelomey pursued his visions. He dressed well, spoke confidently, and accomplished much by pandering to one military request after another. Oh, you want a manned space station for spying? With a defensive cannon on board? No problem! Chelomey just whipped out drawings right and left. "The most amazing thing," detailed one of his engineers, "was how we tore ahead, skipping even the initial drafts, immediately going on to the working plans stage."

His road map for spaceflight was so grandiose, Chelomey explained, that having some extra brick-and-mortar resources would sure help. Khrushchev bought in further, and that's when the bureau takeovers came into play. His eye had always been on Semyon Lavochkin's enterprise, but not until the leader's death did Chelomey sense an in and go for it. His self-important orchestrations affected thousands of technicians, assemblers, engineers, secretaries, and custodians. Several Lavochkin refugees wound up retasked to a small, winged space glider. Others labored over antiship cruise missiles. Who in the industry knew where they'd be officing next week?

Vladimir Chelomey built his rockets and his empire and was immersed in tons of projects when Khrushchev went on vacation in 1964 and came back to find himself removed from office. Snap! Just like that. A seemingly instant overthrow had actually been months in planning.

The sails deflated quickly. With haste Chelomey's projects began vanishing from official itineraries—and funding schedules. People abruptly felt less afraid to back-talk him. Everything he did came under enormous review: his plans, budgets, personal accommodations. Some wanted to outright eliminate his very design bureau. Of late it's been said that Chelomey's greatest contribution to the Soviet space effort was confusion.

Exactly one calendar day following Khrushchev's removal—on October 15, 1964—the re-re-named Lavochkin Design Bureau quietly disassociated itself from anything having to do with Vladimir Chelomey. They stopped working on his ridiculous space glider and packed up all the drawings. Only now they had practically nothing left to do.

Maybe Sergei Korolev had been attracted to Lavochkin's bureau because of its attitude. Over time the place had resolutely compiled a history of engineering the impossible. Of defying odds. And that kind of track record was in dire need at the moment.

See, Korolev had a dilemma. He was too busy. As chief of his own design bureau—Bureau Number 1, no less—Korolev had been responsible for putting the first human in space, Yuri Gagarin. The Soviet government loved him for it. The world had ooh-ed and ahh-ed. Then Korolev had launched other men, a woman, and then three men in one spacecraft. Next he wanted to beat Apollo to the moon with a manned landing. That was great and all, and the governmentals endorsed his commitment, but like spoiled brats they also wanted more. Spy satellites, communication satellites, lunar rovers, plus more unmanned flights to Venus and Mars. The list kept growing.

A man of great inner strength, not even Korolev could absorb all these burdens and survive . . . much less have anything work properly. As of late he'd racked up an abysmal record: 1 for 19 on planetary launches alone. Rushed designs contained blatant inadequacies. Things failed with embarrassing predictability. Korolev's sleep-deprived acolytes dragged themselves through the assembly bays from one in-progress to the next, pinching ninety-minute catnaps in side rooms before straggling back to the latest headache.

Rules began to slide. A big no-no was smoking in the wrong place— yet mountains of cigarette butts appeared in dangerous locations because nobody was taking the time to find a safe spot to light up at. They were all too tired to care. In this kind of environment, easy mistakes happened. Somebody accidentally detonated the separation mechanism between two parts. An exhausted tech installed spacecraft cables wrong and started the thing on fire. One Luna probe blew up in a test chamber. "Our workload was becoming too heavy," summarized an engineer. "Something had to be done to bring the workload under control."

Therefore, in order to sanely focus on the man-to-the-moon effort, Korolev carved off slabs of his work and parceled them out like sides of beef. The satellites went one direction and were fairly easy to kiss good-bye. But the unmanned probes had always occupied a special place in Korolev's heart. They couldn't go to just anybody. And he might have come to a crossroads on them if not for the Lavochkin Bureau. Those guys were smart. They could build just about anything. They could succeed. And due to Chelomey's fall, they were now available.

If not Lavochkin, then who?

"It's time for us to make a complete switch to the piloted program."

Korolev spoke to his assembled team. "We are sending a man to the moon in about three years," he continued. "During that time, Georgiy Nikolayevich is supposed to land so many automatic stations on the moon that there won't be any room left there for the Americans!" (Internally, any Luna was referred to as an "automatic station.")

By March '65 the Lavochkin Design Bureau's transition to independence had been completed. That July, Korolev made his one and only trip out there—meeting with the bureau's director and other top engineers to discuss the handover. Posters hung on the walls of Babakin's small office like science fair exhibits, depicting improved concepts for lunar and Martian spacecraft. Korolev smiled warmly; a fine new home.

That day the people of Lavochkin received a most wonderful gift: liberation from weapons of war. And the responsibility for fulfilling a nation's entire program of lunar and planetary exploration. Peaceful science in the heavens: Korolev called it "his dream" and impressed upon everyone assembled that this gift, this privilege, could easily be revoked if the people before him failed in their efforts. *Everyone, your new top priority: soft-land a spherical Luna on the moon to take pictures and measurements. Get going.* Korolev then hit the bricks and in six months would be dead.

"It is a good future for Lavochkin Association," said Georgiy Babakin at the time of the handover. "A good future."

Fiction couldn't have scripted a more crooked path. Yet that's how a gaggle of wooden-airplane makers got into barnstorming the solar system.

6. There and Back Again

Asking America to provide us lunar samples
would just make us beggars.

—A Soviet scientist justifying why his country
needed its own pieces of the moon

Almost the first thing that Georgiy Babakin did in revamping the way-ward Lunas was to mandate a comprehensive process of ground testing. Now, after some eleven failures it might seem obvious to at least turn your creation upside-down before launch and see if any screws fell out. But that rarely happened, and much of the reason had to do with the cultural politics of the time. It was a strange paradox; Korolev's design bureau enjoyed relative ease in justifying big-ticket items like gold-plated diodes and exotic titanium alloys. But test equipment? The party chiefs didn't get it. They failed to appreciate the need for thermal chambers or shake tables or sensitive measuring instruments. Big honking *rockets* brought glory to a nation. Now go launch them; didn't you people learn by doing? Ask for any of that testing stuff, wrote one engineer, "and you would hit a wall of incomprehension."

So instead of using rigorously vetted equipment, Korolev got to roll the dice. Major pieces like radios or navigation systems often arrived so late that they had to be flown directly to the launch site at breakneck speed. Only there would his team find out if stuff even powered up. Luna's automated control system, as a lowlight, incessantly failed the most cursory of pre-launch inspections. Over three previous launch attempts this dicey slug of obstinate machinery had to be either repaired or replaced five whole times.

But things radically pivoted at the beginning of 1966, when Lavochkin anticlimactically put one of these recalcitrant balls on the surface of the moon. Known as *Luna 9*, it extended a small camera and snapped touristy surface pictures—a deed the Americans wouldn't match for six tough months. Under Babakin, engineers had comprehensively overhauled the guts of the spacecraft: modifying parts and pieces and moving whole assemblies around, culminating in a revamped machine that operated on much more solid footing than ever before.

. "The way we landed it!" shouted a fifty-year-old Babakin after touchdown. "As if into a cradle!"

Truly, a feat that stunned the world (and, intriguingly, one that came only after Korolev's death). A key member of Soviet space efforts, behind-the-scenes supervisor Georgy Tyulin referred to this Luna success as "an inspiration" and assigned most of the credit to Babakin's tireless efforts: "His thirst for knowledge was as great as his disdain for academic diplomas."

Two months later Lavochkin fired off the world's first orbiting lunar probe. Summer gave way to autumn and two more went. During this period Babakin grappled with twin launch failures, but they had nothing to do with the probes themselves. He nailed an on-the-surface encore in December '66, firing back panoramic imagery from *Luna 13*. Overall, a stunning turnaround from the Korolev days.

When he spoke of Babakin's contempt for education, Tyulin knew his associate well; the Lavochkin chief designer indeed held no great respect for pure academics. Quite the contrary. Babakin universally preferred getting his hands dirty to wasting time in classrooms. Any day of the week.

It almost doesn't make sense. Wouldn't Babakin's position have outright demanded that he be a scholar? An individual who'd compiled the most far-reaching academic record possible? Awash in diplomas and degrees and doctorates? Today Georgiy Babakin is regarded as an organizational and electronics genius—a man able to wholly digest the most obtuse technical frippery and excel in the process of applying it. He operated on his feet, driven by a fire in the belly.

Yet he was hardly a scholar. From a very early age Georgiy Nikolayevich Babakin seems to have been infatuated with radio—a trait not coincidentally shared by many of his peers. In the context of this pretelevision, pre-Internet, pre-Twittering era, radio was truly an entity of magical abilities. People congregated around them in groups; an important program or speech might bring friends and neighbors over for a communal experience akin to today's Super Bowl or World Cup. The American writer E. B. White characterized radio as "a pervading and somewhat godlike presence" of the times that transcended the physical box of tubes and wires. It was otherworldly. Voices from the sky! *The* fastest method for disseminating news. When fed-up revolutionaries overthrew Czar Nicholas II in 1917, the parents of two-year-old Georgiy would have heard about it over the radio.

Babakin's father died only a year later. What remained of the family struggled to eat and survive Moscow. Dessert came only on Sundays: cranberry jelly. But radio held young Georgiy's attention like nothing else. Unsatisfied with merely *listening*, he had to know every last detail: What were some different ways to build one? Who made the sounds? How did they come out? How far could the sound go? He asked the kinds of questions that schoolteachers couldn't always answer, which begins to explain the boy's patent apathy toward the offerings of the Moscow educational system. He got into amateur radio—that is, communication between hobbyists for the sheer purpose of enjoyment. ("Amateur" indicates purpose, not competence; amateurs don't sell commercials or try to profit from broadcasts.)

In what was surely one of his few trysts with formal education, Babakin subsequently enrolled in classes offered by the local Friends of Radio society. At seventeen, he obtained work as a senior radio technician at the Moscow Telephone Company. Within a calendar year Babakin moved on to the newly formed Moscow Radio Broadcasting Company with the job of installing equipment at Sokolniki Park—some of it designed by himself. From there he bounced through another outfit or two before the army netted him in January '36. Compulsory military service was law at the time, and besides, the cavalry needed radio operators. Babakin tried to adjust. One July day six months later the Red Army kicked him out because his heart was in bad shape. Congenital defect, they said. Babakin was twenty-two. Undeterred, he married Anne Goyhman in 1937 and managed to pass his tenth-grade exams—the same year Semyon Lavochkin acquired the tumbledown Plant 301.

Only four years later Germany invaded. Most Russians refer to World War II as the Great Patriotic War, and in the beginning it went quickly downhill. Panzer tank crews rolled to within twenty miles of Moscow proper; they could see the Kremlin's spires in their binoculars. So many able-bodied Russian men went to fight that over a hundred thousand surplus women, teens, and elderly shoveled out massive, tank-eating trenches around Moscow as others threw up steel barricades. The entire city dangled by its teeth as the nation gave over practically every civilian industry to wartime defense. In the middle of this hurricane, treading water, Georgiy Babakin was excused from direct combat because of his weak ticker. He supported the war effort at various electronics labs by perfecting the detonation of explosives by radio. And when military brass needed a way to remotely discharge smoke grenades for troop camouflage, Babakin delivered. Unrelenting weather and supply-line troubles helped stem the tide of Panzers, and beyond that the Wehrmacht remained woefully unprepared for the resiliency of Soviet citizens. Moscow held.

Once the shooting died down, Babakin involved himself in the up-and-coming missile defense industry. In particular he was intrigued by the automated control systems responsible for accurately delivering a warhead thousands of miles away. After all, they were based on radio. It was unprecedented, exclusive work that sent Babakin to cross paths with various missile projects—as well as Korolev—until he rolled through Semyon Lavochkin's front door in 1951.

The new man alighted within a hodgepodge of atypical shops, encountering many coworkers who'd been reared in prestigious engineering schools with years of formalized lectures, paper-writing, and exams behind them. Officially Babakin remained "in the capacity of a student," even while accepting supervisory and other high-tier responsibilities. "He was essentially a self-taught person," elaborated Georgy Tyulin. "Sufficiently gifted to attain a level of education that no academic institution could have provided." Within nine years, even after he acquired the post of deputy chief designer for guidance systems, protocol still dictated that his occasional call to the Communist Party begin with "Private nontrained Babakin is here . . ."

He weathered Semyon Lavochkin's death and the Chelomey histrionics before finally carving out time for a college degree. The diploma came in 1957, as Babakin pushed through his early forties—the same year Korolev orbited *Sputnik 1*. By the mid-1960s, Georgiy's son Nikolay Babakin had joined the Lavochkin Bureau as part of his university diploma work. Nikolay's wife, Alina, also came aboard, working on sample-return missions alongside her father-in-law. "He was very glad that myself and my wife work with him in one company," smiled Nikolay. "We had joint problems, joint questions. It was very interesting, and it was good time for all of us."

Fade-up on spring, 1968. Snow melting in Khimki; bright sun, greenery appearing. Outdoor enthusiasts flocking to the Khimki Forest Park, which offers twenty-five hundred acres of lush foliage that is home to natural springs, hundred-year-old trees, and gobs of wildlife. Only a couple miles south, the Lavochkin conjurers methodically readied their next lunar flight. And for the sake of the country's prestige it really needed to work. Barely one year prior, a cosmonaut had been killed while returning to Earth in the new Soyuz manned spacecraft. Designers unearthed a savage flaw in the parachute deployment system and therefore regarded an upcoming American flight with morsels of bitter contempt. As a top Soviet space official confided to his diary, "I have to admit that we are haunted by U.S. intentions to send three astronauts on board *Apollo 8* around the moon in December." The Soviet population needed more confidence in their ambling space program. More glory. And right then, only Lavochkin was positioned to deliver.

In preparation for the Apollo climax, NASA had recently started orbiting the moon with a handful of ships named *Lunar Orbiter*. They snapped tons of high-quality surface pictures to be used in identifying landing sites. But the *Orbiter*s were also flying much more recklessly than anticipated. The error rate on their circuitions was something like ten times the expected amount. Engineers couldn't find a thing wrong with *Orbiter*'s design. This certainly didn't bode well for accurate navigation, and it sent people like Chris Kraft into high-octane fits. What the devil was going on?

Turns out that the moon challenges all visitors with a conspicuously uneven field of gravity. It's "lumpy." Imagine Earth like this: you're out for a morning walk and partway down the road not only are you heavier, but you lean to one side. Walk a little farther and it changes again. Such is the character of our gray pal in the sky. The variances aren't much—roughly half a percent—and they don't shift around geographically, but they'd only been discovered two years prior by *Luna 10* and certainly hadn't been studied. Gravity, of all things, was suddenly a wild variable. Even today, our moon remains the most gravitationally wonked-up place of any yet measured in the solar system. It's like that because of all the asteroid and mete-orite impacts that have gone on there for billions of years. This resulted in pockets of dense material building up—with gravity measuring stronger in those impact zones. Nothing changes the situation. On other worlds, active geology slowly churns their substructures like a giant dirt blender and smooths out the variations.

Worthwhile space missions are crammed to the gills with experiments in order to maximize every usable second of flight time. No exception on *Luna 14*—intended for high orbit and fine measurement of these gravita-tional "mass concentrations." *Luna 14*'s outing would also help trajectory engineers better understand the mechanism of transfer between outbound flight and lunar orbit. (Such knowledge might lead to more accurate tar-geting or perhaps improved fuel use.) One divergent test featured greased-up gears cranking around. The parts weren't linked to anything else; they just spun in place and would do nothing to aid the ship's navigation, tem-perature control, radio communications, or other experiments.

Luna 14 flew that April and the little nipper worked very well. It mapped lunar gravity, tested radio signals, and yes . . . twirled around little gears that weren't connected to anything. As missions go it wasn't terribly sexy—no cameras, no landing, no Soviet coat of arms symbolically planted on the surface. But the country's space missions had been setting a bad prece-dent: too much money and energy wasted on outings with extreme bling yet few credible accomplishments. Flying to make headlines, to be the first in whatever inane new category had just been deemed important. *Luna 14* marked a cosmic sea change and the public never cared. But Georgy Tyulin remembered an immediate crush of geologists and chemists fran-tic to analyze data from this one flight alone. Also, "The designers gained much practical experience by studying the performance of their equip-ment during launch, flight, and operations," Tyulin went on. "This expe-rience came to good use."

Luna 14 also represented the end of Korolev's original design. By early '69 the Lavochkinites were ready to bring home lunar samples. They'd assem-bled no less than five next-generation, two-story machines. *Their* creations, *their* offspring . . . not a rebuild of someone else's cast-off remnants. With such an obscene amount of equipment on deck, people increasingly began living in their offices, testing bays, launch facilities. Home life disappeared.

7. A Luna sample-collecting spacecraft endures testing at Lavochkin. At upper right perches the drill on the end of its swing arm. The vacant return globe sits at top center with its support package underneath. Author's collection.

"Most of the workload," observed Tyulin, "fell on the shoulders of Babakin, his deputies, assistants, and flight controllers."

In particular, the dinky return vehicle was going to have to be one of the lightest and simplest things ever constructed. Even its absolute minimum configuration embodied many, many parts: let's start with a container for the moon dust, which sounds obvious but maybe isn't. It had to have a heat shield. A radio transmitter. A parachute. A triggering system *for* the parachute. It would need some kind of battery—one unaffected by the long wait from assembly through launch and a four-day outbound trip, cooling its heels all through another day on the surface, and then surviving lunar liftoff . . . before working perfectly the very first time.

But heat shields and parachutes wouldn't be necessary if the return ship failed to hit good ol' Earth. During the trek back its flight path would undoubtedly require a couple tweaks—modest nudges. Babakin sighed. That meant tacking on an arrangement of steering rockets able to thrust in any direction. They wouldn't have to be large but they certainly would *be there*—not to mention the tanks feeding them, the fuel inside the tanks, valves, piping, etc., etc.

It got worse. To really know the ship's position with a large degree of certainty meant beefing up its electronics and cramming in more equipment. Lamented one engineer, "All this made it practically impossible to deliver lunar soil back to the Earth." Why? Too much weight.

But one man emerged from the bowels of academia clutching hope. Materializing from the shadows, dusting himself off, Dmitri Okhotsimsky contacted Lavochkin with his game-saving idea. The jowly-faced and bespectacled man headed a team over at the Institute of Applied Mathematics. And for some time they'd been studying this problem of lunar return, which is intriguing because so many simply ignore the challenges of homecoming. People often make lists *before* traveling . . . but who makes one to come back? Wasn't the hard part getting there? Don't you have everything you need already? But ask any high-altitude mountain climber about the return trip and you'll get an earful about how that's when most of the accidents happen. Ask a deep-water scuba diver: people die because they didn't plan how to get back up. Returning is often an afterthought, but not for mountaineers or divers and certainly not for Dmitri Okhotsimsky. He was a numbers guy. He liked math. And one of his major interests happened to be applying it toward the simplification of journeys through space.

Of late, Okhotsimsky had been feeding punch cards through his institute's gargantuan Strela computer. It filled a room. The device's vacuum tubes masticated seventy-five kilowatts an hour while performing two thousand computations a second, and like this it eventually spat out a pile of numbers onto wallpaper-sized printouts. Okhotsimsky grinned. Someone like him understood and appreciated these numbers like others appreciated Nabokov's stylistic wordplay, and with figures in hand he contacted Lavochkin with an elegant antidote to their difficulties.

Roads home from the moon are plentiful, explained the numbers man. *And among all the possibilities there exist a select few that do not require corrections of any kind. Using these, the process is simplified. Launch at the optimal time and you'll come straight home.* Babakin perked up. That meant no little thrusting rockets, tanks, or fuel, didn't it? One individual on the team celebrated this breakthrough as "an unexpected solution." They could drop the gyroscopes and the additional electronics. They had a chance after all. Morale improved. Yet Babakin no doubt appreciated how Okhotsimsky ducked the word *easy* and instead chose *simplified*. A whole lot of tedious preparation separated those terms. Nobody had ever attempted this before.

"We were on the very margin of our capabilities," is how another teammate put it.

The exact clockwork machinations of the process would still have to be thoroughly ironed out beforehand, as everything relates to everything else. Lavochkin wanted the return vessel to set down on the barren steppes of Kazakhstan—about the emptiest plot of land inside the Soviet Union. They wanted to land during the daytime. They also wished to track the thing as it approached, meaning the inbound flight path would have to occur over Soviet territory.

However—as Okhotsimsky pointed out—that wish list joined a whole string of dependencies stretching back a quarter million miles to the lunar surface, dictating *to the second* when the ship would have to lift off for home. That worked backward further still to a head-shakingly narrow landing zone: Lavochkin would have to put 'er within six miles of certain preselected points on the surface. "All of them are around sixty degrees east of longitude," explained another team member. "Why? Because the moon is rotating. And when we are in the eastern hemisphere, this rotation of the moon, it adds a little bit of pulse for liftoff." Well, in order to set down *there*, the outbound flight time and speed and position would all have to be perfectly teased out, culminating at last in a determination of when to blast off from Earth in the first place.

Constraints on top of restrictions meant Babakin had to plan in reverse.

Two weeks after Borman and his *Apollo 8* crew read from Genesis in lunar orbit, a panicked meeting convened right at the Kazakhstan launch facilities. It opened with a top minister pleading, "How can we get out of this mess?"

Instead of an answer, questions buzzed about like feral gnats. What could they do to somehow deflate the significance of *Apollo 8*? What public face should be displayed? Opinions ran frantic circles through the distressed attendees. One official floated the idea of a thirty-day manned marathon in Earth orbit, as a kind of demonstration of Soviet capabilities. It got panned.

A number of hastily generated resolutions poured forth. They'd tackle a manned space station, currently plodding through development. The surreptitious effort to land cosmonauts on the moon would also remain—though most agreed that in Apollo's wake it served no real purpose. (This illuminates a curious facet of the nation's space industry: stopping. All the endless resolutions and decrees and other formalities contained no provisions for terminating the work.)

And, in something of a stunner, Lavochkin's moonscooping effort jumped to the front of the line. This reshuffle enjoyed widespread support from the Academy of Sciences, whose members likely did not appreciate the ensuing subterfuge: every Soviet newspaper, along with every radio broadcast and TV program that spoke of it, would mend the country's reputation by simply explaining that automatic lunar flights were the original plan all along.

One official haunted by *Apollo 8* was General Nikolai Kamanin, head of the cosmonauts. Kamanin maintained a private diary that remained utterly free of rhetoric or doublespeak—unlike the government he suited up for each morning. No matter what might have been uttered during the January launchpad proceedings, or endorsed by bureaucrats, Kamanin saved his real feelings for that diary: "They cannot possibly get into their heads the very simple thought that it is impossible to answer the piloted flight of *Apollo 8* with a flight of an automatic machine. . . . Any automatic machine cannot possibly be a satisfactory answer. Only landing people on the moon and successfully recovering them on Earth would serve as an answer to the triumph of *Apollo 8*."

Under this new plan, Lavochkin's opening salvo materialized in late February '69. This one might've gone the distance if not for a problematic booster that cannibalized itself barely nine miles from the pad. "We could see the launcher ascend," reminisced testing specialist Oleg Sokolov, "leaving behind a white inversion track in a bright blue sky." As his eyes followed the slithering vapors' climb, *Luna*'s booster started rattling. The undesired motion built to all-out epileptic convulsions hard enough for the rocket to shred its protective nose shroud, whereupon huge pieces of it crashed into the lower stages. This precipitated a catastrophic destabilization and loss of control, blowing the entire stack sky-high only two seconds later—and less than sixty seconds into the entire mission. Neck craned upward, squinting, Sokolov observed a different and quite unwelcome spectacle.

"A beautiful red and black flower was by now blossoming in the sky," he mourned.

For spacecraft designers, one extraordinarily frustrating aspect of their work is a complete lack of control over the launch vehicle. They've given themselves—professionally, physically, personally—to that tiny creation up in the rocket's nose. The one piece of equipment giving this whole endeavor any purpose. And if the booster starts malfunctioning, absolutely nothing can be done by them.

"At the first instant when a flaming, smoky ball is swelling in the sky, the brain of the specialist cannot absorb this fact," continued Sokolov. "Instead, one asks 'Why' and 'What next,' which the subconscious mind displays, as on an emergency panel, the only possible conclusion: 'It is the end.'" Artfully generating white and black contrails, *Luna* fell.

Infantrymen dispersed into a smoldering debris field to recover whatever bits they could. Trash went for miles. The work was tentative; rockets contain explosives like kerosene and hydrazine that are wickedly toxic and, after a crash, are usually splashed all over hell and back.

The men kept looking. One guy stumbled upon a charred assembly of wheels, which, beyond their modest size, looked to be straight off a farm tractor. Or a baby carriage, maybe? Soldiers never got briefed on what the pieces *were*. Elsewhere someone came across a portable tape recorder. The thing still worked, and as it came to life the melodious Soviet national anthem brayed out over the steppes.

Finding those scraps was great and all, but what the troops really were after was a twenty-four-pound chunk of radioactive polonium. This stuff makes acid look like Kool-Aid. Polonium is highly toxic: *way* more dangerous than rocket fuel or even hydrogen cyanide. Inhale ten nanograms of the stuff and you're toast. It's more unstable than Charles Manson, spitting off deadly alpha particles while heating itself to well over nine hundred degrees. And here these men were, deliberately looking for it. What was something like that doing in a moon rocket? It never turned up.

Lavochkin shot again in April and lost another one. Two months later came their next try. Minutes into ascent, one of the booster's upper stages failed to light. Total dud. It was high enough in the atmosphere that the probe incinerated during descent and this time left nothing to go collect.

Luna 14's exhaustive study of uneven gravity had instilled confidence that guidance experts could set *Luna 15* upright on the moon's dusty surface. It flew next, reordering Chris Kraft's to-do list and sending Frank Borman through that protracted session of expensive long-distance phone calls. Imagine the change in attitude toward manned spaceflight had *Apollo 11* aborted while *Luna 15* succeeded!

Babakin tried again after *Luna 15*—and then *again*—to no avail. The obstinate launch rockets possessed a number of defects and were ruining his plans by failing to leave Earth. They were overhauled and eventually cleared for flight. But before trying once more, something else had to happen. As with every sample-return attempt, grand math poo-bah Dmitri Okhotsimsky needed to drive this next flight backward and establish when the launch had to occur.

Like a reverse movie he started with the daylight recovery in Kazakhstan, took *Luna* up high to fold the parachute back inside, and regressed through the atmosphere during a time when the approach would occur over Soviet lands. Snapping back from there, his reams of math planted the ship on lunar soil, rewound the sample collection, then unlanded the ship. More equations took it up into orbit, about-facing to Earth, then added speed as the cast-off Proton rocket stages began tacking themselves back on one by one. The ship retreated through Earth's atmosphere, tanks refilling, arithmetically reuniting with Proton's first stage, and then finally dropped down onto the launchpad, where all the flaming exhaust went back up inside. *Stop!* What's the clock say? *That's* when they'd blast off. Where *Luna 16* was concerned, that exact moment would occur on September 12, 1970, at 6:25 p.m. and fifty-three seconds, local time. Okhotsimsky gathered his notes. Would there be anything else?

Right after launch Babakin hopped a plane and beelined fourteen hundred miles to the main control center in Crimea. It lay smack on the north central coast of the Black Sea, near an otherwise picturesque resort town called Yevpatoria. Bellying up to the facility, Georgy Tyulin described the flight's initial progress as "smooth." There they loitered, glaring dry-eyed at monitoring equipment as the ship calmly took its expected five days to reach the target. And Tyulin plainly knew he could offer essentially nothing in the way of assistance should the situation take a nosedive. *Luna 16* was out of his hands, relegating the middle-aged military man to the role of idle observer. "As the mission progressed," he recalled over the days of transit, "the emotional stress among those involved became noticeable."

Ventures like these are partitioned into logical segments, and Tyulin closely scrutinized *Luna 16*'s progression from one to the next. That first day the ship puffed its thrusters to effect a minor course correction. A couple of days afterward it encountered lunar gravity and started the long, gradual brake into orbit. Tyulin continued. "Whenever a phase drew to a close, there would be sighs of relief and occasionally thunderous applause." Its orbit next dropped to barely six miles above the highlands. Away went the deadweight of saddlebag tanks: another milestone. And the people of Lavochkin crept ever so much closer to that invisible line signifying the furthest that predecessor *Luna 15* had gone.

The main engine erupted, burning 75 percent of what fuel remained and cleanly killing *Luna 16*'s leftover speed. Gravity took over and yanked the ship down like a cinder block, screaming through forty thousand feet, then twenty; eight thousand feet to three. All in the machinery's hands now and no re-dos, electrical current flying through diodes, radar blasting the surface. Tyulin and Babakin monitored their automation playing out on a two-second delay. At two thousand feet a trigger went to light the descent engine, which—nine hundred, seven hundred, four hundred—kicked off at sixty-five feet. Six stories off the moon. Four tiny braking engines took over; so as not to disturb the site they cut out less than ten feet up and, free-falling, the craft plopped onto the surface just like that. One ship upright on four legs. They were down and safe in the Sea of Fertility.

An odd, expectant stillness took over—like the dulled atmosphere following a car crash. Okhotsimsky's math hung in the air as if it were smog on the roadside. *Luna 16* verified its health and established the local vertical. Over its radio a command then arrived from Earth. Arm swung out, rotated down, mashed drilling tube against surface. After completing this

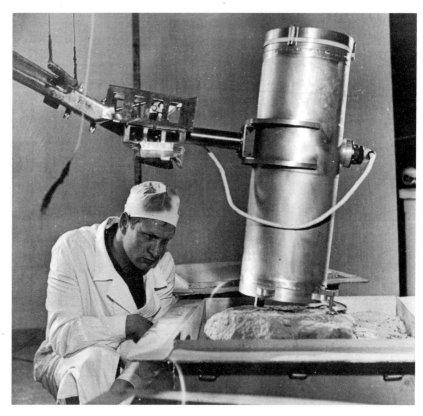

8. A tech monitors one of the Luna drills as it mates against a pretend lunar surface. These drills could bore through solid granite. Author's collection.

task it stopped, awaiting further instruction as telemetry—electronic status reports—flew back to the Soviet Union.

Technicians verified the drill's placement, confidently advancing to their next step in the program. Another command flew up into the silent abyss and told a switch to move.

Circuit complete, humming, energy, toothed cylinder spinning to life. A hundred and forty watts of power buzzing through two electric motors. At 508 RPM it bored into virginal soil, percussive and pressing, 2.2 inches per minute, lubed by special grease designed to progressively surrender itself to the vacuum of space.

Not far from Georgy Tyulin, an enraptured Oleg Sokolov followed *Luna 16*'s progress. "I remember very well how attentively we listened to the telemetry information reports when the tubular drill was digging into lunar soil, hearing that the resistance was increasing with the depth, and then getting a sudden report that the soil resistance sharply decreased." Uh-oh. A change like that could be bad or good. The drill might've broken or punched into a hollow of some sort.

Fourteen inches down they stopped. The drill had been whirling for seven long minutes.

To the quiet room someone asked, "Maybe we have drilled our own leg?" A definite possibility. *Luna 16* augured blindly; nobody could see the bit's position or even if it was in fact boring into the surface of the moon. They had to make a call.

"Not our leg," an engineer finally yapped back, "but maybe ejected tanks," referring to the cast-off saddlebags. Presently another command went up and the drill began ascending. An inch of precious soil fell out. Up it continued, arcing over, pivoting, transferring its minings to the twenty-inch-diameter globe enthroned at the summit of the rig. All this for three and a half ounces of dirt. There. It was in. Hatch sealed.

And then they waited, all activity temporarily ceasing. The return capsule wasn't to lift off until both moon and Earth had rotated into Okhotsimsky's precisely calculated moment in time. It would ascend blindly, as it had while landing. TASS did announce another victorious soft landing on the moon—but left out any other details. They weren't home yet. Babakin retreated to his Khimki office; he couldn't do anything more at the control center, anyway.

In *Luna 16*'s case the departure time didn't arrive until twenty-six and a half long hours after touchdown. A ring of explosive bolts then fired and the twenty-inch ball impulsively spouted upward, riding a small cluster of spherical fuel tanks with rocket engine geysering underneath. This engine had been designed to work only one time but to work perfectly, and it did so without pause. Right then the moon was over the Atlantic Ocean and not the Yevpatoria control center. Information came by circuitous means—dribbling in through a Soviet tracking ship prowling the waters off Cuba.

After expending its fuel the ship was going fast enough to break away from lunar gravity. Earth's gravity took over and the ball further accelerated. Over the course of three days it slowly drew closer to the blue skies and temperate grasslands of rural Kazakhstan, carrying the hopes of many expectant individuals.

Thirty thousand miles out the engine and fuel tanks let go, leaving just the lonely ball. Four hours later it hit the atmosphere, dropping stats no human would ever care to approach: eighteen thousand degrees Fahrenheit, 350 Gs. It fell for a bit, top cleaving away, parachute opening with two red, sausage-like balloons, four whiskered antennae, all unspooling: broadcasting, smiling almost, summoning Lavochkin's finest to *Come get me; I'm home.* Quickly a tracking helicopter picked up the signal, following the now-charred ball as it pillowed down right on target. Eight-thirty in the morning and home again after twelve days. Just as predicted. A recovery team swarmed over it like ants on an apple.

Exulted Tyulin, "When signals were received confirming the safe landing of the spherical capsule back on Earth, the expressions of joy were boundless." The year 1970 marked the one hundredth anniversary of Lenin's birth. The entire nation was in full prep for the occasion, with a spree of renovation and new construction and general sprucing up. Now this!

Soon a light-beige phone rang in Babakin's cluttered office. The chief designer groggily levered it off the hook and tried to summon coherence because *this* phone represented the most important of the four or so roosting on his desk. And Babakin was exhausted. The last few days he'd been essentially living here, pushing through fatigue in order to stay abreast of the many tasks facing him. The voice reaching Babakin's ears belonged to Dmitri Ustinov, secretary of the Communist Party's Central Committee.

To be clear, the Central Committee was not your average bureaucratic hellhole. From the highest of levels, it directed all of the government's activities. Think of it as *the* major policymaking body in the entirety of the Soviet Union—electing the oligarchic Politburo, or executive branch. The Central Committee issued the nation's marching orders, meaning that when its secretary rang up Babakin, the latter man really needed to be paying attention. Yet he struggled that morning under the workload; an associate in the room with him described Babakin's speech as "slightly confused." Secretary Ustinov offered up congratulations and that was effectively the end of the call. Babakin let the handset clatter and faced his guest. He was looking at Mikhail Marov, a planetary scientist.

We all tend to remember some particular aspect of a special occasion. Perhaps it's the standout food, a great joke, the postcard-perfect weather,

9. Taken after *Luna 16*'s return on September 24, 1970: in the front row, bottom left, Georgy Tyulin sits next to Georgiy Babakin, at center, with Sergei Afanasyev on the right. All three men were so joyful that they almost smiled. Author's collection.

or some funny reaction. And on this morning of the Lavochkin Bureau's successful return of moon dust, one specific memory lingers in Marov's brain all the way to this day.

"I remember the shining with happiness eyes of Georgiy Nikolayevich."

As the sphere cooled it enjoyed a flight to Moscow, a quick visit to Lavochkin, and then a police escort back through Moscow to the Vernadsky Institute of Chemistry. Those twin red sausages, extending from the parachute compartment like overfilled condoms, were meant to serve as indicators—visually standing out better than the ball itself, which otherwise was the color of burned toast.

One of Lavochkin's premier metalworkers carefully sliced open their charred re-entry capsule. Most of it was filled with batteries, a radio transmitter, and the parachute compartment. Ignoring those for the moment, technicians extracted an inner cylinder holding their booty. Then—after being safely transferred to a perfectly clean work receptacle filled with inert helium—out from *Luna 16* came the material. To a degree it paled, in comparison, to the dozens of pounds of samples already returned by Apollo. But these three and a half ounces nevertheless belonged to Soviet citizenry alone. In between peeps through the windows the team hunched together for a photograph.

If *Luna 16* accomplished only one thing beyond the snatching of moondust, it was reinforcing the public assertion that this country was *not* engaged in a race to the moon—that they never built a manned landing program, that automated space machines had always been their sole intention.

Victorious Georgiy Babakin, bringer of overdue Soviet glory, would in the near future most definitely not be catching up on sleep. Anyone outside the nation's guarded space industry holding any assumption that *Luna 16*'s mechanized exploits represented the pinnacle of robotic space accomplishments would have been speechless after learning of what was just about to happen.

7. Sitting Cosmonauts

Could not the money spent on the Apollo program have been
spent more effectively by creating an analogous USA
program of moon research by automates?

—Soviet engineer Boris Rauschenbach

Planning for this next big thing had taken a massive step forward in 1968. That spring a secretive telegram had gone forth to every one of the dozen-odd complexes forming the country's diffuse network of space mission tracking facilities. They're fairly regimented kinds of places, with little room for boneheads. Any officer with the grace to be posted at one had already distinguished himself with intelligence, maturity, common sense, motivation, discipline. None of them got to see that telegram when it came through, but their supervisors did. The small piece of paper requested "top-class military engineers," as part of it read. "Young but experienced. Sporting and in a good state of health."

Subsequently, forty or so preselected candidates received notices. They'd been invited to a meeting in Moscow, the particulars of which were not disclosed in advance. It marked the beginning of a riddle, for the meeting was not a meeting at all; everyone found themselves at—*Huh? The Institute of Biomedical Problems?* Yup, for a checkup. They got their vision tested. Their hearing. *What was this about?*

Soon the group dwindled; anybody with lame ears or iffy eyesight failed to make the cut. Their appraisals got specific: How quick was a man's reaction time, how sharp his mental focus? How rapidly and accurately could he process information flying at him in little bits and bursts? Nobody there was dumb, but the dumbest guys fell away. Summer replaced spring. The survivors went elsewhere in Moscow, encountering another series of demanding trials. Clearly, whomever had been ordered to fill seats was after some rather sharp pencils.

The profligate process persisted. Who had the best memory capacity? Who stood out? Some left the room and never came back. After they'd been going awhile, a few of the remnants wondered if they weren't being screened to become cosmonauts.

But that wasn't adding up. The selection criteria didn't favor pilots. Nothing went too deeply into aeronautics or how much stick-and-rudder time a guy had. It came off as more balanced. The players behind this whole charade seemed intent on ferreting out healthy, motivated guys who could pay really close attention to something, make rational determinations in the blink of an eye, and then implement what they'd decided without any emotional hang-ups.

As summertime wore on the indecisive ones dropped off, then the most unsure, until seventeen of the fittest, quickest, and arguably smartest individuals remained. They were put together in a group, not knowing what would happen next. Presently, a man none of them had ever known or seen stepped before the assembly to deliver the shock of their lives. Fashionably clothed and dragging heavily on a cigarette, the man dispassionately stated that his name was Georgiy Babakin and he had a proposition for each and every one of them.

"Comrades," he went on, "the officers in the Soviet Union developed a program for the exploration of the moon." But absolutely none of them would be flying in space. They weren't becoming cosmonauts after all. A team of brilliant proletarians, the group learned, had leveraged the power of socialism to create a technological marvel. Something absolutely unprecedented. *And you have been selected to* operate *this marvel—remotely commanding the first vehicle driven on the surface of the moon.*

Babakin smiled down upon their bewilderment. He deadpanned, "Who wants to participate? Ten minutes to think," then excused himself from the room.

One recruit, a whip-smart thirty-year-old named Vyacheslav Dovgan, lit a cigarette while pondering his choice. *Join, or leave?* Years later he recalled the absurdity of the situation. "I mean, a smoke—and decide!"

When Babakin returned, Dovgan elected to stay aboard but three others resigned. That left fourteen holdouts. To them Babakin inquired, "Who would like to become a *driver*?" This question, implying that more would be involved than just driving per se, did not permit another ten-minute smoke break. Seven hands punched the air, Dovgan's among them. That was it for the questions. Meeting over. The remaining men now blindly moved on to the next phase of training for this new and unforeseen technology.

Remember how the Soviets were *also* going to send people to the moon? Just like Apollo? Yeah . . . easier said than done. Those in charge of safely landing bona-fide humans faced a bitterly serious problem: their equipment wasn't real great. It operated on the absolute bleeding edge of pandemonium. Despite years of effort on their gigantic N-1 moon rocket, it still transported less payload than Apollo's Saturn V—*much* less, to the tune of a hundred thousand pounds. This meant a vulgar difference in capability: while the Apollo lander carried two men plus three squares a day plus hammocks and personal knickknacks (and, later on, a freakin' roadster), with the N-1 a lone cosmonaut would head for the surface in what amounted to a man-sized Pepsi can. There just wasn't enough of a weight allowance to build anything more. The lander joined other elements of a kludged-together lunar scheme driven entirely by what their N-1 booster *couldn't* give. The Soviets started later than Apollo, didn't have its money, and needed everything: launch facilities, simulators, lunar suits, recovery plans, and oh yes—a decision on where to go in the first place.

"We were selecting the landing sites," explained geologist Alexander Basilevsky, who spent months doing exactly that. Numerous factors affected the touchdown point, but above nearly everything else the mission planners dearly craved *flat* and *smooth*. Since engineers were too busy coercing all that iffy hardware into operation and didn't know jack about the moon anyway, they went galloping through the nation's universities to beg academic help. That's how Basilevsky got attached. His primary tool? Start laughing: it was America's five *Lunar Orbiter* spacecraft and their gorgeous catalogs of imagery. "We used them a lot," he remarked. With the U.S. government advocating a "civilian" space program, *Orbiter* pictures were not in any way classified and the Soviet government appeared only too happy to stick its arm in the cookie jar. Basilevsky and his colleagues hovered over poster-size reprints, inspecting them with magnifying glasses. "We were counting craters, counting rock fragments, making calculations—how

many craters on square kilometer, and so on." He snickered. "And generally it is a very boring thing." Yet his results went directly into estimating
how much fuel the landing ship might carry in order to perform last-second
boulder avoidance. "If he could see that some safe areas are around," Basilevsky described a cosmonaut's approach, "he could turn his spacecraft a
little to the right, to the left, or further."

But issues didn't end there. Since the ship was so flimsy, what if it met
with damage upon landing? What might the luckless cosmonaut do then?
Call his travel agent? Panic?

*Lunar Orbiter*s worked great for general mapmaking. But their high-
altitude cartography lacked the fine detail required to isolate safe landing
zones. They needed more. Well, went the reasoning, after tagging their top
two candidate spots, how about sending unmanned rovers to those areas?
They could be driven around by remote control—imaging whole swaths
of countryside, backward and sideways and probably upside-down if necessary. With new favorites in hand, engineers next advocated sending—of
all things—an *empty* man-rated lander to plop down within their *second*-
favorite zone. The nearby rover could serve as a beacon for the incoming
ship to line up on. And once the ship berthed, the rover could circle around
to inspect this new arrival. Did it land in good shape? Anything broken?

Once all that hardware was down and settled and thoroughly checked,
waiting cosmonauts could finally, mercifully, blast off from Earth to their
own lunar destiny. The second lander would be piloted down to everybody's number-one site, cosmonaut hunkered inside as the other rover circled *him* like a shark while checking for damage. Only with an all-clear
might the spacefarer embark from his craft to plant socialist footsteps on
the barren old world.

What if his lander breaks? No problem! Hike over to the other one; it's
a spare. What if the landers aren't within walking distance of each other?
No problem! Add controls and a seat to each rover. What if the guy runs
short on air? No problem! Mount some tanks on the rovers, too. Draftsmen hurried to revise their drawings. The rovers got steering controls and
reserve oxygen tanks, and naturally they got bigger and heavier. Ultimately
this plan dissolved into dust—but it evinces the insane layering of options
that people felt driven to.

A large measure of complexity might have been dispensed with by just making better stuff at the outset. But remember the state of affairs: a capitalist, competitive society this wasn't. In April 1969 the heir to Korolev, Vasily Mishin, got called on the carpet to personally explain things to Soviet leader Leonid Brezhnev. Apollo was supposed to try for the moon that July—but Mother Russia couldn't even get her N-1 rocket to fly straight? *Why weren't we more ahead in space?* demanded the general secretary. Mishin had no option but the truth. Deftly he explained that every manufacturing plant struggled with substandard organization. Quality control was abysmal, in part because nobody had any incentives for doing better work. Production facilities lay scattered everywhere; some of them faced obligations to make wildly differing kinds of things and couldn't specialize. *What else were they supposed to do?* In response, quantity: robot taxis backing up backup moon landers.

Derogatory statements are occasionally made about the quality of Soviet-era technology. And yeah, there's some real justification for that. Their computers were slow. Soviet cars left *much* to be desired. But let no one ever say that the nation regarded its cosmonauts as expendable. They never went to the moon because Mishin and everyone underneath him could not unequivocally guarantee the safety of their high flyers.

In early November 1970 a slim, bespectacled man kissed his wife, hoisted a rucksack, and headed out from his apartment to join the afternoon Moscow hubbub. That day the weather was great; temps just above freezing with light wind. A good day for travel. After five minutes of walking he reached a city bus line and hopped on. One or two stops down, the bus intersected a subway station in southwest central Moscow. Roughly twenty minutes and one train change later he got off at Kurskaya Station and made his way over into the Kursky Rail Terminal. There the man rendezvoused with a small handful of friends, who all purchased tickets and clambered aboard.

Shortly thereafter the train departed, rumbling southward from Moscow, gaining speed past Podolsk, past Serpukhov. The men dined together in the same coach—sharing food and conversation and more than a sizeable amount of alcohol. Excitement ballooned in the air around them. Anticipation. Tula flew by, then Orel. An hour before midnight the conductor came through, dousing lights. Aboard the lurching snake they stretched out and caught a few winks; this twenty-two-hour trip wouldn't end until morning.

The journey continued south, winding past Belgorod and Kharkov, wee-hour darkness occasionally interrupted by bright flashouts and noise from other trains roaring past in the opposite direction. As dawn approached they brushed the western flank of the Sea of Azov, rumbling across a narrow strip of land into the blunt precipice defining a near island jutting into the Black Sea's north end. Three-quarters of the way down it the train, at long last, halted before an arched white limestone station accentuated by a three-story clock tower. This was, and is, the city of Simferopol. The Crimean Peninsula, where the city is located, lies within today's Russia and is a touristy part of the world, filled with many resort areas. But our travelers had not come all this way for beach time.

In Simferopol they left the train, only to board a tumbledown charter bus. Its schedule? Unadvertised. Its final destination? Unmentionable. From the station's parking lot the bus driver grinded onto Gagarin Street, then hooked left onto KIM Street. The slender, high-curbed road threaded through residential areas but the driver took a couple of curves and in short order they were briskly angling northwest on the road to Yevpatoria. Now he moved at a rapid clip over the narrow stretch of concrete. These are wide-open prairie lands teeming with farm fields and the unassuming Simferopol Airport. Understand that this road did not actually have an official name; around here they were all like that. If in 1970 you were headed from Simferopol to Yevpatoria (or an interim stop along the way) and someone asked what road you were taking, it was "the road to Yevpatoria." If you were on the exact same road but headed the other direction you'd have been taking "the road to Simferopol." And that's how it worked out there. Travel maps of the time faithfully depicted the roads and number of kilometers between towns but included no road names.

The bus driver hung with the road to Yevpatoria only a few miles before jogging leftward onto a nondescript byway leading west over a small rise, past a dirt jogging track and school to where a large gate suddenly obstructed his progress. On either side of it a concrete wall trailed away into the countryside. From seemingly nowhere, a uniformed guard brazenly confronted the infamous Crimean wind to shuffle over and verify paperwork. It all seemed in order, so the guard handed everything back and opened his gate. The driver nosed on through and down into a shallow, low-lying settlement that was purposely invisible from anyplace on the main highway. Just ahead, past a threadbare soccer pitch on the left, they rolled through the shadow of a regally high cylindrical redbrick water tower that could well have been plucked from King Arthur's castle. The road bent, then forked. The driver swung right, ambling down a straight, narrow lane with a pistol range off to starboard. Trees now filled the periphery on either side, unremarkable buildings modestly peeping up from behind them. Another gate loomed ahead but the driver had stopped anyway, his diesel-powered people mover having alighted before a four-story hotel.

The door creaked open and everyone maneuvered out, half pushed by wind, filing inside to claim rooms. No rush just yet; they'd come a few days early—strung out from the trip yet alert, and wanting.

Next morning after breakfast the group stepped outside and approached that second gate: two large, green steel panels the size of garage doors that completely blocked the road. A guard emerged from his little tin-roofed shack on the left side of them and everyone withdrew ID. Not too many people saw the other side of this gate—it required special passes different from the first, back by that school.

Satisfied, the guard swung open a barred, narrow door on the sidewalk. The group proceeded through, ambling alongside a main thoroughfare before encountering yet another gate decoratively festooned with circles and rectangles in a most unappetizing shade of baby blue. From the small one-story office attached to it another guard came out and checked IDs. One by one the visitors stepped through another barred side door before hanging a sharp left down a secondary road that fronted a noticeably sparse area of town. Pint-size white shacks lay dotted about, some with hemispherical domes on their roofs. Very *very* few outsiders ever made it through that third gate.

After ten cumulative minutes of walking they came to a bland, two-story, white, L-shaped building accompanying a wide-open field to the south—an altogether different kind of field from every other they'd passed on their long journey here. A scorched field: black and charred and devoid of Crimea's tall native grasses and wildflowers. One instead dotted with craters and boulders and other riprap, which all seemed conspicuously out of place. Several hundred feet away a gigantic radio dish carved its outline from the sky. The Moscow men had never been here before yet smiled because they'd finally arrived.

Huffing up low steps to the L-shaped building came the wife-kissing

10. Welcome to Shkolnoye, the most important space place you never heard of. In 1970 it was absent from every map and forbidden to discuss. Author's collection.

rucksack bearer in a textbook display of purpose and motivation: necktie slightly askew under a sweater vest, massive eyeglasses balanced precariously on a lean, humble face. In this manner, Alexander Basilevsky reported for his first day of what certainly represented an ultimate field trip. As of late the guy had been operating in a fast-forward kind of mode. It'd begun several weeks back when a call came through asking him to choose a definitive landing zone for something called *Lunokhod*, and for God's sake please hurry because they were just about to launch it.

Basilevsky had stopped dead in his tracks. *What* were they launching?

"I think my chief of my lab," recollected the nearsighted geologist, "he probably knew much more than me, but he didn't tell us about these things. You know, there is a good saying, probably not only in Russian: 'The less you know, the better you sleep.'" He laughed at the joke. "But then we received a kind of official request from Lavochkin Association. They told us that, based on ballistical requirements, constraints, they ask us to find good place with this and this longitude, this and this latitude." In collaboration with his associates, Basilevsky labored to comply. It was tough; the criteria didn't match what they'd used when picking manned sites. Yet the group succeeded nonetheless. "We found a quite good place in the northeast part of Mare Imbrium," he continued. "And we said, 'Okay, we should go there.'"

Brisk wind and near-freezing temperatures drove his group inside the Shkolnoye building. It looked like the train station all over again; rebounding humans buzzed every which way. Immediately the new arrivals encountered a local conscript with a practiced awareness of their identities. He began escorting them through a series of cornflower blue- and yellow-painted meeting spaces before trotting up steps and heading down a wide hallway.

Presently they halted before two closed doors exactly opposite one another and Basilevsky inspected the first one. A sign on it said HARDWARE along with some three-letter abbreviation he didn't recognize. It also seemed to be the only door garnished with an armed soldier at attention. To the right of the guard and door a grid of translucent blue-green blocks formed part of the continuing wall. The blocks ran nearly floor to ceiling, shadows playing around behind them. Somebody was in there.

"You scientists—it's your place," the guide brusquely indicated, pointing to the *other* door. In a flash Basilevsky averted his eyes and did as instructed, entering the second room instead. He found a couple of big desks, a mishmash of ugly chairs, and perhaps twenty other academic types lounging around waiting for action. Scientists. He was in the room for scientists; "his place." Trussed up in one corner hung a thick TV monitor, accompanied by a silent loudspeaker. Nothing showed on the monitor screen.

Whatever this room was, was not much. Sighed Basilevsky, "Nothing special." But it'd have to suffice as his virtual home away from home for . . . well, he didn't know how long this all might last. Tomorrow *Lunokhod* would try setting down in the exact spot they chose. And if all went according to plan, Alexander "Sasha" Basilevsky would soon become one of the first geologists on Earth to explore another world in real time.

The morning after his arrival—a week after launch—*Luna 17* cast off its saddlebag tanks from low lunar orbit and thunked down near the north end of the Sea of Rains, a folded something buckled atop. After the engines finished gasping their last and all seemed well, an instruction went up. Slowly in the lunar vacuum, four gleaming metallic planks noiselessly unfolded themselves—one from each corner of the platform. They operated in parallel, synchronized, forming two sets of opposing ramps.

The science room's dormant TV flickered to life and everyone crowded round. What appeared was a jumble of blurry white and gray shapes. Slowly the picture improved, tube electronics warming up. In glaring monochrome Basilevsky recognized pipes and ramps and wiring. His eyes refocused, attention now settling upon what lay beyond that scene: landscapes of uncharted virgin territory that fairly yearned for the warm consideration of a kindly geologist. Twenty seconds later the image refreshed. Same view. Basilevsky stared hard. He'd been waiting, and from his rucksack retrieved a small journal with which to record the ensuing events. Again, eyes to screen. The soil beckoned. It lay there, undisturbed and gleaming in the lunar dawn, jet-black shadows tracing ridges and ranges and betraying even the smallest of rocks attempting to hide. Real estate never before seen by any human. Basilevsky's mouth watered. Another refresh. Still no change. He ogled the image once more, tepidly sentimental that no one would ever again see what lurked behind that camera.

What no one would ever see again took the form of a giant bathtub sitting on eight wheels. The tub held power and cameras and science instruments and had been specially built for traveling the moon by remote control. And this creation, of which the United States quite simply had no equal, now sat patiently waiting a first instruction. Its name was *Lunokhod 1*, the mere presence of which signaled a culmination of more than sixteen years' worth of theoretical discussion, meetings, rejection, surprise, reassignments, drawings, transfers, long commutes, lost sleep, mock-ups, booze, more meetings, test articles, flight articles, marital strife, bad food, and cold tea. Not to mention liquid nitrogen—lots and lots of liquid nitrogen.

How many things never make it off paper? Die in the planning or budget stage? And here it was.

Another command severed the remaining connections between landing platform and rover. Basilevsky stood up and crossed his arms. Waiting. In the dead air he browsed the other expectant faces in that room, all glued to the crappy monitor. They were ready to gather every last bit of data on the moon's chemical composition, soil properties, or cosmic radiation. Basilevsky himself looked forward to analyzing ground imagery. That was all fine and well but nobody had put a steering wheel in *here*. In

11. This is *Lunokhod 1*. The giant *Goldfinger*-looking raygun at top front is actually the steerable radio antenna. The name "Lunokhod" variously translates to "lunar walker" or "lunar wanderer." Courtesy RIA Novosti.

this stupid holding cell. He looked at the screen again. Same image; it still hadn't changed.

A glance over to the doorway. A fellow geologist, Boris Nepoklonov, headed the whole science team, and Basilevsky knew he'd already been operating with some kind of crew. Across the hall must be where the drivers worked and right now where Boris likely was. The command room. But—why couldn't they talk to anyone in there? Wasn't this mission about science? What if they wanted to stop and take a deep look at something? Heavens above, what if they noticed lunar bedrock? Shoved into this dungeon like they were, like brainless cattle, would anyone even be listening?

That's when the loudspeaker cackled to life.

It said, "Brothers, are you ready?!"

Across the hall from Basilevsky and through that forbidden door, occupying a claustrophobic square of a room with a herringbone-patterned wood floor, one of eleven elite men awaited his cue to start the engines. He'd been clapping—in here they all had been, once the landing succeeded—and as the sting died away from his palms Nikolai Yeremenko had the opportunity to reflect that this was it, the moment he'd trained for, all those months of toil and drudgery, unable to tell even his close family what he was up to.

Yeremenko took his place in a straight-backed, wood and metal chair that looked like it came right out of a schoolroom. Before him sat a half-height metal console. It was industrial, functional, and drab as hell. A small work surface jutted out from it with barely enough space for Yeremenko to rest his lean forearms on. Full of indicator lights and oversize needle gauges, the console's centerpiece was an up-angled TV monitor displaying exactly what the scientists were getting across the hall: a scabby, low-res angle from one of the navigation cameras on *Lunokhod 1*'s nose. Four additional cameras had been tacked on, two per side. One set created horizontal panoramas, 180 degrees' worth. The others imaged vertically through a full 360 degrees. All four delivered significantly higher resolution than the front-mounted nav-cams and would supply the imagery for Basilevsky and his ilk to scrutinize. Panoramas took twenty minutes apiece; the first got underway as *Lunokhod* peacefully waited atop its landing stage. "I see the moon's surface!" called one man as the image slowly built. "It's flat. The surface is flat. And it's beautiful!"

Yeremenko's console joined others in two neat rows, arranged at the far end of the room. They faced away from the door, toward an additional TV monitor high on a corner pedestal, with the room's windows just to the left and covered by heavy drapes. Yeremenko and his four teammates had first shift. Five others composed a second lineup, with one spare man in reserve for either group. Never were they thought of as two teams—rather, one team of two shifts. It was part of the mind-set. Way back in training had Georgiy Babakin anointed them "my sitting cosmonauts."

With pronounced slowness the navigation image refreshed once again and, even though nothing changed, the crew gawked. Already their minds had begun transitioning to a perceived mental state of actually being on the moon.

Adjacent to the dual rows of consoles sat an oversized drafting table. And behind all that, at the very back of the room, sat a few assistants—plus most of the remaining crew members (two of the crew, including Vyacheslav Dovgan, were at that moment racing to Simferopol aboard a passenger train). "The surface in the landing area was smooth," indicated one of the idle men. "And the conditions for roll-down were good." Whoever chose *Lunokhod*'s port of call had done their job.

Hang on—five whole guys to steer this thing? Well, while one did just that, another kept tabs on the rover's vital signs: angle of inclination, battery levels, condition of science instruments. All in the domain of the flight engineer. A third parked himself at the drafting table, accessorized with a right-angle ruler on a cantilever arm. This man functioned as navigator, charting progress with the deliberate attention of a mapmaker. Another man constantly nudged *Lunokhod*'s pencil-beam antenna in order to keep it locked on Shkolnoye. The fifth guy held dominion over everyone else on duty: commander. And make no mistake, this would not be some elaborate charade of a video game. Driving anything takes work. Ask a Predator crew: how hard can it possibly be to fly unmanned drones through frontline combat eight thousand miles away while reclining in squashy armchairs at a Las Vegas command post? You'll get an earful about exhaustive focus and the tolling stress—no matter the physical separation and loungeful accoutrements.

The finished panorama indicated that nothing obstructed their rover. Over two hours after landing, it was time. A switch got flipped, and everything they said would now go out over the building loudspeakers, as well as down onto audiotape.

Recalled Yeremenko, "After applause and many congratulations, Babakin came up to us and asked, 'Brothers, are you ready?!'"

Seriously? They'd been practicing for two straight years.

"Ready!" cried Yeremenko, with a touch of emotion.

Howled Babakin, "Saddle up!"

Now commanded Yeremenko, "First speed, forward!" A man in back responsively noted the event in a massive logbook: his first entry of many. One row in front of Yeremenko's console, the short and round-faced team driver Gennady Latypov gripped a chrome-colored joystick, thumbed the button on top, and oh-so-carefully began easing *Lunokhod 1* down its ramps.

Each crew member wore a lightweight blue jogging suit with white accent stripes on the collars and wrist cuffs. Such roomy loungewear would help mitigate the steady hours of focused concentration.

Across the hall, Basilevsky adjusted his glasses, watching the screen (and now listening to some faceless driver) as it updated. They were moving! Another bit . . . steady as she goes . . . almost . . . almost . . .

Latypov's heart rate shot to 140.

When *Lunokhod*'s front wheels touched, a disembodied loudspeaker voice informed everyone that they'd just contacted the wrong place. Shouted the voice, "*Lunokhod* has landed on the surface of the Earth!" Promptly it corrected itself: "The moon!" Everyone burst into applause.

All the way down now. Off and clear of the landing stage. A command went up and gradually the top of the bathtub hinged open from the back, like an oversize toilet seat. On the lid's underside, a carpet of solar cells ravenously gobbled daylight, juicing the batteries in *Lunokhod*'s belly. They'd been installed in a charged state but now needed a good topping-off. Basilevsky characterized them as "buffer batteries," which is a nicely compact way of describing how they ingested fluctuating current from the solar cells and pushed steady streams of clean power to the rest of the moon car.

First the crew headed south, crawling along slowly in one of two modes. The safest involved driving a preprogrammed distance: "travel half a meter," for example. This got used the most. The other, "continuous" mode utilized an approach of "go until told to stop" and represented an altogether gutsy way of driving something from almost a quarter million miles away. Near Yeremenko's hand sat a button. If anyone gauged that *Lunokhod* might be headed to a place it shouldn't, the commander could slap his button and halt the vehicle.

Latypov tweaked their position. To the right of his TV screen sat a purposefully simple arrangement of four large arrows pointing away from each other in cardinal directions, like a compass rose. The arrow tails converged in the middle on a two-by-two grid of lights. In this fashion Latypov had before him a straightforward display indicating whether *Lunokhod* was stopped, turning, or proceeding straight ahead. Over to the left of his TV, humongous needle gauges reported the steepness of the slope being traversed and the rover's degree of side-to-side tilt.

View was everything and they didn't have enough of it. The fixed-position nav-cam pointed straight out and couldn't gimbal down—forcing the crew to deal with a nasty blind spot. So in a manner of speaking, *Lunokhod* did not possess the dexterity to see its own toes. And the low sight line was awful. Think about crawling through a meadow on your hands and knees while trying to gauge distances or appraise the forthcoming terrain.

On top of those dwelled the refresh problem. The rover carried a backup nav-cam immediately next to its primary, and neither was capable of full-motion video. Still frames dribbled in about twenty seconds apart—a rate that could be varied only slightly, driven by the limits of technology. Add to that three more edgy seconds for the radio signal to go round-trip. Altogether, it equaled the team not seeing exactly *where they'd driven to* for several chest-grabbing moments. The men certainly weren't frantic—after all, they'd trained this way—but already they felt the hemorrhage of energy from continuously memorizing every approaching feature. *Slow, slower.* Over the course of that afternoon the bathtub gradually inched away from its landing stage and that was as fast as they dared go.

Presently a massive set of lapels entered the crew room, tugging the uniform and pendulous girth of Deputy Minister Georgy Tyulin along behind. Loitering near the glass-block wall, he quietly schmoozed with the spare crew and tempered his feelings about *Lunokhod*'s performance thus far: "During their first attempts to drive it on the moon, they used up excessive amounts of onboard electrical power." How come? Nothing here was much different from training.

It occurred to him that maybe the squad couldn't get it together because of interference. A clot of prescreened Soviet journalists had come to witness and report and were seriously getting in the way.

"Despite strict rules to the contrary," Tyulin went on, "the visitors kept crowding around the *Lunokhod* operators and their TV screens, inquiring about features on the pictures and making analogies with driving a car on the Earth, where closing your eyes for twenty seconds is paramount to joining the afterlife."

Tyulin looked at the drivers and back at the invaders. Irately he picked up the story: "Although conversation in the control room was prohibited, some visitors volunteered a running commentary." Voices piled atop each other like rugby players. For as much as they'd been through, the drive team had never trained with a bunch of prattle-mouthed rubes hovering over them like wasps.

"The operators' patience was beginning to run out," described Tyulin, in something of an understatement. "They were perspiring from the stress and the heat emitted by the control instruments. Their pulses reached the 120–140 mark." Throughout all this, *Lunokhod* was supposed to keep moving. But the crew's productivity was sliding off a cliff.

Lavochkin deputy Vladimir Panteleev jumped on a chair and administratively cleared his throat. "Everybody get out of here!" he screeched. Party over, the journalists dispersed.

After moving sixty-six timid feet they stopped for the day. Cumulative distance could be measured via a ninth "odometer" wheel trailing just off the rover's back end and fitted with spiky treads to reduce slipping. Yeremenko and Latypov and the others abandoned their consoles, leaving an idle *Lunokhod* to soak in blasting sunlight. Engineers wanted a full Earth day for additional battery charging, meaning that Basilevsky had a chance to unwind. He and Boris Nepoklonov retreated back through the weather and two security gates to their lackluster hotel accommodations. Five-star they weren't.

"We stayed four people in one room," said Basilevsky, "with women and men restrooms in the corridor at each floor."

The scheme for a remote-control moon lab was not a new one, and it did not start life as towel boy for manned landings. Rather, Lunokhod's heritage ambled backward over a rumply ribbon of time extending at least sixteen years. Click those heels together three times and return to 1954—a time when *Brown v. Board of Education of Topeka* ruled segregation to be illegal. A time of Elvis Presley's first recordings, not to mention the separation of Vietnam into north and south. Roger Bannister violated the four-minute mile that year. And Senator Joseph McCarthy got asked whether or not, at long last, he had any sense of decency left.

Within Soviet lands, many scientific minds had been theorizing about lunar exploration—with a bevy of speculative design to fulfill that need. Their most versatile idea involved roaming the landscape with some kind of automatic car. It was totally blue-sky thinking because in 1954 nobody knew how to build that, and they sure didn't have the wherewithal to cross 239,000 dead-black miles in order to use one.

Even so, people love contemplating what might be, and a light-utility-style vehicle supported everything they could ask for: tons of experiments on a mobile platform, rolling anywhere you want. Perhaps under the impression it'd be going into battle, they envisioned a tank: rugged, all-terrain, armored. In some literature it acquired the noxious term "tankette-laboratory." Some concepts featured solar cells, including automatic ways to constantly face them toward the sun. At that time in history broadcast television was just beginning its popular expansion, and one group advocated the inclusion of TV cameras, which "will permit scientists on the Earth to observe the lunar surface and the lunar sky," using TV "to determine the safest path for the movement of the laboratory." They proposed loading the rover with "various automatic instruments, transmitting to the Earth their readings on the state and properties of the lunar atmosphere and the lunar surface." They took a stab at the tank's overall mass, which wasn't terribly far removed from that which actually flew. One drawing published at the time indeed depicted a gunless tank—crawler tracks ringing its exterior, with power supplied by an internal combustion engine!

Eerily, one article foreshadowed what would come to be official Soviet policy: with the advent of these mobile laboratories, "serious initial investigations of the moon, sufficient for carrying out the next stage—the mastery of the moon by man—are possible in principle." Only a few years later, Sergei Korolev's team plunged into their own rover designs. And these guys had rockets that could go the distance.

Three days in, Basilevsky and Nepoklonov headed back over to reclaim their places in the bland science room. Both were on loan from the same guy—a round-faced geologist named Kirill Florensky. He sported thick, horn-rimmed eyeglasses, a hairline operating at very high latitudes, and an intense curiosity about meteorite impacts. By 1967 his Department of Lunar Geology had been assembled inside a relatively new Moscow organization known as the Space Research Institute. There Florensky oversaw roughly fifteen individuals spread among two major disciplines: geology and cartography. Nepoklonov came to him as a mapmaker—and in addition to heading Lunokhod's science team would inventory the panoramas and manage their analyses. The only scientist even considered for crew-room access. Whenever the rover's end finally came, Nepoklonov would distill its raw imagery into comprehensive maps of the lunar terrain.

12. On the left, Alexander Basilevsky examines Lunokhod panoramas in the science room with Boris Nepoklonov. Neither gussied up for the camera. "At Soviet time scientists used to dress a little bit formal," assured Basilevsky. Courtesy Alexander Basilevsky.

Cartographers live for uncharted territories, and into one a fully charged *Lunokhod 1* now took off. It went in the logbook as "Session 102." The numeric broke down into first lunar day, second communication session. Once again Basilevsky trained his eyes on the glowing TV screen. "My involvement was inevitable," he suggested of his time on Lunokhod. "Our lab was the only professional group in the country working on surface geology of the moon."

For much of their professional lives, geologists labor in relative obscurity—heading out into the field, analyzing rocks, writing papers, guiding students, presenting at conferences. And Basilevsky's career had been following the same kind of pathway. "I was interested in minerals," he noted of his earliest passions. "Beautiful minerals, which were in dirt or deposits where I was working."

To most, however, that's all so academically mundane. His world really started to germinate when those first requests came through to establish cosmonautic ports of call—the manned landing sites. Every question about lunar terrain went to Florensky, and his unassuming little department inadvertently sculpted a monopoly. In short order, the Lavochkin Bureau essentially became dependent on the group's recommendations. For everything. "Including geologists of our lab into the Lunokhod science team was done quite automatically," conveyed Basilevsky, speaking of his rapidly evolving career.

He welcomed the transformation. "It's not that at any given moment somebody *needs* you." And this, in a nutshell, is how things were different. A newfound reliance on his team filled the man with an awareness of purpose he'd never before experienced. "We felt that they *need* us," he applauded Lavochkin, the cosmonauts, and even the Kremlin bureaucrats. "They *needed* our results."

Watch it! Craters ahead! When the rover was in motion, any image appearing on the monitors represented where it *had been*, up to twenty seconds ago—an altogether unfair delay. Circuiting through the building, Georgy Tyulin could practically catch a nap between video-screen refreshes, and in that time a strip of dark shadow might turn out to be some hugely deep crater. As such, the crew shied away from using *Lunokhod*'s continuous drive mode. If Yeremenko called a pause the instruction leaving his console would have to race down through the bowels of the building and out across the black field and over to the antenna and then up it and to the moon and *Lunokhod*'s own antenna and down *that* into the belly and the main computer for interpretation and finally a wheel stop. Four point one seconds. For Yeremenko to receive word back that *Lunokhod* had actually ceased motion took at least another three. It's driving with closed eyes and mushy brakes. That second day *Lunokhod* advanced 295 feet, while the third saw 328. With concern Basilevsky noted how the crew's desire to barge ahead superseded that of doing methodical science.

The navigation image updated, fresh crew in place, Vyacheslav Dovgan now handling the joystick. (Along with Commander Igor Fyodorov, he'd been late for the landing due to a mandatory Moscow briefing on *Lunokhod*'s science experiments.) While driving they employed a clipped, antiseptic style of communication that sounded right off a nuclear submarine. "This is 101 reporting on the situation," Dovgan stated to Fyodorov at call sign 103. "Twenty degrees left of the course, a stone. Distance, five meters." Back when training was just getting underway, everybody talked at once—blabbering out data over the radio loop, trying to report every single thing on their screens and gauges. But nothing ever really got communicated because no one ever listened to the other guy. Discipline and tight syntax followed.

The high-contrast TV picture facing Dovgan wiggled slightly from side to side in analog imprecision. "Straight ahead, a crater. Diameter, nine meters. To the right, fifteen degrees, a gap." Another screen refresh. "Decision: will turn left sixty degrees to avoid both crater and stone, and then regain the straight-ahead direction." Dovgan swallowed. The precision taxed his faculties. Navigator Vikenty Samal lodged no objection to Dovgan's plan. Fyodorov okayed the move. Thumb on joystick. Rolling. Antenna operator Nikolai Kozlitin lightly tapped his direction-changing buttons to stay in touch. The better the radio link, the less noise coming through in the pictures (not to mention the diminished number of errors in their data signals). Samal laid pencil lines onto the poster-sized chart beneath his forearms. Flight engineer Albert Kozhevnikov noted the rover's voltage levels and temperature from his mammoth computer console. Detour complete. Big breath. That's how every move went; all five laboring together as a single organic whole.

Slowly yet certainly, *Lunokhod*'s drive crew acclimatized. And, from Dovgan's perspective, the encroaching lunar sundown marked a noteworthy increase in team cohesion. "By its end," he reported of this first day, "stiffness in crew actions, which we'd observed earlier, had completely disappeared." A well-earned, practiced edge began creeping into their maneuvers. "Movements became more confident." Already they had the hang of it—with Dovgan even noticing tonal changes as they spoke to one another on the intercom loop. "More airy and spirited," he felt.

They wrapped day five by zigzagging around to find a nice level parking spot. The rover's arrival had come during lunar dusk, as it were, and an inhumanely cold night was about to set in for two long weeks. During that time *Lunokhod* would have to brave a dreadful period of hibernation. Would it come back to life afterward? Engineers gave Lavochkin a ninety-day "warranty period," meaning they expected the thing to persevere through three lunar nights, max. After that all bets were off.

Realize that an entire lunar day runs approximately one Earth month—four weeks. For two of those weeks the sun is "up" on the moon, and for the other two it's down. No sunlight on the lunar surface means nothing's lighting up the solar cells on *Lunokhod*, which by extension means not enough power to move or run a science instrument or do much of anything. And it's mighty cold up there when the sun goes down: 250 below, Fahrenheit. "At the nighttime, it is so cold that if you don't have a heater inside, everything could be frozen," explained Alexander Basilevsky. "The batteries—they had liquid, so that liquid would be frozen." Insulation splits. Wiring cracks. Rovers break.

Closing the lid helped warm things up by sealing over the massive thermal radiator sitting at the top of the tub. Whatever heat lingered inside would thus be temporarily retained. But that by itself wouldn't keep the home fires burning.

Erupting from the tail end of *Lunokhod*'s body, like some giant pimple on its butt, hung a twenty-four-pound can of polonium. Next to circus peanuts, it's some of the most dangerous stuff on planet Earth. Polonium is nasty—radioactive and toxic and murderous—but its natural decay generates free heat and that's precisely what the idea was in using it. (A comparatively mundane element like uranium would never produce enough warmth for two constant weeks of sustenance—unless so much was crammed inside *Lunokhod* that it couldn't possibly get off the ground. You need material with a rapid period of decay.) An arrangement of pipes arterially wended their way through the rover, fans circulating air to all extremities. Normally the fans and pipes expelled *hot* air and kept the buggy from overheating during those tropical lunar days. But after the sun went down it had the opposite problem—*not enough* heat. So at the back of the rover this piping intersected the polonium and voilà, instant heater.

A flight engineer verified that the lid had indeed closed and that *Lunokhod*'s internals were warming up. Tired, Alexander Basilevsky packed his rucksack and walked to the bus, initiating a long journey home to Moscow to try and come down from all the hoopla. In two weeks he'd return to see if dead things really could come back to life.

8. Cauldron of Contradictions

I won't give you any advice. You're the specialists, you figure it out!

—Sergei Korolev, to the engineers of Institute 100

The "tankette-laboratory" took its own sweet time coming together. In March '63, Sergei Korolev had issued an edict for rover construction to begin—which was all fine and well until Korolev's people sat down to wrestle with how to actually do that. Their first problem centered on mobility. Rovers have to rove, and they sifted through every imaginable option. Tank tracks. Wheels. They appraised one that inched along via ski-shaped "feet," alternating steps. What was more important—navigating boulders or not bogging down in loose soil? Maybe the job needed something totally out of the box, like giant snowshoes. Nobody could draw a bead on *how to move*. One of the project engineers bemoaned their predicament: "It was not possible to design a remote controlled lunar vehicle able to travel over a terrain of dust, sand, *and* rock," he confessed. "We had to find a single option and make a decision." And of course, lunar probes had previously never needed to *drive* anywhere after landing; they were always just balls with things springing out of them. But now Korolev's bureau would craft a rock-solid kick-butt ultra-stable all-terrain lunar hot rod entirely from scratch?

Absurd. Futile!

It hit somebody: what about the tractor people?

Of course, the agrarian yet mightily industrialized Soviet Union had shitloads of tractors laying around. Who can forget the unforgettable Stalinets-80 or the rough-n'-ready T-60? Simply designed and dependable as hell, those things could go darn near anywhere that wasn't under ten feet of water. Soviet tractors took the pain and gave. With these attributes in mind,

Korolev confidently approached the Institute for Tractor and Agricultural Machinery Building. Months later the place responded by telling him to forget about it. The idea was "impossible," as they phrased it. They'd built a mockup. It sucked. Nobody was ever going to put a robot ATV on the moon.

Korolev grimaced. Things like this tend to delay projects.

That summer a man 450 miles away from Moscow and Korolev, who knew nothing about the moon or lunar rovers, was busily engaged in the gritty theatrics of trying to make his air cushion work. The guy's name was Izrail Rozentsveyg, staff engineer at an enormous technical and mechanical plant in Gorolevo known as the All-Union Scientific Research Institute No. 100. It operated throughout the southwestern confines of Leningrad over many acres of offices and machine shops and testing labs. These days Leningrad is called St. Petersburg, and on a map this second-largest Russian city is tucked underneath Finland, just to the right of Estonia.

Officially, Institute 100 was not an institute or a manufacturer or even a place. It was not civilian but a military plant—utterly secret and therefore *nothing*; it wasn't there. Insiders referred to it as "a mailbox." The facility's big thing was making tanks. An entire department there absolutely loved creating them, and the Soviet army had come to be very thankful for their putting forth the effort to invent such good ones. During the World War II siege of Leningrad, Institute 100 tanks often rolled directly out the factory gates and up to German positions.

But Rozentsveyg did not build tanks and neither did his boss, a charming and slightly built departmental head named Alexander Kemurdzhian. Both occupied a completely separate wing known as the Department of New Principles of Movement, which is where the air cushion came into play. This venture aimed to synthesize tanks with hovercrafts—"capable of overcoming water bodies, wetlands, soft bottoms," described Rozentsveyg. Military strategists ached for such a vehicle. "Unfortunately, the four years during which we worked on this project did not yield positive results." By mid-1963 it'd turned into a catch-22 of a wild goose chase because they couldn't get a hovercraft to carry the required munitions and armaments while at the same time meeting specific weight limits.

Without warning that hot July day, Rozentsveyg got pulled into Kemurdzhian's office and sworn to absolute secrecy. Only a couple of hours before, he learned, a trusted representative of the space program's myste-

13. With beret on and head cocked slightly, thirty-three-year-old Izrail Rozentsveyg stands at dead center. Behind the group rests a prototype "hovertank." "The picture was taken outside the city, on the lake, where tests were carried out," said Rozentsveyg. Courtesy Izrail Rozentsveyg.

rious chief designer had paid a visit. *The guy who put up* Sputnik? *The dog? Gagarin?* Indeed. He wanted to maybe collaborate on some kind of new-fangled moon machine—one that could actually drive around up there under remote control. For the very first time, Rozentsveyg heard that the chief designer's name was—*Shh!*—"Sergei Korolev."

"Why did Kemurdzhian trust specifically me with this secret?" wondered Rozentsveyg aloud, many years later. "Probably because I was the one working with ultra-light materials, or because I was one of the most experienced designers of the department. Or maybe just because we were friends."

And why Korolev had singled out *them* wasn't real clear. "The institute had never worked in aviation and space," Rozentsveyg acknowledged, "and completely lacked experience in the creation of vehicles for flying." Their bread and butter was tanks, which—yeah, okay, traveled over varying kinds of difficult terrain . . . but the similarities ended right about there. "Tank designs did not have such stringent requirements for weight, sterility, and for ultra-low environment pressure. The conditions under which the tanks had to work were extremely clear and understandable," he added. Furthermore—if something in one of them broke, a soldier could just hop out with his toolbox and fix it (under nominally appropriate covering fire).

Their being a military facility probably had something to do with Korolev's choice, though. "In our country," Rozentsveyg continued, "it was believed that military departments' experts were better qualified. The possibilities of such institutions were greater; they were better provided with materials and had access to information stolen from the West." Still, ah, that tractor shop had passed on the whole thing? Maybe they should do the same.

Institute 100 deferred a decision on accepting; they needed time to mull it over. Rozentsveyg didn't know beans about the moon, so for the next month he visited libraries and tried to cram his brain with whatever scraps could be found. He talked to astronomers and geologists, who all had opinions on the moon—though nobody had yet landed anything on it to examine the conditions firsthand.

"Our customer," he laughed of Korolev's design bureau, "believed that the rover chassis was a completely solved problem." One prominent engineer had even lectured him, "Do not complicate the issue. It should be an ordinary bicycle!"

"Didn't feel that way!" chided Rozentsveyg.

The tractor institute shipped over their dud mockup. "I understood the reason for their failure," Rozentsveyg charged after having a close look. "From the very start they decided that the chassis should be on caterpillar tracks." On each side of the mockup, a belt of heavy interlinking plates wrapped around giant cogs, which in turn joined with multiple suspension arms. Above this arrangement it wore a half-spherical turtle shell, making the whole contraption look straight out of an Ed Wood movie.

Caterpillars were an obvious choice, he supposed—a known quantity, but also a complicated and uninformed one. "Without consulting, without contacting the specialists, they decided to play it safe." Rozentsveyg didn't understand the exact way to build a lunar chassis, but he knew they could sure do better than this.

Toward the end of August, Kemurdzhian culled a group of fifteen or so experts from the various departments to jointly determine whether they should continue. The assemblage included metallurgists, electricians, transport specialists, and plenty of tank guys. As Rozentsveyg put it, "Nobody at that time could answer the essential question: What *is* the lunar soil?" Solid answers would tell them whether to go with tracks or wheels. And once a determination had been made, how would the power plant operate? Using what kind of fuel? What special preparations would metal-on-metal parts need in order to avoid fusing together in a vacuum? How would the electronics have to be prepped? Also: how to "drive" this thing from such a huge distance?

Throughout the remainder of '63, Kemurdzhian's group worked the situation. They met with Soviet astronomers to discuss likely compositional aspects of the lunar surface. They went to the nearby Pulkovo Observatory to stare at the moon through telescopes. "We were unable to really see anything," remembered one attendee. But the men succeeded in digesting a significant amount of information on these previously unknown topics.

Said Rozentsveyg, "The final technical report issued at the end of the year allowed us to formally demonstrate the fundamental possibility of creating such a machine." They thought it could be done. "And not only the chassis itself. We discovered a whole field of opportunities to do research, including the study of properties of the lunar soil." They whittled the basic locomotion options down to two—a wheeled version and one using crawler tracks. Skis and snowshoes were out.

During the spring of '64, Institute 100 took on a noticeably different appearance. The number of people assigned to the rover effort increased to more than fifty. Testing stands began rising inside cavernous work bays. Engineers sorted through options for high-spec electric motors capable of functioning in the moon's extreme environment. An oval test track went in; trucks arrived bearing tons of pumice, sand, cement powder—every analog for lunar soil. Ferrari had a test track; now Gorolevo did too. Of particular interest was how caterpillar tracks might handle turns and cornering on these uncommon surfaces.

Everything they did occurred inside a bubble. "We had no opportunities to learn what was available abroad, in Europe, in the U.S.," lamented Rozentsveyg. They didn't have sacks of American dollars laying around—only rubles, which, outside the border, didn't get a guy very far. "We could only dream about imported equipment, which was highly appreciated in the country, but for which foreign currency was required."

Months later, on May 31, 1964, Korolev and five others visited the institute for a highly anticipated meeting in the director's office. Korolev's wife also came in tow. Appearances by someone like the chief designer were ordained with the utmost in priority and importance. Most rank-and-file employees got the day off. The big meeting's guest list was rigidly controlled, down to who got to handle key documents, who got to have dinner with him afterward, and where they'd be sitting at the restaurant.

"And now it was necessary to show to the visitor how much the institute was ready."

Lively discussion was struck up on the two base configurations. Korolev overtly preferred tracks, owing to the uncertain nature of the surface. Kemurdzhian smiled; he also was thinking tracks and recommended as much to his visitors. On the walls around them hung posters of different conceptual designs. Accompanying graphs laid out estimated costs—including some specific kitchenware the institute foresaw needing: more lab space, vacuum equipment, testing chambers.

Kemurdzhian presented a report that took half an hour. Then Korolev maneuvered his flabby gut from the chair and strolled around browsing posters. While up he launched into a discussion of the "Terms of Reference," or what could be thought of as the rover's design criteria. They'd been written by his own men and specified a six-hundred-mile operational range, achieving speeds of over six miles an hour. In previous meetings with Korolev's subordinates, Institute 100 men had daintily expressed concern over delivering such high standards—favoring a more conservative set of metrics instead. "Our disputes for decreasing the requirements for the vehicle were always met with a vehement resistance," remembered Rozentsveyg.

Looking at nobody in particular, Korolev crinkled his nose and, to everyone's mute stupefaction, abruptly denounced the terms. *Exaggerated claims*, he blared. The task at hand was not to race along for hundreds of miles at top speed; it was about threading through uncharted lunar landscapes. *This is about exploring!* He sat back down.

The meeting closed with a plan to revise the terms and move forward and then they were basically done talking. After collecting his wife from the director's lounge, Korolev and his entourage toured the adjacent workshops—reviewing the impressive infrastructure already committed to the rover project—before finally heading out to eat. The name of Izrail Rozentsveyg hadn't made the dinner list. Although he owned a car, his journey home entailed a succession of three public buses, eventually reaching a 430-square-foot apartment shared with four others. Elsewhere, Korolev's group proceeded to a large private feast with many toasts of brandy. Afterward they took in Leningrad's Russian Museum before flying out on a private turboprop.

Meetings begat meetings; the "Terms of Reference" were distilled into more manageable specs. "There is a project brief, there are some developments," inflected Rozentsveyg. "We got the confidence that all this was serious, that we had to continue working. That we should get rid of the air cushion and work entirely on the project of the lunar rover."

At lower levels, even an informal decision still hadn't been reached on wheels versus tracks. People had their biases and favorites and other made-up reasons for preferring what they did. "We *wanted* to use caterpillars," argued institute engineer Pavel Sologub. "We used to make tanks, and we loved tanks."

"Psychologically, the caterpillar was close to developers' hearts as they were mainly tank men," admitted Rozentsveyg. "There were people who believed that *only* the caterpillar was able to 'walk' on the moon." But to him, anyway, tracks presented a bevy of inadequacies. "The caterpillar was still quite heavy, unreliable, and required more energy," he listed out. "We had a very big shortage of power, weight, and size!"

Korolev had a lot on his plate, and already-spotty rover development quickly fell to the tail end of priorities. After all, the Communist Party expected him to land cosmonauts on the moon, and that was not exactly a part-time job.

RED CLAIMS HARD MASS COVERS MOON

LONDON (Reuter's)—The moon's surface is covered by a deep layer of porous material like hard cotton wool, not thick dust, as hitherto believed, a top Soviet scientist said Saturday.

Prof. Vsevolod Troitsky, a doctor of physics and mathematics, in an interview with the Soviet news agency Tass, reported on experiments conducted by himself and other researchers at the Soviet Institute of Radio Physics.

Rozentsveyg and three associates paid Dr. Troitsky a visit in January 1965. They talked about the issue at hand and, in Rozentsveyg's words, "tried to convince ourselves that the scientist was correct." Eventually they did just that, resolutely foregoing caterpillar tracks in favor of independently suspended wheels.

"It became clear that wheels were more reliable," echoed Pavel Sologub. "Caterpillars could get stuck, and that would ruin the whole mission. And we couldn't afford to make a mistake." As upstanding a man as he was, Alexander Kemurdzhian later conveniently forgot that he'd backed caterpillars for so long.

They whipped up a model chassis, hanging wheels off the corners of a rectangular frame. Okay, not bad . . . although it still didn't seem to be headed anywhere past mediocre. But then, a genius move. Smiled one participant, "We placed a Japanese video camera on it and controlled the machine from a distance using a television."

Expectantly the men watched their "tank" rumble around on everyone's best guess of the lunar surface. It moved, it climbed, it traversed—all guided by rudimentary controls parked before a low-res TV display. Something clicked. At that moment, they jumped a mental barrier to declare, *We can do this.*

Now, let's be clear here: the prototype's hastily welded frame was too heavy to fly. No science instruments were aboard. This thing plainly would not have survived the lunar environment. *Nothing about it at all* was "flyable." But after that camera went on top, everyone knew they could build a car to drive on the moon because they could now see it in their minds' eyes. With every boulder bouldered and crater crossed, the effort inaudibly transcended fantasy to become potentiality.

Even with a pimped-out camera, one rough-and-tumble prototype went

14. The prototype Lunokhod rover undergoes agility tests. "The wheels should not be inflexible," characterized Izrail Rozentsveyg of their evolving design. "They were supposed to be made resilient, to increase the area of contact with the surface, and to reduce ground pressure." Author's collection.

only so far. The real rover's frame would have to dynamically move and compensate for abrupt terrain changes. Undulate like a Jeep doing ballet. They therefore needed to cook up the world's most versatile automotive suspension system, and along with it some kind of self-protection mode—built-in smarts to ensure the rover would automatically halt prior to roaring up too steep of an incline, or before tilting too far to one side. Sologub contemplated how to run all this on the allotted power budget of three hundred watts. "Can you imagine?" he grumbled. "It's the energy of a lightbulb. It's very very weak. The energy of a lightbulb was supposed to power the Lunokhod under the extreme conditions on the moon!" Golly, the air cushion had never needed to be *smart*, and pieces of that thing hadn't exactly fallen together all by themselves, either. They were going to have to come back to that one. Kemurdzhian latched the problem in his brain and set the controls to low tumble.

Up for grabs was the number of wheels. The rover needed enough so that if some of them broke, bogged down, or dropped into a gap, it could still push on through. Many factors influenced what might seem an otherwise easy decision: unevenness of ground, desired torque, flex, gear ratios, weight. From all those and more tumbled an arrangement of eight twenty-inch-diameter wheels. Hallelujah, they had a configuration.

The wheel decision came just in time for Institute 100 to lose their customer—and potentially their whole project—as 1965 saw Korolev transfer his lunar and planetary work to Lavochkin. And realistically, this was a very good move because Lavochkin was hungry. Energized. Galvanized. They assumed overall responsibility for managing the moon car, along with creating and instrumenting its body. They also solidified Institute 100's role as prime chassis developers.

Praised Rozentsveyg, "Now there were real horizons associated with the lunar rover."

The question of what brave fantasies might sit atop that chassis now fell into the hands of Lavochkin's star engineers. Raw hunger and energy, unfortunately, do not make technical obstacles much easier to overcome. Rozentsveyg's initial hope soon mixed with despair as Lavochkin struggled to absorb and comprehend the project's scope. Blueprints, mockups, boilerplates, hope. Babakin sifted through the dregs of his malnourished inheritance the way one would rummage through destroyed mementoes from a flooded house. Was *anything* worth saving? Could *anything* be done with all this half-thought-out slop from Korolev? The rover was nowhere near "ready to build," as they say. Not even close. He supposed that the chassis was on its way, but most everything above it—the body, power plant, thermal control—could stand to be reengineered. Painfully Babakin elected to till the fields and start anew.

The remainder of 1965 only filled with more disappointment. "In essence, the year was lost," professed Rozentsveyg—largely due, in his opinion, to Lavochkin's transition from missiles to spaceflight, combined with their gestational sample-return efforts. "This somewhat weakened the attention to our joint project."

Their outer-space Rolls Royce was supposed to roam over an unmapped landscape that, only because of *Luna 9*, had just been seen for the very first time. It was to do this in the midst of daytime temperatures soaring over 240 degrees Fahrenheit . . . and then somehow stay warm even when the nighttime low hit minus 290. It had to offer a method of informing earthbound controllers, in near-real time, exactly where it was going and whether its commands had been received and correctly processed. And what about the science? God, the science. Already those guys were lining up with experiments. They wanted to study cosmic radiation. They wanted to precisely measure the Earth–moon distance. They wanted to grind into lunar soil and zap it with radiation. They wanted to study galactic X-rays. They wanted to take very-high-resolution panoramic photographs. They wanted everything.

Georgiy Babakin thought about all of this. What he really needed was magic.

Years after it all ended, after the rover cashed in and everybody went home, Georgy Tyulin sat down to reminisce. In particular he spoke about the uncertainties during that first week of December 1970, as daylight approached *Lunokhod 1*'s position on the moon. Light gives life and soon they would know.

"The question arose whether the lid would open again during sunrise." Tyulin was institutionally noncommittal as to his own opinion. "The technical leadership under Babakin and Milovanov held many meetings to analyze the results of the previous lunar day. Would the *Lunokhod* ever live to see another?" (At that time, A. P. Milovanov functioned as the director of Lavochkin and Babakin's immediate supervisor. Someone needed to maintain the bureau's direction of work, offer guidance, and fish for new projects. That was Milovanov. Chief designers like Babakin did not run a bureau.)

On December 9, just after lunch, an answer stood before those assembled in the tidy Shkolnoye control room. Hot, pure sunlight began gradually carpeting the Sea of Rains. As the drive team ended their midday banter and assumed stations, every project scientist except Boris Nepoklonov remained curtly sequestered across the hall, and Alexander Basilevsky still wasn't happy about the arrangement. "It was not allowed," he said flatly of his joining the control room proceedings. "There was a soldier standing in the door." Maybe that door wasn't locked, but it sure was closed.

Tyulin recalled the scene on *his* side of the hallway: "When the operators sent the first telecommand, the lid refused to open." Uh-oh, was it dead? "They sent another command, and this time the cover did open." Brainwaves. Power flow. Nav-cams winked back on. Eyesight. Alive! Reported Tyulin, "The second lunar day broke to the accompaniment of applause from the control center." Basilevsky heard it through the walls and loud-speaker and managed a smile himself before settling down to wait on the first new panorama.

Within hours of lunar sunrise, creeping light progressively warmed the gray ground by over 480 degrees. *Lunokhod* shook off its chill. The first session back felt like a Lazarus miracle. One Earth day later, though, during Session 202, a whole big pile of trouble came truckin' on through. High sunlight blaring down on the moon made the near absence of shadows particularly hazardous, and driver Gennady Latypov bulldozed right into a huge crater.

"Gennady gave an order to stop the vehicle." Vyacheslav Dovgan felt he knew exactly where Latypov miscalculated. "But he didn't activate STOP. He shifted from second gear to first gear. The *Lunokhod* continued forward. He thought it would get through the crater without any problem." But the dirt was too much. They were stuck.

Catcall from the back: "Whoops! He just drove into a crater!"

See, the rules had gotten all loosey-goosey again. Georgy Tyulin explained. "Keldysh had invited a number of people to witness the travels of *Lunokhod*. These were journalists, academicians, and scientists who were reasonably well-versed in space technology." Just like the postlanding ruckus, these supposed VIPs were once again interrupting the crew with banter and pointing and *What's THIS button do?* and now the rover had potholed so deeply that it engaged the automatic cutoffs in the wheel motors. Crew-room noise ricocheted. The temperature in the room went up: an increasing multitude of distractions. These rabble-rousing visitors had been expected to stay well behind the drafting tables, but it didn't last.

Seethed Dovgan, "Impossible to concentrate!"

Babakin had been off to a side, keeping quiet. Processing. The response had to be diplomatic yet unambiguous. "I ask everyone to leave the premises," he informed the crowd, plainly and succinctly. "Everyone, without exception. And I too will leave. The crew is well trained." Only Nepoklonov would remain with them. Babakin latched the door tightly on his way out, and Basilevsky figured that now he'd probably never get in that room.

Things like this frustrated him to no end because the drive crew—not to mention all those "guests" in the control room—hadn't spent years interpreting lunar features. Like *he* had! "When the surface is rough at high sun," complained the geologist, "it's especially bright! When it is more smooth, it is not so bright." They should have known to be more careful! How easy would this have been to avoid? Had he, ahem, been shoulder-to-shoulder with the drivers—lending his practiced eye and commentary—they would not have sandbagged in a pathetic hole!

Methodically the five proceeded in workmanlike fashion: closing the lid, jostling *Lunokhod* slightly, reviewing its video picture, trying alternate maneuvers. Two hours became six. No change. It almost seemed like a lost cause. Somebody called *break* and the team limbered up during an impromptu seventh-inning stretch.

Seven and a half hours. Eight. A nudge here, tweaking there, and in an agonizingly slow fashion their intrepid adventurer began to withdraw from the crater. It—*they*—were going to live to drive another day. After *Lunokhod* was finally out Vyacheslav Dovgan noted, with some annoyance, that the extraction had required nine diligent hours of microscopic attentiveness.

The day's work had been shot to hell, so everyone vacated their respective rooms for the big end-of-session assembly. One happened every day in the center's meeting room, located near the front entrance and containing a chalkboard plus three TV screens of its own. In filed an already-smoking Babakin, plus the crew, plus the technicians and scientists. Everyone was hungry.

Basilevsky found a place with Nepoklonov as the engineers spoke first. "Everything worked okay," they said of the Shkolnoye facility's overall health. "Radio communication was okay."

Lavochkin people went next, bursting with stats: distance traveled, voltage levels, temperatures, number of panoramas imaged. Although it was kept quiet at the time, *Lunokhod*'s brakes had failed—unfortunately, in the "on" position. It'd happened soon after landing stage roll-down, and the rover had been muscling along despite it.

Scientists began taking turns, articulating discoveries buried in the reams of computer printouts being continuously delivered to the science room. One instrument hanging underneath *Lunokhod*'s tub blasted X-rays onto rocks and soil to discern their composition. They were finding lots of iron and aluminum, explained a member of the X-ray team.

The geologists got their turn. "Panoramas are very interesting for us," reported Basilevsky in a mild kind of way. That's all he had for the time being.

After the meeting broke most everyone headed off to the hotel. "Everyone" included the drive crew, and the walk took a good ten minutes plus gate checks. So Basilevsky strategically leveraged the opportunity to start making himself known to Dovgan and Yeremenko and the others. "After working session was over, Lunokhod crew get out," he indicated. "We could approach them, we could talk to them." And more than anything it was a risk: scientists are clipped from very different fabric than military types. These men all lived under the same government and spoke a common language, yet they existed in two separate universes. Would the drivers blow him off? Tell him to get lost?

But his overtures were met with warm reciprocity. And as paths continued crossing—in the hotel, the can, at tea, during meetings—these two parties from opposite sides of the hallway would slowly come to be on a first-name basis. "There was no formal, 'Let me introduce myself,'" recalled Basilevsky. "It was somehow more informal."

The hotel rooms were cramped and cold. But they signified down time. "When we came back to the hotel we could boil tea, we could have snacks then." Like anyone, Basilevsky appreciated the chance to kick off his shoes and unwind; the drive team had bonus access to a private steam room. "In the morning we could go to the canteen and take breakfast."

After five solid Earth days of effort they hit lunar noon. When this happens, the sun is directly overhead for about seventy-two hours and ground shadows are nonexistent. "When you don't see shadows," cautioned Basilevsky, "everything looks as very smooth. But you know it is not smooth!" That made things dangerous—the harrowing crater incident had been too close. During lunar noon, all operations temporarily halted. "So everybody was free from the work!" Babakin announced that he had other squirrels to sauté. The chief designer wished them well and departed for Moscow, leaving his deputy Vladimir Panteleev to represent Lavochkin.

The geologists had three days to kill, and Basilevsky really wanted to do it someplace else. "Frankly speaking," he remarked of Shkolnoye, "it was boring to stay each day behind the wire fence. It's always soldiers, officers, so it is boring."

The locals told him, "Go to this place called Gurzuf." It lay south, directly on the coast of the Black Sea—about two and a half hours from Simferopol. He and Nepoklonov piled on a bus and rumbled down to find a small resort town smack in the middle of off-season.

Gurzuf offered ideal temperatures, pine-clad mountains, lush vegetation. Tourists in their own country, they strolled about on pathways with low stone railings drizzled along the water's edge and rock faces pushing out into the water. Picturesque Bear Mountain loomed in the distance. The surroundings revived them. They invigorated them. "We could go to café, we could see the sea, we could go along the shore," said Basilevsky, who enjoyed time to decompress with his friend. "It was just relaxing. It was beautiful."

Upon their return to Shkolnoye the lengthening lunar shadows had grown to the point where everyone could resume. Humming with power, *Lunokhod 1* obediently took off—truly going where no one ever had. By that point six Americans had already walked on the moon, but they sure hadn't been able to explore it for as long.

The rover halted for more experiments. Underneath their eight-wheeled sedan hung a little wedge-shaped knuckle, the idea being to thrust it down at the ground and *twist twist*, measure the soil's strength and resistance. It took awhile to use. During the hour-long intervals, Basilevsky had nothing to do and usually vamoosed from the confining science room. "I was free," he said in an uplifting tone, "to breathe a little." Sometimes he and Nepoklonov would stretch their legs outside. Within the third perimeter fence all the buildings were connected by paved narrow walkways and random shrubbery. They could hop off the path and hike through open meadowland and sparse trees. "Chat with my colleagues." In multiple places the meadow had been implanted with concrete-lined stairwells leading down underground to heavy locked doors. Beyond them existed a subterranean network of cable raceways linking the different buildings. Occasionally soldiers would clamber on the high structures of the big antenna dish to refill its cooling system or to clean or perform some other service, and Basilevsky could watch them until it was time to head back inside.

Barely one Earth month later the rover began pushing up against the end of its originally projected life span. "We guaranteed only three months!" warned Lavochkin engineers. But it kept on ticking as the drive crew fulfilled a grand circuition that wended back to the original landing site. And there it was! Tracks and ramps and tanks and tubes, all waiting patiently for eternity. Georgy Tyulin sighed. Finally, it was all going so well.

Over the ensuing months *Lunokhod* operations fell into a cadenced pattern:

15. Haunting and still, *Lunokhod 1*'s descent stage is revisited by the rover in this detail from one panorama. Author's collection.

five days on, seventy-two hours off during high noon, followed by another five days before nighttime. "Typically, in the beginning of a lunar day the working session started in the afternoon," Basilevsky recalled. Those initial sessions might only go a couple of hours, with subsequent ones lengthening in sync with the levels of sunlight. Yet Earth and the moon rotate at different speeds, meaning a shift in each day's start time. "So if today we started at 5:00 p.m., tomorrow at 6:00 p.m., next day seven, and so on." What a blow to the circadian rhythms. A 7:00 or 8:00 p.m. start in the middle of a lunar day meant Basilevsky and company might remain in their corner of the world until five o'clock the next morning.

"Of course," explained the geologist, "from time to time I was getting out for the restroom!"

He decided to confront another festering stickler. Anyone outside of a uniform couldn't help but notice that the chief function of *Lunokhod* did not appear to be the conduct of scientific experiments. Rather, it seemed to be more about tallying miles on the odometer.

Everyone *did* appreciate the high-quality panoramic photographs. As Basilevsky chuckled, "Because panoramas then go to the newspapers and everybody knows, including you Americans, that we are great." Where the hang-up came, then, was in the fact that panorama generation meant halting *Lunokhod* for a good half hour at least. Ratchet the parking brake. It would sit there, immobile for the duration, as its television imagers swept the landscape like invisible searchlights.

But protracted idleness is inherently unpopular with military folk. "Lunokhod is not Luno*stop*," Basilevsky was informed, curtly, on more than one occasion. "We should move. We should show that it is effectively moving."

By lightly shifting the rover a second, nearly identical panorama could be made and the two then combined to create an image in three dimensions. Under a stereoscope they were utterly stunning, and the geological team wheedled management into a few. But it got old waiting another half hour for the cameras to painstakingly image what amounted to the same darn thing.

"Hey, listen," went the typical rebuff. "We had one panorama. Why?"

Frustrated, Basilevsky eventually approached the colonel to whom the crew commander reported for a simple demonstration of the power of 3D. Strictly speaking, the colonel had not yet imbibed.

"I took one of these stereo pair, these two panoramas, put under the stereoscope, invited the colonel and said, 'Look.' It's psychological." Basilevsky jabbed a finger at the images as he lectured. "It's very strong. You just, instead of just a picture, you see that like stones like get *up*. And craters get *down*. You see 3D!"

The colonel went wide-eyed in astonishment: "Oh!"

With that subtle maneuver Basilevsky emerged victorious from his skirmish. "And since that time he was very positive!" More panoramas would now be coming.

After much nudging and needling from Mstislav Keldysh, a sensible draft plan finally accreted in 1966. It encompassed a roving lunar scientific laboratory that could be manufactured within the realm of existing Soviet technology, launched on an existing Soviet booster, and controlled with an existing Soviet communications network. The plan did not assume *perfect* or *ideal* technology—just what was on hand. It did not involve guesswork. It was refreshingly realistic.

The atmosphere at Institute 100 had metamorphosed. First of all, its name changed to Institute for Transport Machinery. Many abridged that to TransMash, recognizing how the Russian suffix -*mash* is a catchall term for "vehicular engineering." For those assigned to Lunokhod, the style of work also changed. It was much more serious: "We were put in a room," stated one engineer, "closed off from prying eyes. This is where we set up our drawing boards. Access to our offices was forbidden."

He wouldn't be leaving any time soon, either. "We fixed up the offices so that we could sleep there," said Alexander Kemurdzhian of their amped-up workload. "We brought in mattresses, sheets, blankets, and called that part of the plant the 'Char-Mash Hotel' because we usually manufactured chars, which means tanks." Indentured servitude became the norm; explicit permission had to be granted in order for someone to even leave the plant.

To produce the rover chassis they'd been granted the astronomical budget of 4 million rubles—about $3.6 million in the mid-1960s—and spent a goodly percentage of that to add on. It was all fine and well to build your average war tank inside some regular assembly bay, but in space little pieces of debris can float into the wrong thing and kill it. Out came the checkbook. Up went a 129,000-square-foot utilitarian edifice nicknamed "Sphere": clean rooms and sticky walls and filtration systems and dust masks and thick books filled with sterility procedures. Everyone started running around in white coats like a bunch of dietitians. Also, the rover would have to function in a near-total vacuum and at extremes of temperature. Izrail Rozentsveyg well knew what happened to moving parts in such conditions: they fused together. "Liquid and plastic lubricants evaporate," he dismissed. They needed to invent new grease that didn't do this, or find a way to treat metal with innovative coatings that didn't bind, or come up with something else entirely.

Every potential solution would have to be tested inside specialized, airtight enclosures that could be pumped down to nearly zero atmosphere. Widget goes in, air comes out, and people watch through thick portholes to see if it bites the dust. For some early tests Rozentsveyg's associates flew nine hundred miles down to the Institute of Low Temperatures in Kharkov and used their facilities. But it got to be a pain, commuting. Into Trans-Mash rolled flatbed trucks loaded with high-buck vacuum chambers and piping and valves. But these gadgets weren't just fancy toasters that plug into a wall. The vacuum state inside a chamber is typically achieved by using cryogenic materials; liquid nitrogen is a perennial favorite. In the beginning, Rozentsveyg had people bring it by hand in large Dewar flasks. So inefficient. He got the bright idea to stage it all in one spot and plumb the entire building for liquid nitrogen: "Just like in your home—open the tap and fill!" Rampant testing guzzled the stuff like mad, and the facility could never operate at full potential.

Still, they moved forward.

The number of people working on the chassis multiplied into the dozens and then into the hundreds. Many came straight from colleges and technical schools. "It was very important that young engineers were not 'tainted' by tank experience," conveyed Rozentsveyg. "They worked in accordance with new requirements, using a modern stock of knowledge!" Anyone in the shop with an advanced degree earned approximately twice as much as those without, and people in charge of departments always had degrees. "For example, the head of the lab received up to 400 rubles a month and could consider himself 'wealthy,'" Rozentsveyg explained. "A skilled designer received no more than 160 rubles a month." Figure 13 percent taxes, ten rubles for rent, and nothing terribly exciting to buy. That left enough to put fish on the table and see a movie every once in a while.

New blueprints came forth. Each of the eight wheels would function at the beck and call of a direct-current electric motor in its hub. Designers had been at a loss for how to slick-up the intermeshed reduction gears within . . . until stumbling upon a revolutionary hybrid they termed c-5. Under high heat and pressure it melded iron powder with glass to create an alloy that could be formed into parts containing *their own* lubrication. Two c-5 gears gnashing together in lunar conditions spawned enough heat to melt the glass particles and form a protective film at the points of contact. That's right: liquid-glass lube. It seemed ideal, but final validation would have to come from space itself. So TransMash arranged for select assemblies to deadhead on *Luna 12* and *14*. That's what those twirly do-nothing parts had been up to up there: vetting design assumptions. Another problem down.

The possibility existed that their off-world ATV might jam itself up on a rock, or worse. How soon a few cosmonauts might be available to come push it out still wasn't clear, so each axle also contained a small explosive charge that could be detonated by remote control. It was a permanent step—the wheel forever rendered passive—but TransMash overdesigned so that the rover could still make headway even with only two good ones on a side.

Now the plant needed to complement its wheels with an exceptional breed of spoke. Pray tell—across the breadth of the Soviet Union, where were the most lightweight and strongest of spokes to be found? Why, underneath the bodies of champion Soviet cyclists! (Like that hunky Viktor Logu-

16. Note to Land Rover: ill-suited for mud or snow, these babies positively shine when tearing through lunar scree. Here a tech bolts wheel to chassis. Courtesy RIA Novosti.

nov!) *Lunokhod*'s came from the State Bicycle Plant in Kharkov. Installers laced them into wheels made of fine wire mesh and stubby titanium blades.

In a high-walled room fifty feet on a side, laborers overhauled the test track—raking away the sand and cement powder and implementing an obstacle course of rocks and dirt and divots and ditches. They covered it with truckloads of Armenian pumice and rolled out the bouncy-bottom chassis, which at this point had nothing more on top of it than a triangular metal framework. From this armature a giant wiring umbilical arced upward and over to a gondola holding two men and controls, rolling atop an inner oval of small-gauge railroad tracks. In this fashion, engineers could shake down their hot rod through a series of endless laps and loops, and gradually the bugs began to dissipate.

So much cutting-edge stuff and yet so much gravel-road backwardness. Juxtaposed with their freshly scrubbed, state-of-the-art operation, Trans-Mash's working conditions seemed positively abhorrent. Rozentsveyg labeled this a "cauldron of contradictions." "We ate badly," he said, as only one of many examples. Frontline workers could partake from either of two main cafeterias. "The usual food, very monotonous and nonnutritious," came his allegations. "You could buy kefir, a glass of liquid sour cream, dried fruit compote. We did not see any fresh vegetables." Thursdays had cod. Rozentsveyg generally avoided the whole scene altogether and just brought his own meals every day. Department heads like Kemurdzhian got a few perks in their sequestered eatery. "A much more interesting table! They cooked for them separately. Fresh beer and cognac was always served. And the cost was comparable to the one in the canteens for ordinary staff." When Rozentsveyg traveled to any of the plant's dozen-odd subcontractors, he'd stick his head in their cafeterias and find that it was the same deal everywhere. Certain Soviet cities didn't allow foreigners of any kind, and with interest he noted how almost none of the restaurants in those places offered any kind of meat.

"All the time, we endured."

TransMash delivered a finished chassis near the end of 1967 and what rolled into Lavochkin's workshop resembled art. This thing was made of the best materials money could buy. It worked flawlessly in a vacuum. It could climb twenty-degree inclines and ramble along side-slopes of forty-five degrees. The automatic fault-protection system constantly measured its own angles of travel and would stop everything in a heartbeat if these limits were reached. All in all, the chassis turned out better than anyone could have hoped.

So much for "impossible."

After their guests left, assemblers transferred the newly received hardware to a prep area. On top of the chassis, techs lowered seventeen hundred pounds of machined metal bathtub whose everyday shape did nothing to indicate how utterly complex it really was. To make weight, Babakin had specified lightweight magnesium alloys wherever possible. Deep within, a pressurized compartment supported the rover's brain, radio, power plant, and thermal control system.

Come the summer of '68, at long last, Lavochkin was ready to drive a complete machine. "The rover was tested," as Georgy Tyulin picked up the story, "on carefully chosen terrain whose topography, in our view, closely resembled conditions on the moon. Excepting of course the gravitational pull." Naturally the terrain they sought lay nowhere in Khimki or close to any stop on greater Moscow's Metro subway line. No, it waited thousands of miles away in the barren emptiness of the Kamchatka Peninsula. The active volcano Gorely, in particular, is not only uninhabited but rife with scrabbly pumice. Lavochkin flew a rover out there and took the recently selected drive crew along with.

"It was not of course an absolute replica of the lunar surface," conceded Mikhail Malenkov, who spent years at TransMash with Izrail Rozentsveyg. "What was important were the *characteristics* of this surface. Its capacity to affect the reactions of the motors and chassis."

"It was a unique vehicle," chimed in Pavel Sologub. "The Americans hadn't even thought of it!"

A first attempt to send one came during that frenetic period after Christmas when the Soviets were dying for virtually any tangible response to *Apollo 8*. A Lunokhod went up in February '69 and almost as quickly came back down—forming that kooky debris field that included polonium and a tape recorder blaring the Soviet national anthem. It was supposed to play right after landing; Earth would be notified of this stunner by way of lunar panoramas with accompanying soundtrack. But instead, the booster's nose shroud had stripped off like a banana peel and the operatic march performed to scrub brush and bemused soldiers, who dutifully gathered every rained-down hunk of litter they could find and ported it all back.

Everybody was on break from *Lunokhod 1* during another two-week lunar night. Georgiy Babakin went for a bike ride with his son on the afternoon of August 1. "I think we made twenty kilometers," remembered his son Nikolay. Two days later Nikolay and his wife had tickets for a cinema festival. Both also worked at Lavochkin and were excited for the festival that evening. But they couldn't find a babysitter.

That morning, within their shared four-bedroom apartment, Nikolay approached his father about the issue. The elder Babakin thought he might be able to utilize a child-care service available from Lavochkin but wanted to rest awhile before dealing with it. Nikolay asked him to stay in touch about the evening's arrangements—then sped away in the family's gray Moskvitch. "I went to company and was working," he said.

A few hours later, Grandpa Georgiy grabbed the tickets and hopped in his company Volga to also head toward Khimki. But Nikolay became worried, as too much time seemed to be going by and his old man hadn't shown up yet. "I'll try to find my father. It was impossible. We had not mobile phones at that time, was many years ago, so I call to his secretary: 'Where's my father? Where's my father?'"

"We don't know," she told him.

Georgiy Babakin never made it to Lavochkin that day. During the trip he started feeling weak and turned back home. In the hallway he asked a neighbor for any kind of heart medicine, then stumbled to his own apartment. Straightaway the neighbor called for an ambulance and then hustled over to Babakin's door. It was quiet. He went in.

"He find my father, dead," said Nikolay. "That's all." An ambulance showed up less than fifteen minutes later.

"It was a shock for me, for my wife. Of course."

Georgiy Babakin had engineered so many unprecedented marvels, yet he never tried producing one to fix his own weak heart. It gave out on August 3, 1971, at the age of fifty-seven.

No one who worked with Babakin denied the man's ability to blend technical competence with unconventional cognition. "At the briefings he could sit with an absent-minded air," remembered his coworker Oleg Ivanovsky. "And then offer an idea that seemed crazy, though later would become an ingenious method." One problem lunar-trajectory planners had constantly faced was the moon's uneven surface (which is separate from the issue of uneven *gravity*). When and how the spacecraft should come in for landing depended to a large degree on knowing its precise altitude. Today that's no problem at all; computers are small and powerful and can deal with the approach radar throwing them change-ups. But back then engineers didn't know what to do. They lacked the weight allowance and space to install computers able to account for varied surface topography.

Babakin approached the problem from a totally oblique angle. "Okay," his men were told, "let's pay no attention to this." He instructed them to treat the moon as if it were a perfectly smooth marble—no surface features whatsoever. The descent engines should be provided with enough extra fuel and maneuvering ability to deal with any last-second radar input. Most engineers would never even entertain such cavalier hip-shooting, but that approach with *Luna 16* is how it finally brought home the bacon.

Soviet Russia's most prestigious burials were almost always in the Kremlin Wall. Babakin found peace elsewhere—nestled in a horseshoe bend of the Moscow River, at the cemetery of Novodevichy. Close by lay Nobel winners, cosmonauts, artists. Nikita Khrushchev is here, in what's regarded as the country's *second*-most-prestigious burial location. It's a tranquil spot, more parklike than anything. Visitors walk from site to site on paths fronted by dense foliage—accented further by a majestic seventeenth-century convent sprawling across the north end. The fallen don't get traditional headstones with sterile text chiseled into low, flat slabs. Here they are honored with original and tastefully sculptured monuments, which typically involve a stonework rendering of the person's likeness. They get art.

At the time of its creator's death, *Lunokhod 1* still gamely chugged along. According to Basilevsky, the demise of Lavochkin's great chief designer had little real effect on the modern tankette. "There was no big impact, at least on Lunokhod and Luna sample-return missions," he affirmed. "Everything was preplanned. Everything was going smooth." What testimony to superb project management.

Communist Party officials had always rejoiced in their success at preserving national security by confidentially suppressing information about Babakin's very existence. That secret no longer needed to be kept. "The Soviet Union has announced the death on August 3 of Georgiy Babakin, identifying him as head of a design office responsible for work on lunar and planetary probes." So claimed the August 1971 issue of *Flight International*, published in Britain. "He is thought to have contributed extensively to work on the *Luna 16* lunar soil-retrieving spacecraft and on Lunokhod. He had been connected with aircraft and spacecraft design since 1949."

That right there was the entire article. That's all the West knew of Georgiy Babakin.

9. Buy-In

He needed somebody who could make it work.

—Patricia Ann Straat, deconstructing Gil Levin's staffing choices

Although the events of that day were already receding in time, Gilbert Levin remembered them sharply. First, a phone call. Subsequently an envelope had arrived in the mail, postmarked February 1969. It contained three sheets of paper, adorned with a familiar sweepy logo in the upper left-hand corner of page 1. Levin treated the pages carefully. They confirmed what had been stated during the phone call and were not, in any way, junk mail:

NATIONAL AERONAUTICS AND SPACE ADMINISTRATION
Washington, D.C. 20546

Dear Dr. Levin,

I am pleased to inform you that you have been selected to participate in the planning phase of the 1973 Viking Lander as a member of the Active Biology Team. The members of the Team are listed in Enclosure 1, and the role of the scientist and functions of the Active Biology Team are given in Enclosure 2.

Levin's eyes wandered down the page. Paragraph 2 covered a basic schedule of meetings, compensation for expenses, and other matters. He came to paragraph 3:

The Langley Research Center (LaRC) has Project management responsibility for the Viking mission.

Not Marshall. Not JPL. Interesting. He flipped over to page 2:

The Viking Science Active Biology Team is responsible for the search for life using an integrated instrument capable of providing data interpretable as evidence of active biota on Mars.

Next came a list of six individuals and their professional affiliations. Levin reviewed the names:

Wolf Vishniac, Department of Biology, University of Rochester

Norman H. Horowitz, Bioscience Section, Jet Propulsion Laboratory

Joshua Lederberg, Department of Genetics, Stanford University School of Medicine

Gilbert V. Levin, Biospherics Research, Inc.

Vance I. Oyama, Life Detection Systems Branch, Ames Research Center

Alexander Rich, Professor of Biophysics, Massachusetts Institute of Technology

As always when recollecting this moment, a warmly satisfying mood overcame Gil Levin: his dear Gulliver would finally visit alien lands and test for life. It was a euphoric feeling akin to those earliest days—when his first experiments had proved successful, along with the ones after them and the next after those. But a vaporous period had then arrived, when nobody knew if they'd ever really fly. How easy it would've been to just shelve the work and move on. But now, all these years later, America was finally—improbably!—planning the big mission. It said so on paper.

See, as Don Hearth's Voyager had made its way to the paper shredder, a funny thing happened. Virginia's Langley people—freed from that horrendous amalgamation of temporary California offices—had returned east with holes in their hearts. They'd created a good program to reconnoiter Mars, yet Congress had pulled the plug because Voyager—though impressive—was flawed due to its gargantuan size and imposing cost. If something was ever going to actually leave Earth and reach Mars with all bills paid it needed to be more modest, more practical. So, after unpacking, the Langley crew had sat down at their practical Hampton furnishings and begun wishing-up a Voyager derivative. Nobody told them to do so. And nobody requested any money for the effort, either, because they didn't have to. Unlike JPL or GE or Avco, the Langley Research Center was not a contractor. They were already part of the government, operated on salary, and could therefore pursue whatever their little type A engineering brains desired. And curiously enough, Hearth's old boss Ed Cortright had recently become director there. If anyone wanted to rise from Voyager's ashes, it was Big Ed.

Mere months after returning from his European sabbatical, Hearth got a surprise request to visit Hampton. *Come down*, said the Langley guys. *Let's meet about something we've been kickin' around.* Artfully, they'd put a hook in the water and now Hearth slowly circled, low-level intrigue registering within him. "These guys are good," he rationalized of his interest. "They're talented people." And they must have something hot. He chomped the bait. Hearth and Oran Nicks arranged for a NASA plane, buckling in alongside John Naugle. The latter man functioned as NASA's associate administrator for space science and was as interested as anyone in examining foreign worlds close-up.

Following their arrival, Langley people ushered the trio into a conference room adjacent to Cortright's office. He had no way of knowing it right then and there but in three years Don Hearth himself would claim the Langley directorship and move into that very same next-door office.

Identically thick packets began circumnavigating the room. "Here's some options," smiled a fellow named Jim Martin as he began spelling out what they had in mind. Hearth paid attention. Martin looked like one of those substitute math teachers from hell: stout and crew cut, physically intimidating, with utilitarian horn-rimmed reading glasses that were straight off the clearance rack. Probably born in that necktie. But Jim Martin was not some humorless scab who enjoyed commanding others to solve for x. His resume celebrated years in aviation and engineering circles. Some say that Jim Martin's success came about only from his sensible and communicative approach to running aerospace projects. Others maintain that fear played an important role. As in, Martin was sensible and communicative, but if his mind was made up you *would lose*; he'd never hesitate to dominate any situation where he felt his own approach should carry the day. Nobody disputed his prowess as a genuine leader, or his charisma. And Martin now beckoned his guests to peruse the materials just handed them.

Localized silence as everyone flipped pages. From behind wire-frame eyeglasses, Naugle reviewed the material. Hearth thumbed his own packet. Evoking Voyager, Langley was proposing a combination Mars orbiter-lander.

For a name they suggested "Viking." Half the size of Voyager. Cheaper. Simpler. Easier to develop and coordinate. None of this fly-on-a-Saturn-V hokum, either; the center recommended using a modest-sized, flight-proven, known commodity of a booster called Titan. All in all, Hearth felt mildly attracted.

Someone asked how much the scaled-back plan might cost. Langley was thinking in the sub-four-hundred-million range. *Not too big a bite, eh?* Having once choked on a $2.2 billion Voyager Mars flyer, John Naugle's eyes began sparkling. Hearth noticed and immediately glanced over to see that Oran Nicks's were, too.

"By God," one of them whispered. "We can have an orbiter *and* a lander. We can do it." That snake charmer Martin had spun a trance. Quizzically Hearth swiveled around. Was he the only one not being hypnotized?

It sounded promising in part due to the grand-slam Langley had cracked with their recently ended Lunar Orbiter project: yup, the very same one supplying all that high-quality imagery used by Alexander Basilevsky. Between August '66 and '67, Langley had orchestrated the single most triumphant space project so far of any nation. Five launches. Five perfect flights. On time, on budget. And managing space missions wasn't even the kind of thing Langley typically did.

Everyone finished their initial read-through of the Viking packet. Hearth pondered that cost estimate. "Where'd the number come from?" he wanted to know.

Glances. Half smiles. He got a side-steppy, noncommittal answer, which made for an uncharacteristically imprecise response from Langley's normally detail-oriented folk. But Martin's trance evidently held because nobody pressed the issue.

During their flight back, John Naugle sidled over to Hearth. Quickly Nicks ambled up. Naugle accessorized his nearly bald, spherical head with enormous sideburns that hung down his cheeks like drapery. They made him resemble one of the Founding Fathers. Now he asked, "What do you think?"

"Well," volunteered Hearth, "it sounds pretty good. But I don't believe the cost."

"Why don't you believe the cost?"

Hearth erupted from his seat. "John, we've been lookin' at orbiters and landers on Mars for *years*," he snarled. "It's gotta cost at least six hundred to seven hundred million dollars! Not counting the launch vehicles!"

Nicks flapped his hands in the air like a distressed penguin. "No no no," he protested. "I think they know what they're talkin' about."

Disbelief swirled around Hearth. *This is the exact same kind of thing we all called Voyager,* he charged back. *All the same traits. Except on a smaller craft!* Heavens above, size alone couldn't cut the price down to Langley's fire-sale estimate. Every orbiter-lander study that HQ ever made had closed with a final price tag approaching $1 billion. They'd been remarkably consistent like that, every dang one of them.

Despite the chasm separating those estimates from Langley's recent pitch, Nicks persuaded Hearth to tag-team with him in advancing the idea. Hearth went along because he felt NASA's planetary efforts to be stagnating; ground-level Mars investigations were an important personal goal of his.

With brilliance and skill the men sold it to Congress, and Viking miraculously joined NASA's budget at $364 million and change for a projected 1973 launch. Still, Hearth felt misgivings because that amount of money signified one of two things. Either it was considerably below what everyone really believed it would cost—and therefore deceptive—or it was the amount Viking actually wouldn't exceed so long as nobody ran into a single unforeseen problem whatsoever at any point between napkin sketches and end of mission. Hearth snorted at the second option. "I'm sittin' there as director of planetary programs and saluting and it goes in at that number," he remembered. "But I just knew damn well that there was a buy-in goin' in." Hearth swallowed. "And I think deep in his gut Oran knew it, too." From the standpoint of Hearth's seasoned logic, not even the virtually faultless Langley Research Center would be able to orbit and land on Mars without encountering any trouble. The task before them represented something too new, too thorny, too dicey. He continued, "You never have a hundred-percent technical success during design and development. Things are gonna cost more because they're gonna be more complicated than you think they might be—because there'll be technical issues, schedule delays. Things take longer. Time is money." It'd always been like that in any space project. Or military one. Springing up out of left field comes a wad of technical snafus that nobody ever anticipated and *snapcracklepop* you're over budget.

"But if you said that at the beginning you wouldn't get it approved!" Another laugh burst from Hearth as he sought to justify the maneuver. "Geez, this was a way of gettin' something back in the program."

For a totally camouflaged price, America had successfully bought into landing on Mars. Now it was up to Hearth, Nicks, Cortright, and the whole Langley team to see it through. No mere conference-room salesman, Jim Martin would head up all day-to-day oversight of Langley's vision. It specified two Viking launch packages—each dropping one landing craft while its companion remained high above in orbit to act as a radio relay and operate additional experiments. Four ships total, christened in typical Langley fashion: *Orbiter* and *Lander*. No majestic name? No splendor? The label "Viking" had apparently emptied their idea jar.

Brimming with engineering excellence, albeit crappy naming skills, Langley nevertheless wasn't set up to actually construct space hardware. *Well, who should build* Orbiter? Langley debated a multitude of possible surrogate mommies; again and again they kept coming back to the Jet Propulsion Laboratory. At that very moment, the Lab was thigh-deep in actualizing a next-gen Mars orbiter for launch in '71. Okay, their attitude wasn't perfect, but JPL certainly did possess the facilities *and* the experience. Assuming some oversight, who better to construct *Orbiter*?

Next a suitable custodian had to be picked for the *Lander*s. After a grueling battleground process of grisly attrition the contract hit Denver and the Martin Marietta Corporation in late May '69—besting twenty fountainheads originally solicited by NASA. Some regarded Martin as an odd choice. At that time, one of the biggest things the company had going was a design-build contract for the Disney World monorails. Another chunk of their enterprise dealt in gravel and cement production. They had little experience in building spacecraft and zero in soft-landing on other planets. Only six years beforehand, Martin had finished dead last in the competition for Voyager study contracts. *This* place was going to build a Martian lander?

Well, things happen. Eight years before, the Glenn L. Martin aircraft company had tired of dealing with headaches unrelated to their product. They'd output some amazing warplanes, like the B-26 Marauder and the *Enola Gay*, which dropped the A-bomb on Hiroshima. Success pushed them into aerospace with the Vanguard and Titan launch boosters. But companies that operate solely as government contractors have essentially one customer. Engineering excellence proved no match for a congressional budget cycle, so the Martin firm sought to diversify. It found a match in the building materials powerhouse American Marietta, and a hungry new company took root. They wanted Viking like no other project and insisted it was within their capability. Time would tell.

Of course, Viking meant nothing without science. Much of the luggage slated to fill its trunk smacked of conventional gear like weather stations and cameras and atmosphere sniffers. But *the* key objective bridging Voyager and Viking had always been the search for extant life on another world. With John Naugle's casual announcement of impending flight opportunities came a frantic melee for slots on an as-yet-undefined package of biological study. People went wild; over a dozen motivated individuals desperately wanted one of those few seats to Mars.

Subsequently Naugle's committee distilled its half-dozen finalists, each of whom received those identical letters in the mail. What a slog. For years they'd all lingered in limbo, wondering if a mission would ever pop from that overweight bureaucracy huddled on the fifth floor of NASA HQ. Geez, how long had Wolf Vishniac been trying to hop a ride? Over ten years, wasn't it? What a long time to sit on your thumb.

Only four of the six parties would supply an actual life-detection experiment. Offered finalist Josh Lederberg, a geneticist, "Alex Rich and myself both did not want to be tied down to a particular experiment because, you know, that would be years of very detailed commitment." Instead they'd serve as advisors. At one point Lederberg had been in the running with his own brainchild. But then he let it go. "We both felt that there was a lot that we could do in terms of the general overview of overall scientific direction."

Levin hadn't been at all certain about reaching the winner's circle. "Oh, I was not always confident; I was always worried," he said of the nail-biting interval between proposal submission and that welcomed sliver of U.S. mail. His newest new company had been at it for only two years; in '67 Levin had abandoned Hazelton Labs for a self-owned startup called Biospherics. "Competition closed on us many times in many ways from big corporations, prestigious universities." So many with so much better credentials. He'd even been up against Nobel laureates. "And here we were, this little company that had just started up, and the only thing we had going for us was the experiment worked so well!"

Elation gave way to frustration. After all the talk and snake charming and big promises and wink-wink negotiations, Langley got busted on their cost projection. After only five months of development the originally approved $364 million had shot up to $606 mil, and that wasn't even counting launch vehicles. Don Hearth really *did* know how much programs cost. Two months later John Naugle postured before Congress, trying very hard to justify an up-to-date guesstimate of $750 million . . . and to do it without getting lynched.

A remorseful Naugle went for the mea culpa. "We underestimated the weight of both the orbiter and the lander," he acquiesced.

In late November '69 President Nixon signed off on the fiscal 1970 appropriations. He did so after $299 million had been lopped like shrubbery trimmings from NASA's overall budget. Once again, the plan to scout for Martian varmints hung inside a dense gray cloud of uncertainty while headquarters went on a pork hunt. First they inserted a comma after all Saturn V assemblies beyond the current one in progress. With mere pen strokes this effectively truncated further Apollo missions. HQ also deferred the 1973 Viking launches to '75. In a strange twist, this drove program costs higher—while assuredly doing little to boost morale among Viking's hive of worker bees. But American taxpayers wouldn't have to ante up until later, so it looked good on the balance sheets.

Setting sail in '75 meant longer flight times and a more complicated route through space. Planners at JPL swallowed hard and threw out their suddenly useless trajectory diagrams to begin anew. And four Martian biology teams now had twenty-four extra months to kill. They'd end up needing every minute of them.

No matter how pleased Gil Levin had been to score a place aboard Viking, another downer caught him: involuntary name change. No longer would the experiment be known as Gulliver. "NASA thought that was too cute I guess," he intoned, "and the public wouldn't understand that. And they thought it should be a more scientific name, and somehow they thought 'Labeled Release' was that." The new appellation—often abbreviated as LR—made perfect sense . . . so long as you were a grizzled industry insider. *Labeling* is a trade expression for the use of radioactive markers in chemistry. If bacteria ate them, these markers would be *released* into the air. Levin winced; only governments could so thoughtlessly strip cleverness from a name.

The guy also faced a major staffing hiccup. He had a business to maintain; his cardinal efforts always went obligingly toward the funneling of more traditional projects through Biospherics—strangling whatever time he could spend on ~~Gulliver~~ Labeled Release. Up to now he'd had a full-time assistant working for him named Mary Francis Thompson: "dynamite," as Levin put it. A genuine right arm. She and a junior man carried out whatever variations on the experiment protocols Levin managed to architect.

Unfortunately, Thompson hadn't stuck around for the next act. She cut loose around the time Levin got his mailing, so he advised the senior chemist at Biospherics to begin trolling around for another right arm and to do it fast. Shortly after Levin issued his directive, a telephone rang at the desk of Patricia Ann Straat. She picked it up and engaged in a brief conversation with a man who explained that he was looking to hire a person with her qualifications into private industry. Would she please come discuss?

"I have no idea how he got my name," Straat later asserted. "I wasn't even slightly interested. But I decided it would be a good experience to go down and interview, which I did." Truthfully, she wasn't real keen on the idea of entering private industry. But six years of biochemistry at Johns Hopkins, every day doing the same thing in the same department, had really taken its toll. "I was getting a bit tired of characterizing enzymes and wanted to do something exciting," she mentioned. So Straat had been dangling her resume around in various directions. "If I kept staying in jobs like this I was never going to get my horse farm, which was my dream!" So why not see what this guy Levin had to say? They arranged a time for her to visit Biospherics's office on Wyaconda Road in Rockville, Maryland.

After half an hour's worth of chatting, "I found him intellectually fascinating. He was just full of good ideas." Until then, Straat hadn't heard that people were seriously gearing up to find alien microbes. "He talked about this life-detection experiment that had just been funded, and he had a couple of other things going, too." So much bubbling away inside such a nondescript one-level building. "A whole new world!"

Nevertheless, Patricia Straat was not the kind of rubber-spined follower to impulsively leap from one half-baked decision to the next. She told Levin they'd be in touch and went home to think about it.

He rang back only a few days later. "I have no choice but to offer you a job!"

Out of pretty much every human on Earth, Gil Levin felt that he desperately needed the capabilities of Patricia Ann Straat. She didn't deny it: "My expertise was so well matched to what he needed!" No mere biochemist and biophysicist *combined*, this woman had already spent years mastering the very technology that Labeled Release hinged upon: radioactive isotopes. "I was an enzymologist, and I used them to follow reactions." Cave explorers will sometimes toss a dye pack into an underground river to see where it comes out. In the same way, isotopes act as tracers, highlighting pathways the eye cannot otherwise discern.

Straat circled back to Biospherics for an encore visit. "I wanted to know," she continued, "what the company was going to do for ME. So we had a second interview, but this time I interviewed *him*." Like a relentless prosecutor she interminably drilled Levin on where the job might take her and what the benefits might encompass. "When Gil talked about all of this, it was SO different from anything I had done. And it sounded like just a whole lot of fun." What this man Levin proposed to do really struck her as not only unprecedented, but hugely desirable. Two days later Straat informed Levin that he had a deal.

Right from go Straat fell on a hamster wheel. And rather immediately, Levin cataloged her quick mental processing of basically any given situation. "She was so effective," he remembered, with obvious fondness. "It just took a conference, maybe a few minutes each morning, and she was able to go ahead and do the whole thing." He let a giggle escape. "Of course, it wasn't always my just telling her what to do. She's feisty, and she would tell ME what to do, and a lot of the time she was right!" He laughed again, as if to wonder how come he'd been so lucky to have happened across her.

Straat padded the office's back rooms, pencil and yellow pad hoisted. Each Viking *Lander* was to contain one unified, integrated piece of hardware comprising the quadruplet of chosen life-detection experiments. They'd share a common method of soil delivery, omitting redundant parts—not to mention the pesky variable of who got what soil. This approach also provisioned the same bank of electronics across four otherwise independent devices. It centralized the gathering and reporting of results. It reduced complexity. It made things lighter.

But this new whatever-it-was would never seamlessly embrace an unmodified Gulliver (or Wolf Trap or Carbon Assimilation, for that matter). No way in hell. As Straat told it, "The experiments had to be made compatible with an instrument which hadn't yet been designed." There were all sorts of integration gotchas that Levin had never had to address. Like the sticky strings: they couldn't feed four mouths. Or what about the deal with gas collection. Gulliver had used special filter pads to corral any radioactive gases let off by bacteria. Once an hour while the experiment ran, these pads had to be changed—then dried and examined. "That was how we tested the early experimentation, and that was how we did it in the lab," Straat recounted. "Totally incompatible with flight hardware."

And speaking of, they needed to get on a plane. Martin Marietta had wasted little time subcontracting various *Lander* elements out to other companies. One got the computer, another the cameras, a third the radio. One was already hard at work producing a "bioshield" to completely enclose each *Lander* before launch, as part of the sterility procedures. Another company focused on just the dirt scooper, because Viking needed more than sticky strings. All told, eleven major subs held responsibility for differing pieces of the total machine.

Straat and Levin's flight took them to California. About six miles due south of LAX sat a campus of modernist buildings called Space Park: the Redondo Beach facilities of TRW. This high-tech manufacturer of automotive and aerospace electronics had been hired to construct Viking's life-detection hardware. Everyone there called it the Biology Instrument. TRW would also be providing the *Lander*'s miniature weather station, although that'd leverage different people from a separate division.

Straat dropped her things in a loaner office on the ground floor. She then proceeded to learn that TRW had gotten a little ahead on design—and hadn't exactly done so in a collaborative fashion. From one intense meeting through another (Straat: "They were *never dry*, believe me!") the TRW guys anaerobically spewed through hordes of game-changing yet already-set-in-stone details. Back in Rockville, Biospherics worked to save time wherever possible. They'd prep several experiments and run everything at once: different nutrient blends, different controls. But TRW had to think minimal. "The first problem was that we could only run *one* sample at a time," denounced a harried Straat. It'd already been decided! *Arrghh* . . . already one single experiment took days. Okay, but maybe the engineers didn't know that.

Of the group she inquired, "Any way we can make it so the active and the control run in parallel?"

"No."

Gee, that stung. Pat Straat was learning that space missions require a shoestring application of resources. Everything's always so close to red-line. Metal parts are shaved down, wires thinned, opulence eliminated. If too much solder was used on its circuit boards, Viking might be too heavy to fly. By necessity TRW had to focus on reducing weight, space, power demands—whatever. Double- or triple-up on anything possible. And to that end each team was going to have to get what they got and deal with restrictions. Because they sure kept coming: Gulliver's little filter pads definitely had to go: too impractical. Norm Horowitz probably wouldn't get the small window he needed to channel sunlight into his testing chamber. It went on and on.

"You *have* to have a minimal level of system integration. Or nothing would work," rationalized Josh Lederberg. "That was imposed on us whether we liked it or not." TRW's use of shared, common assets required the scientists to compromise with each other to a significantly tighter degree than any really were interested in. Unencumbered by not having to worry about his own gear, Lederberg sat back to observe. "At various stages, some of the people threatened to quit if they didn't have more control over their own local area," he said. "I know Norman was very uncomfortable about the idea of having to justify his ideas to Vance and Gil. I can understand his feelings."

Subsequent trips revealed more and more constraints, more discouragement after every meeting. "They went ahead and designed without our input, and we learned we had to live with it whether we liked it or not," grumbled Straat of TRW. Perhaps the biggest downer: "We could only have one nutrient." Maybe not a deal killer, but supremely exasperating all the same. "That was another disappointment."

In the Gulliver days, Levin had always assumed he'd be able to exploit a variety of nutrient blends. For all the up-to-date research about Mars, nobody had the slightest idea of what might compose its terra firma. So the idea was to send different recipes: one with the simplest compounds, others with varying amounts of water, diverse sugar types, assorted vitamins, and so on. Proteins are formed by twenty distinct amino acids; why not send each one individually? "We would have liked to have had a *hundred* different test conditions," wished Patricia Straat. But the Labeled Release part of the Biology Instrument—as it began coalescing inside TRW, anyway—contained only four test chambers. And a single tank for its nutrient, called VMI: Viking Medium Number One. The ship had no room for a Two.

Having to choose one formula meant relinquishing a Gulliver hallmark. Levin spoke of a concept known as "chirality." Think about your hands: congruous, yet dissimilar. One matches the other only in mirror image. It's the same thing with molecules—a detail Levin had always meant to capitalize on. Perhaps the reverse of something doesn't seem all that different, but molecules are surprising. The "right-handed" carvone molecule, for example, tastes like spearmint—while its "left-handed" counterpart fills your mouth with the taste of caraway seeds. And this kind of specificity extends into the biological world. "All living material uses only left-handed amino acids, right-handed sugars," Levin articulated, speaking in a biologist's shorthand. So at the very least, they really needed two nutrients aboard—separating left- and right-handed sugars and amino acids, on the outside chance Martian life differed from ours. "It was in our original proposal," he lamented, "which we were told could not be accommodated because the instrumentation would have to become too complex and heavy."

Only one mixture could fly, leaving Straat to establish its exact composition. Her magic elixir also needed to be capable of merely surviving the trip. "It wasn't just that you whip 'em up in the lab and give 'em to the soil," she illustrated, speaking of nutrient preparation. Every Viking biologist had reviewed the same list of qualifications. "They had to go through a couple of years of storage. They had to survive all the heat-sterilization procedures." Again, more restrictions never even considered back in Gulliver's day, when all anyone needed was an empty ball field.

Straat organized her thoughts in pages of notes and took a first whack at the formula. One with limitless appeal seemed unattainable. She leaned toward the most basic compounds, or "substrates" as they're called, because they were more likely to be favored by primitive Martian life. One early favorite was glycine. It's a versatile, sweet-tasting amino acid that functions as a key building block of protein and gets used a lot in things like animal feed.

"We collected a wide variety of bacterial cultures and tested them *extensively* with candidate substrates," she explained, trying to draw a bead on how different blends of soup made little bacterio-critters behave. She also said, "We wanted to choose nutrients that did not give false positives." Martian soil, as only one variable, could be acidic. To Straat's horror, a few of her test nutrients reacted with *sterilized* acidic soil to produce results identical to that of active biology. Acetate was one. "So we couldn't use that; that gave false positives." They also wanted glucose, an everyday sugar. But under the prelaunch heat-treating regimen it would caramelize and form a useless sludge.

What else? Aboard Viking, little sealed ampoules would hold VMI, to be punctured one at a time for use. "They were going to build the ampoule out of a stainless steel that had copper in it," articulated Gil Levin. "And copper is poisonous to microorganisms—or many of them. So I argued with them. I finally won; the nutrient would be stored in a glass ampoule."

As months went by, the days grew longer, Straat and Levin committing more and more of their waking hours to advancing, correcting, refining, improving. Flights to Redondo became more and more common. Straat learned she could catch a 7:00 a.m. out of Baltimore and still make TRW by twelve o'clock—then hop a red-eye at day's end and return. Outside of her apartment, a neighbor bumped into her early one morning and commented, "You look especially nice today. Where are you going?"

"Los Angeles. I have a noon meeting."

Next morning she and the neighbor crossed paths again. "I thought you went to Los Angeles."

"I did!" She gave a tired laugh.

Yet the fact that she and the other experimenters were involved at all during this stage demonstrated one hard lesson absorbed by NASA. Many scientists, while otherwise comfortable building their own lab equipment, genuinely suck at producing flight-grade hardware. It's too specialized and fragile, too difficult. Only a few years beforehand, with Voyager Mars breathing its last, scientists at Berkeley had taken it upon themselves to build an instrument for use on two Mariner flights past Mars. One instrument failed completely—with JPL more or less predicting the entire time that bad things were going to happen. So researchers typically handed off their precious design to some specialty fabricator and then turned into nervous wrecks hoping the outsiders understood exactly what it needed to be. This separation tended to produce rifts, anger, bad feelings, bad publicity, and sometimes equipment that worked but didn't correctly perform the experiment. For the express purpose of reducing such strife, John Naugle had lobbied hard to involve the Viking experimenters in hardware construction from day one.

Levin and Straat continued their weary journeys across the continental United States. Back and forth between TRW and Baltimore, over and again. Red-eyes and airline food. Meetings, discussions, revisions, paperwork. Living out of a suitcase. Reams of paper, crossed and crisscrossed again with pencil lines, calculations, errors, scribbles, erasures, corrections. Sweaty and cramped hands. Recipes. Lists of considerations, problems, things to bring up with Gil over dinner, or while flying. "I designed the laboratory programs and instructed the technicians how to do it and analyzed all the data and wrote all the reports. *And* kept Gil informed." Free time disappeared. Friendly get-togethers decreased, then fell off the bottom of the schedule. Eating food directly out of the packaging. Less and less sleep. All for one teensy device, so simple in concept yet so menacing in execution.

"The experiment became my baby."

10. "Prepared Area"

An extraordinarily beautiful and cozy small town—where there
was always cleanliness, accuracy, and military order.

— Shkolnoye native Anna Dzhuly, when asked to
describe her town in one sentence

Towns and cities are established in various ways and for differing reasons.
Many sprout from bent-river settlements that expand and evolve over time;
certain sites might've been good because of the water supply, or rich topsoil,
or the fishing. Shkolnoye, however, was conceived as an entirely utilitarian entity. A deliberate town, born from pure necessity. It began life at the
dawn of the space age, in 1957, when Soviet planners realized the impending need for a string of facilities to track and control their upcoming fleet
of satellites. To that end, roughly one dozen outposts went up in a loose belt
spread across the greater girth of the Soviet Union. The positioning of each
was driven by factors that usually don't matter in construction—things like
launch site proximity and uncluttered sight lines, not to mention overlap-
ping coverage with the other stations. They needed to be attached, at minimal cost, to the existing layout of highways and power and phone lines.
They also needed to be inconveniently located, so as to avoid prying eyes.
Consequently, many went into quite sparse environments. Ministers and
party officials could've cared less whether the sites offered woodsy exercise
paths or sun-drenched views of the countryside. These places were for soldiers and work—not spas and yoga!

Seamless project execution did not follow. One facility located close to
a river had to be moved when the river flooded. Another never even got
finished because construction workers couldn't bore through the local per-

mafrost to install footings or service tunnels or much of anything else. Perhaps to throw off CIA spies, each was cryptically known as a "measurement point," and in bureaucratic Soviet fashion the plain in the middle of nowhere that is Shkolnoye became Measurement Point Number 10. The town's name literally translates to "school," which may or may not have also been part of some broader facet of misplaced deception. Indeed, the only building visible from the main road, and the only one outside of any gates, was and is a school.

Into this vacant scrubland came power, sanitation, concrete, glass, people. Far on the west end they built a gigantic steerable antenna dish, 105 feet across. A few hundred yards to the north of it went up a smattering of unlabeled service buildings. They filled with the antenna's power infrastructure, controlling electronics, and recording equipment; umbilicals snaking through underground tunnels. Double-row barbed-wire fencing surrounded the entire complex to become the *Technical Zone*, third gate in. Just to the east rose up a barracks and motor pool and mess hall and parade grounds: the *Administrative Zone*, accessible via that green second gate. And then one more hop to the right saw apartments and playgrounds go in, a post office, and even an outdoor swimming pool. Behold the *Residential Zone*, set behind only one gate. Arranged like this, the most confidential facilities were the farthest from the road and the hardest to get to. Such a little place, it didn't even have a main street—just a handful of back roads that never seemed to converge anywhere.

It was ready for habitation and so came the radio techs, the operators, the maintenance crews—along with various other personnel. Workaday solders occupied a set of barracks in the Administrative Zone. Married officers would perform their duties and then retreat east at night through the gates to the Residential Zone to raise families and warm the place up a little. Bachelor officers had their own dorm nearby. On free days, trips could be made down into Simferopol—forty-five minutes by bus to catch a movie or shop the shops or grab a train for someplace even farther away. The rockets began flying and the probes started beeping and everyone in Shkolnoye felt a snug sense of purpose. It worked. The collective might of socialist labor had triumphed yet again.

So in many ways the town had already been hopping years before Lunokhod ever came on the scene. The place was high tech and secret, yet with

17. Shkolnoye comes together in this image taken by an American spy satellite on October 4, 1965. The sports arena and school are at the extreme upper right. The road to their left rises and then dips just before the first dwellings, effectively concealing Shkolnoye from the road. Author's collection.

an upbeat human side that truly began to fall in love with this blessed little slice of Earth originally carved out for military reasons. As one resident exalted, "*There*, was a paradise."

Isolated within a bland and secure room nobody could talk about, three fences deep inside a hush-hush town left off the map, the five-man Lunokhod team inchwormed along a hostile surface more than a quarter million miles away from them. How dearly did Vyacheslav Dovgan miss his wife, not to mention the core emotional support that dwells in familial ties and close friendship. He couldn't and didn't tell anyone the truth about his activities. Well, almost. "My parents knew what I was doing," he admitted, explaining that they were supposed to stay cadaverously quiet about it. Once his daughter sent him a letter. It showed up addressed to "The driver of Lunokhod Dovgan Vyacheslav." Shucks!

The ongoing seclusion cut deeply in part because Dovgan knew this area well. Of all the places in the world to perform these top-secret duties; he'd grown up just down the road in Simferopol. "All my friends were there; I went to school there." How much worse did that make things? During lunar nights he could break away and catch up with his buddies, but only to a point. "It was particularly hard for me to keep my mouth shut." Laugh with the chums. Reminisce till it hurt. To those asking about your current assignment, maintain vagueness. And then head back through those gates to commence yet another lunar day.

Dovgan found the driving experience itself as otherworldly as any terrain they roamed. "It was a strange steering method," he suggested. "Because an image appearing each time on the video monitor didn't resemble the previous one. We had to 'play in' this work to feel the lunar rover movement, as if from the inside. It is hard to imagine something similar on Earth."

An image from *Lunokhod*'s nav-cam lit up the screens. What looked good? Where to go? As Dovgan illustrated, "Three to five seconds were usually required to make a decision." Commander Igor Fyodorov second-guessed his driver on occasion but typically respected Dovgan's judgment. They punched in commands to roll a bit: six feet. Twenty seconds later came the image refresh. Left by twenty degrees. Refresh. Three feet farther. Refresh. Twist left again to avoid a rock. Refresh. Behold the live-action filmstrip. How tough and slow might walking be if you could open your eyes only once every twenty seconds? And if your vision had been restricted to looking through paper-towel tubes? From training, Dovgan had conditioned himself to incrementally memorize features. "When we were looking ahead, and thinking of the obstacles that we did see, we also had to remember what was just behind!" Drive another couple feet. Now forget what you just saw and memorize the next picture.

"Everything was fine if you had correctly analyzed the situation, the various parameters, and taken the right decision."

It made no sense to duplicate Lunokhod's control room elsewhere just for straight classroom instruction, so the class came to the room. Remember that blackened field sitting outside? The rock-strewn, out-of-place one? In the beginning it was all grassy meadows like everything else. But then in '68—around the same time Dovgan was enduring crew selection—landscapers marked off a hectare's worth, grooming it into a reasonable approximation of the lunar surface, including undulations and dozens of craters in every size.

Now it just needed the proper surface, and for that it received all the care and attention of the Versailles gardens. Away went the grass and dirt,

18. Vyacheslav Dovgan maneuvers *Lunokhod 1* across the moon's surface. Gauges to his left display pitch and yaw angles the rover leans at. The center console holds the TV screen, marked with reticule lines for estimating distances. His four-arrowed panel indicates active wheel motion and direction of travel. Author's collection.

scraped clean, replaced by truckloads of coquina bricks. This slightly bizarre kind of rock is formed by naturally compressed invertebrate shells—quite common in coastal areas, easily mined, and super cheap. Whole Crimean neighborhoods were built from this stuff. In Shkolnoye, crews permanently "borrowed" enough from nearby construction sites to line every ridge and feature in the field. Next came a topping: dark-painted rocks and grit and dust ladled out to the farthest corners of the plot. There: the Lunadrome. A classified American intelligence report of the time included a map of Shkolnoye detailing its various buildings and antennae. The Lunadrome boundary had been labeled "PREPARED AREA," with no apparent insight as to what it'd been prepared *for*.

To accompany it, Lavochkin delivered a trainer machine encompassing a flight-ready chassis with electronics and cameras but no lid of solar panels. Instead, a thirty-six-foot, two-hundred-pound umbilical connected it to the control room, and away they went. "A lot of operations were practiced," reminisced Dovgan of their prep: running zigzag up and down the

19. On the Lunadrome, driver Gennady Latypov poses with the trainer. Sticking out from its side like two soup cans with their lids touching are the panoramic cameras. Courtesy RIA Novosti.

turf, holding a straight line, navigating peaks and craters, avoiding obstacles. All utilizing that trainer just a few hundred feet away.

"We could have seen it, but the curtains were closed." Dovgan smirked at this irony, yet he ultimately praised his instructional environment. "The drivers and commanders learned to very accurately determine the distance to obstacles in the 'lunar' surface, the diameter and depth of craters, the width of cracks, the sizes of stones." Perhaps the biggest problem with the Lunadrome was its propensity to collect discarded cigarette butts, which had to be fished from the outermost craters with sad regularity.

The Jackie Stewarts of lunar autocross managed to get themselves stuck again in April. They were toodling right along, no worries . . . until *Lunokhod* suddenly dropped into the most evil of craters—ungodly steep sides and loose fill—and it could have been the end right there. Total rover quicksand. They flicked off protection mode, then slammed it forward—strong ahead, grinding up the twenty-four-degree crater wall, struggling, pushing 90 percent wheel slippage. But the machine wasn't going anywhere. Tilted open like it was, *Lunokhod*'s toilet-seat lid sandbagged any progress because too much weight sat over the rear wheels. Everyone finally stood down for a moment to weigh options. As Dovgan remembered it, "The crew took a risky decision to close the solar panel and get out blindly." *Lid shut? Confirmed.* They leaned on the joystick again, forward, wheels . . . churning . . . dust . . . electric mixer spinning dry cake batter . . . motors hot . . . working . . . and it popped back up on top.

"Getting out was extremely difficult," shrugged a nonchalant Dovgan, recalling the Herculean efforts. "All ended well." True, the buggy had emerged in one piece—but also exhausted. They reengaged the self-protection, then left *Lunokhod* alone for a couple days; solar cells guzzling light to recharge overtaxed batteries. Across the way in the science room, men donned sport coats and gathered paperwork.

Everyone headed out for a much-needed respite, back again two days later: living on borrowed time, five stretchy months into a totally open-ended mission, sixty days beyond *Lunokhod*'s original design life. Alexander Basilevsky had no idea when it might end. "It was major job," he said of this mission and its importance to his career. "It didn't destroy any plans." Of course it didn't, because he'd canceled them all—and reckoned on sticking around until their shining Cadillac finally kicked the bucket.

A couple of other scientists wanted to halt and poke the soil. Boris Nepoklonov collected Basilevsky and headed out for another stretching of the legs. Typical day in Crimea: wind folding the long native grasses. Birds warbled. Soldiers rumbled on by in an open truck, hauling flasks of liquid nitrogen with which to cool the waveguides for the big antenna.

While traversing the Lunadrome, Basilevsky suddenly whipped out a camera. The presence of such an object was strictly forbidden, a supreme violation of the rules, yet both men got a juvenile kick out of the idea. They stood there clacking shots of each other until patrol soldiers recognized what they were doing and raced to cut it off. *Ay! Top-secret buildings in the background!* Next thing they knew a quite humorless man came storming across the playa directly toward them. Adopting an innocent tone, Basilevsky later admitted, "We were caught by local KGB person and it was little scandal." The agent, first name Felix, physically stripped the film from the camera and marched off and that was the end of it. No gulag. Walk continued.

Until mid-June, *Lunokhod*'s performance was flawless. It peacefully slumbered through another lunar night but then—after reviving for a ninth day—status lights on the control center panels flicked over from "normal" to "satisfactory." Instantly Lavochkin engineers knew what this meant: well into the autumn years, their silver chariot was about to hit winter.

They also knew exactly what was happening because hot stuff stays hot for only so long. The decaying polonium had lost much of its potency. Beyond that, the rover's silver-cadmium batteries were capable of only a finite number of charging cycles, and their overall capacity had sharply diminished. With a grimace Vyacheslav Dovgan zipped on his tracksuit for another round at the controls. When the sun fell in two weeks' time they might never hear from it again.

Curiously, that didn't happen. The July work session came and went with little emotion. *Lunokhod* no longer performed at 100 percent but everything still ran; by the armful, scientists gathered reams of details on radiation and soil density and chemical makeup. Basilevsky got his photos. Then in late July, as another lunar day kicked off, the Soviet Ferrari experienced something of a visitor when three Americans journeyed to the moon in a cone-shaped spacecraft. One stayed in orbit while two landed, unpacking humanity's *second* wheeled vehicle on the moon's surface. This one carried men from *Apollo 15*, who remained for nearly sixty-seven hours before rejoining their crewmate Al Worden in orbit.

"As the three of us flew over the lunar surface," recalled Worden, "continuing to study its features before heading home to Earth, I took some planned photos in the direction of *Lunokhod*." He didn't know exactly where it was but understood the approximate location to be northwest of *Apollo 15*'s own site by 450 miles or so.

Like many, Worden appreciated the rover's general function and accomplishments but knew zip about the personalities behind it. His thoughts continued. "It couldn't do what humans did on the lunar surface, but it sure could cover a lot of distance, and work a lot longer. It would have been fun to ride around on the little guy and see the places it explored. It was too tiny and far away for me to see, but I wished it a long life as we slipped over the horizon." Then the Apollo men went home. A month later, up went *Luna 18*—another quiet attempt at returning samples. Not long after initiating the drop from lunar orbit, it crashed; official Moscow dispatches blandly classified the landing as "unlucky," which was altogether not untruthful.

In mid-September the Shkolnoye team closed down *Lunokhod* again, wondering as always if this would truly be their last contact. Just in case, they proactively parked the rover with its French-made laser reflector facing Earth. *Luna 19* then made the scene in late September—conducting an orbital mission to further examine space radiation, magnetic fields, and our moon's kittywompus gravity. The super-short interval between *Luna 19* and its crashing predecessor implied a backup scooper, and many Western observers kept waiting for the thing to attempt its own landing. They waited for a very long time.

Down on our moon's unevenly pockmarked surface, the lunar day began to fade. Temperatures dropped along with the sunlight, dipping way too low for the rover's depleted polonium to keep pace. The feeble contraption did not despair, or cry, or become lonely. It was too far gone already, its debilitated mind blurring to the situation. And sometime during the next two weeks a parasitic wraith of bitter, piercing cold approached, clambering insect-like across *Lunokhod*'s helpless self—bony, sharp ice fingers clawing witchily at the seals between lid and tub, between motor and axle, camera and mount, in frantic efforts to pierce, gash, maim, and get in. Low temperatures imperceptibly crept through the rover's meticulously designed chassis, enveloping suspension members, antenna mount, camera lenses. An eternal subzero hug. The brilliant machine mounted no defense but felt no pain as it numbly succumbed and slowly froze in place.

On the next lunar dawn they tried calling and got no answer. They tried again and then again. *Lunokhod* had flatlined. Word went out to every scientist on the project, informing them not to bother coming down to Shkolnoye. The crew of Lunokhod, the quick-sharp brainiacs who drove and drove and drove, packed their bags and went home. As eulogized by a wistful Vyacheslav Dovgan, "The operation of the rover on the moon ended in a natural death at a very old age." And death so came not because their creation had shed its will or courage but because it simply could no longer keep itself warm.

Comparing Lunokhod to Apollo is not only unavoidable but difficult, if not impossible. They were two completely separate programs, with wildly varying design requirements and mission specs. Not to mention goals. Really, they had only two things in common: both went to the moon, and while there both used a laser reflector to measure the Earth-to-moon distance.

Apollo astronauts conducted a plethora of experiments. They laid out seismometers for detecting moonquakes. They propped open foil sheets in order to collect solar wind particles—material then packed away for return to Earth. And of course, live astronauts enjoyed the unfettered luxury of hand-selecting rock specimens to bring home. No contest there.

Yet the Lunokhod program performed broad-scale examinations of its own that Apollo never could—ones encompassing nauseatingly iterative rounds, boundless stretches of terrain, and vast periods of time. Try telling a human that he'll be on the moon for ten months solid, running the same experiments over and over. Go ahead, write it into the flight plan: X-ray the soil at twenty-five locations. Document surface strength with five hundred measurements over the course of six unique miles. Carefully map ninety-six thousand square yards of terrain and collect 211 high-definition panoramas while in the process of doing so. Good luck with that.

But these stats are exactly what *Lunokhod* amassed with absolutely no griping, refusals, or hysterics. Not too shabby. In terms of the scope of their scientific explorations, the Apollo and Lunokhod programs stand as nearly perfect complements.

Alexander Basilevsky, the geologist from Voronezh, returned home to his wife. And a divorce. He sort of saw it coming. "You know," offered the man, with a touch of sentiment, "it's not very good for family life when for about a year you are two weeks at home and two weeks out of home, two weeks at home, two weeks out." The couple never had children.

The efforts of Izrail Rozentsveyg and his TransMash associates were celebrated with medals and long vacation outings and even a Certificate of Invention for a Lunar Rover Chassis. The acclaim ended just about there. Based on their work, Rozentsveyg's division generated presentations for conferences in Rome and Tokyo—but the actual authors did not attend. "Much to our regret," he said, "we were not allowed abroad. Jews in general were not allowed; feared that secrets will be given to Americans." He shook his head. "Not even allowed to enter the Czech Republic!"

Although the engineering particulars had to stay under wraps, Basilevsky and Nepoklonov and the other project scientists did not face such restrictions or blanketing secrecy. Mission findings resultantly washed out into the world's scientific conferences—helping to fill cracks in our knowledge of this closest celestial neighbor.

"The Americans were extremely respectful of the science we accomplished in our country," extolled a prideful Alexander Kemurdzhian, who would remain at TransMash for the duration of his career.

"Everyone is capable of doing extraordinary things," he insisted. "Each in his own way."

11. Laying Eggs (Somehow)

For everyone's sake, I hope they have landed instruments
and are receiving data. If that is the case, it will be a fantastic
accomplishment that we ought to take our hats off to.

—Caltech geologist and *Mariner 9* scientist Robert Sharp,
immediately after the Soviets laid a probe onto the Martian surface

While theoretically possible any time of year, excursions to Mars are most feasible about every twenty-six months. That's when the God of War briefly aligns with us in a fashion that makes for decreased fuel requirements and flight times—along with a correspondingly dramatic increase in payload size. Mission designers call this kind of alignment a "transfer opportunity." They also call it a godsend. And 1971 offered the most favorable Mars opportunity in ages, with only thirty-five million miles to cross. Planetary launch schedules are dictated not so much by budget cycles or even politics but by existing celestial mechanics that no one can change.

Lavochkin's Martian battle plan had been in the works ever since mid-1967. Twin ships were to orbit the Red Planet and drop sacrificial entry probes to help determine the best method of landing. Nobody was yet sure whether to use parachutes or rocket engines or big rubber bands or what.

Seven months into development, these two *Mars-69* crafts were very nearly out of control. Look at just the propulsion trouble: as the machines burned fuel, their centers of gravity would shift in undesirable ways; the rigs might not remain stabilized. Or even on course! Cancerous problems materialized with the fuel tanks themselves. Lavochkin's design specified elastic membranes lining regular metal tanks, which helped control the distribution of fuel in a weightless environment. But after a few months in storage the liners tended to crack and leak—bad juju for a spacecraft taking half a year to even reach its destination.

"Because of the shortage of time," remarked one frustrated participant, "we were unable to find the proper solution that would guarantee reliable sealed membranes." They needed another approach. Months flew by. *Mars-69* endured umpteen design changes and fixes and other revisions, to the point where engineering simply was not able to keep pace. A flightworthy craft eluded them all.

Still two and a half years away from his fatal heart attack, Georgiy Babakin opted for an unlikely track: reboot. As in, discard the entire three-year-old design and completely start over. Thirteen months before launch! "Surprisingly," reported Lavochkin designer Vladimir Perminov, "the decision of Babakin did not depress the team. On the contrary, it seemed that the whole team got new inspiration. The pace of work, although quite impressive before, was increased further."

Strictly speaking, the Mars transfer opportunity did not care about Lavochkin's state of readiness. It'd close regardless of whether they were ready to go. As a result, comrades one and all set up cots by their desks to grab random hours of sleep. Lavochkin's in-house cafeteria kept the lights on 24/7, doling out free grub to anyone in need. Nobody got paid overtime, nobody bitched, nobody walked out.

With the days running obscenely short, assembly teams completed both ships and crated them off to the launch facilities without delay. Everything arrived in time to witness the first N-1 moon rocket sneeze into a gazillion pieces just over a minute after liftoff. It was February 21, 1969. The blast shattered windows up and down the hotel quartering Lavochkin employees. Outdoor temps measured twenty-two below, Fahrenheit, and the hotel's pipework iced over almost immediately. Handymen raced around installing new windows. That helped stem the heat loss, but replacing every damaged pipe and radiator wasn't going to happen any time soon. A line formed to requisition portable electric heaters. To a degree they worked, but they offered limited reprieve, managing to keep the average room temperature around freezing while simultaneously presenting a total fire hazard.

"Nevertheless," recalled another man, "people did not give up and continued to work to prepare the spacecraft for launch. It was a real challenge!"

Cruelty plays out in strange ways. All that selfless effort went for naught when both ships left the pad but unexpectedly returned to Earth—each victimized by its own booster mishap. Neither even made orbit. Draftsmen, welders, fitters, electricians, assemblers . . . the crew had killed themselves while readying these viable, science-driven spacecraft that ostensibly *would have worked* if given the chance. Now Lavochkin's Martian assault faced real trouble. Inside of two years they wanted to be first on scene with a soft-landing vehicle: survive, take pictures, record measurements. While America's new Mariner would merely orbit the Red Planet, Soviet engineers intended to inaugurate an on-the-ground *station*. They still needed to regroup and probe the atmosphere . . . but a grand touchdown would never happen if they couldn't figure out how to do it safely.

Up and down Lavochkin's hallways, the problem mushroomed into a swirling black hole of brainpower, unprecedented mental yoga disappearing over its event horizon, falling into the genesis of a solution to landing on this foreign world. *Anything* they could learn about their target—anything at all, the slightest bit of detail—would only tease out gray areas. Refute or reinforce assumptions. In the engineering world, mortal souls like Perminov knew that guesses could ruin his day.

Thirty-eight-year-old Vladimir G. Perminov had taken his education from the Kazan Aviation Institute, graduating in 1954. From there he'd transferred directly to the Lavochkin Bureau and immediately submerged himself in the business of designing a space plane for Vladimir Chelomey. And then in '65, Perminov had attended that fateful meeting where Sergei Korolev had bequeathed to Lavochkin his entire program of lunar and planetary missions. With some sentiment, Perminov recollected Korolev's appraisal of their charts and posters on display that day. One of them depicted a plate-shaped Martian lander serenely glissading toward pay dirt underneath a taut canopy of fabric. Quietly Korolev had commented, "The landing should be performed by the engines, without parachutes." The young, fresh-eyed Perminov bashfully reminded the chief designer how Mars's thin atmosphere was entirely conducive to such an approach. But Korolev had never responded.

In the four years since, Perminov had replayed that weird scene in his mind several times. Why didn't Korolev trust parachutes? The guy know something he didn't? *Nah* . . . every scrap of design documentation had been turned over to Lavochkin. And parachutes made sense. The biggest gotcha Perminov could think of was fouling: after you land, a billowy chute can settle atop the probe and block its operation. A parachute can't exactly be directed to fly off somewhere else. Or can it? Perminov reappraised Korolev's statement at face value. He'd said "the landing." Should they be thinking about this more in stages? Is that what the guy had suggested? To him, was "landing" somehow separate from "descent"?

While draftsmen sketched out new frames and supports and tanks and assemblies, trajectory planners weighed flight options. A repeat of the '69 mission profile was still needed, in order to augment Lavochkin's rather basic grasp of Mars's orbital and atmospheric properties. But it seemed such a waste to blow the golden 1971 alignment on a lot of reconnaissance. After much discussion the bureau settled on three launches. One would lift off a couple of weeks before the others, hauling along no provision to land—but plenty of extra fuel for a long stretch in orbit. The Mapmaker. A resolver of unfinished business. During flight its constant reporting on the position of Mars in space would help answer key questions: How can this planet be reached with a minimum expenditure of energy? What's the best approach for the other two launches?

And then, before the stragglers dropped into orbit, they'd release 790-pound doodads to barrel through the Martian atmosphere. Somehow. Downward they'd plunge at speeds of thousands of miles an hour before tumbling onto the surface like nothing ever happened.

After a (somehow) perfect landing, radio antennae would pop out like party favors, instruments coming alive for studies of wind, temperature, soil. Not to mention photographs! Just imagine: courtesy of Soviet technological superiority, enjoy the world's first pictures of the Martian surface—while American tin cans remain stuck up in boring orbit!

It sounded great, but of course everything had to be approved. So in late May '69 a small faction trooped through north central Moscow to Mstislav Keldysh's office, located within a building of the Institute of Applied Mathematics. In walked Perminov and Babakin and the impressively uniformed Georgy Tyulin, along with several reps from some of the involved ministries. As offices go it was quite intimate and Perminov, for one, appreciated the surroundings. Keldysh could have easily scheduled any meeting at the blandly cavernous Academy of Sciences, but these digs were more cozy.

An upbeat Keldysh soon voiced his approval of *Mars-71*. With some disdain Perminov later noted how Babakin agreed to use a new radio system on the spacecraft even though it wasn't as good as their current one. In a surprising moment of deference, Babakin's choice had stemmed from a friendship with the new equipment's lead designer. Everyone at the meeting approved this change, but not because of some intimate understanding of the strengths and weaknesses of each radio design. They just took Babakin's word for it. Perminov knew why Babakin wanted to make the switch . . . but he kept his mouth shut.

Back in Khimki, he mentally filed the radio issue and started in on other changes to their legacy design. Orbiters and landers share common transportation and spend part of their lives physically attached. But each is a very different animal, and building these things is like building anything high-tech. Over the years, design and performance improve. The twin '69 ships functioned well, but servicing them had been a different story. All the primary electronics lived within an airtight chamber deep inside the ship's pressurized core. Interconnecting wires ran through complicated airtight sockets. If anything inside that chamber needed service, forget your next meal. Disconnect all those cables from all those specialized sockets and uninstall the entire central core. Open the chamber of horrors. Perform the service. Flawlessly reverse every step to reassemble. "These procedures led to a great waste of time," recollected Perminov.

He threw the doors open. Anyone with better ideas was encouraged to present them; all comers welcome. The redesign went to a young engineer who first stretched Lavochkin's existing spherical fuel tank into a long cylinder. On either side of it he tacked rectangular solar panels. The dreaded electronics chamber became its own entity—a snub-nosed cone dangling below the fuel tank, modified so as to provide sweat-free access to the equipment nestled inside. Perfect! Lastly the engineer balanced a lander on top of everything. The orbiter's framework supported it, yet it easily popped off, like a champagne cork. Ultimately this arrangement would morph into the base configuration of every Soviet planetary craft until 1984.

While the orbiter redo had been essentially straightforward, all bets were off when it came to a landing machine. They knew some fundamentals. It had to survive that final hit from any angle, so what always seemed to work well were designs that opened up after touchdown. Maybe cube shapes were easier to make or fit parts into, but if they hit wrong on a corner, that could spell the end. So every lunar probe had been modestly egg-shaped. That way it could bounce and roll after hitting, to dissipate some of the shock. Four pie-shaped wedges atop the exterior would then spring open like flower petals. Even if it landed completely upside-down, this arrangement would cleverly right the machine. Turning around an egg is so much easier than flipping boxy things with corners, which further justifies the design.

In Russian, eggs are *yaitsa*. And Ol' Mother Hen Lavochkin now had to lay two of them onto the surface of Mars. Gently, please!

In America, elementary schools do a fun science unit. Each student receives one fresh egg and the challenge is to protect it during a twenty-foot fall from a balcony or high ladder. Some kids build little parachutes; others bundle their eggs in layer after layer of bubble wrap. Everyone takes a turn dropping while the group collectively laughs about the outcomes and *Geez, man, did you see what happened to that last one?*

But Lavochkin needed much more than bubble wrap at twenty feet. The problem broke down into stages. First came entry. The probe would hit at transit speed, thousands of miles an hour. For several years now aerospace engineers had understood the principle of the blunt body. To enter a planet's atmosphere, common sense might dictate the use of something needle-like: poke a hole and slip through, right? But the *opposite* worked best: mostly flat and very slightly rounded. Eggs weren't shaped like that, so Lavochkin needed to fit them with disposable heat shields to use and then throw away.

Mockups and wind-tunnel simulations led them to settle on a broad and profoundly shallow cone, sides sloping away at 120 lazy degrees. The roomy heat shield dwarfed its payload, and at ten and a half feet in diameter it just fit within the Proton rocket's nose shroud. Think of the landing egg as a human head, and this heat shield takes the form of a Chinese rice-paddy hat sitting on top. Odd maybe, and certainly not pretty, but good engineering doesn't care.

More complications. In order to proceed along into orbit, each *Mars-71* would have to maintain speed and release its lander while still twenty-eight thousand miles out from the planet. And understand that landers can't just tip off the side of the orbiter like a dislodged rock and plummet down. For the big breach they actually need an uptick in velocity, plus a way to stabilize their position. Here, Lavochkin applied Frisbee principles. Disciplined Frisbee throwers angle the disc in such a way as to maximize lift. It is thrown with a given amount of force. A Frisbee spins, offering stability to that angle of travel. Each of these principles applied well to Martian *yaitsa*, and like Frisbees, they would go in with boosted speeds and angled spins.

Lavochkin now addressed the dilemma of descent. By the time *Mars-71* finished violating the atmosphere, it'd be hurtling along at three and a half times the speed of sound in a configuration no longer befitting its new environment. So in a blink the machine had to origami into a more suitable formation and descend in one of two basic ways: glide or fall. While complicated, the former offers control. Wickedly ungoverned, the latter offers simplicity. Both end up on the ground. Which was best?

Engineers like control, and gliding down made tons of sense. But the technique depended on a slew of aerodynamic provisions that hadn't been factored into the *Mars-71* design at all. Each egg's center of gravity would have to be shifted. Perminov didn't think they had enough hard data on the atmosphere to design a glide, so Lavochkin went with the falling-rock approach.

There—done. Okay, falling egg. Parachutes were a logical next step, but how big? How many? They were engineers, not skydivers, and they farmed the work out to a separate institute that focused exclusively on parachute landing systems. Mostly the place handled military applications—like chucking tanks out the back of cargo planes—but had expanded into the space business. They'd built Yuri Gagarin's parachute, for example.

Definitely consider their product to be a *system*. So much more is going on here than just circles of fabric and string. Parachutes must be sufficiently lightweight yet strong as hell and sized appropriately to the load. A highly reliable mechanism of deployment must be provided. The chute must be designed to smoothly emerge from its housing, to cleanly deploy while not being torn away. Throughout descent it must provide stability as well as the obvious reduction in speed. None of these things happen by accident. Even a child's toy model rocket contains a parachute *system*, albeit a simple one.

Unfortunately, the Institute of Automatic Devices, as it was known, had one serious hole to climb out of. Only a couple of years beforehand, cosmonaut Vladimir Komarov had been killed when the parachute system aboard his *Soyuz 1* capsule failed to properly deploy. Right on the heels of that accident came two additional high-profile miscarriages—although nobody died on those. The bad streak resulted in the sacking of the institute's chief designer and rattled the place down to its core.

Now here came Vladimir Perminov, young and expectant, with his needs: brake an egg without breaking it. Within the vaguely understood Martian atmosphere a spacecraft would need to be slowed from thirteen thousand miles an hour down to approximately fifteen. From there, Lavochkin could handle the actual impact.

The institute guys swallowed. *Come again?* Some fairly tall orders had come through the gates, but nothing like this! Long ago they'd once made a chute for use above the speed of sound. Once. But the straight-faced weirdo sitting before them was politely requesting insanity. *Deploy at thirteen thousand miles an hour? Are you kidding?* In the entirety of aerospace history such a parachute had never been created. The Khimki man told them, *No joke; that's the flight profile.* And since there didn't seem to be any more questions, Perminov excused himself to rejoin other crises already in progress.

By that point everything was more or less taking shape. Lavochkin had the orbiter undergoing assembly and test. They had a lightweight *yaitsoh* frame all built out. They had a dense, resin-coated rice hat over the top of it. Workmen now seated the egg and hat into a donut-shaped base designed to hold the eventual parachute system. Underneath that they installed a crossbar framework, spanning the hat brim with a giant *X*. Onto it went a modest solid-fuel rocket, to light fifteen minutes after orbiter separation and notch up the lander's speed by a few hundred miles an hour. After that happened, the gizmo would next have to be oriented for contact with the upper atmosphere. To the expanding assemblage, designers added bottles of nitrogen and four puny nozzles capable of tweaking the spacecraft's position with gassy little toots. Once the correct angle had been achieved, a different solid-fuel rocket would set the hat spinning and impart stability.

Lavochkin reconvened with the Institute of Automatic Devices guys, who, in spite of some preposterous requirements, had nonetheless scratched up a plan. A hundred seconds after *Mars-71* dropped inside the atmosphere, rice hat having slowed the goods to thirteen grand or so, fifteen square yards of fabric would unfurl to stabilize and further brake the probe. This "auxiliary chute," explained the men, would kill the speed to just under

20. Behold the *Mars-71* lander configuration. Rice hat atop egg: wouldn't it have been obvious from the very beginning? Courtesy RIA Novosti.

two thousand miles an hour before automatic controls set it free. Metallic lanyards would then pull out 167 square yards of megachute to swell open in the thin Martian air and slow everything to bicycle speeds. Lavochkin told them everything sounded great; it just needed testing.

Simulating other planets is tough. Back during the Mars-69 program, engineers had slung test models underneath humongous ascension balloons and let 'em go. Past a hundred thousand feet, radio signals cut away the balloons and lit solid-fuel rockets to run the models up to entry speed. Then the parachutes came out. American engineers were doing more or less the same thing with their own Viking test models. And that somehow bothered everyone in Khimki, but not because of copycatting. It was because of the test itself.

So what if America tested in the same manner—was it a solid-enough technique? Did it accurately reflect the conditions of entry and descent? What were they forgetting to consider? Absent Mars-69 data hampered many decisions, and Lavochkin's philosophy called for beating the hell out of a design. In the case of pyrotechnics, for example—miniature explosives to sever connections or deploy instruments—one never went in any space-craft until performing flawlessly twelve straight times.

Lavochkin crammed one-fifth-scale egg models into the noses of two-stage M-100B rockets commonly used for meteorological research. These puppies could hit the edge of space. Launch rocket, release model, free-fall to speed, deploy parachute. What happens? Institute men crowded the test range and after fifteen tries concluded that the main chute tended to collapse. Was it coming out too early? Too late? Was it too big? Shaped wrong? Every assumption in their design would have to be reexamined.

While the parachute techniques underwent a complete overhaul, Lav-ochkin turned to the critical end moments of descent and landing. Nobody wanted the false sense of security associated with flying seventy-six million miles and ducking inside the Martian atmosphere—*Yay, we made it*—only to biff in the final seconds. As Perminov soberly noted, "A soft landing is the most complex stage of any flight." It's true with airplane travel as well; the landing is the one part of the trip when everyone stresses.

Landing with the main chute attached could easily tangle up each egg in a circus tent's worth of fabric. No experiment would stand a chance. There-fore, very close to impact, the egg would need to hack loose and put some distance on the chute. This could happen with a bunch of automatic com-mands. But . . . how much *time* those commands would need for execu-tion became the next sticky wicket. Time translates into altitude. The more time needed, the higher up the egg has to be . . . but the harder it'll hit.

After much discussion, and some heavy math, a sweet spot appeared to lie about a hundred feet off the ground. At that height, if the chutes did their job, the craft (probably) wouldn't be dropping any quicker than fif-teen miles an hour. Right at that moment they'd have just enough time left, and be low enough, to cut free.

But in order to do *that*, an egg would require some way of *knowing* how far off the ground it was. Cut loose too high, and instead of photo-graphs you'll get an omelet. Well, okay, they could bolt on hardware to blast the ground with radar and measure distances. Although precise, it'd add weight, not to mention complexity, so instead they went with a much more basic radar altimeter.

This part of the problem was now mostly solved. A hundred feet up, their liberated egg would be in free fall. What happened after that was going to be . . . what?

No question, *Mars-71* needed some kind of shock absorber. *Luna 9*'s air bags had worked great; what about using them here? Other engineers shook their heads. Any one of those solid-fuel rockets could burn through an air bag. They'd never last. What else, then? Big springs? Pillows? Some squishy gel?

Perminov finally advanced his killer idea: Styrofoam. What if, he proposed, they surrounded each *Mars-71* lander with several inches of the stuff? It was lightweight and took a beating. They'd have to find some way of clearing it from the moveable petals, but that might not be so difficult. Engineers waved the green flag and Perminov raced off to slather his egg with foam. Eight full inches went onto the bottom alone, with a thinner coating up top.

More testing ensued. Foamed-up eggs went joyriding in a centrifuge. Still worked. Like cans of unmixed paint they endured runs in specialized machinery that shook the hell out of them. No failures. For entire days at a time eggs sat in test chambers at low pressure and high wind, temperature constantly ramping up and down, all to simulate real-world operation. Every single time, the lander performed as advertised. Things looked promising.

Despite the passing grades, Perminov once again asked himself if the tests were good enough. He really wanted to ice the cake with a full-up simulation—crashing the lander onto fake Martian landscapes at different speeds, from various angles. Wouldn't that be great?

Enter catapult.

True professionals, Lavochkin concocted the ultimate egg-abuse accessory. They built a pure torture machine, first crafting a lengthy slide that hinged at the bottom. Just off the slide's low end sat a large pad of rocky dirt—the pretend Martian surface. Beyond it, installers vertically hung a giant trampoline. With such an arrangement the terminal drop could be simulated from proper impact speed. Technicians perched fully operational eggs atop the slide and let go, watching like interested house cats. One at a time the eggs would come barreling down, wallop the pad, then ricochet into the trampoline—rebounding, arcing up and over, tumbling, clattering back down onto the pretend surface again. After two or three eggs, it got to be quite a rush. Since the slide hinged it could be winched up to produce faster descents and more perilous impacts.

Every egg survived. "Tests showed that foam plastic provides a proper shock absorption and protection of the capsule during landing," Perminov reported. "The simulation of all flight conditions was made." Despite such brutally inhumane cruelty, each egg automatically and properly shucked its cover, unfurled every petal, righted itself, and sprang to life. The instruments deployed and the radios came on. Cameras began making pictures. The soil analyzer kicked into action, broadcasting its analysis of the fake Martian soil.

The Institute of Automatic Devices came back around with reworked parachutes. Techs installed them in five lander models and independently brought each down from the very edge of Earth's atmosphere. Everything worked swimmingly. On occasion they'd play the temperature card—chilling an egg way down prior to a test run or baking it virtually red-hot. No matter the temperature or the angle of impact or whatever, each machine continued to function as intended.

"A whole cycle of testing operations was made without any failures," claimed a giddy Vladimir Perminov. "And we became confident that the automatic station could accomplish the tasks planned for it." On technical merit the overall scheme was approved and at long last they had confidently secured a front-to-back method of landing on Mars.

Mariner 8 beat them off the pad; it was May 8. Six minutes later it beat everyone to the garbage bin after an upper-stage malfunction sent the thing careening into the Atlantic Ocean. Lavochkin's orbiter went up next, on May 10—about the same week Alexander Basilevsky got busted for shooting photos on the Lunadrome. As with most planetary spacecraft, *Mars-71S*'s booster first took it as far as low-Earth orbit (the *S* meant *sputnik*, or "satellite"). And what typically happens—even today—is that a planet-bound vessel, still attached to its final-stage booster, repeatedly orbits while undergoing a check to ensure that all is well. Departure from Earth orbit then happens not only with confidence but at the precisely defined moment necessary to hurl the probe down its mathematically determined course. Nobody launches to where Mars is—rather, they launch to where Mars *will be* in the six months or so required to get there.

An hour after takeoff, *Mars-71s*'s final-stage booster failed to relight for the kick out of Earth orbit. Unlike *Mariner 8*'s failure, though, the mission wasn't exactly dead just yet. Technicians started appraising the situation while probe and booster looped harmlessly around the globe. Fuel problem? Computer problem? Reams of data streamed back from sensors installed all up and down the stack of hardware. And refreshingly enough, this problem wasn't too hard to uncover. For whatever reason, no command had been issued for the stage to fire up again. To unstick this mission, a tech at the control center simply had to key in an eight-digit radio code telling the booster what to do and when. He did so—backward, unfortunately. And at that point they were really sunk. First one gone.

"It was a human factor, not technology, that was responsible for the error." Perminov couldn't help but feel some angst. "We lost the opportunity to launch the first Martian satellite. Besides that, we lost the radar beacon that provided information about the position of Mars in space." Nineteen sixty-nine all over again.

They rallied. *Beat America off the pad! Beat them to Martian orbit!* Both nations raced for the same transfer opportunity. Starting nine days later, Lavochkin's twin orbiter-lander combos began leaving Earth and met with victory; no launch problems whatsoever. Once underway they received the unexciting names *Mars 2* and *3*, while the failed orbiter became *Cosmos 419*. Nearly eight times lighter, *Mariner 9* set out only two days after *Mars 3*. The fact that this wimpy American offering had been designed only for orbit remained a prideful topic in Khimki.

Over the next weeks Perminov caught up on sleep as day-to-day control transitioned over to a stable of in-flight managers. Everything ran well enough until just over a month after launch. And then one morning Perminov's phone started ringing—uh-oh, Babakin's dedicated line. "Come urgently," beckoned the senior man.

Perminov materialized at Babakin's office door to find his boss pacing, tiger-like. He looked even more frantic because the room was so small— eighteen steps by nine, according to Babakin's son Nikolay, who had plenty of occasion to visit it himself. Beyond a framed portrait of Semyon Lavochkin, the room had not one decoration.

"I just spoke with Timonin," began the chief designer, anxiously puffing away on another cigarette. Every morning since launch, Lavochkin flight manager V. G. Timonin had delivered a presentation on the health of each spacecraft. And right through the day before, every report had dripped with positives.

Chin tilted up, Babakin systematically exhaled a fountain of wispy white smoke into the air. His normally dapper suit was a little rumpled. "Communication with both *Mars* failed last night," he sighed. Each ship's primary radio transmitter had stopped working. But then, oddly enough, the backup on each ship *also* failed after a short period of operation. Seductive commands went forth to the transmitters, attempts to entice them back into the land of the living. But no luck. Flight controllers had thrown up their hands and called an SOS.

Perminov couldn't fathom the changeup. "I was amazed by Timonin's news," he recounted. For one, everything had been running so smoothly! But even stranger—*twin, identical* failures on two separate spacecraft? What were the odds?

For a brief moment the men sized each other up, nonverbally replaying that meeting in Keldysh's office when Babakin agreed to use the new radio design. "Get the team together and fly out to Yevpatoria immediately," instructed the chief designer. No spacecraft maintains perfect radio contact. Signals dip in and out and must, as our planet rotates, be continually "handed off" to another station down the line. Lavochkin's tongue-tied Martian twins would next be in range of Yevpatoria station, and of course Perminov couldn't go there directly. First he'd have to jet into Simferopol Airport. Grab a car for the road to Yevpatoria, buzz Shkolnoye, and careen past Yevpatoria itself before reaching the station, which was actually much closer to the town of Vitunye. A fifty-mile drive, all told, on ridiculously narrow roads. Urgently Perminov worked the phones. Across town the radio-system contractor pledged to send four people as well. Men scattered.

After collecting two other Lavochkinites, a harried Perminov galloped over to the airport. It was late June—high tide of the vacation season and rather impossible to buy plane tickets for such a prime destination as Simferopol. The Council of Ministers wisely maintained a block of tickets in reserve for themselves, and Perminov tried like mad to lodge his talons onto a few. No luck.

In desperation he raced down to the Kremlin and rang up Georgy Tyulin. The deputy minister had not been aware of Lavochkin's acrobatics and received a truncated synopsis of lowlights. *Mars 2* and *3* were in trouble, he learned. A team really needed quick transportation to Simferopol. Any ideas? Tyulin knew about some other ministry airplanes sitting around idle at Vnukovo Airport. He told Perminov to grab one, so the engineer hung up and motored twenty-one miles southwest to the hangars. Despite their status as ministry-only planes, each giant metal bird still read "AERO-FLOT" on the side.

The troubleshooting contingent piled aboard a forty-four-seat Antonov AN-24 turboprop and shot off. With plenty of space to move about, the trio spent their entire 741-mile flight combing through every known scrap of data and roughing-out a best-guess plan of attack. Upon landing in Simferopol the men huffed down steps and into the terminal, only to get practically steamrolled by a line of porters barreling past them in the opposite direction. In cinematic synchronization the three engineers swiveled around to watch a silent opera. Every porter was mutely trying to comprehend why, in the absolute middle of the vacation season, a nearly empty airplane had just arrived from Moscow.

Just over an hour later, the men screamed into Yevpatoria's complex and huddled up with the management team in residence. Everyone compared notes. Perminov flipped through records of the most recent ship-to-ground communication sessions. The Lavochkin guys recommended a few procedural changes. Perminov noticed Sergei Afanasyev lurking about the facility but learned he was there to supervise the manned *Soyuz 11* flight that was currently orbiting Earth. Afanasyev held the title of minister of general machine building, which was an intentionally muddy way of identifying the head of the nation's entire rocket- and missile-building industry. Somewhere over the years Afanasyev had managed to earn the nickname "Big Hammer" due to his responsibilities and customarily intimidating approach to fulfilling them. He was a fiend, but fiendish for overly positive reasons, and one who got results.

That night each *Mars* probe finally swung into range and Yevpatoria started lobbing up different commands. Nothing seemed to work and the frustration level ramped up.

To appreciate their predicament, understand that planetary spacecraft carry two types of radio antennae: so-called high-gain and low-gain. Each more or less accomplishes the same thing, but in different ways. The high-gain variety resembles a mini satellite dish. Using it enables copiously swift rates of data transmission—like having a super-fast Internet connection. But it sends and receives a very narrow signal beam, meaning that high-gain radio antennae must be precisely trained onto a target.

Switching over to low-gain results in comparatively slow data rates, but the broad signal washes over everything it's pointed at. On Earth, low-gain works well on undulating terrain with many obstacles . . . while high-gain signals thrive in places like open prairie land. Spacecraft designers include both because above all else they want to maintain contact with their ship no matter what. So the basic strategy is high-gain whenever possible. And if you can't stay locked on, change to low.

Even with both ships carrying both kinds, *Mars 2* and *3* remained largely incommunicado. Most of the night's work was in vain, although little tricks got them fleeting snippets of connectivity. It was something. Reported a stoic Perminov, "A few straws of hope appeared for reestablishing communication." But he knew that hope was never something to rely on.

Abandoning sleep, the group worked straight through the night and the whole next day without pause. As night came on, the skies of western Crimea darkened, and soon both spacecraft arced into range again. Outside, a manually triggered siren wail spooled up to max volume. As it died, the nearby bouquet of antennae dishes trembled and then smoothly rose. More commands went up, utilizing differing approaches. The effort began to show promise. Turned out the radio systems hadn't totally failed after all. "The second night was productive," continued Perminov. "We identified the operating conditions in which the duplicate transmitters worked." This hard-earned discovery enabled them to isolate when and how the primary radios operated, putting each *Mars* probe back into business.

"The exhausting work was completed." Perminov felt warm satisfaction creep over him. "For two days we had not slept at all, and now could get some rest." After he woke, the busy minister Afanasyev wanted a status report before turning his full attention back to *Soyuz 11*, due home the very next day. All three men aboard it would perish on earthly descent when a vent in their spacecraft opened prematurely. Twenty-four hours following the tragedy Perminov and his team appeared back in Khimki.

Summer's end arrived. Russian weather began its predictable change. On Mars, however, the weather changed like nobody'd ever seen. Beginning in late September, ground observers watched through telescopes as a vast storm of opaque dust slowly enveloped the Red Planet. Inside of three days it spread two-thirds of the way around the entire globe. Then on November 19, sad news: *Mariner 9* had won the race into Martian orbit. Although that's as far as it would go—the machine carried no breakaway landing module.

"It will be very interesting to see what kind of data they collect on the surface," mentioned JPL director Bill Pickering of the Soviet efforts. "And how they measure the dust storm that is still raging."

Come late November the Mars flight program dictated another course correction. This maneuver comes with the territory because no spacecraft ever flies perfectly to its destination; somewhere along the way little twists of the steering wheel always seem to be needed. In order to do this, both *Mars* ships—like any planetary ship—carried little rocket nozzles on their frames, pointed in opposing directions and firing in specific patterns. Lavochkin had preprogrammed them for autonomous operation, and in this realm the absence of knowledge left by *Mars-71S*'s fizzling was definitely felt the most.

Mars 2 faithfully executed the maneuver—three times, in total, over the course of flight. Only it hadn't needed to make that third correction. After its second tweak the ship had been perfectly on course. Six days later, *Mars 2*'s egg-and-hat arrangement unlatched itself to begin the four-and-a-half-hour solo dash to the edge of Mars's atmosphere. It was out of position and already doomed.

Had the situation been better understood . . . and with more advance notice . . . Perminov's team might well have been able to orchestrate a fix. "Could we have avoided these results? Definitely yes," he suggested. "We would have activated the Earth-based control system and the flight would have been controlled by commands from Earth." But this didn't happen, in part because of the time delay for radio signals traveling between Earth and Mars. In 1971, even with the two planets so close together, nobody would know the ship's exact position until three minutes and six seconds after it'd already *reached that position*, and by then it'd be too late. The *Mars 2* lander came in steep and fast and obliterated itself on the surface before the elaborate descent procedure ever had time to activate. Utterly disheartened, Perminov ladled measures of blame onto the schedule. They didn't have near enough time, he insisted, to wring out every permutation of the spacecraft's programming. And they never ran simulations of how the ship would behave if its real position already matched that which it was trying to acquire.

"We just did not have time," he mourned.

Similar problems did not befall its twin. Five days later, *Mars 3*'s lander disengaged itself to begin the long descent. Four and a half hours after separation, the only remaining foamed-up Weeble in the entire solar system hit Mars's uppermost atmosphere. Spinning like a rifle bullet; seared like a steak. They were through, entry accomplished, rice-hat away. Now drogue, line of fabric stringing out the top, tethered by ribbons of metal, opening, whistling in the paper-thin wind. Slowing, slowing, five minutes till touchdown, POP went the pyros, drogue lines lengthening, donut-shaped package freed from the egg top, stretching out on metal ribbons of its own. Springing, then taut. Battery. Coming to life, simple instruments began reporting Martian vital signs: temperature, wind speed. Radio chatter flying up and away, storms of electronic snowflakes fluttering back toward the orbiting mother ship.

POP went the donut, main chute unfurling out—bouncing open but restricted at first so as not to overload the fabric. Slowing, slower. Cue experiment. Down on the probe's absolute bottom, a thin tube laid through the foam shell began sampling Mars's atmospheric pressure. Unleash main. Pyros. Constrictive ropes fell away. Canopy! Plump and full; one good main. Slower, slower. Getting down to freeway speed now. Landing radar on, blasting, finding ground. Down, down as planned, the invisible black line approaching. A hundred feet to go.

Now! Explosive charges severed metallic ribbons linking chute to egg. Chute cut free, starting a timer while lighting up its own small rocket package to get the hell out of Dodge. Fifteen seconds on the clock as *Mars 3* free-fell on its own and it all came down to this at twenty-six miles an hour, twelve seconds, eleven. Altimeter cued ground-facing solids to life, firing, dispensing a final cushion. Impact. It took the pain, survival, foam worked. Far enough away, the entwined parachute-and-rocket gizmo crashed itself in a lovers' suicide. Two, one, zero, and timer ran out. Deep inside *Mars 3* a gas cartridge emptied itself into a rubber bladder sandwiched between petals and foam. Two seconds later high pressure liberated the protective cover and four petals yawned open, points touching the Martian surface.

*Show*time.

Sterilized before launch, the entire rig began powering up—breathing life into thirty-five pounds of instrumentation. Cameras flickered to life, starting line by line to record the incontestably first Martian surface image, transmitting it home. Fourteen and a half seconds later the lander died, yet for the next three minutes and six seconds Perminov and his colleagues would not know this, as the pen-plotter they stood watching traced out those very same lines imaged by their dream machine. "Of course there was great enthusiasm!" beamed a scientist who was also present. "When you don't see the signal, and then suddenly you see it on the screen!" He could barely contain his emotions. "I would say one of the deepest enjoyments, one of the *greatest* enjoyments that you can experience!"

They looked at the printout and saw gray noise and nothing else. Fourteen and a half seconds after beginning its work the plotter stopped. And at that point Vladimir Perminov knew all too well what had happened.

12. How Low Can You Go?

The Russians claim to have landed on Venus, Bruce!
Is that possible?

—*New York Times* reporter Walter Sullivan, waking up
Mariner scientist Bruce Murray with a 6:00 a.m.
phone call on Thursday, October 19, 1967

They had nothing—zero imagery. *Mars 3* had died right in the middle of its big shiny moment. Technicians reran the picture data and all anyone ever managed to extract was more gray noise.

"Search for signal *by all means*," called out the chief designer for the radio system. He was in command of his emotions, yet antsy.

"We tried all antennas," continued the no-longer-beaming scientist, who'd been so upbeat only thirty seconds before. "We tried to find out what could happen, because . . . okay, maybe antenna was wrong, maybe the amplifiers, you know there is receivers, something, our receivers? And, but no way. Yeah. It was frustrating." Somewhere between two and three hours later, Georgy Tyulin ordered everyone to give up.

Today some confusion persists over whether or not *Mars 3* took the first photograph of another planet's surface. At the time, TASS celebrated the egg's transmit of information to its mother hen, which in turn relayed the data to Earth. Accurate enough. TASS further reported that "video signals" had also been delivered, although they "were brief and suddenly discontinued." And that, well, is sort of true. At least one frame did indeed make it back home. The image in question is filled with classic TV snow, punctuated by a thick horizontal band of white bisecting its middle. This white is not what everyone focuses on. Rather, angling upward and to the right from it is a distinct and extremely low-contrast triangle shape. The rest of the picture is garbled. For that canted triangle to be the Martian horizon, *Mars 3*'s camera would have had to lay tilted on the surface by a good forty-five degrees. It's certainly possible—even discounting the craft's self-righting petals—but this image fails to make the grade on multiple levels. Without any context, show the picture to someone. Anyone. What do they think it is? A wedge of Roquefort? Evel Knievel's takeoff ramp? Absent serious mental leaps, the image cannot be interpreted as what some purport it to be. It's too undefined, the supposed horizon too vague.

"Essentially it was noise," admitted one Mars teammate. "It is really sad." *Mars 3* did not return any surface pictures. It had died on arrival.

The agony of failed lander transmissions cut deeply. Much more deeply, in fact, than a measly photograph. Now the Soviets wouldn't get to show off their big fat secret, unrevealed to outsiders until the 1990s. A wonder of engineering and determination that had come directly from those same hands that produced the Lunokhod chassis.

In addition to its camera, the fertile *Mars 3* egg had also carried a small rover. By modern standards it was puny and underpowered and almost pointless. Its level of finish alluded more to weekend Erector-set playtime than serious engineering. The rover did not bristle with capability. It held no camera or life-detection gizmos or weather station. But it nonetheless reached the surface.

After *Mars 3* had unfolded and righted itself, a cantilevered boom would have unsprung and somewhat abruptly somersaulted the nine-pound, dictionary-sized gadget upon Mars's surface. Maybe this happened; nobody knows. Then, under a single watt of power, two side-mounted ski- feet would have inchwormed the little papoose along: lift, body up and forward and down, skis rotate up and forward, down and pushing off again—a fifty-foot umbilical trailing along behind. Should the bitty guy have thumped into rocks larger than it, a levered bumper on its nose was to halt forward motion and cue a sequence whereby the rover would back up several steps, turn slightly to one side, then attempt a go-around. Every five feet it'd automatically stop and twist a small metal knuckle in the dirt to measure soil properties—same as on *Lunokhod*. Had the *Mars 3* lander camera performed as intended, it would've imaged the rover and its tracks.

One of the more disappointed parties in this whole affair had to be Izrail Rozentsveyg. After all the success and hoopla of Lunokhod, TransMash's expertise had been called upon once again—this time, to create an entire vehicle. The new rover wouldn't have to operate in a vacuum, but the thin, dry Martian atmosphere wouldn't make things any easier. Rozentsveyg explained that metal parts rubbing together break up carbon dioxide and liberate huge amounts of oxygen that immediately attack metal parts. "We had to create special greases," he explained, and even those had only a short working life.

Lavochkin began their autopsy. Near as anyone could tell, the radio failures likely involved heat—although that conclusion had more to do with deductive reasoning than hard data. A smoldering trail of clues wordlessly meandered along the side of the ship and up to its high-gain antenna dish. Immediately behind this area sat two smaller low-gain antennae resembling fat ice-cream cones. Quite likely, it began to seem, the high-gain dish had absorbed so much heat that it gravely damaged the two low-gain cones before winking out. (This theory did not go unprotested; the equipment in question had been assembled with pure-silver solder and was supposedly good to thirteen hundred degrees.)

Nevertheless, above the high-gain dishes of later kinfolk went a simple cloth sunshade. The antenna design per se never varied. But no radio trouble ever rematerialized after those little pieces of cloth were installed.

Pigheaded Mars continued upon its merry way through space, oblivious to the migrainal ruminations in Leningrad and Khimki and Moscow and equally unmindful of the pathetic transfer opportunity it would remit in two years' time. This upcoming 1973 alignment of Earth and Mars would mean dieting down to lighter-weight spacecraft. Designers therefore envisioned four discrete ships—two orbiters, two landers. A veritable Martian armada, setting sail for battle with an undefeated opponent.

But if Vladimir Perminov had reckoned on washing his hands of disappointment, he would have been dead wrong. In a ghastly combination of incompetence and ignorance and blasphemous corner-cutting, these four spacecraft would be doomed prior to ever leaving the ground, their fate lasciviously sealed while still in assembly. And left to explain it all would be one man—a total fish out of water, utterly miscast in a role that he'd involuntarily occupy for the next fifteen years.

Luna efforts continued in earnest. Come early September 1971, *Luna 18* crashed right at the end of its automatic descent in what is largely thought to have been an attempted sample-returning encore. Just over three weeks later, *Luna 19* flew the requisite quarter million miles only to loop around in orbit— returning imagery and science data over the course of its four thousand circu-itions. But no moondust. (A totally unsexy flight, though orbit *was* the plan.)

Over four months passed with no word from behind the Iron Curtain about any space shots whatsoever. The vulgar silence finally broke on Val-entine's Day, 1972. Tucked inside page 2 of a north Texas newspaper, right next to an announcement canceling the Ladies' Day Club's next meeting ("lack of sufficient registrations," FYI) was this:

SOVIET LUNA 20 TO ORBIT MOON

MOSCOW (UPI)—The Soviet Union today launched Luna 20, an unmanned spaceship, toward the moon, the Tass News Agency said.

TASS went on to bill *Luna 20* as conducting "further exploration of the moon and near-moon space," but seasoned reporters already knew this to be lingo for a touchdown attempt. They were right; with textbook execution it landed six days later and only a hundred miles north of its cousin *Luna 16*.

Facts, as they often did, began dribbling out in a series of carefully scripted press releases. News of sample drilling soon hit Western papers: "Because of the great strength of the rock, the drilling was done in sev-eral stages with intervals during which the drilling rig was stopped." Thus continued TASS's overly massaged narration of the chancy events playing out so far away. In actuality, an extremely dense surface nearly broke the drill; ground controllers perspiringly halted and restarted the proceedings many times so as not to burn out their equipment. Almost thirty hours after landing, the ship finished its surface activities. Two days later it came roar-ing back through Earth's atmosphere and soon hung underneath a bright orange parachute. Almost home!

For as stressful as the operations had been so far, engineers now felt even greater reason to worry. Their tiny return capsule—all that remained of a six-ton rocket—had ingloriously found itself caught in the midst of a brutally severe snowstorm as it plummeted directly toward the half-frozen Karakingir River. Lunar highlands had been nothing compared to this.

21. The sample chamber from *Luna 20* is slowly extracted from its return capsule.
Courtesy RIA Novosti.

Pilots circled in their gargantuan Mi-6s—helicopters so rudely huge they have *wings*—as the little trooper ploomped safely down on a tiny island. An island? Recovery crews tried snowshoeing to it. They piled into off-road jeeps. But uncooperative Siberian weather didn't permit any real forward progress. Their meek little capsule, a nation's pride, sat completely unattended for an entire day and night until the storm blew over and it could finally be retrieved along with the single ounce of priceless moondust that it contained. Published articles mentioned nothing about recovery troubles— only that the charred ball had descended within a "preset" recovery zone.

In a refreshing show of détente brought about partly by the efforts of Frank Borman, seven-hundredths of an ounce of the *Luna 20* haul were exchanged for samples from *Apollo 15*. Yet the state-run Soviet press couldn't resist one final dig at the Americans. Said *Pravda* on February 25, "Moon rock returned by *Luna 20* is expected to be at least one billion years older than rock brought back from the lunar sea areas by *Luna 16* and the U.S. Apollo astronauts."

In the Soviet Union, all men were equals—but all moondust apparently was not.

Schoolkids are tantalized by the idea of swimming to the bottom of the pool. Down there it's mysterious and exotic and dangerous—in their eyes, anyway. To ride on the zenith of life, to exist on a higher plane, all you have to do is get there. They stand at water's edge in logoed cargo shorts or frilly character one-pieces and dare one another to go for it: to push deep down, down underneath the inner tubes and kicking feet to where you're alone, defenseless in a hostile world of blurry sounds, pressure squeezing the ears. Your head might pop. You could run out of air, drown and never come back and the lifeguards will forget about you and go home. All for a quick touch of that roughened floor. More daring kids go straight for the drain. It's that most exclusive of subsurface real estate where the water is deepest, the pressure highest. A spastic, serpentine struggle all the way down. Those with no hang-ups eschew dime-store goggles and force their chlorine-burned eyes open, or they do it the uber-creepy sightless way. Wrinkly preadolescent fingertips brushing discolored metal grillwork, lungs burning in an about-face, frantically thrashing upward to the comforting light and air and civilization. Back from the void. Their fiscally unbuttressed reward? Bragging rights. *I was there, I touched.*

Enigmatic, alchemistic. The utterly recondite, necromancing netherworld of swimming-pool bottoms; that is where heroes dwell. Only babies play by the surface.

Venera 8 sat there quietly on the bottom. Not of some apartment-complex swimming pool, but on the bottom of the airless, eye-burning, head-popping atmosphere of Venus. Upright, intact, operating. It was on the ground. The planet had just received its most recent houseguest: a faceless, brownish, cauldron-like wonder that had exchanged millions of rubles and engineering man-hours for a total working life of approximately two hours. What contrast to its equally daring twin that had never escaped Earth orbit. They were not children but resulted from the ambitions of youthfully eager minds that were similarly unafraid to strive for the bottom. The kind of people who had never outgrown that rush of going down there and touching something exclusive and somewhat forbidden.

Due to its size and brightness and nearness, Venus, throughout history, was long regarded as paralleling Earth in its climate. If Venus is closer to the sun than us it must be warm, and warm planets undoubtedly have oceans and foliage. So went the logic. Okay, the days were long: 243 Earth days per; one single day on Venus actually takes longer than its year. But that wouldn't make a difference . . . would it?

Venera had just landed. Winds blew quite calmly; a gauzy yellowish-orange haze permeated the scene. Light levels approximated an overcast earthly day. If the ship had had a camera, which it didn't, its view would have ranged over half a mile. Presently a puck-like device sprung out from its top and landed nearby on the scorched granite surface, trailing a short tether. This functioned as the craft's main antenna, and soon details of its permanent new home began flying earthward—tales to banish any whimsical thoughts of lush tropical gardens or of humanity ever conceivably visiting in person. Where to begin? How 'bout the daytime high: 878 degrees Fahrenheit, phew. Add ninety atmospheres of pressure—1,323 pounds per square inch. Reaching that on Earth would've required a swimming pool nearly three thousand feet deep. This place wasn't an oasis; it was the inside of a kiln. So . . . any ten-year-olds up for a *real* challenge?

High temperatures began creeping in, slowly working their way through layers of insulation covering the kettle's exterior. *Venera* was good until about 160 degrees. "Essentially the lifetime of the lander directly depends on how fast the temperature inside will go above these limits," articulated one mission participant. And soon the heat reached a dodge—wads of a chemical compound that absorbed heat like sponges do water and gave the machine a 20 percent extension on its life clock. "You have to isolate them from the ambient environment," continued the man, describing how critical it is to separate electronics from hellish temperatures. "Because otherwise they just will not work." The strategy therefore hinged on keeping everything as cool possible for as long as possible.

In sum, the metric was, "How fast will you die?"

Venera 8 marked only the second time one of the Soviets' meaty tubs had knowingly set down intact on a world celebrated for its glassy brightness and outward beauty—and not at all celebrated for the abounding number of complications involved in reaching its nefarious geology. Several days before taking the plunge, a refrigeration system chilled *Venera 8*'s innards down to five degrees above zero. It then unlatched from a mother ship, hit the atmosphere an hour later, and opened a parachute at 180,000 feet. Special ties constrained the canopy to a narrow diameter—a configuration known as "reefed"; upon opening it doesn't jar the fragile payload and makes for a greatly reduced risk of canopy blowout.

The drop continued, barreling through high clouds. In vaporous curtains they hung over Venus in suspension, enveloping it in thick blankets of foggy bewilderment. The condition prohibited any Earth-based investigations from determining what might exist at the surface—one more reason why *Venera* had come. Its onboard light sensor noted that brightness levels had now plummeted at least threefold. Strong winds came along and blew the ship horizontally in an unexpected side trip that would eventually cover some thirty-seven miles. It drifted on, unconcerned, the downward-pointed radar exposing jagged peaks of terrain. Whoa; Venus wasn't a glass marble after all. Another instrument licked the high clouds and pronounced them to be made of sulfuric acid. So many traits of this planet seemed so totally out of whack with the rest of our solar system, or even common sense, and *Venera* hadn't even landed yet. If acid clouds weren't enough, just check the speed of that cloud layer; within ninety-six hours it rotated once completely around Venus. What else might be there, way down deep near the drain?

Halfway, wind speeds plummeted and the light levels began to even out. A layer-cake atmosphere now seemed likely. From here on in, however, the ship would not be enjoying some pleasant escalator ride. Just under ninety-nine thousand feet its restrictive ties melted through as temperatures climbed and *Venera*'s parachute inflated to full breadth. Squeezing pressure now multiplied as the craft sank deeper toward landfall, a scrawny, submerged ten-year-old with plaid trunks and scratched-up ill-fitting goggles and a boogery nose kicking downward like mad, arm outstretched, eyes squeezed tight, wondering if and when that roughened pool floor would finally materialize. Fifty-five minutes after initiating descent, *Venera* thumped onto the surface and automatically severed its parachute lines.

Venera 8 was not the first. It alighted with such apparent ease and discovered what it did because of forerunners. A year and a half prior, during the closing weeks of 1970, *Venera 7* had skydived into the planet's viperous atmosphere with the singular goal of hugging the ground. As such, its creators overdesigned it to function at one thousand degrees and 180 atmospheres. After consulting with submarine builders, they fabricated a perfectly spherical, rugged yet smooth canteen with no surface welds or other potential weak spots. Bulky insulation and a thickened hull left practically no room for complex experiments . . . but that was not the point of this one.

Game time came in December 1970 as *Venera 7* went headfirst into the maelstrom. A flyaway top exposed parachute moorings and science instruments. Two classically geek-dad, rabbit-ear antennae flipped out over the side and downward to begin reading altitude.

A dozen miles off the ground, *Venera 7* swayed violently back and forth until the battered canopy gave up with two miles still to go and released its cargo into free fall. Ignorant of peril, *Venera* dutifully reported on fast winds unexpectedly moving backward. Then the kettle whacked Venus at thirty-eight concussive miles an hour and bounced. Signals dropped out, muscled back full-on for an instant, and then went completely silent again. The big show was kaput. To the shock of all involved, no other decipherable measurements had come from *Venera* save the wind data, which itself had been derived from studying changes in the radio link.

Nevertheless, the Soviets knew they had it. As did America: "For the first time, a man-made object landed on another planet and returned data to Earth." So went part of a U.S. Senate report that burned through hundreds of pages of stats and hearsay trying to figure out what in the dickens the Russkies might be up to. Militarily speaking, a benign flight.

One of the mission scientists was struggling through his PhD thesis at the time, involving a somewhat esoteric treatise on Venusian winds and the movement dynamics of parachutes. "It was quite unusual behavior," noted the man, Viktor Kerzhanovich, of *Venera 7*'s rock-a-die-baby. Shortly after flight operations shut down, he began daily visits to a smallish city about twenty-five miles southeast of Moscow. There, at the convergence of Gagarin and Tupolev Avenues, sprawled a gigantic aerodynamics research facility that included a number of wind tunnels practically big enough to hold the Olympic Games in. This is where part of the *Venera 7* autopsy would occur. Technicians began dissecting the parachute's actions under load, working to unravel its mechanism of failure during those critical moments of final approach. "You have to know the behavior of the parachute. Otherwise you can mix the wind effect and the parachute dynamics effect," stressed Kerzhanovich. "We needed it."

Some thought the canopy had melted; others reckoned it tore. "But parachute was not changed much from *Venera 7* to *Venera 8*, as far as I remember," he countered. "It was the same material. And they didn't fail on *Venera 8*."

Doggedly the entire group kept at it, Kerzhanovich enduring a five-hour round-trip commute every day of the week: first the Metro subway, next a train, then finally a stint on the bus. "In the Soviet time we overworked a lot—it was quite usual. At that time my company would not pay for the hotel if you are so close to Moscow."

They modeled different failure scenarios to judge what best fit the evidence. "I was sitting there in this wind tunnel for maybe for a couple of months," Kerzhanovich went on. And one explanation finally bubbled to the top. "It was not the parachute," he revealed, "but it is point where the parachute is attached to the spacecraft. Failure was *there*." The vessel used four such mounts, and after sixteen minutes of equable descent—with less than sixteen miles to go—two mounts had given out and induced the phantom swaying. Fifteen minutes later the remaining two surrendered, and that was the end of another Venus lander.

What happened after it hit?

An incredibly faint signal from *Venera 7*'s recorded telemetry had persisted for almost twenty-three minutes after landing. Strange; it only sent temperature data. Normally a mechanical switch on the lander rotated through a swath of readings—clacking in turn through altitude, pressure, and other bits of interest. But the switch had somehow gotten stuck on temperature.

One of the men involved later remarked how thankful they all were that the switch hung up where it did because temperature data could be correlated with properties of the radio signal to restore the missing altitudes and pressures and conclusively establish what the hell happened. It took a month, but experts finally managed to extract whispers from the dead. After impact, the mortally wounded *Venera 7* had rolled to one side, enduring a ninety-two-atmosphere surface pressure. Its antenna now faced away from Earth and was transmitting at a strength between 1 and 3 percent of normal. Soon the brown bucket breathed its last.

Venera 7's rollover prompted designers to add that jack-in-the-box antenna to pop away from the tub and broadcast in all directions. And less surface pressure than expected translated into a reduction of the design's overall beefiness—leaving more weight available for surface studies.

Researchers were now set to abandon the idea that Venus might have oceans. Today it sounds far-fetched and laughable, some weird joke that even kindergartners would see right through. But until these *Venera*s went out, the notion had remained theoretically possible because nobody'd been able to penetrate the Venusian clouds. They were too thick, water vapor in Earth's own atmosphere further complicating the task. You basically had to go out there.

Venera 7's born-again results chalked an improvement over its forefathers'. Over a year prior, *Venera 5* had made it out of Earth orbit with no trouble. Five days later a blizzard tore through the Soviet launch facilities in a demonstration of winter that would've completely shuttered Cape Kennedy. Instead of going home, Russian pad workers reviewed their schedule. Within ninety-six hours *Venera 6* had to go, clearing the way for a Soyuz flight's impending reuse of the exact same pad. Nobody even blinked. With mittens and *ushankas* in place, the collective might of socialist labor cleared away truckloads of white frosting and every launch happened precisely on schedule.

The descent tub, or kettle, represented only a single component of each *Venera*'s overall structure. A big cylinder of guidance and control equipment formed the mother ship's core, with a large, mesh high-gain antenna on its belly. Solar panels jutted out from either side, accented by a large flowerpot-shaped engine perched atop for course adjustments along the way. Then, tucked underneath it all, the descent tub hung like a ripe apple. Engineers collectively referred to this as "the stack"; both were identical.

In mid-May '69, *Venera 5* severed four thick metal straps and its apple fell from the tree. It barreled in steeply, the plump orb enduring much higher deceleration forces than its predecessor. Friction crippled speed and the sensors came alive. From under a parachute came reports of high clouds and high wind. After *Venera 5* sunk below the clouds, the wind stalled out. CRACK. Twenty-seven atmospheres ruptured its battle armor with at least fifty-three thousand feet to touchdown, and *Venera 5* retired from the game. One day later its twin made the plunge—dropping farther yet faring no better, to end in a *Venera 6* face-plant nearly two hundred miles away from its martyred relative. Each had lasted in the blistering environs for less than an hour.

All in all, not bad. Shy Venus seemed to have a way of slowly revealing itself, as if in striptease, and the effect largely resulted from a basic evolution of technology. As inherited from Sergei Korolev's design bureau, the original *Venera* had not exactly been met with rapturous joy. The craft was entirely too cumbersome, its mechanicals incommodious. It had more problems than the South Vietnamese government.

Lying there, cold and inert and practically abandoned in the arms of adoptive parents, whimpery *Venera* begged for improvement. Lavochkin obliged. They stripped it down to its underpants and commenced rebuilding nearly from scratch itself. Only the basic shape remained. They reinforced its pressure vessel. On the mother ship they got the bright idea to meld the radiator into the high-gain antenna—clearing excess weight and sensibly placing *Venera*'s cooling mechanism on the side facing away from the sun. The craft's radio complex behaved more like a recalcitrant Airedale than quality electronics; Lavochkin disciplined the equipment until it behaved. During ground tests the whole ship went to hell and back. It responded. It got better. They coaxed and charmed and beat and cajoled and ended up with something worthy of flight. Boris Chertok served Korolev for years as one of his key engineers. And of Babakin's effort he commented, "You have to give credit to his staff, who found many flaws in our design and systems."

It was ready to go.

In June '67 the *Venera 4* launch went smoothly. Every instance of radio contact occurred as expected with no electronic histrionics. And what might it find? Would Venus turn out to be the lush, tropically warm and humid paradise that some had always predicted? Or would she prove to be the victim of a devastating "runaway greenhouse effect," as thinkers like Carl Sagan kept yammering about?

Boris Chertok had never reckoned on attending *Venera 4*'s descent. True, early Venus flights had been part of his domain, but he'd involuntarily washed his hands of it all nearly two years prior when everything lunar and planetary had gone to Lavochkin. Venera probes had almost entirely left his short-term memory—until the day beforehand, when Korolev's successor Vasily Mishin had rung Chertok and ordered his butt on a plane to witness the landing attempt "in person," meaning at Yevpatoria station.

Another Crimea trip. After flying to Simferopol he drove northwest and started hitting the major resort areas after thirty miles. Wordlessly he navigated past their legendarily luxurious hot-spring mineral spas and lakes of mud. Their top-shelf hotels. Beaches ran for miles upon end; everyone outside of his dirty car windows was having fun. At dinnertime Chertok arrived in Vitunye, straightened his tie, and found most of the permanent

22. Two unidentified techs inspect printouts of received data from a spacecraft; their primitive machinery sounded like mechanical cash registers. As Boris Chertok commented, "The mission control centers at Cape Canaveral and in Houston seemed like a fantasy to us." Courtesy RIA Novosti.

crew already in bed because the next communication session would begin at four o'clock in the morning. Overnight he managed to grab some rest and then finished breakfast in time to join the proceedings by 5:30 a.m. It was still dark outside.

The facilities were as advanced as Soviet technology and politics allowed them to be. For example, they couldn't process and display flight data in real time; operators made do with ink pens tracing squiggly lines onto narrow strips of paper tape. They also had secure phones and telegraph machines.

Some of the equipment dominated a large, hot master control room that had been effectively partitioned in two by the arrangement of a large sofa. At the moment it was occupied by Mstislav Keldysh, in extremely low gear, who'd flown a red-eye from Moscow and kept dozing off despite the excitement. Georgiy Babakin rushed between control panels—feverishly scanning for trouble—though little could've been done about it.

"Forty thousand kilometers to Venus!" hollered Revmira the wonder woman, her distinct voice blaring through the intercom. She occupied another room entirely and spoke with rich tones into a microphone. *Venera 4* approached its hot date and the craft's speed quickened. Any minute now the fishbowl-shaped lander would unstrap itself from the stack and plummet into swirling clouds. A deadly mating, like those of black widows.

"Twenty thousand kilometers to Venus!" sang Revmira again. "Onboard voltage . . . fourteen-point-five volts!" Without her, these updates would not have been possible because Revmira was the only person, in the entirety of Yevpatoria station at least, who could glance at the abstract squiggles of telemetry being drawn onto paper tape and instantly translate them into usable information. Please, comprehend: without Revmira, nobody would know what-all really had happened out there with *Venera 4* until many days or even weeks later, when all the telemetry had been laboriously decoded in bulk. Nobody would know how fast the ship was closing on Venus, its onboard power situation, or anything else really, *at the same time that data was coming in.* No way in hell. For this rare talent, Babakin jokingly called the woman "our computer: the MIRA-I!" and tried to hire her away many times.

The station waited. A hundred and twenty days since launch and it was coming down to these uniquely tense moments. Facing her wall of electronics stood Revmira: slightly plump, with pleasant features and shortish hair tucked behind the ears. Her overused white lab coat hung loosely off broad shoulders.

"Separation command!"

"Loss of signal!"

"We have separation!"

From here on in they'd get flat silence, until the eight-hundred-pound lander popped its chute and started broadcasting. Noise levels rose in the control center. Babakin told everyone to hush up.

Several delicate minutes later:

"We have a signal!" Revmira again, master of ceremonies.

"We're receiving from the descent module!"

A pressure meter lit up. An altimeter. Two thermometers came alive, one functioning at high precision within a narrow range of temperatures. The second had a wider gamut but less accuracy. Electronic floodwaters burst and information started pouring in. Eighty-five thousand feet high, *Venera 4* gossiped of the one and a quarter Earth atmospheres and 172-degree temperature. Hot enough to roast a pork loin. Within fifteen minutes the values jumped and then jumped again only eighteen minutes after that. Five and a half atmospheres at 330 degrees; cookie-baking temps. Wasn't that about the limit of the pressure meter? Spelunking inside Venus's undergarments, *Venera 4* had entered some odd territory indeed. Chemical results washed in: 90 percent carbon dioxide atmosphere. Less than 7 percent nitrogen. Chertok cocked his noggin: *Surprising.* Half an hour after those readings, one pressure sensor went off the scale as the ball endured a deceleration of 350 Gs while meeting with increasing resistance from a thick, doughy atmosphere and *Venera 4*, as later deduced, literally began coming apart at the seams. Now 482 degrees: hot enough to melt tin. Now 518. The last reading from its pressure meter said 9.3 Earth atmospheres, redefining the planet as more boa constrictor than fairy-tale princess. Venus liked squeezing things very hard. The entire signal disappeared; *Venera 4* must've crash landed. Yevpatoria erupted in emotion.

"Now it is clear that these flights have not been in vain!" loosened Babakin, violating his own you-talk-I-spank policy. "No one is going to start planning piloted landing expeditions to Venus!"

The signal flickered back and then dropped out again. Forever. Ninety-three quick minutes had elapsed since the broadcast started; years of work for an hour and a half of storytime. But *Venera 4* proved to everyone in that room that the effort had been worth it. Down there inside the Venusian recesses lay something waiting to be discovered. There had to be a way to make landfall again—but in good working order.

Watching it all happen in front of him—the excitement, the amazing real-time results cascading forth, the handshaking and hugging and backslapping—Boris Chertok could only thank his lucky stars that he'd been subpoenaed to attend. So often they'd launch and have to brave another heartburning round of disappointment. Their booster would vomit, the stack would miss its target or outright fizzle. This time had been different. The scene in Vitunye offered nothing short of an uplifting, inspiring spectacle.

At that moment, only those inside this very room knew the real truth about Venus. America didn't know, or Brezhnev, or even the guards out front. What everyone had learned during these past two hours would be disseminated—quickly—but for the next several minutes Chertok belonged to an elite fraternity who knew things the rest of the world didn't. "This was perhaps one of the happiest days since the flight of the first Sputnik," as he later phrased it. "We learned more about the secrets hidden under Venus's clouds than science had discovered during preceding centuries."

Fresh news eventually went across the telephone lines from Vitunye to Moscow and thence proliferated to the rest of the world. One American report summarized the Venera program to date by noting that "a growing reliability is appearing, and a continued dedication to such missions should provide improving returns." *Venera 4*'s exploits became the confetti of scientific conferences and papers and discussions, and right about then is when outside analysts got hung up on the Biggie.

The Biggie was this glaring uncertainty regarding altitude. *Yevpatoria station assumed a landing.* Right after *Venera 4* stopped transmitting Babakin had shouted, "We sat down!"

Keldysh opened his eyes. "Let's not rush. I think it is still far from the surface," he suggested. "There are quite different conditions than we imagine."

The story went in every direction. Jodrell Bank affirmed to news outlets that the ship had indeed touched down. A Soviet communiqué retorted that it did not, followed in short order by a second announcement that reversed the first and said Oops, it actually did. The international community barked up a hot fuss: nobody had the data to prove such balderdash, and a landing would be a huge deal. Revised wording later dribbled out from behind the Iron Curtain, timidly suggesting that *Venera 4* had alighted on top of a very tall mountain. Again: bestial outrage. During a series of meetings in '68 and '69, *Venera 4* results went head-to-head with those from the American *Mariner 5*, which'd flown past Venus only one day after *Venera 4*'s self-immolation. Before the assemblage, Soviet astronomer Arkady Kuzmin faced off against Carl Sagan, Bruce Murray, and a slew of others.

"Venus must have great high plateaus," asserted Kuzmin, calmly. "*Venera* must have landed on such a high place."

Prodded the Americans, "A plateau sixteen miles high? Isn't that rather improbable?"

"Let me tell you about 'improbable things,'" berated Kuzmin, modestly inflamed. "What would be the chances that the first German bomb dropped on Leningrad would kill the only elephant in the Leningrad zoo? Yet that's exactly what happened."

In the face of such unassailable logic, Murray and Sagan discontinued the conversation.

But Kuzmin was bluffing; his own experiments showed that temperature data from the lander didn't match up with popular models of the surface. And there was more. American radar surveys had long ago determined Venus's position in space—as well as its diameter. This data lined up with *Venera 4*'s atmospheric profile only if Venus's ground level were situated many miles lower than where it was already more or less known to be.

Furthermore, if the *Venera 4* temperature and pressure graphs were merely shifted to higher altitudes, then any discrepancies reconciled almost perfectly. With some reluctance Kuzmin's group acceded to international naysaying and revised their findings: when *Venera 4* proclaimed 85,000 feet, its true height had been closer to 180,000. *No* landing. Although failing to reach the nadir, this big brown tub had nevertheless plunged far down into the pool's deep end.

Georgiy Babakin penciled a note: *Use better altimeters.*

The eventual success of *Venera 8* would never have occurred without the string of sacrificial brothers in arms that'd gone proudly prancing off the diving board in advance. They enabled *Venera 8* to go where it did, and do what it did, and as waves of vitriolic heat continued their relentless march into its belly, the machine forwarded home priceless nuggets of data about Venus's ground composition. Planetary geologists squealed like swimsuited grade-schoolers because they'd finally touched, had finally rubbed electronic fingers on the bottom for just long enough to formulate a picture of what lay all the way down there. Odd . . . the tub didn't appear to be perched on a solidified river of volcanic rock, as some had predicted. Rather, it was a dense slab of granite. This marked the first-ever on-scene report of Venusian surface conditions.

Remarkably, the sky also appeared to be much brighter than anyone anticipated. They could send a camera and see for themselves this three-dimensional representation of hell only one planet over.

Fifty minutes after touchdown, *Venera 8* finally yielded to the heat and pressure and its radio transmitter shut down.

If the bottom of Venus had a drain, the remarkable Soviet urns never found it—though a forthcoming generation of newbies would certainly look. *Venera 8* was the last of its kind, perishing on July 22, 1972. Sadly, the London Zoo's giant panda Chi Chi also died that very same day.

13. Three Mistakes

I did not warn anybody. It was a little aggression from my side.

—Alexander Basilevsky, outlining his party-crashing
actions during work on *Lunokhod 2*

Immediately after *Luna 21* set down with *Lunokhod 2* atop, Basilevsky inquired as to whether he might be able to join the crew-room proceedings. That got a thumbs-down. He retreated to the science room in a stew.

Two days later, with the new moon car well underway, Basilevsky made his move.

"I will do it," he told himself.

It was time. He'd had it up to here with the barfy politics. With the ridiculous notion that *achievement* equaled *distance traveled*. Their wunderkind was capable of so much more than mere ambulation. Why even go to the moon, if its most intriguing features were at risk of not being studied? "Governments," he complained, "they don't listen too much to scientists. They need political success." But hadn't that already been achieved via *Lunokhod 1*? Here they were over a year later, back in Shkolnoye, January 1973. If anyone asked *him*, a little change was pretty goddamned overdue. Time had come for the authorities to receive input from someone able to follow geologic trails of evidence. To interpret those cracks and craters and piles of gray rubble and comprehend the story they silently uttered to the ages.

"I just took a chair from the scientist room," he went on, hoping that everyone would find some way in their hearts to forgive what he was about to do.

All excitement over the landing had dispersed. Everyone else had nicely settled into their routines. More exasperated than confident, Basilevsky strode across the hall to the crew room. As usual it was blocked by a uniform, who took pause to face down this hundred-pound scarecrow glowering at him. "The soldier didn't know what to do with me. I was very serious, and he didn't know who I am. Maybe I am big boss?!" The metal chair twisted awkwardly in his fingertips. "And he just, like, moved away a little. I came in, and the crew knew me, and said, 'Oh, priviyet Sasha!'" (*Priviyet* means "hello"—a very informal way of saying so, no less; the way a close friend would talk.) Basilevsky parked his chair at the rear of the room and defiantly crossed his arms.

"So okay, I will be sitting *here*. Okay!"

The occupants regarded him briefly and then turned back around to resume operations. Minutes passed. Nobody kicked him out.

"And there was not any scandal."

Occupying the crew room did not for one second mean that he was in any position to start blurting out instructions. That would've been a complete breach of protocol. At its core, Lunokhod remained a military operation. Civilian Basilevsky had no rank and certainly no authority. For him to argue otherwise, and be granted such privilege, would've set an awkward precedent and urged the proceedings one bitty step closer to anarchy. How soon, then, would all the other scientists come barging in to demand one thing or another from their own personal agendas? Granted, Dovgan and the others had smiled their hellos, but the overall procedural structure had not actually changed. "Drivers would never listen what I am saying them," agreed Basilevsky. "And even their commander on shift would never listen to me. They would follow what their *colonel* said them—and their colonel of course listened to Ivanovsky."

His new approach leveraged politics: use the current Lavochkin rep in attendance, Oleg Ivanovsky, to position Basilevsky as an unthreatening scientific advisor offering mere guidance. From there, gradually coax Ivanovsky into whispering recommendations to the colonel: "Suggesting something like general direction—to go *there*. And also we could say, 'Okay, let's stop here.' And look more attentively at something."

Above all else, Basilevsky didn't want the plan to get trashed. See, the first time around they were frankly just driving—timidly exploring the area proximal to *Luna 17*'s landing site. "Reconnaissance," as he put it. "Trying to understand what is around." With their big southerly loop they'd acted like wandering tourists, returning eventually to the barren *Luna 17* descent platform. "And then went to the north," he continued. "Working around the place and just waiting that we may find something." No set route had been meticulously plotted ahead of time. "We did not have the long-term plan like to go to *that* place, to *that*," he elaborated. There was no itinerary, no hit list.

"With *Lunokhod 2*, we *had this plan*." Months of effort went into it. Conspicuously improved lunar imagery—much of it courtesy of Apollo— had inspired Soviet geologists to scour the surface details anew, in search of some magic locale with just the right combination of diverse features.

Now, they couldn't set down on mountain ranges; the journey still had to begin from a nice big pancake of an empty landing zone. And engineers put *Lunokhod 2* at exactly the desired spot—inside a cosmic vacancy that is Le Monnier crater, right on the eastern shores of the Sea of Serenity. This meandering lowland separates two geologically distinct areas that scientists were itching to visit. On one side lay the "mare," or flat "seas." On the other, highlands. The excitement came from what surprises might be found inside that transitional zone and how the moon would be different *there*. Basilevsky's muscling in on the crew room sought to guarantee that any potential geologic revelations did not go to waste. To have spent all that time choosing such a great location—only to watch *Lunokhod 2* blow past all the sights? Just to rack up mileage?

"We knew *where* we landed." With grand excitement he rattled off destinations and objectives one after another. "If we go south, we come soon to the highland area—long highlands." Apollo photography had uncovered many interesting features to the east, and they'd be heading over that way, too.

"Maybe we could observe outcrops!"

To share in this excitement, first understand that lunar outcrops are something of a rarity. "When you are on the surface of the moon, usually you don't see any rock outcrops. You see just regolith, regolith, regolith. You see rocks," said Basilevsky. Regolith is boring old dust and soil. "Practically no outcrops. Outcrops are only on the slopes of big craters."

Outcrops are *not* boulders. The moon is practically covered in boulders, most of which are borne of *cratering impacts* like good ol' meteor strikes. Inside the resulting crater, any boulders tend to be embedded somewhat in the gray soil, while those thrown clear are usually much more exposed.

What differentiates outcrops is that *they* contain very old and undisturbed material that hasn't been created or otherwise influenced by meteor impacts or other external forces. Outcrops are original. They offer a journey back through time to the origins of the moon itself.

During the rather brief *Apollo 11* moonwalk, astronaut Neil Armstrong professionally followed his to-the-minute flight plan. Except once. Late in the walk Armstrong knowingly and deliberately stepped away from the TV camera he was supposed to remain in front of, shuffling over to photograph and examine the walls of a crater.

For what reason? Why would a highly trained and fantastically procedural man, in this unique position, disobey like he did? Armstrong later wrote that he thought the crater walls might contain a rock outcrop. "I felt the potential gain was worth the risk," he rationalized. So the mere possibility of an outcrop is why the commander of the first manned lunar landing blatantly violated the rules.

If only *Lunokhod* could roll up to any old crater and frisk it for outcrops. But no matter which room Basilevsky sat in, nobody was going to let an irreplaceable rover get too close to any big craters. They're dangerous beasties. It could be the kind of magic trick nobody wanted: the incredible disappearing rover. So the Shkolnoye geologists pinned many of their outcrop-flavored hopes on this impending eastward journey. And for these kinds of reasons a self-empowered Alexander Basilevsky stepped into the Lunokhod facility every working session as a man of purpose.

"We had beautiful program to work with!"

They were currently heading south, toward the nearest highland point visible from *Luna 21*'s touchdown spot. *Lunokhod 2* retained the basic shape of its predecessor: large tub with fold-open lid. As thermal control goes, the lid was a brilliant idea—but also a problematic one. "Movement with the lid open was no pleasure," injected TransMash engineer Mikhail Malenkov. "The lid moves the center of mass to the rear wheels, thereby overloading the rear wheels when climbing up steep slopes." He pointed out that with a fully extended lid, the vehicle's overall length has effectively doubled—and eight wheels now have a wide beaver-tail appendage hanging off their back end.

"The lunar rover, with an open lid, becomes a very unwieldy structure."

Still, the machine at their command represented a distinct evolution of the species. *Lunokhod 2* weighed more and contained more experiments than its predecessor. The front nav-cams had been tweaked upward, offering improved perspective. It carried a third navigation camera, at chest level. The solar panels were more efficient. It could roll at twice the speed. It handled larger obstacles. Imagery came in faster. Overall it was *better . . .* excepting one minor detail. While working, the drive team constantly referenced a series of gauges displaying *Lunokhod*'s angle through two axes of motion. Some indicated to what extent the vehicle nosed up or down, while others showed left-right tilt. "Readings of these sensors were used to assess the situation and make decisions," added Malenkov. "Especially in cases where the driver did not see the horizon." If the rover approached too extreme of an angle, these gyroscopic "heel and trim" sensors would automatically call a halt. But on *Lunokhod 2* they weren't functioning. At all. Malenkov explained that the original contractor had been replaced at a rather late point in the game. "Development was unsuccessful," he benignly affirmed, which was one way of saying that the delivered system broke down while still in transit to the moon. The drive crew would have to rely solely on their own interpretations of the TV images to know how much they tilted.

The southward push continued. To the crew, Basilevsky pointed out how surface soil always deepened when approaching larger craters. They could be rolling along, leaving barely perceptible wheel tracks of only an inch. Then before anyone realized it the track depth would increase to seven or eight inches and turn lumpy. *Caution!* he'd urge. *Large crater nearby!*

They studied everything: soil characteristics, photographic panoramas, chemical compositions. One new experiment was the ultraviolet telescope—an upward-pointing device measuring that portion of the sky's spectrum between visible light and X-rays. (Using one on Earth is practically meaningless, as vast amounts of UV light are filtered by our atmosphere.)

No matter the findings in those panoramas, or the quality of science readings, the top brass remained most interested in racking up distance. *How many meters today?* they always wanted to know. *How many kilometers total?* "It was big political pressure," said Basilevsky. He loves to tell a story about how they once earned "free" distance. It starts with him forgetting something. They'd been traversing a geologically curious highland area—planning all along to stop and have a whiff of its surface composition. Ahead of time Basilevsky had been suggesting, "We need to have chemical analysis of this." But while they were there he forgot to ask, so the drivers kept ambling on down the highway and it wasn't until a good kilometer later that the geologist finally remembered. *Uh, would it be possible to get a reading from back there?*

Everyone relaxed for a beat. "Okay Sasha," the crew commander offered. "You wanted to make analysis there, we will do it." In a flash his driver 180-ed and dropped into *Lunokhod*'s existing wheel tracks. Following those, they retraced the trail at full speed, made it back in record time, and got the readings after all.

"We measured good chemical measurements. We found more aluminum in that than was normal." Everybody came out a winner because, as Basilevsky put it, "The bosses were very happy because they could report, *Okay, today we made* TWO *kilometers!* It was like a record, but it was little trick!"

Reaching the highlands capped an end to this lunar day. If their plan held, the travelers would spend the next couple months investigating them before striking out east. Prior to boarding the Simferopol train for Moscow, Basilevsky and his cohorts made sure to stock up on liquor. "Crimea is good place to buy wines," he advised. (A true understatement, because it's the Napa Valley of Asia. Frank Borman even made a point to swing through for some tastings.) On the return trip the geologists always consumed more alcohol than they did coming down, while trying desperately to reserve at least some of the Crimean stock to enjoy at home.

Basilevsky stared out the grimy train window, letting his droopy head rattle against the glass. Diminutive riverbeds twisted through the countryside. He found it intriguing the way they completely dried up in the summer and formed steep ravines. They'd made this trip many times, but each ride greeted them with unique views, as Crimea has amassed a surprising number of landscapes and turbulent climatic zones. Entire seasons can change within hours. Nighttime revealed isolate, faraway lights floating in the dark—settlements and farms and small towns—and before long they'd reached Moscow once again.

For the next two weeks Basilevsky and Nepoklonov could savor a little catch-up time. Whenever *Lunokhod* was "on" the scientists never got a full night's sleep. After a session ended they'd go racing back to the hotel and grab a snack and review what'd happened and maybe catch a low number of winks and then it'd be back into that dreary room the very next day—perusing data and steeling themselves for another two-fisted round of action. This mission imposed a real-time environment that embodied something of a new challenge for any scientist. Think about how it usually goes: an experiment is performed in a controlled laboratory setting. Surrounded by an environment for data collection. It's all meticulously planned out in advance. Afterward, the researchers still face deadlines for analysis and publication, though they typically don't have to contend with manic urgency. Here, the direction of *Lunokhod*'s next tracks could well be determined by a scientist's overnight findings.

"It was exhausting," conceded Alexander Basilevsky.

While everyone recovered, a *Lunokhod 2* wheel sensor reported –193 Fahrenheit, while another up on the tippy-top of the radio antenna said 361 above. Imagine designing a car that had to operate with a 550-degree temperature differential between headlights and trunk.

The break offered Vyacheslav Dovgan his own opportunity to reflect. After their selection in '68, the seven who wanted to actually *drive* had traveled to the Gorelovo suburb of Leningrad. There, for an intense month, TransMash engineers schooled them on the chassis and led technical discussions about exactly how it functioned. They explained the various modes of driving. The fault protection. It was like grad school. Everyday motorists didn't have to contend with the intricacies of carburetion and transaxles, but Lunokhod guys weren't getting off so easily.

After Gorelovo, these wannabe drivers next journeyed to Khimki for a reunion with the other seven—who'd been immersed in their own specialized track of learning at the Lavochkin bureau. For them the curriculum had been all about radio systems, batteries, camera control. And with everyone together in one large group, the tough lessons continued. Instructors had really stacked their curriculum: metallurgy, thermals, wiring schematics. Testing bays and testing techniques. Heavy stacks of blueprints. Geologists like Boris Nepoklonov lectured on the lunar environment. Dovgan attentively gulped every crumb of information, "trying as far as possible to learn more about our natural satellite," as he put it.

The men dissected Lunokhod models while striving for fluency in this outlandish machine they'd soon command. "You must know the entire vehicle," preached one mentor. "Little will make sense if you study only buttons—what to press when going forward and when going back. Behind each button you should see the entire scheme, and the logic." Such effort was apparently too much for three of the candidates, who quietly withdrew from training near the end. Eleven remained, and no more would quit.

Afterward, everyone had headed down to Shkolnoye. More drills and classwork. Familiarization with the control facility. Lunadrome exercises. What a blur. And now here was Dovgan, underneath the Crimean dusk, wrapping up a friendly volleyball game inside the Residential Zone while all those memories washed gently over him. He had that victorious first mission tucked tightly under his belt, was well into another, and savored the pleasure of deciding how else to spend his remaining free time until the lunar morning came once again. Vyacheslav Dovgan was in a happy place indeed.

"Okay, let's change." Both doctors had approached the colonel, advising him to swap crews. From day one they'd hovered near the men—observing, taking notes, vigilant for trouble. And all signs indicated a need for fresh brains.

On this new session the team had been going for a couple hours—prowling along through highland areas, tweaking their antenna, logging temperatures—maneuvering via the flickering filmstrip before them. Neck fatigue, eyestrain. Metal-bladed desk fans whirred in their faces and moved stale air in convective circles. Five sets of eyes drying out. As noted by Dovgan, "Practical driving required exceptional coordination of the entire crew."

Their navigator hung with the action. Continually he updated his ground plot with *Lunokhod*'s current location—sliding a thick plastic architect's ruler across poster-sized pages, snapping charcoal lines to indicate the most recently traveled meter. Pencil to paper, twist compass, sketch crater sitting four meters to the left. Sharpen pencil. There was always something to note down, some detail. Pepper in that clustering of boulders. Keep it to scale. Don't smudge.

Conversation levels plummeted. Now the crew spoke only in clipped truncations of their normal chatter and patter, which is exactly what bothered those two physicians from the Institute of Biology and Medicine. Their presence—which once again spoke volumes about Soviet concerns for personal well-being—was strictly to monitor the crew. Russian culture has much to do with stoicism and heartiness, and this drive team comprised

23. In the midst of the crew room hunkers Boris Nepoklonov at left, assisting the efforts of Lunokhod navigators Vikenty Samal, in the middle, and Konstantin Davidovsky. Courtesy RIA Novosti.

some of the best men around. Could they really be expected to put up a hand and announce, "I'm tired!" over an open PA system reaching halfway around the Technical Zone? The toll of toil could not be denied. "Practical experience in steering," recalled Dovgan, "revealed a peculiarity. The working capacity of all crew members dropped sharply after two hours of work." Fatigue had set in, their response times growing while *Lunokhod*'s progress slowed to a crawl.

From his roost in back, Alexander Basilevsky noticed how even these doctors, standing right there in the room, weren't allowed to interact with or directly instruct the crew. Everything had to run through either Ivanovsky or that colonel—and only then did the word go out. Efficiently the five surrendered their controls and the other group took over. No complaints; no nothing. "It was not their decision," observed Basilevsky of any shift change. They just stopped and switched.

Five droopy men retreated to a private side nook in another part of the building. First each took a minute to unzip his jacket-top and remove the "bra" of sensors that continually transmitted heart rates, blood pressures, and respiration. Having one of these on meant that the medical men could objectively monitor stress levels in real time as the vital signs chattered out onto rolls of paper tape. Each man's jacket lapel also held a little five-pointed red metal pin-badge trumpeting "USSR" in contrasting letters. During their initial trip into Crimea, Dovgan and Igor Fyodorov had found them at a newsstand. With Babakin's permission these "unique mascots" had become a standard accessory on the warmup suits.

Next, to a table overflowing with snacks and drinks—indulgences that understandably provoked small twinges of jealousy from others in the sparse building. "It was not for us," commented Basilevsky of the exclusivity. "We didn't have any facility to eat at work." He and Nepoklonov always waited until after returning to the hotel. "They even had something special for the crew," as Basilevsky remembered it. "They had so-called oxygen cocktails. It was water saturated with oxygen. So, they said that if you drink it, that oxygen goes to you not only through your breathing, but through your stomach too." He guffawed at the idea. "I think it was their little invention!"

Onward—tottering across the surface, third lunar day, seeing the heretofore unseen. At the service of its masters, *Lunokhod* snapped panoramas, climbed slopes, measured radiation and magnetic fields, snuffled the dirt . . . once even sinking in up to its axles. Basilevsky now enjoyed open dialogue with the crew. "We should make here good analysis," he'd say, cuing the drivers to fresh-looking craters with crisp rims and steep slopes. Only 20 percent or so of the craters in this area had such characteristics. They saw plenty of small, shallow ones—ten feet in diameter or less—that were completely littered with rock fragments. A sure sign of formation from an extremely low-velocity impact.

With the area seeming to have been more or less explored, they now struck out to investigate firsthand what Apollo photography said lay eastward. The locus of Basilevsky's hopeful outcrops, it's known as a rille. That's German for "groove," and on the moon this feature can be identified by a long, meandering crack or depression in the surface.

Rilles are further siloed into a couple different groups. *Apollo 15* had landed near the kind that forms when a cold, dead river of lava collapses onto itself. That's a "sinuous rille." The one *Lunokhod 2* headed for can be described as a "linear rille" and on-orbit photography suggested that it might contain a graben. This refers to a long fault line depressed into the ground—a feature born from tectonic plates in motion and the reason why it fits a different category. Graben may well contain lunar bedrock: the moon's original crust. Geologic gold!

They covered much ground during this time, rambling across flatlands and placid undulations—dodging the occasional bowl-shaped minicrater—before crossing a gentle depression. Every change in the rover's bearing meant another crew discussion, another pencil line on the nav chart. *Lunokhod*, full of life, Formula 1 champ, purred right along.

As they finally approached the southern end of their objective, the terrain drastically changed. Basilevsky picked up the story. "We were moving to the east," he oriented. "And then we approached to the graben." This particular fault line has come to be known as Fossa Recta, and the turf doesn't just suddenly drop off into it like a cliff edge. It comes up slowly; they played on the periphery. It's a literal slippery slope, where continuing may seem innocent enough until you've gone too far. They kept rolling. Basilevsky put up a hand. "Let's stop here. Let's stop here," he signaled.

The geologists liked this spot. "Because there were very new morphology," recounted Basilevsky. "It was a lot of rocks, so it was very new and interesting area." One fuzzy nav image rolled to another. They'd come perhaps fifty yards; main fault line right ahead. Very near it the terrain sloped dangerously, thirty or thirty-five degrees. On both sides of it, angular rocks and small boulders freckled the landscape. Past the column of boulders, in a no-mans-land where their trusty rover could never go, the surface dropped precipitously a good fifty yards to the bottom. This is as far as they'd come.

Sang Basilevsky, "Okay! Let's make here panorama!" He wanted everything and didn't know where to begin.

Dovgan could barely process each request pouring forth from this madman in the back: "He kept exclaiming, 'Wonderful, this is it! Stop, look at this, show me that!'" Panoramic image data trickled back from Fossa Recta, bathing Shkolnoye's giant antenna dish, waves of electric impulses following underground lines of cabling to a room in the bowels of the control center. A runner handed off printouts to the crew room. Basilevsky unrolled them onto the nav tables. A magnifying glass, a squint.

Wait for it . . .

Jackpot. Lunar bedrock!

"It was good interaction between geologists and the crew," he dotingly recalled. Fossa Recta bedrock: a formation that likely wouldn't have been discovered without a stout bridge of common ground between scientist and crew.

"They listened to us!"

A kid at Christmas, Basilevsky gestured at the screens: talking, pointing out regions of interest, babbling on about features, involuntarily leaning his body in the direction he next wanted to go. The terrain had to be inspected, measured, documented. It had to be understood.

Focusing so intently on those TV images, Basilevsky's mind psychologically uncoupled from his earthbound body and replanted itself inside of *Lunokhod*. As if he was somehow now *inside* the tub and peering out through its cameras. In this altered state of consciousness, any sense of time utterly disappeared. "The working session ended quite late—maybe at five a.m. or six," he said. "And I get out after the session, and I could see the moon in the sky. I could see Mare Imbrium, and it was for me like splitting of my brain or my conscious. I see the moon, it was there, but *I was there too!* I had that feeling and it was very strong."

Basilevsky needed to unplug—to savor some tea and enjoy a bit of quiet solo hiking through the trees. Something tangible to plant both his feet on Earth again.

This third lunar day transitioned into a fourth. Oleg Ivanovsky abdicated his position to another Lavochkin man by the name of Felix Babich. Four months in, they'd already gone three times farther than with *Lunokhod 1*. Everybody felt in the groove. Come late April 1973, with the newest lunar day half over, they merrily prospected northward along the east side of Fossa Recta—having pushed through terrain with flattened, upright boulders that made the area look like a cemetery. And that's when it happened.

On this stretch they'd been using the "continuous" mode—where *Lunokhod* advanced until told to halt. The sun hung almost perfectly behind them. "So we couldn't see shadows," noted Basilevsky. "In that case the surface looks, for you, just smooth."

Without any warning a crater materialized before them. The driver hit STOP. But his command took three seconds to ping. *Lunokhod* rolled six feet.

And plunged.

The crew winced. It was totally avoidable. They'd become too brave, too complacent.

"We get into this crater," lamented Basilevsky. "It's mistake number one."

If the tilt sensors had been working, they would've known how much slope these crater walls presented. Looked about thirty degrees. Maybe? The drivers wanted to unlock protection mode and go for it.

"Make panoramas!" warned Basilevsky, like a sideline coach. "Understand where we are!" Right next to him sat Nepoklonov. Both men vociferously advocated a gathering of more information on the exact shape of their newfound prison. The crater struck them as between sixteen and twenty feet across, though they couldn't be sure. And *Lunokhod* wasn't much shorter than that.

The request got dismissed. No pictures.

"We didn't do this. It's second mistake."

The crew began slewing the rover around, forward-back-twist, forward-back, trying to find a good spot to have a run at the side. Basilevsky shook his head. The open lid gave *Lunokhod* a tail-heavy girth of nearly fifteen feet. They were in *way* too small an area for this. This was bad.

"Close the lid!" he panted.

Forward-twist-back and the driver backed *Lunokhod* right into the crater wall, spading dirt onto its solar cells. Immediately the power output dropped by 20 percent. "Not dangerous. Not a problem," someone offered. But that wasn't true. Right then their magic car was doomed, no matter whether it escaped the crater or not.

"We didn't close the lid," mourned Basilevsky. "Third mistake."

Today, space machines and their handlers are much more sophisticated. After chugging for over five years, an American rover on Mars called *Spirit* managed to quicksand itself in thick red dirt. And before trying a single darn thing, the flight team stood down to gather more info. From every conceivable angle and view did *Spirit* image itself, and nobody had to guess what in the world might have gotten stuck or how. Engineers then mocked up the exact predicament using simulated Martian soil and a duplicate rover. In this fashion, various techniques could be developed and micrometrically tested before trying anything out on the real deal. They spent over eight months analyzing the situation and judging different approaches. And they never got the rover unstuck, but it sure wasn't because of rushing or guesswork.

Basilevsky was right. The Lunokhod controllers should've taken panoramas and mapped out the situation. They should've closed the lid. Panoramic shots would've provided invaluable detail on the crater's height, breadth, and overall threat. When dirt fell on the solar cells, a method likely could have been developed to clean them: drive uneven slopes, rock the chassis back and forth. They had the Lunadrome right outside. It was there for things like this. Panoramas in hand, the crater could've been duplicated and the training rover dropped inside. These may seem like obvious steps, but that is the cruelty of hindsight. And the price of being first.

Instead of doing any of the above, *Lunokhod*'s crew stomped on the gas. And within an hour's time they managed to extricate their pride and joy.

An unseen clock now ticked. They could pick back up again, driving on as planned. That is, until the day's end approached and time came to close the lid. They *had* to close it; otherwise *Lunokhod* would freeze. But when the lid swung up and forward, nothing would halt its dumping of soil over the top of the radiator. This is a piece of equipment whose sole purpose in life is to shed heat.

Basilevsky underscored the delicate situation. "Lunar soil is a beautiful thermal insulator," he said, on something of a down. The worst possible substance.

More than likely the rover would persist through its slumber, but when they opened the lid again, *Lunokhod*'s radiator wouldn't be able to clear the dust. It hadn't been designed with a way to do so. Even after years of development this was still only the second one out, and machines always have a way of demonstrating to their creators any sort of design-related black holes. So, like a motor underneath thick woolen blankets, their *Lunokhod* would overheat and sputter and that'd be the end.

Basilevsky wanted to abandon all sense of safety and head straight for the mountains. Their sedan was going to eat it anyway; why not tackle some risky stuff they ordinarily wouldn't?

He sprang into action, approaching Babich and the colonel.

"Okay," he said. "*Lunokhod* will die."

They regarded him with silence. Military guys do that sometimes.

"But let's die *with music!*" It was a classic Russian phrase, analogous to going out with a bang.

"Let's go," he pitched, "not along the smooth surface, but let's go to nearby mountains!"

The bosses explained that they were afraid to go in that direction because of the dangers. "No," they told him. "No risk." And their decision was final.

The accident had happened overnight between April 19 and 20. In the next session they didn't push far; everybody had sort of wilted. "The driving was very minor," admitted one man. April 22 marked the lunar day's end, and it was time. They parked their wheeled bathtub—*Kemurdzhian's* bathtub, *Rozentsveyg's* bathtub, *Babakin's* bathtub—with its French reflector glass facing Earth. Then the crew looked around at one another and regretfully delivered the instruction to seal *Lunokhod's* roof. Nobody saw or heard it, but the telemetry showed motors in motion and everyone knew exactly what was happening up there. At 16 percent speed it came: thick, clumpy soil sliding across the solar cells and down, falling into the tub where it forever and for all time coated the precious radiator.

Two weeks later they returned; a full week into May already. Robert Menn took over for Babich as Lavochkin's head rep in Shkolnoye. No newcomer, Menn had witnessed the crew-room fracas during *Lunokhod 1*, when Vladimir Panteleev yelled at the unwelcome journalists to vamoose. (Menn's take on the incident is that *Babakin* wanted everyone out—yet his refined self felt uncomfortable getting on a chair to yell. So instead he'd quietly communicated his desire to Panteleev, who got stuck with the dirty work.)

Basilevsky double-checked with Menn—still no mountains. The big shots just wanted to play it safe with any time remaining. He grimaced and sat down.

After the lid opened, their clock ran faster. And that first session back offered little in the way of exploration. "It was mostly checking systems," recalled Basilevsky. They got back to it in earnest over the following session—an evening one devoted to lunar magnetism that broke less than half a mile of new ground. And then the clock ran out entirely. Beginning with the next session, *Lunokhod's* on-duty flight engineer noted that his vehicle's internal temperature had soared above 116 degrees Fahrenheit. "It's a lot," commented Basilevsky. "So it was obvious that it is the end." They parked it facing southeast, toward the sun, and collectively agreed to surrender.

Further attempts to resume radio contact did not bear fruit. Basilevsky then penciled a final entry in his journal: "May 11, 1973—No response from Lunokhod 2," and shut the book.

"So, we died without music."

A reporter who knew the crew was allowed in. Quietly he approached the shift commander and whispered, "Igor?" But the commander did not hear, for his mind was still on the moon, right there with his beloved car that never again would turn a wheel.

Killed by a goldilocks crater: not too big or too small, but just the right size to swallow a Lunokhod. The crew took it maturely. Observed Basilevsky, "Of course they were sad. But nobody was yelling, crying. No. It was just, they kept it quiet. Was sad." The drive team switched off their desk fans and powered down the consoles. Navigators rolled their charts.

For what he didn't assume would be the last time ever, Alexander Basilevsky packed for home. He'd spent nearly two years exploring the moon; rather an interesting twist in life for the man whose passion could be traced directly back to poor eyesight. "When I was in high school," he reminisced, "I and a friend of mine at that time, Vovka Shibanov, we were dreaming to do something related to the seas, to the oceans." Maybe oceanography? They looked into it and quickly discovered a gotcha: that line of work carried a strict vision requirement. Uh-oh, both men had terrible eyesight. "It obviously was not possible for us. So we decided that we may go to be engineers in ship-building. And we even started to plan it very seriously." They'd head to Ukraine and join an institute up in Nikolaev City.

But less than a month before their departure, another little speed bump reared itself. Shipbuilding imposed almost as stringent vision requirements as oceanography. They weren't going to be able to do that, either.

"Why don't we try to become geologists?" It was Shibanov's idea. "It's very interesting, very romantic, a lot of adventures!"

Basilevsky was game. "Okay, let's try." The two applied to a local college and together wended their way through classes and exams. "But when we graduated from the university, I started to work as geologist in central Russia, and he started to work as geologist in the Soviet far east." They never did collaborate professionally, but they did find their passions in life.

"He and me, we like to be geologists."

Out among the diverse terrain of Kazakhstan, Basilevsky settled in to his own routine. Digging in the dirt, blackened fingernails. Dry hands, dirty hands, banged-up hands. Crags and crusts and reefs and rubble and slags and slabs and shelves. All the while those same questions tumbling through his brain: *How did the rocks get here? What story did they tell?*

He wasn't asking himself what the rocks might be like on other worlds; the idea of *extraterrestrial* geologic research was nowhere to be found in any of his cranial cubbyholes. As proof, Basilevsky offers his 1965 geologic field trip into the Ural Mountains. The men had just finished a day of work. "It was summer, it was quite north," he said. "So the long long evenings, we were around the fire talking." The leader of their party had already retired to his tent and was listening to a radio. Suddenly he bolted from it and dashed out to the group.

"Listen! Americans flew by Mars!!"

Nearly everyone stared at the guy in utter disbelief. Honestly, though, it didn't do much for Basilevsky. He told the instructor, "Okay, that's good," with little emotion. It just wasn't where his head lay at the time. "I was quite neutral to our space achievements. I was proud of Soviet successes in space, but that time it was absolutely not interesting to me. Geology and geochemistry were areas of my professional interest."

Where things changed, however, was with his invitation to leave geologic fieldwork and complete a PhD in Moscow. There, Basilevsky's advisor installed him in a wedge of academia known as the Vernadsky Institute. "And I started to do some experiments in experimental petrology," he outlined. Petrology is the study of conditions under which rocks form.

It was a decent gig. He made friends with another student across the hall, whose instructor began taking notice of Basilevsky's aptitude and work ethic. But the failed shipbuilder himself never noticed this attention. "And when my PhD project was over, I didn't find good interesting job."

But that instructor across the hall, a certain Kirill Florensky, held on to his memory of that impressive student and not long after received instructions to form a group at the Space Research Institute—a group that would be able to find lunar landing sites for cosmonauts. He had multiple slots to fill. The man rang up his former student, who in turn connected him with Basilevsky—out mapping rock formations in the middle of blasted nowhere. Over a fragile phone link they discussed the potential assignment. *Would you be interested in coming to work for me?* asked the elder man.

Basilevsky told him, "Yeah. Let's try." And from then on the nearsighted geologist began to increasingly feel the warmth of people who actually *needed him.* "It was very interesting," he fondly recollected. "It was time when me and my young colleagues, our careers started with something *very* special. We were selecting landing sites for Soviet manned expedition to the moon."

With a flicker of inflection, he attached, "It never happened."

Soviet space engineer Boris Rauschenbach can't help but weigh his country-men's lunar exploits against those of the United States. "After the successful implementation of this scientific program," he offered of the Luna-Lunokhod combo, "we can ask the question: were the piloted flights to the moon nec-essary, if all the scientific data and materials could be delivered by auto-matic space vehicles?"

He says it like robotics were the plan all along. He's busted: Soviet Rus-sia built a manned lunar program and couldn't make it work. Cosmonauts were never going to the moon. By the early 1970s, it was definite. The pro-gram hadn't just been mothballed, it was dead. Executed. Soviet politicos were openly lying about such a notion having ever existed. They switched to Plan B. Soon the order came forth to round up any remaining hardware from the N-1 rocket and smash it into unrecognizability. Even so, many claim that the Soviets actually came out ahead because they explored the moon and returned samples at a fraction of the cost of sending people. And by definition, they risked no lives.

Yet many of Rauschenbach's own countrymen—those who examined samples from Luna, even, or occupied the science room in Shkolnoye—would say that any comparison with America is blatantly unfair. One exam-ple: during their hikes across the moon, two *Apollo 17* astronauts discovered *orange soil* and took a sample of *just that* to bring home. Nobody had ever seen anything like it! (The color resulted from pockets of extremely old volcanic glass beads.)

In comparison, a Luna brought back . . . whatever its drill came down on top of. The clump that *Luna 20* pinched might well have had the most amazing dirt on the whole moon right next to it and no one will ever know. It was a blind grab. Yeah, *Luna 20* had a camera, but not to help choose a sampling site. It was there to monitor drilling operations. The camera worked only in black and white. It couldn't zoom in on the ground. And even if it could've, the drill arm wasn't articulate enough to be so discern-ing in its pick. All in all, quite a far cry from placing trained geologists on the moon to appraise its surface with human eyes.

"Robots," Georgiy Babakin once said, "can do everything. But they can-not give *their impression*."

Alexander Basilevsky dreams of the transient hope that would have been *Lunokhod 3*: partially built, never completed, and now sitting almost forgotten in the dinky Lavochkin museum at Khimki. An expensive and utterly unutilized showpiece. From Basilevsky's viewpoint, it's cause for outrage because this machine represented a quantum leap in capability. "We discussed our desire to have a robotic arm with Lavochkin people. And they promised us that *Lunokhod 3* will be with that arm." Bolted to one side of the tub, it would've enabled scientists to choose a particular rock, or wad of soil, and hoist it up to a much more sensitive instrument than previous rovers had carried. "Engineers," he divulged, "they were working on it, and they were quite close."

An addition like this would've quelled a core problem of imprecision that was endemic to the original rovers. Look at their soil analyzer. It hung underneath each machine and pointed straight down. The experiment irradiated a region of ground to determine its chemical composition but did so to a fairly large area—almost three feet square. And in order to analyze a certain patch of dirt, they had to be able to drive over it. That restriction alone excluded whole expanses of terrain, not to mention larger rocks. A Lunokhod might've managed to park atop orange soil, but it still wouldn't have been able to sufficiently isolate the material.

"The robotic arm could take a sample and bring it *to* the sensors, *to* the analyzer!" preached Basilevsky. Here was a solution! What they'd been pleading for! Choose the exact bit of dirt—a specific rock!

The vision fills his dreams, yet he dreams most passionately for the grand excursion called Sparka—teaming upgraded Lunokhods with new Lunas.

"Sparka," explained Basilevsky, "means 'something done by two.' By a pair." Using it, they'd go on safari. "So the plan, which was supported by engineers, was that *Lunokhod* with robotic arm lands, collects samples, goes like several kilometers or maybe even hundred kilometers. At that time it was already understandable that we can do it." Along the way they'd halt at intriguing rock formations or soil pockets and get a sample of basically anything they wanted. With the arm and color cameras they could be like *Apollo 17* and get *just* the orange soil. Or scrape out a piece of that graben. Possibilities abounded.

The rover would complete its journey at a waiting Luna, which rockets on homeward. Nestled inside its womb is a superior collection of *selected* and *documented* lunar samples. No more blind, random snatching. Basilevsky considered it realistically equivalent to what the Americans had. "We would be almost the same comparing to Apollo," he hoped.

But Sparka never left the drafting table and *Lunokhod 3* never flew. Basilevsky is of the opinion that the Space Research Institute lusted over America's plan to send their Viking to Mars and quickly lost interest in pretty much everything else. "For them, the moon was very boring," he charged. "So the resources were directed to missions to Mars."

Sparka's equipment was already flight proven and reliable; only the specific techniques had to be finalized. They could've been cherry-picking lunar samples, just like the Apollo boys, and sending them on back. They could have flown higher-resolution cameras. Better instruments. They could have done so much more.

And this is what bothers Alexander Basilevsky the most.

"With Lunokhod, we only *started* to do science."

14. Devil from Redondo

A horrendous undertaking.

—Loyal Goff of NASA's Viking Program Office,
on the Viking Biology Instrument

Unfettered and indiscriminate in attitude and behavior, the Looney Tunes Tasmanian Devil had nothing on Viking's Biology Instrument. Although quite beyond control, the cartoon Taz was at least more or less predictable— putting him squarely ahead of what TRW had on their hands. As the design of Viking's life finder had accreted and evolved, the insubordinate machine morphed beyond that of mere convolution into a spastic, blurrily moving target that eluded even the most rudimentary crosshair lock. It spat in the face of its handlers: rupturing valves and fittings, splitting open chambers and hoppers, locking up, conking out. All without warning. One seemingly innocuous design tweak often precipitated a costly domino effect of alterations that sent techs racing to contain them like grass fires.

Nonstop changes became such an ever-lengthening tapeworm that whole procedures went into effect to stem the tide. Gil Levin well remembered this firebreak approach. "If ever we wanted to change any little thing, you couldn't just call 'em up and tell 'em," he said. "You had to execute a change order. And they charged for that." Levin strove to contain his modifications like everybody else. Although "NASA was trying to get you *not* to change, but NASA was making changes also!"

Four years till launch.

In late October 1971, TRW finished readying down-and-dirty mockups of the Biology Instrument for its first major review. The autumnal date represented a three-month deferral from Viking's original schedule and most

assuredly failed to endear the company to other subcontractors. By then
the overall estimated fee of preparing two flight-ready Biology Instruments
had surged from $13.7 million to a gag-inducing $20.2. Engineers at TRW
begged off, arguing that nobody could ever have predicted just how mind-
bogglingly complicated their little Erector Set would become.

Worldly events rolled on by as if flights to Mars never existed. Walt Disney World had just unlocked the doors. One day afterward came Soul Train's
inaugural syndicated episode. People toured Cinderella's Castle and danced
to Eddie Kendricks in pure oblivion to the emotional gymnastics being
called to order inside TRW's Redondo Beach conference facilities. Reps came
from Langley, Martin Marietta, NASA. They emptied coffee urns and wore
a lot of ties. They sat around tables in discussion for extremely long periods
of time. And the scheduled three-day event demonstrated much more than
just runaway changes or licentiously amoral cost projections. Viking's life
sniffer faced peril on several fronts. Just like *Cannon* actor William Con-
rad, its weight had risen to alarming levels. The mechanical assembly that
handled used-up soil and nutrient had become formidably overcomplicated.
One of the more disturbing issues, noted project manager Jim Martin, was
that in several areas the failure of any given component virtually guaranteed
an unrecoverable seizing of the entire apparatus. Only three months beforehand he'd put forth an edict: no single malfunction would be permitted
to incapacitate more than one experiment. Hadn't anyone paid attention?

As 1971 wound to a close, things started coming off. Working with
Biology Team leader Harold Klein, TRW deleted a plethora of suddenly
excessive pumps, gas-delivery modules, and experiment chambers. All the
related valves and wiring also came out. But the damn thing was still mor-
bidly obese and prone to spontaneous breakdowns. That following January,
another tense meeting brought news that Viking's special box of love had
now topped $33 million with no end in sight. The only thing TRW could
think of to restore sanity involved the exeunt of at least one whole experiment. A maddened Martin concurred. Be it Horowitz or Vishniac or Levin
or Oyama, one wouldn't be leaving Earth.

Josh Lederberg appreciated Martin's rationale—once suggesting that "an
effort to sustain all four would probably prejudice the entire mission"—
but ignorantly wondered aloud why Viking hadn't just been made larger
to begin with. (Pro tip: *never* make suggestions like that to aerospace engi-

neers.) Unavoidably a committee formed, with the idea of reaching judgment on who'd get axed.

When Harold Klein found out he was supposed to head this group, he cornered the two nonexperimenting scientists (who were also group members). "It's obvious you two are going to be the swing votes," alleged Klein to Josh Lederberg and Alex Rich. "You are the only ones who don't have an obvious and selfish interest in this regard."

Lederberg and Rich shared a quick glance. This was unexpected.

"You two had better advise us on what to do," wagged the frumpy Klein, "and then maybe we can get a team consensus."

If anyone didn't enjoy the sour turn of events, it was Lederberg—who, at that moment in time, likely would've preferred to remain immersed in his genetics research. A dozen years earlier he'd won the Nobel Prize and didn't need any Viking-themed stressors. "The procedure by which this was done was a very painful one," he asserted of the deliberations. "It is not a very pleasant experience to have that responsibility. But I figure that in a certain sense, that was what we were there for. We were there for those kinds of hard decisions."

The committee set about gathering specifics to formulate an opinion. What was the state of everyone's instrument? Who'd encountered the biggest problems? "It was terrible," remembered Gil Levin of the two-month period between Martin's pronouncement and the unwelcome verdict. "We were *always* the underdog." He felt exposed because the other three came from huge universities with entire departments to address whatever anomaly came up. Compare that to hole-in-the-wall Biospherics, with Levin as owner/operator!

Finally, Lederberg and Rich wrote John Naugle outlining two major arguments for choosing the project they did. And come mid-March '72, Naugle rang up Wolf Vishniac to delicately inform him that Wolf Trap would not be visiting Mars. In a follow-up letter to his ousted candidate, Naugle wasted little effort on sugarcoating. The review panel thought Wolf Trap to be the one experiment of the four offering the lowest potential for scientific return. "More difficult to actually build into a problem free device," indicated one part of the letter. Naugle then closed his guillotining communiqué by expressing a desire that Vishniac find a way to continue his participation in Viking.

Wolf Vishniac couldn't grasp the news, couldn't digest it. The very first player to ever run with alien life detection had just been yanked off the gridiron.

Dropped from NASA's payroll, Vishniac melded back into academia. "I simply must place my priorities on my university work," he explained to Viking's chief scientist, Gerry Soffen, in a note the following year. "The consequences of my change in status in the Viking Team have been far-reaching as you know, not to say disastrous."

Only years later did Gil Levin feel comfortable expressing his true feelings about Wolf Trap. First off, its tiny incubator required copious amounts of liquid water—a real swimming pool. Scolded Levin, "We knew *that* wasn't the case on Mars." But then came a decidedly fatal flaw in the experiment's behavior. "When you put soil into water it settles," he indicated, matter-of-factly. "But after a while some of it starts rising again. And that would be interpreted as microorganisms."

Levin's sentiments were echoed by Josh Lederberg. "It was a very un-Martian environment," he alleged of Vishniac's little world inside his testing chamber. "The whole experiment depended on growth in a liquid medium at temperatures with fifteen degrees Centigrade." That's a warm spring day. "There is no place on Mars that has that habitat." Lederberg also found fault with how Vishniac's experiment regarded changes in sample cloudiness as indicators of life. "It relied on organisms being able to be separated from the soil and the dust particles that were in it." He reckoned that Wolf Trap carried a very high probability of returning false positives.

"We felt that of all the errors to make, that was the worst. It would not be responsible to go into a mission that had an uncontrolled opportunity for a false positive result." Perhaps not surprisingly, these objections were of the same flavor that had been noted in Ames's review nearly eight years before.

Ultimately, some felt that Vishniac's true strengths were to be found outside of the project, in other capacities. "He had an opportunity to use himself to a better advantage," endorsed Lederberg. "His thinking about ecosystems was more important than that particular experiment."

At least TRW had been making progress. By December '72 assemblers had coughed out three hardware mockups, one for each experiment, operating similarly and utilizing the same kinds of processes as the flight ver-

24. Patricia Straat in battle with TRW's Labeled Release hardware mockup. "Each of these tests took days," she pointed out, "because the start-up sequence took several hours. And the cleanup at the end of a test cycle took a lot of time." Courtesy Patricia Ann Straat.

sions would—without actually *being* the final product. For Labeled Release, soil had to be manually spooned into a little cup, which in turn was strung to a nutrient bottle, Geiger counter, and supporting electronics and collectively held in what amounted to a deep, heavy metal tray. It all had to work under Martian conditions, so after the soil went in, a thick, two-foot-high, bell-shaped glass jar was lowered over the entire shebang and cinched down real tight. Only then could the interior be brought down to low temperature and pressure using a huge, vertically standing control panel. Every phase of a test sequence still had to happen manually. And, as TRW had promised, only one trial could run at a time.

Having briefly returned home, Pat Straat bunked in at JPL for two solid weeks right on top of Christmas, learning hands-on how to operate the LR mockup. Seven ingredients made up her final nutrient recipe. Each had been chosen primarily because of its wide appeal to microbes (especially primitive ones). Sweet glycine had made the cut, along with lactate—responsible for everything from the flavor in sourdough bread to the burn in your muscles during exercise. She ran gobs of experiments with different soils and analyzed data and wrote reports and scribbled memos and despite all this barely-above-water thrashing did not lose sight of the overarching question: *Will this hardware be capable of conducting the experiment?*

Overworked TRW had also given up on building any kind of skylight or sunroof into Norm Horowitz's testing chamber. So in place of true sun, the Carbon Assimilation study would have to use an ultraviolet xenon lamp to encourage photosynthesis. But to the horror of Horowitz and his men, this type of light reacted with water vapor and his radioactive gases to spawn *at least* three organic compounds that could be interpreted by their machinery as presumptive of life. One of them, for example, was the common preservative formaldehyde. Without delay the group introduced a small filter into the lighting system, which fixed the issue. They'd caught this one . . . but what else might pop up? And when? Would they discover something worse after it was already on the way?

Two and a half years remaining.

In early '73, Straat returned and spent ten weeks in California beating up the massaged hardware. Clusters of sample chambers pirouetted in small tight circles, miniature valves opened and closed, helium flushed through on command. Better, but not perfect. "Found lots of different problems," related Straat of the headway, "and things that didn't work right." The effort was like rolling big on a game board and moving far ahead, only to land on a spot that sends you back ten spaces. "I wrote lots of memos, and I talked to Gil every day on the phone, and then we made changes." Experimentation always begat yet another pricey hardware mod. So many of the alterations involved pipes, fittings, wiring, or valves. Each required written approval, another change order, another charge. Each sending TRW fabricators reaching for another virginal block of expensive metal alloy, to be lathed and milled into the next iteration of some part.

"We all had design problems," recalled a member of Horowitz's team. "We all had people camped out down at TRW workin' the problems."

Things matured to the point in mid-April where Straat felt decently comfortable venturing home for a quick respite. She checked out of her rented LA apartment and flew back east to refamiliarize herself with dusty digs and the Biospherics home office. TRW phoned regularly to keep her informed of any breakthroughs. They promised to have an improved unit together by October, and when October rolled around Straat indeed received a call:

"They'd had all kinds of problems and had to postpone it for a month."
Weeks later TRW called back asking her to please come that November.
Everyone had been running hard and they'd have another variant ready for
action—the first test of all three together in a flight configuration, no lie.

Straat's heart sank. Why now? "Opening foxhunt was the first week-
end in November," she pined. "I missed it. And foxhunting was my sport
and it almost killed me." She threw open the closet door to kiss her outfit
good-bye: derby with yellow vest and canary pants, black boots, and white
socks. After longingly caressing her black coat, Straat abandoned the closet
to endure another plane ride to LA, another drab apartment she rarely saw,
and yet another round with uppity hardware.

Almost in simultaneity, Langley director Ed Cortright appraised the
unappetizing situation that TRW had landed itself in. Choking on their
own excrement. Any failure of contractors to deliver operational equipment
on time reflected badly on a center—*his* center. With an incendiary letter,
Cortright firebolted TRW general manager George Solomon. "You are currently beset with a rash of technical problems which further threaten schedule and cost. It is clear that if the job were on schedule, there would be more
time to adequately cope with the necessary fixes." Cortright acknowledged
TRW's substantial efforts to date but nonetheless recommended "heroic
action" on Solomon's part.

As Straat prepped herself for new testing cycles, TRW's own delivery
schedule slipped even further and Jim Martin introduced the contractor
to his little slice of public humiliation called the Top Ten Problems. This
indecorous moniker applied to those aspects of Viking that credibly threatened the integrity of its mission, launch vehicle, or date of liftoff. Appearing
on the Top Ten meant things were real super-duper bad—though Martin
clarified to Cortright that there were no *penalties* for those who made the
list. No Top Ten appearance should ever equate to "a mark of poor performance," Martin conveyed. But it *did* mean that special attention would
be coming someone's way.

Subsequently, Cortright lobbed another 8½-by-11-inch grenade at TRW's
Solomon, prophesizing a "potentially catastrophic" situation if the roller
coaster didn't stop rollercoastering in a mighty big hurry. Then Cortright
found someone else at the company and ripped them a new one, too. "It
is imperative that you bring to bear on these problems the most talented

individuals you can find," he catapulted at TRW VP Rich De Lauer. "I must believe that you have not yet applied your maximum effort, for which there is no longer any substitute."

Within its sprawling facilities TRW maintained a huge, airtight chamber for stress-testing its space hardware. Technicians lifted the very first complete, flight-like Biology Instrument and secured it within. Everyone left, sealed the door, and slurped out enough atmospheric pressure to simulate Mars's wispy one. The temperature inside plummeted. Then, showtime: dirt tipped into a small blender atop the hardware. Little tines whirled up to speed, pulverizing the coarse, dark material. Underneath, valves automatically winked open as gases flowed, clarinet-like, in and out through them. Puny carousels rotated undersized sampling chambers into position. Dirt began trickling gently down toward the chambers, which stuck on their carousels as numerous valves and seals gridlocked and triggered a chain reaction of unstoppable damage back upstream through virtually every facet of the instrument.

Patricia Straat swallowed hard.

"All three of the experiments totally, utterly, completely failed."

Shortly after his expulsion, Wolf Vishniac had embarked on a trip. More time seemed available these days. Once again he journeyed to Antarctica, to a crinkly expanse of terrain adjoining the Ross Sea. Vishniac spent his days exploring this, the ice-free Asgard mountain range, as its frigidly desiccated landscape represents the closest known terrestrial analogue to Mars itself. (Asgard is essentially a very, very cold desert.) He collected all manner of samples in order to better appraise the state of microbes on our southernmost continent. As a favor to Gil Levin he even toted along a roadworthy edition of Labeled Release to run directly on-site. The experiment had to be operated manually, as opposed to Viking's version, but worked the same.

Bacteria *thrived* in the continental wastelands. No surprise to Norm Horowitz, who'd discovered that 86 percent of his own samples from the area contained some variant of microbial life—although Horowitz didn't conduct those studies firsthand. "I never went to the Antarctic myself," he confessed.

Working alone one afternoon, Wolf Vishniac slipped on the ice and fell hundreds of feet into a crevasse. Viking's would-be fourth experimenter was dead. On the birthday of one of Norm's assistants, no less.

After the November testing catastrophe, senior NASA and Martin Marietta staff descended upon TRW and forcibly took over management of the project, coup-style. They initiated a crash program to ferret out every single identifiable glitch in the Biology Instrument—and then correct it by any means necessary. Okay, so from a top-level perspective, what seemed to be its primary failing? "The design didn't work!" hollered Pat Straat. And soon she learned she wouldn't be leaving Redondo any time soon. Even today she keeps a written decree issued by Jim Martin during this period. One line of it ordains, "The science team will remain in residence until these experiments are ready for flight." And Martin's edicts ruled supreme. Over the course of subsequent review, some eighty major headaches came to light—including a nasty revelation that certain chemical detectors were oversensitive to things they shouldn't be, like temperature and brightness. Not good! Straat wrote another IOU to her pillow.

The Viking manager's follow-on action sent even grander waves of discontentment crashing through Redondo Beach. "Jim Martin came out there, furious, and started talking about throwing biology off. And it ended up by his saying, 'We're gonna throw off the two worst experiments.'" Straat abhorred the situation thrust upon them. "Basically what he did," she complained, "is he pitted us against one another to see which experiment was better. Well . . . it turned out they were all so bad, they were trying to figure out which was *least worse*!" Throughout the deliberations, Straat remained at TRW with her assistant. "I, who had gone out there for two weeks, never got back for a year and a half. Really!" She laughed at her predicament, describing how the pair slaved away in an unending stream of nights and weekends, keeping a grinder of a schedule that "you wouldn't believe: eighteen hours a day, seven days a week, to get this thing up and running." TRW supplied them with a continually updated LR model for evaluation and detailed two staff engineers to work at Straat's direction. "When something needed being done to the experiment to move it along, you were there to do it whether it was at 3:00 a.m. or what." To LR, by and for LR, Straat and her cohort became indentured servants. "We literally *lived* that experiment. We lived it seven days a week, twenty-four hours a day."

All this despite a possible eviction. "I stayed in daily contact with Gil," she reiterated of the anxious scene. "I would let him know what happened. And we would talk it over and try to figure out, you know, what's the best thing to do." Throughout TRW's other hallways and workrooms, Horowitz and Oyama each maintained similarly embedded crews performing identical ambulations—all in the same pit of alligators. "When it came to choosing which experiment was worse, or least worse," recounted Straat, "we were all just really, *really* sluggin' it out there!"

While Straat attended her all-day sparring contests, writing and arguing and presenting, Gil Levin stoked the home fires in Maryland—driving hard to not get kicked off the United States' only scheduled Mars lander. It soon became a naked process of dog-eat-dog one-upping. Occasionally Levin's phone would ring with chief scientist Gerry Soffen on the line— demanding some obtuse justification as to why *they* should remain aboard versus the other flunkies. Sometimes the exchanges curdled.

"If you don't get out here right away your instrument's gonna be taken off!" Soffen would yap into the phone, hapless Levin dropping everything to find a plane for California to dissect whatever triviality threatened to hand them the short straw. Once, the entire Levin family had just arrived for a vacation when Soffen rang their hotel. "You get your ass out here tomorrow or it's *gone*," he snarled.

"Defend your position," commented Levin—quite wearily—on the rationale for such impulsive trips. "Defend why your experiment should not be taken off." Endless justifications over the smallest details. Out of everything he endured in fifteen-plus years of LR development, Levin identified this narrow and dark period as the most genuinely stressful.

Both Vikings were scheduled to leave Earth in August or September 1975—less than twenty-one months away. To have even a supernatural chance of making those dates, TRW faced a thorny situation. After finishing Martin's mandated redesign, they'd have to build and test new mockups while simultaneously crafting the actual flight hardware. It couldn't get done otherwise. So any deal breakers would likely be identified *after* the ships were already on their way. By February '74, more than one independent review had forecast the instrument's delivery as realistically no earlier than July 1975—darn close to missing blastoff. From Jim Martin the word soon ricocheted out: please look into flying without the Biology

Instrument at all. Analyze contingencies. How would a foot-square empty hole in its belly affect Viking's center of gravity? Its handling and balance in the Martian atmosphere?

Engage afterburners. "Everybody pulled together like crazy," recalled Straat of the frenetic forced march that pushed through one brutal month after another without pause. She'd given up on regular meals and circadian rhythms.

But in the ugly face of death came change. "At some point during that time, we all started working as a team. And it was really one of the most glorious experiences." A triad of divergent agendas unified, collaboration fostering a breakthrough in operational workmanship. "And finally, it became clear that all three experiments were coming back together again." Martin withdrew his threats. Nobody else got kicked off after all.

Half a year later—February '75—TRW staged round two. Into their large chamber went a revamped Biology Instrument, patched to outside controls, with the idea of running it for two straight months through a complete end-to-end simulation. The absolute minimum amount of time needed for even a basic electrical and pneumatic shakedown of the thing was an entire month. But to that, programmers had inserted a full minute's pause between every single command. This would buffer the instrument's complex machinations while simulating the heinous time delay to be encountered during the real mission.

Heavy doors closed and the chamber was once again drawn down to Martian temperature and pressure. Heaters and detectors fired up on cue, carousels spinning with Rolex precision. Morsels of dirt tumbled through piping into chambers. Valves hummed and curtsied with bursts of gas and nutrient. But Straat fretted for the next two weeks, pondering why Vance Oyama's seemed to be the only experiment generating useable results, while she and Horowitz got gibberish. They called it off. Technicians normalized the chamber pressure and ventured inside as if entering a minefield. The resulting disassembly and inspection betrayed a miniature gas line plugged with solder. Also, two naughty plungers had failed to break open Straat's glass bottles of nutrient. Techs repaired LR and whatever'd gone wrong with Horowitz's stuff, then shoved it all back in to resume testing. Same deal: results from Oyama, but zippo for anyone else.

Finally the two-month run finished and everything came out for a post-game check. As TRW handlers began uncoupling and unfastening, it basically looked okay from the outside. "When we opened them," remarked Harold Klein of the Biology Instrument's tiny chambers, "we could see soil spewed all over the insides. There had been an explosion." Klein couldn't believe how poorly everything was performing, and so close to launch. "We have not yet had a successful integrated test with soil in the instruments," he complained. Loudly.

A brand-new son-of-crash program ensued, TRW engineers having long abandoned any sense of normal workdays. In 24/7 shifts they cut, crimped, threaded, bolted, welded, wired, brazed, and soldered on the redesigned hardware—linking pieces almost too small for human hands. This wasn't science, it was watchmaking: Soil chambers the size of penlight batteries. Tubing that resembled spaghetti. Bottle-cap carousels. Three months remained until the bus left for Mars.

A fair amount of criticism originated from those Viking scientists with more traditional experiments aboard. Long vetted and delivered, the widgets for geology, weather, and photography all sat installed and perfectly ready to go—freeing these participants to kick back, pop a cold one, and observe the Chinese fire drills characterizing every rascally moment of Biology Instrument preparation. Many already did not appreciate how the biologists seemed to receive more attention. And budgeting. Some naysayers wondered aloud how things might have been different had NASA pursued a more structured approach to Mars exploration.

"If we'd gone in steps," carped an idle Viking scientist, "we'd know what was in the atmosphere of Mars *now*."

His geologist colleague totally agreed. "We could have sent atmospheric probes or hard landers with chemical instruments to Mars, for the cost of the over-runs on the biology instruments alone!"

That prompted a man on the Biology Team to fire back.

"You don't seriously think Congress would have spent one billion dollars just to do *geology* on Mars?"

With Pat Straat still haunting the West Coast, people at Biospherics worked to flesh out their burgeoning compendium of reference soils. The effort continued that which had begun years prior with Levin and Gulliver, in the days of teammate Horowitz. If and when LR alighted on Mars, its results would mean nothing without context. How did different soils compare? How strong was the average positive response, versus a weak one? How quickly did radiation curves typically shoot up a graph? When did they level off? All the teams were doing it. Said Norm Horowitz, "You have to get a background of experience so that when something comes down from Mars, you don't have to sit around and decide what it means." Levin wanted a catalog thicker than Sears Roebuck's—and accordingly made it his employees' objective to gather, test, and index as many soil varieties as humanly possible.

Off they went—tramping high-kneed through the Eastern Seaboard, gear in tow, collecting all manner of samples and hoofing them back to the lab. Biospherics maintained a six-unit automated LR model and kept it going continuously. Levin leveraged the Bell System, ringing up colleagues at universities around the globe. Packages materialized: African soil, Asian mud, loamy gatherings from a barren stretch of Mexico. "We got samples from the Gobi desert. Everyplace!" To preserve their native condition, each had to be gathered in a highly structured, protected, and isolated fashion. *Documented* samples. Levin next hit up the space agency. "We got NASA to send us bonded soils from all over." Some, from the bottom of the world— Antarctic 542, Antarctic 726—had been collected years beforehand by outside researchers and long certified as organism-free. After wending through LR, the "clean" Antarctic 726 gave a weak but positive response.

"So we were able to detect microorganisms in some of the Antarctic soils where people had thought they were sterile!" Levin felt euphoric. He swore that in thousands of tests, they never received even one false positive. Or false negative. "When we got a response," he insisted of any positive outcome, "we *proved* that it was living, because the duplicate sample in the control was killed by heating it." Another detail for their reference catalog: *to what extent did heating affect the control samples?*

That wasn't all. As detailed by Pat Straat, "You want to test a *naturally sterile* soil—so you know that the heat itself isn't doing something funny." Gosh, what's naturally sterile? Recent volcanic eruptions near Iceland had created a brand-new island the locals called Surtsey. Almost immediately after its formation in the late sixties, biologists visited the spit of land and gathered samples. Biospherics dropped two into LR and found them to indeed be free of any bacteria. Into Levin's hands also came a tiny pinch of lunar soil. And? "It gave no response whatsoever."

25. One of the finished Viking Biology Instruments is examined by TRW techs. Not a single flight-ready version was ever tested inside a working *Lander*, or even a model of one. Courtesy NASA/JPL-Caltech.

By the end of May 1975, TRW delivered up-to-date equipment—plus a recommendation to Jim Martin that he remove the Biology Instrument from his Top Ten list. It was one of two remaining holdouts. Viking's life-detection machinery wasn't so much finished as overdue. The actual flight units destined for Mars couldn't even be tested because that would've meant destructively disassembling the parts to clean everything.

They sure weren't perfect, but they were there. Each formed a stunning example of what happens when mechanical stubbornness collides with human determination. Inside a thirty-four-pound metal box no larger than a truck battery rested forty thousand individual parts that didn't give a gnat's toot about coalescence. Dinky ovens, gas bottles, train-track carousels, nutrient-containing vials, Geiger counters, one lamp, dozens of valves—plus twenty thousand transistors—sat on the absolute bleeding edge of doing absolutely nothing. Their total as-delivered cost now topped fifty-nine million smackers—over 400 percent more than originally estimated.

Prior to installation on their respective launch rockets, one step remained. Something critical. If the whole point of Viking was to find life on Mars, they couldn't very well carry along any from Earth. Both finished *Landers* were enveloped within "bioshield" membranes and seared for eighty hours at 233 degrees Fahrenheit—enough to slaughter any remaining microbes that had managed to stow away throughout all the white-glove assembly. In test after test this tropical regimen had managed to overwhelm the Biology Instrument and both onboard computers, as well as many other spacecraft electronics. Now it was happening to the real thing. The cost of sterilization alone ran approximately $232 million. That was fully one quarter of Viking's entire budget and over half of Langley's earliest divination of total project costs.

Buy-in? You betcha.

On an otherwise unremarkable Wednesday, in August '75, Viking 1 left the ground. Its twin followed three weeks later.

Remarked Norm Horowitz, "I didn't know whether the darn thing would fly."

15. The Boy to Be Beaten

Let's be honest. Do we all really believe that landing a
single human being on the moon will be a priority? Can we
surpass the Americans in this, or perhaps we should be
thinking today about Mars?

—Mstislav Keldysh, speaking to a group of
space engineers in January 1969

Roald Sagdeev hated his new job.

Begrudgingly he'd accepted it only three months beforehand. The work involved space flight, which he never wanted anything to do with. His interests did not involve space. He'd never thought much about Mars. Or Venus, or for that matter the moon. He hadn't been educated in aerospace engineering, space technology, space science, or even space physics—and what Roald Sagdeev really was, was a man infatuated with physics. Things like that really buttered his muffin.

Nevertheless, here he sat inside a stuffy Kremlin meeting room, wasting a lovely June day to suss out the readiness of four individual yet very similar *Mars* spacecraft. From the womb of Lavochkin, these next-gen offspring were already built, tested, and mated with boosters. A month down the road, all were scheduled to initiate a veritable assault on Martian secrets with two orbiters and two landers.

Although it represented the first one Sagdeev had attended, this particular meeting stood as nearly the last in a bone-dry series about the ships' preflight status. There was a lot to discuss. To put it mildly, none of the probes had encountered smooth sailing along their respective roads to readiness.

The simultaneous prep of four individual vessels had led to eight strung-out teams working twelve-hour shifts.

"Some of the instrumentation was not ready, it was not delivered, was not tested," remarked Sagdeev of the development process. "You know, lot of pressures, because of delays." But truth be told, these sorts of issues are nothing out of the ordinary for any kind of high-tech stuff. With all of them finally awaiting launch, each spacecraft had since come to symbolize a triumph of engineering and miniaturization. In the minds of Lavochkin they were darn-near perfect. Except for one teensy-weensy little detail.

Sagdeev regarded the meeting room as nice enough. One wall had columns lining it; a white marble sculpture of Lenin garnished the other. A dozen officials who ran various plants and design bureaus occupied a central U-shaped table. Lining the walls sat row after row of chairs for second-tier participants, bringing the overall head count to at least fifty. It was getting kind of warm in there; Sagdeev's bulky glasses kept slipping down his nose.

The agenda ticked along. All four Proton booster rockets were in great shape. Launch facilities were totally ready to go. Every flight trajectory had been properly vetted and programmed. Most of the concerned talk now focused on a low-level technical issue—some kind of trouble with electronic components inside the spacecraft themselves. Paperwork had long been floating around calling out the failure of certain microchips during qualification tests. But Sagdeev hadn't joined the proceedings until now and therefore didn't know anything about that. He glanced up from his notes; a man in front had taken the floor. "It looks like there is an internal defect," the guy was saying. Sagdeev asked for clarification, and very soon the almost illegal oversimplification of that man's statement would become crystal clear.

He represented an electronics plant in Voronezh, about three hundred miles south of Moscow. The chips in question used a transistor identified as the 2T-312, made by the truckload at his facility. Now, understand that transistors are one of the true building blocks of electronics. They're what cells are for biology. Well before the early 1970s, transistors were very commonplace and the methods used to produce them quite thoroughly understood. So, certainly by the time of *this* meeting, they were not a bleeding-edge piece of equipment by any stretch. Practically a commodity! But they did have to be made a certain way—using key ingredients like pure silicon, with gold or platinum contacts. It's a reliability thing. These very small parts depend on connection integrity. The transfer of electricity between them must be perfect every time. On the *Mars* ships, they got used in *everything*: control systems, actuators, science instruments, timing, cameras.

Seeing as how the proper functionality of a multimillion-ruble spacecraft hinges upon thousands of transistors each the size of an office staple, they really ought to be made well. But the Voronezh plant had been trying to save money. In their misguided attempts to do so, they swapped out gold leads for cheap aluminum ones and ran the whole production batch like that. The things still worked, but only temporarily. At some point down the road corrosion would spread, inhibit operation, and fail the chips. They'd bring down the house.

Posters went up around the Kremlin meeting room and the Voronezh man gestured at them. Extensive calculations had shown the failures to occur one and a half to two years after manufacture. The chips inside *Mars 4, 5, 6,* and *7* had all been made about a year prior. This wasn't an *if*. It was a *when*.

Sagdeev couldn't believe what he was hearing. The presenter seemed very sure of himself; his numbers and logic rang true. If they launched next month, the ships would almost reach Mars before unreservedly face-planting. That didn't make any sense at all! Other posters displayed various options. Going at this *safely* meant delaying every launch in order to replace the thousands upon thousands of 2T-312 transistors liberally used throughout the probes. Fresh production runs would take a good six months—after which point the ships would have to be completely disassembled and retrofit from stem to stern. "Ruled out immediately," commented Sagdeev. "Most of the hardware already was integrated and chips were deep inside. You cannot touch any more, open all these boxes!"

A swap out meant postponing until the next Mars opportunity in 1975. But the Soviet program of space exploration did not operate in a vacuum. America's Viking flights had just been delayed from '73 to '75, offering the competition an at-bat.

Sagdeev framed it like this: "We knew very well that technologically, Vikings were far more superior than our instruments, and the whole mission of Vikings was much more advanced." It boiled down not to science, or even common sense, but to rivalries and gamesmanship. "So even if we would have been successful two years later at the same time as Vikings—

successful with *our* definition of success—the whole mission was inferior to Viking mission." They *had* to get to Mars before Viking. Upstage America in any way possible. Replacing all those gobs of chicklets would kill the chance.

Best guesses put mission success at fifty-fifty. What should they do? Opinions bounced around, voices rising. "It was a quite serious discussion," Sagdeev continued. "It's not every day such things happened." These ships were time bombs. How the hell did they—and especially *he*—get into this situation? Why did he agree to this goddamn job?

Mere weeks ago, Roald Zinnurovich Sagdeev had been practicing his chosen craft of plasma physics—whistling happy tunes at a place with the unassuming name Institute of High Temperatures. Within the huge outfit, Sagdeev orchestrated a small band of physicists—*theoretical* physicists—afforded wide latitude in exploring whatever subject seemed worthy of investigation. They were not *experimentalists*, who actually built lab instruments and ran tests. The two groups are complementary. Sagdeev's operated in a nonlinear kind of world where math and vigorous free-form discussion unite to resolve unanswered questions about natural phenomena. Ball lightning? Dark matter? Come right on in. Answers may never materialize—or they may suddenly pop from nowhere. Once, Sagdeev was attending a conference of theoretical physicists in Italy and some of them took a break to go swimming. He'd been chewing on a puzzler about shock waves that just didn't make sense no matter how he turned it around. Sagdeev dove under the surface and immediately rushed over to a friend after coming up.

"I solved this problem!" he crooned. The solution had flashed into him just like that—and could now be tested (by an experimentalist) to see if the approach held up.

Ah, physics. Sagdeev had greatly enjoyed his workplace over the past two years, and life in general. Until one day when his phone rang with a secretary from the Academy of Sciences on the line.

She said, "Professor, Keldysh wants to talk to you."

Wha—the president of the academy?

A moment or two later the Man himself came on. "Could you come to me?" he asked. That was it; Keldysh said nothing more. The president had courteously framed his request as a question, when it really wasn't a question at all. Mstislav Keldysh wanted to meet in person versus talk on the phone. In order for Sagdeev to do that he'd have to leave his office, get the car, drive at least forty minutes southwest—all the way into downtown to the academy—locate parking, and then go inside and find Keldysh. Ugh.

Before dropping everything for a face-to-face, most people would probably want to know what the meeting was about. Sagdeev didn't ask. "That's usual in the academy," he dismissed. "When you get invitation from the president of academy, he doesn't need to explain why he invites you. Always take it as something important." Immediately Sagdeev halted his activities and commenced the trip over.

If Moscow has one thing, it's architecture. The Academy of Science's Presidium occupies an eighteenth-century mansion; Napoleon spent his last night in Moscow there. Sagdeev parked and took a few practiced moments to install the steering wheel lock and remove his windshield wiper blades. Then he hoofed it up to the second floor and into Keldysh's otherwise relaxed office. Rows of oil paintings hung on the walls—former academy presidents, whose solemn appearance now functioned as inspiration to not screw things up for the next guy.

Keldysh never bothered with schmaltzy overtures. "He didn't like very long sentences," mentioned Sagdeev. "Everything was practical. Very short." And with a generous measure of surprise, rank-and-file Sagdeev learned that Keldysh envisioned him taking over the position of director at the Space Research Institute. The what? Sagdeev knew very little about the place and certainly held a less-than-favorable opinion of his country's efforts in space. He judged them from the angle of a scientist—that is, a blue-blooded researcher curious to learn everything possible. In this regard, the national program struck him as woefully lacking. "There was a bias in favor of technological spectaculars, almost without any intention to support science," he opined of the program up to that time. "It was more the show for political reasons."

Sitting before Keldysh, however, Sagdeev kept quiet. No telling which direction this would go. A bunch of questions came to mind, but he asked only one: "Do I have time to think over this proposal?"

"Yes."

"How much time will you give me?"

"I think one week should be enough for you." Sagdeev puckered. Answers like that signaled an end to the proceedings.

On his return drive, various thoughts coursed through the head of Roald Sagdeev. First and foremost came the paradigm shift. "I was thinking that it would bring a complete change to my life. I was like a free artist, you know, theoretical physicist with small group. I had a chance to pick up any interesting topic to work on." He really enjoyed that unstructured aspect of his career. If he gave Keldysh a Yes, the pleasing environment would vaporize.

"I would not any more control my own life."

He spent the rest of his afternoon back at the Institute of High Temperatures. Then Sagdeev adjourned home to his wife, Tema, and informed her that the workday had involved a few unexpected twists. Their kids appeared: thirteen-year-old Igor plus their daughter Anna, age nine. Tema herself was the daughter of a theoretical physicist who dealt in plasma research. Sagdeev spilled the beans on everything that'd happened and what little he'd been able to gather about his possible new digs.

The Soviet Union's Space Research Institute functioned as a branch of the Academy of Sciences. It was a fairly new place—having come into existence only in May '65, with the express goal of representing scientific interests in the country's expanding space program. To a degree it echoed the core mission of the Office of Space Sciences at NASA HQ: advance the *exploration* of space past any testosterone-fueled "Got There First" missions, and fly more true science. In order to fulfill his job requirements, Sagdeev would have to diplomatically "sell" the pedantic military-industrial complex on the worldly relevance of something as superficially mundane as science experiments. Tricky! From the government's viewpoint, things like atmospheric pressure sensors did not intimidate other countries. Proletarians of world communism were not united by analyzing magnetic fields. The Space Institute existed to promote such disciplines. Its very birthright should've put Sagdeev at ease. But creating the place and fulfilling its mission were two different things.

While he'd been talking, the expression on Tema's face slowly changed. Both kids also picked up on their dad's overly negative tone of voice.

Remembered Sagdeev, "I think that my family immediately understood all the implications."

At the very least, they'd find a new apartment closer to the institute. At the very worst, the new job would suck. *Why does Keldysh want ME?* he kept wondering. Roald Sagdeev was not some space apparatus designer or industry veteran. Whatever he had picked up about the Venera or Lunokhod programs came from the state-run newspapers. Wouldn't a hundred other people have made better sense? The physicist never pressed for answers but felt pretty confident that Keldysh wanted, as Sagdeev put it, "Fresh blood. Younger people." He was one of the few remaining full members of the academy not burdened with some kind of large administrative responsibility. That could have something to do with it too.

Keldysh had given him a week. Several times during the course of it, Sagdeev came very close to rushing the guy's office and telling him to forget about it. Easy to say, and perhaps easy in principle to accomplish. But as he later indicated, "I knew that the ultimate pressure to force me to accept the offer might be overwhelming."

Sagdeev responded a few days early. He'd do it, because he didn't seem to have a choice.

The Space Institute's outgoing director, an aging yet entirely competent Mr. Petrov, seemed well aware of his imminent removal and arranged for Sagdeev to shadow him for a couple weeks. Afterward, Petrov would fully relinquish his duties but had no immediate plans for dancing straight into retirement. "He stayed in the institute as a head of one of scientific departments. So he was always available," noted Sagdeev. "I spent a lot of time with him. He was introducing me to all the issues; that is what I was learning. I was introduced to other staff members, and so on." Quickly Sagdeev understood his predecessor to be an exceptionally generous and friendly man.

The pair toured offices and meeting rooms, newbie Sagdeev pumping hands and trying his best to learn names. Mr. Petrov's lean, six-foot frame and abnormally thick white hair towered over most every subordinate. He smoked the entire time. Petrov also had a habit of talking nonstop, for reasons that soon became clear: it prevented anyone from slipping in any dissent or negativity. A carefully evolved tactic. After several days of observation, Sagdeev assembled the impression that Mr. Petrov was not retiring so much as being replaced due to his perceived failures at managing the institute.

They kept walking around, at one point traipsing by the ubiquitous marble bust of Lenin on display. Sagdeev's feet grew tired. The place was massive—over twelve hundred people already at work on various classified projects the world might never hear of.

Down a long corridor decorated with pictures of rocket launches and then past a Sputnik model, Mr. Petrov led the way into his office. Eventually he'd migrate to a different section, leaving Sagdeev to inherit this space. It appeared fairly grandiose. On the second floor of a multistory building, the room's middle was dominated by an enormous T-shaped counter with the director's chair sitting where the two lines intersected. This served as a combo desk and conference table, with paperwork and four rotary telephones spread about. Floor-to-ceiling bookshelves covered one wall. On the side opposite, giant windows opened out onto a sprawling deck. Petrov gestured down the hall. Those offices held other deputies plus housekeeping, construction, financials. About half a dozen people—all the administration—worked out of this floor. A nearby kitchen served tea and snacks. The KGB guy had his own space three doors down. Sagdeev cocked an eyebrow. The KGB guy?

Petrov ignored him and collapsed into a chair. For the new director's benefit, he now began painting a large and rather unfiltered view of Soviet space science. First off, he lectured, everything is controlled not by institute members but by high-rolling Communist Party bosses and other governmental bigwigs.

Petrov dragged heavily on a cigarette. "You, poor boy, will be dependent on *every*—even the most absolutely insignificant—bureaucrat everywhere," he cautioned a fidgety Sagdeev. "Those fellows will tell you what you have to do. They will draft and approve every bit of the planning." He went on to say that anytime something went wrong—which in this big machine was often—a scapegoat would need to be identified for the blame and fallout. That was easy in the space industry because only one existed: the entity that Sagdeev now headed. The favorite scapegoat. Petrov referred to their institute as "the boy to be beaten."

What culture shock. Such a long, far cry from the friendliness and camaraderie inherent in theoretical physics. Sagdeev unpacked. Decorating one's office in Soviet Russia was nothing like today's cubicle accessorization. People kept things very stripped-down and typically didn't even bring in pictures of their own families. Nobody had Zen rock gardens or posters of cute little kittens dangling from tree branches with "HANG IN THERE— IT'S ALMOST FRIDAY!" Nooo way. In *this* office, inspirational portraits of Brezhnev and Lenin adorned the walls. Sagdeev carted in a few plants.

And of course he embraced the bookshelves, which could slowly fill with important volumes.

During subsequent weeks, Roald Sagdeev marveled at just how many undertakings already filled the roster. There were so many wannabe projects—like, for example, a nutty scheme to land on Phobos, the biggest of the two Martian moons. Or what about the open-ended agreement with the French to fly some smallish weather balloons on Venus? Enough paper projects to last ten years or more—leaving practically no room for any agenda of Sagdeev's own. "It's not like I will come, will have ideas, let's do something *new*, no! I had to be responsible for fulfillment of something which was scheduled, planned long before," he denounced. "That was not very pleasant news." Sagdeev made the observation that in commercial industry, by comparison, this predicament wouldn't be construed as unusual. For example, someone might take over the management of a beverage factory about to release a new lime soda that's been in the works for eight years. "It's normal," he continued. "But for *scientists* to take a job to do this kind of thing, to sacrifice his or her own creative scientific interests and ideas, it's tough! That was my problem."

Director Sagdeev wondered how the institute's efforts held up against the competition's. "I wanted to find out about the substance of this huge amount of work and compare it with what I knew about American program. So my first thing was to go through from one project to another." He rounded up a smattering of staffers. For both U.S. and Soviet flights they reviewed the types of science experiments performed, the equipment used, its relative intricacy, and how much money had been spent.

Truth can hurt. "The final outcome of this working group was very pessimistic," he announced. "I came to conclusion that situation is not so rosy as Soviet mass media was painting it." The budgetary gulf almost took his breath away. "The difference was striking," he recalled of the disparity in expenditures. Only fifteen million rubles a year were being devoted to scientific flight hardware. In 1973 that approximated US$12.4 million—a pittance by NASA standards. As Sagdeev realized, "Maybe fifteen or twenty times more was spent in America."

He next turned his attention to the issue of longevity. Before him sat a large graph, prepared by his underlings. One line charted typical American lunar and planetary missions of that period, indicating the length of time that their instruments generally lasted after launch. A contrasting line traced the same metric for Soviet flights. It looked embarrassingly short.

"The difference was almost an order of magnitude," he groaned. "You can see how much longer they collect the data. It is a *quantity* lifetime but it translates into the *quality*. If your spacecraft, or the hardware, is capable to survive only few months, or maybe a year . . . then from the very beginning you will have to *exclude* missions which would require much longer time to fly." This basic limitation would significantly constrain his later efforts.

After digesting every result, Sagdeev arranged for a series of posters to illustrate the reality in meaningful ways. Around he went with them to high-level bureaucrats. "This is the situation," he began, to everyone who'd listen. In all these colorful space missions there did not seem to exist any significant dedication to quality science returns. Nobody in high places gave a rip about science like they should have. Instead, "it was like a little piggyback passenger on top of military missions and on top of political spectaculars." Point made, Sagdeev folded his posters.

"We cannot sustain real competition," he warned, purposefully, and then took a seat. "That's it."

After their visitor left, the bureaucrats would look at one another and always, as Sagdeev later learned, give the same response: "Why is this young man coming and bothering us?"

In no way was the Space Research Institute proving to be some utopian haven of progressive scientific endeavor. Gradually Sagdeev recognized the presence of multiple and disparate camps—almost high-schoolish cliques, really, with arrogance and bias displayed by all. Over in one corner sat the astronomers, wishing only to loft enormous telescopes into orbit and peer out near the edges of the universe. Why do anything else? Such people carried their noses high before the institute's contingent of earth scientists—those keenly interested in studying our home planet's geology and layered atmosphere. Another corner held the lunar and planetary guys, who'd already flown various sensors and detectors and -ometers and other trappings. A quartet of new spacecraft were apparently in the works to orbit and land on Mars; Sagdeev had a meeting coming up to discuss their readiness.

He also found procurement to be a real eye-opener. Requests would come through for some specific gadget—a camera or radiation detector—and part of Sagdeev's job was to arrange for its construction. What should've been straightforward equipment sourcing instead bled out into a sluggish underworld of closed doors and barefaced inaction. Sagdeev learned that, generally, public (or otherwise "unclassified") suppliers were nowhere near qualified enough to build at the high standards required by the Space Institute. "Expertise could be found only inside the military-industrial complex," he sighed. But the problem there was that anyplace he went tended to be hugely overbooked already and wasn't usually interested in new jobs. "Why would they need a little contract from someone, when they will get a fat contract for something related to military?" Research geeks simply didn't rate much attention. And quickly the realization came that to get anywhere in this crazy arena, Sagdeev's new outfit should learn how to build its own stuff. He added that to the bottom of his lengthening to-do list and then drove up to the Kremlin for that meeting about the four *Mars* ships.

After the Voronezh plant manager finished laying all his bad news on the table, the assembled participants had to make a go/no-go decision. Should they fly?

In retrospect it seems obvious. There's absolutely no chance to fix things after launch. Plenty can go wrong on space missions when every single part functions perfectly, and half the people in that meeting could practically hear little timers ticking down on all those crappily made transistors.

But an external force had unwittingly conspired to oblige the launches. Offered Sagdeev, "We knew that two years later, Viking would do something. We wouldn't be able to compete on Mars." He described the mood in that room as "our last chance" at the Red Planet. "Nobody wanted to accept delay for two years." The group's collective attitude swung in one direction only: with Viking in the mix, it was now or never.

They recommended launching. Sagdeev rubbed his taut cheeks.

"I thought, 'It's Russian roulette. What's going to happen is unpredictable.'"

16. How to Buy a Computer That Does Not Exist

We don't have a culture for resigning.

—Roald Sagdeev, telling an American friend why he
couldn't just quit his job

Fifteen years after the tsar's overthrow, math teachers Zinnur and Fakhria Sagdeev named their first son after the South Pole conqueror Roald Amundsen. Four years later the growing boy met his newborn brother, Robert. Neither name represented the family's Muslim heritage in the Tatar Republic, but Roald's parents never worried much about conforming. They didn't even live in the homeland—preferring Moscow for career reasons. Besides, the American explorer Robert Peary long claimed to have been first to reach the geographic North Pole, and wasn't that something to commemorate as well? When two more boys later came along, both received traditional names more in line with the Sagdeev family heritage. Roald asked why. His parents explained that they'd run out of poles.

When young Roald was five, his father's weak heart prompted the clan to move 540 miles eastward—back into the Soviet-controlled republic of Tatar. The unfortunate health news came as a serious emotional blow to Zinnur Sagdeev, who fancied himself a competent wrestler as much as a gifted mathematician. The city of Kazan held half a million people and the Sagdeev family took up residence in its downtown area. That might sound cramped and blandly modern, but not so in Kazan. Their single-story freestanding brick house offered three rooms plus an attached barn. Electricity arrived within a few years and everyone luxuriated in the magic of radio. The family didn't possess a receiver per se, just a cone of black paper wired in series with cones at other dwellings. Somebody at one end of the wire controlled the actual receiver, which at that time delivered but a single station.

"The story about the beginning of the war came through such a radio," underscored Roald Sagdeev.

Nazi Germany blitzed the Soviets in late June 1941. The Wehrmacht never got anywhere close to Kazan; volunteers nevertheless began excavating a defensive trench clear around the city. With new school textbooks out of production, lessons were taught using old, pre-Stalin ones. Vividly Sagdeev recalled his teacher instructing them to cross out the names of certain political figures and blacken over their pictures. At night, house and apartment windows also had to be blacked out. Life became strained in many ways. "It was a shortage of almost everything," he continued. "It was my assignment, everyday assignment, to go to stand in the line for the bread rations."

Roald got into chess, then soccer. In colder months, people strapped blades on their shoes and went ice skating. "Everyone had toys," he also remarked. "I probably remember much better the toys of my brothers!" Despite crowded Kazan and marked-up books—despite rationing and bland food and the potential for spies and an enemy who wanted to shell him into oblivion—Sagdeev recalled a decidedly enjoyable childhood.

His parents cultivated a generous library in spite of the sardinious accommodations. "It was big fun, you know, to try to understand what these books would tell me. Some of these books were already textbooks for college students. Math, for example. So it was a great challenge to try to understand what they say." Up to then, every math problem assigned by his schoolteachers had been a cinch. But lately—while settling into his early teen years—the trend had shifted to a discomfiting number of zingers he struggled to lick. More and more, the adolescent Roald perused his family's reference library in search of guidance. Kazan University had a special evening math program, and he opted into attending. Roald also became more and more intrigued by physics, keeping chess in his back pocket as a hobby. There weren't enough hours in the day to satiate his curiosity.

Red Army troops claimed Berlin in late April 1945 and the Kremlin declared war on Japan only a few months later. As Soviet forces thrashed through Manchuria that August, they reclaimed ethnic Russians who'd split during the 1917 revolution. Some of these people were jazz musicians and returned with their skills pleasantly intact. Downtown Kazan had a movie theater called the Electro and it began hosting small jazz concerts in the foyer. Within teenage Roald the events kindled a deep appreciation for this musical genre—redoubled when patriarch Zinnur bought a short-wave radio not long after the war ended. He patched it together with a turntable and speakers, "and suddenly the shortwaves opened the world!" cheered Roald Sagdeev. "I was able to get Voice of America. And the most important impact of the Voice of America was I became an ardent fan of jazz music." Mere weeks elapsed before Japan capitulated and at long last the hard fighting died.

University life now appeared on Roald's immediate horizon. He surprised most everyone—including himself—by choosing physics over math, right at the very deadline for application. "When you have two loves," he explained, "you hesitate. Until the very end."

With bags and books all packed, Roald Sagdeev bid a complicated goodbye to his folks and boarded the train for Moscow State University. His education in physics came complete with laughably mandatory classes on socialist ideology and the armed forces. Failure to pass these could easily garner a lengthy period of military service—forcing Sagdeev to pay close attention even when the material bored him out of his eyeballs. He recalled tousled teachers working hard to keep order in the face of roomfuls of pupils who saw right through the BS.

Sagdeev lived in a dorm and attended classes and at one point studied almost round-the-clock for three months solid in preparation for a grueling exam series. And in the midst of it, the bright Kazan boy decided to become a theoretical physicist—mostly because he liked the free-form aspect of it, but also because he didn't consider himself particularly adept at designing and building scientific instruments. "I think I am a reasonably good handyman," he interjected. "But to become an experimental physicist you have to be a real maestro. You know, dealing with hardware. It's on a completely different level." Sagdeev could fix a door or change a tire, but that was about the extent of it. Theoretical work no doubt better fit his abilities.

"Probably Galileo was one of the last guys who was able to do it both!"

As graduation approached, physics students were eligible for one of two basic career paths. They might end up in run-of-the-mill research at the Academy of Sciences. The other option in those times was, of course, nuclear weaponry. The curiously concentric curtains of secrecy enveloping this work amused Sagdeev and his classmates to no end. Even the facilities were code-named, using "mailbox" to describe a nuclear research institution. Most everyone preferred going into weapons because the job came stacked with higher pay and improved benefits. It was more prestigious.

All Sagdeev could think about, though, were restrictions. If you couldn't even say the name of the place, how big a thumb would you be under? Would guards stand there and watch you take a pee? Near term's end Sagdeev got called into a meeting and told to report for work at a place with the cryptic address of Moscow Center 300. He went back and told a professor about it.

"I am afraid I know where you have to go," revealed the prof. "This is a mailbox."

ONE OF FOUR SOVIET MARS SHOTS WILL ATTEMPT LANDING

Monday, September 24, 1973. MOSCOW (AP)—The Soviet Union, in a rare departure from previous policy, revealed Sunday that one of its four unmanned space probes hurtling towards Mars would attempt a soft landing on the planet.

The disclosure came in a Pravda *interview with Roald Sagdeyev, 41, the new chief of the Soviet space research institute. The interview marked the first time that Sagdeyev, a nuclear physicist, had been identified as the new head of the agency.*

They slid toward Mars, four pucks on ice. Already the spacecraft had been going for weeks and Lavochkin called every few days to check in; Babakin's successor Sergei Kryukov or one of his deputies would brief the institute on whatever up-to-the-minute news had been collected.

Things began to sour a couple of months after launch. Carrying another minuscule rover, *Mars 6* inaugurated the proceedings by abruptly ending its telemetry broadcast. *Bink*, it went off the air. Ground controllers could still issue commands and determine more or less where the ship was. But any supplementary feedback on its health—or even whether orders had been properly received—would not be coming. Desperately they transmitted over and again, plaintive requests flinging through space one after the other, never getting back even a whisker of acknowledgment. From here on in the ship would have to operate off its own preprogrammed instructions.

Time went by; Sagdeev pressed ahead with his everyday duties while keeping one ear on the updates. *Mars 4* suffered next. The probe's main computer bonked and lost the capacity to administrate itself. Then one of the radio transmitters aboard *Mars 7* threw in the towel. What might cut out next? On which ship? "Most often something happens out of the blue," Sagdeev brought up—many decades after having weathered these humiliations. Usually spacecraft out-and-out fail to leave Earth orbit, or simply stop working, or crash. It's a near-instantaneous breakdown—a snap of the fingers.

Sagdeev's eyes lit up as he shook his head and gestured. "Here, it was developing like in a slow movie!"

For his college diploma work, Roald Sagdeev had indeed been assigned to one of the dreaded mailboxes—a nuclear weapons facility. Reaching this particular one involved a trip on a specially designated train that brusquely stopped in the middle of the night between high walls of barbed wire. At the time, Sagdeev was not aware he'd just arrived at someplace called Arzamas-16. It sat more than three hundred long miles east of Moscow and pretty much in the middle of nowhere. Inhabitants called it the Near Volga Office, another cover name for the town originally known as Sarov, which disappeared from maps in 1946 after the weapons work started up.

Everyone shuffled off the train at sleep-deprived half speed. A top resident physicist by the name of Andrei Sakharov explained to the depleted young charges before him that they represented the very first students drawn into the Soviet nuclear program directly from universities, and they better take it seriously. The group had to sign pledges to never divulge anything about what they saw there or the efforts underway. Some unnamed chatty woman had just drawn three years in the clinker for blabbing stuff in a letter to her parents.

Efforts began; many whispered about *the device*. Why code phrases mattered in a gated town full of people all working on the same thing never really got resolved—everyone already knew the term meant a thermonuclear warhead. By this time in the early 1950s, fission bombs were well understood and practically blasé; the United States and Soviet Union alike had deeply entrenched themselves in hydrogen-fusion bomb research, which is what Arzamas-16 did. Each student's assignment represented one piece of the nearly solved puzzle. Sagdeev's responsibility was to examine the conditions inside stars under which hot plasma contributed to nuclear fusion.

Months later, with all chores mostly finished, the students felt a breeze of liberation upon them. After five and a half total years of college they were just about done. What then started was a process whereby every day a few pupils would meet with a special council that doled out postgraduate work. To his general shock, Sagdeev received an appointment to another mailbox near the city of Chelyabinsk: over 1,100 miles from Moscow—nearly 600 miles farther east from Kazan, even. For a month Sagdeev fought the assignment, roping in university professors and anyone else of influence who might be able to muscle him onto a different rock.

He finally found somebody who wrangled his transfer from Chelyabinsk to a mailbox in northwestern Moscow with the typically obfuscating name Laboratory of Measuring Instruments. It was laid out like a campus, with dormitories and various specialized buildings. Sagdeev began there in February '56, and upon seeing the facility's nuclear reactors knew darn well the place had nothing to do with measuring instruments. Once again, his work centered around nuclear fusion—applicable to both wartime and peaceful uses.

Today the world knows how to build a fusion bomb. However—if the correct recipe and procedures are ever assembled, the same core processes could well be a source of limitless energy for the masses. How does fusion work? In simple form, two identical and lightweight atoms like hydrogen are forcibly combined, or fused. The act of doing so releases a predictably small amount of energy. Get *lots* of atoms to combine, and it'll power a city. Maybe that sounds easy enough, but atoms *don't* want to do this. They're repelled by strong electrostatic forces in the same way that magnets are.

Now, these forces can be overcome; all you have to do is barbecue the atoms in question to about ten million degrees. Heat turns them into plasma, which is more agreeable to combining—but the plasma itself must be corralled so that fusion may proceed. The ideal tool for this is gravity, but the only nearby thing able to pull off nuclear fusion using gravitational restraint is the sun. At his new place of employ, Roald Sagdeev investigated how to enslave hot plasma with electromagnets.

Only a year later, even though the whole lab remained top-secret, Cupid still found it. Cupid finds everybody. A mentor introduced Sagdeev to his daughter, Tema. She studied linguistics and was real easy on the eyes. They went dancing, went out to the movies, and formally tied the knot in '59, two years after meeting. Sagdeev was twenty-six. Their son Igor came along one year later and the newly expanded family settled down in a campus dormitory.

Within a year Sagdeev nailed his PhD and the trio shuffled about to wherever his career led. He briefly stinted at the Moscow Energy Institute. Work next took them to a kind of "academic city" even deeper into Siberia than the remote mailbox where Sagdeev's diploma work had occurred. By now he'd been shakin' his bacon in the physics world for several years, and in 1964 the effort garnered him a seat within the Academy of Sciences. His title? A second-tier corresponding member. People don't apply for this; they must be chosen by peers.

Four years downstream, Sagdeev leveled up to full member. He was thirty-six—uniquely young for such an achievement. It came with a new and rather distinguished title: academician. The term originated with Peter the Great himself and denoted a scientist who's made substantial contributions to his field. The honor also came with perks: a virtual doubling in salary and minor celebrity status—nothing to sneeze at in a socialist world where any sort of glitter helped move a guy farther up in line.

By 1970 Roald Sagdeev had had it with almost ten years of narrowly confined nuclear physics research in the hinterlands of Siberia. Emotionally, it squeezed: the walls moved a little bit closer each month. "There was almost no infusion of fresh scientific blood," he lamented. No unfamiliar faces to greet. Infighting was on the rise. Sagdeev longed to find permanent refuge in the arena of nonsecretive, unclassified science. But the mere act of verbally contemplating his departure was enough to ostracize the diminutive Tatar man who longed to practice physics on his own terms. Colleagues made him feel like a defector.

Sagdeev's family soberly retreated to Moscow, where Roald accepted a position at the Institute of High Temperatures. The place had recently formed a small offshoot of a plasma theory lab and he took over its leadership. This accomplished man now enjoyed the freedom of pure theoretical research, but frankly he wasn't sure how long he'd be hanging out

26. Roald Sagdeev combs through his belongings while still in Siberia. Courtesy RIA Novosti.

at the new digs before starting to feel restless all over again. That's about the time Keldysh's secretary phoned, and the life of Roald Sagdeev went around yet another curve.

By the time Sagdeev arrived at the Space Institute, Mstislav Keldysh had been the academy's president for over ten years. "He was a workaholic. Absolutely," Sagdeev characterized his longtime friend and associate. A man capable of near-perpetual activity, Keldysh lived at his desk. Secretaries would ferry him sandwiches while he plowed through material at a superhuman pace: specifications, conflicts, appointments, proposals, and the occasional irate individual. He spoke math like a second language. And when this white-haired academy president called a meeting, everyone had better prepare themselves beforehand.

"There were no intermissions to go to toilet," remembered Sagdeev with a dead-straight face, coloring his remarks with tinges of bewilderment. "We were joking: '*How this guy* is sitting ten hours, twelve hours, without need to go to toilet?'" Certainly, Keldysh seemed happiest when at work and ignored every distraction. Part of what supposedly drove him was a mediocre family life that didn't offer much to go home to. An adult son of his committed suicide, as only one example. The situation began leading him down a path of depression noticed only after he was gone.

But at his office, Keldysh maintained perspective on the challenges facing Soviet science. "He tried to rejuvenate the academy," claimed Sagdeev. The average age of members had slowly been increasing—a trend Keldysh strove to reverse. "And he tried to create special incentives, special rules, special vacancies, for people below a certain age. For young people." Ergo, one of the reasons Sagdeev now did what he did. Keldysh tended to call him at unpredictable times about some detailed procedural matter or technical clarification. Frequently the two convened in person. Sagdeev always hit the restroom first before going in. Occasionally Keldysh ranted about how their country had basically conceded the space race to America. If it was people on the moon, or life detection on Mars, or the first trip to the outer solar system, the United States had them beat.

"If you really feel that we are so far behind, why don't you talk to Brezhnev?" wondered Sagdeev aloud during another crossed-leg meeting one day. "Something has to be done."

Keldysh looked up with somber eyes. "You think Brezhnev doesn't know?"

Virtually every day after coming home, Roald Sagdeev sat to review and discuss his colorfully novel work environment with Tema. Both kids were still young enough that she hadn't yet gone back to work herself. Teacups occupied the miniature kitchen table, sips of hot aromatherapy, ceramic clatters punctuating the conversation. He told her all about the community he'd been encountering. Plenty of smart cookies dwelled there—people well versed in the grungy politics of space, able to navigate the confusing tangle of ministries and special committees and other seemingly ad-hoc yet official entities that all overlapped way too much.

But Sagdeev also explained to his wife that he couldn't fathom why certain others even showed up. By and large, they didn't come off as overly interested in the subject matter. "It was so *fashionable* to work in space," he later said of the time period. "So, many people who are not very serious and good were attracted to get into these places." For Tema he expounded upon the institute's large support staff and how a good number of the inherited populace seemed outright worthless. Just look at Mr. Petrov's original right-hand man. He was, to the new director's vexation, "almost illiterate in everything related to science." Petrov himself had tried to have the guy dismissed. But no use—he'd won a Lenin Prize, which offered much in the way of political insulation from things like hostile termination attempts. Tema fiddled with her glass, confused. It didn't make sense to her. Gently Sagdeev blew on his tea. The institute was only a few years old, he pointed out, and engaged in brand-new avenues of research. There was just no precedent for the type of person to hire, no record of who made a good fit. Just to get off the ground and start moving work through, Keldysh would've needed trustworthy and dependable people, which this particular "scientific illiterate" happened to be. "He was not really a bad guy," commented Sagdeev—just one who was out of his element.

The steam fogged his glasses; Sagdeev wiped them with a shirttail and took another nip. Some of the personalities flopped in the other direction. His lead deputy for engineering issues was nothing less than a seasoned maestro of spacecraft design and operation. This guy knew most every inside trick for making a ship hum and served as a veritable walking reference library. Too bad for his "absolute lack of administrative talent," as Sagdeev put it, coupled with prosaic verbal skills. A useful individual, for certain—but one who required special handling.

Teatime finished, Tema washed up the ornate samovar and glassware while Roald continued on. He was appalled by the tight control exercised over the entire academy by the Communist Party's Central Committee. It had a special department known as the Commission on Exits that seemed to be filled with a lot of judgmental bigots. Anytime someone from the academy wished to travel outside the country it had to go through this agency. "The academy had to send accompanying documents," divulged Sagdeev. "How good this particular person is as a family man; was he always faithful to his spouse or not. You know, this type of thing." Not until they had reviewed the documents—and very often at the last minute, after visas and nonrefundable plane tickets had been issued—would the commission render their final verdict.

"I think probably there were people who had only denials," he mentioned.

The evening at a close, Roald and Tema adjourned to the rejuvenating atmosphere of a cozily inviting bed. Tomorrow would come soon enough. Placing his glasses aside, Roald Sagdeev tried to rest while pondering what Tema must have been thinking about his new job.

"She knew pretty much how tough was this environment."

To Sagdeev's colossal surprise, one of his allies turned out to be the KGB man from three doors down. Remember that the Academy of Sciences encompassed a patchwork of satellite facilities broadly distributed all over the country—its Space Institute being only one of them. Almost none of these places kept a KGB guy on-site, full time, like some frat-house mom. But the institute did, because its highly classified operations required anyone working there to possess top-tier security clearances.

Upon learning of the durable KGB presence only steps away from his own office, Sagdeev rolled his eyes. "You cannot circumvent them," he remarked of Soviet Russia's beyond-the-law secret police. "They would know more about you than you would know yourself." No priggish KGB man cared about Mars's atmosphere, or the surface of Venus, or even if batches of a certain transistor had been royally screwed up and made the whole country look dumb. He was there to preserve security, uphold secrecy, and function as gatekeeper/bouncer for many employee issues. His paycheck was not signed by the director and he couldn't be fired. But in a strange way, Sagdeev needed him. Really, they needed each other.

The KGB guy's name was Georgy, with a hard *G*. Small of stature yet in excellent physical condition, his polite manner and sheer effectiveness had rewarded him with a string of interesting assignments. Georgy's previous post had involved accompanying Soviet ballerinas on oversea voyages. When Sagdeev heard that, he joked that Georgy held responsibility for the country's two most valuable assets: the legs of its ballerinas and the brains of its scientists.

But at the end of the day Georgy still had to wear the KGB hat—part of which meant collaborating with the Commission on Exits over who in the institute got to travel. The first time Sagdeev hit red tape on this he went straight to Georgy. Why are certain people, he demanded to know, who have passed all the required checks and clearances, still barred permission for travel to an international conference?

Well, divulged the KGB man, it came down to what it said in the records.

"You should understand that there are people, ill-wishers, who send bunches of letters and memos to us, calling into question the loyalty or faithfulness of the applicant." No one could eradicate such charges, which were registered and given the status of official.

At that, Sagdeev breathed fire. "You mean there is no way to investigate and eliminate denunciations that come from anonymous bastards?!"

In slow motion the KGB guy shook his head, at which point Sagdeev commenced a hot lecture on the priorities and responsibilities of the Space Institute. How cooperation was of the utmost importance—"Especially if you yourself understand how ridiculous these contradictions are!"

Fresh on the heels of dustups like these came a pressing emergency with cash flow. See, the institute's fiscal year was just about over, and Director Sagdeev had not yet spent all the funds in his budget. "Since it was very difficult to find contractors and to buy something, there were always delays," he outlined. "So towards the end of fiscal year, you will accumulate a backlog of money. If you would be unable to spend it, it would be taken back to the state budget. Annihilated." He made a slash-across-the-throat motion that transcends all cultures and languages.

Already Sagdeev knew more than one horror story of other institute directors receiving derogatory verbal whippings: "You are not doing a good job! Unable even to spend the money you were given!" He felt very highly motivated to avoid *that*.

"So the problem was, at the end of the year, to find some miraculous way: buy anything!"

Now, Sagdeev didn't care to piss away his reserves just to clear the books. Rubles were scarce and—hey . . . come to mention it the institute *could* use an up-to-date mainframe computer. Their existing setup was too overburdened with processing the wads of incoming experiment data, or creating graphs, or running other programs that always needed a ton of heavy lifting. But ordering a computer was like ordering a submarine: it had to be spec'd out from the ground up. Customized. Normally that took months, which was time he didn't have.

The director paced his spacious office—eyes absentmindedly following the lines of bookshelves as he contemplated the accumulating stacks of paperwork, the computational conundrum, and his imminent tongue-lashing should the hoard not be spent. Eventually he called some old friends in Kazan. Over the crackly line he explained his predicament. "Look, guys, you have one of the most prominent companies manufacturing computers," he implored. "Could you help me to spend this money?"

His call got passed around to a variety of individuals. Eventually the head of the local Communist Party took up the receiver and instructed, "Come here." Sagdeev raced 540 miles all the way out to Kazan and a culture that seemingly preferred to conduct business in person. On the way, he laughed at the situation. "It's like asking my tribesmen, you know?!"

After arriving, a thick conversation about computer purchases did not immediately commence. First things first: "Drinks with the big party boss." It's an embedded aspect of Russian culture, and the refreshments are to always be consumed in groups. Ritual complete, additional calls went out to the Enterprise of Computer Technology—the place Sagdeev had mentioned on the phone. They were ready to talk. Everyone piled into cars and drove over.

Sagdeev wasn't sure if this whole effort was a dead end. "Look—this money," he begged. "Please help me. I'm ready to buy." The enterprise guys wanted to help—anything for a fellow Tatar—but simply didn't have any more products. A planned Soviet economy meant they'd long ago built and shipped everything they had parts for.

But people forced to operate within this ponderous economic system were nothing if not ingenious in their ability to manipulate it. On paper and over many hours, the group configured a system applicable to the Space Institute's needs. They put a cost on it. Sagdeev autographed a purchase agreement. This computer was not on the assembly line. Its chassis wasn't sitting over in fabrication. Truthfully, every fabrication room was empty. The silicon for its chips probably hadn't even been mined yet. But months down the road, when parts eventually became available, it'd get built.

Great news, yeah—unfortunately, not enough to satisfy the institute's rather pragmatic accountants, who'd want to know where in the hell it was. But Sagdeev's associates were no greenhorns, and confidently set in motion an accounting end around. They whipped out a set of blank documents and began typing and soon handed their customer a draft to read over. It was some kind of addendum to the main contract and had been worded as if coming from Sagdeev himself: "I, on behalf of the Space Research Institute, ask you to introduce a few specific modifications, nominal, to this computer which I bought." Sagdeev dropped the paper and started laughing. These Kazan guys made it look so easy. What pros. The Space Institute had just bought something with absolutely no projected date of completion, paid for everything up front and in full, and automatically returned it to the manufacturer for a series of nonexistent changes that would conveniently delay its final delivery. And so in this fashion the Space Institute would obtain a new mainframe computer that, by Sagdeev's own estimate, fell at least ten years behind whatever the Americans were currently making.

Paperwork complete, mission fulfilled, Roald Sagdeev began the long trek back to Moscow—where bizarre strategies like these began to figure more and more heavily into his routine.

"It was typical: how to spend a number of extra millions of rubles at the end of year," he smirked. "You can use many different tricks."

Sagdeev hadn't gone to any of the four launches. But as each *Mars* ship approached its destination, he did make a few obligatory showings at the spacecraft control center. Getting there required upwards of an hour of vehicular combat on the Moscow beltway in a boxy black Volga sedan. The sedan was neither owned nor operated by him, because this job came with perks. The institute maintained a whole stable of drivers, cars, garages, and mechanics to work on the cars. The name of Sagdeev's first driver can no longer be recalled, but he was older than dirt and the same guy who used to cart Mr. Petrov around. "Very smart, experienced, *slowly* driving, but was very good caretaker."

His new driver was a thick-bearded Ukrainian named Ivan who knew all the shortcuts and always got there quicker than anyone else. Angling ninety-five untuned horses through the tangle of Moscow streets, working chunky rubber pedals like a double kick-drum, he'd unload Sagdeev immediately in front of his destination, allowing the director to run along without delay to his appointment. Then Ivan would embark on a sometimes fruitless quest for parking. Nearly always, this happened when dropping his boss off in front of Moscow's spacecraft control center. "It was a very interesting place to go," Sagdeev lightheartedly offered of the high-tech facility. "You can see all the space barons there. And in the intermissions people would get out of the room, and there will be a bar open with drinks, some snacks. Everything was there." Over the course of later encounters he realized the setting to be ideal for cementing valuable relationships—not to mention working in the occasional small request for whatever need might have recently come up.

"A very interesting place, you know, for these type of conversations," he revealed. "You always can find someone to talk to."

Like passenger jets they started coming in on final approach. In early February '74 the hobbled *Mars 4* computer never told its maneuvering engines to fire and slow down for capture into orbit. The ship blazed past, at least 1,145 cruel miles away from Mars, and might never have accomplished more except for a squadron of dedicated engineers who managed to power up its cameras only minutes before closest approach. Rapidly *Mars 4* clacked off twelve frames with an ingenious rig that shot 25 mm film and then developed it onto a spool. The resulting images were scanned into a data stream and radioed back at one of ten possible quality levels. In tandem, a separate onboard video camera snagged two wide surface panoramas and queued them up, too—along with data on the local space environment already tallied by other instruments. By the time all this went home the ship had about breathed its last.

Two anxious days later, Sagdeev learned how *Mars 5* had victoriously slipped into orbit. The machine gave an appearance of sublime health— the only one still at 100 percent. Maybe things weren't going to be so bad after all?

Any optimism was short-lived. Making electronics work in the vacuum of space is difficult, and Soviet engineers favored placing them inside special compartments that were pressurized to Earth levels. But seals aren't flawless: immediately after starting orbit, *Mars 5* sprung an unfixable leak. If scientists wanted to finish the entire original work program, a three-month period of observations and data gathering would have to be condensed into three weeks, maybe less. Instructions went up and the ship commenced a paparazzi-like bout of nonstop, frantic picture taking. Scientists perused every one of the eighty returned images at low resolution, then had controllers retransmit the favorites at high-res. The ailing vessel stuck it out for twenty-two orbits—until the very last day of February, when pressure levels fell too low for its internal organs to continue. Only half the fleet remained.

By March 9, *Mars 7* had come within spittin' distance of the Red Planet and properly unloaded its egg, on time, as hoped. On autopilot the lander began drifting toward a perfect Martian entry profile . . . but hadn't avoided the sickness. Fifteen minutes later a bout of confusion wrought by malfunctioning electronics led to a mistaken cancellation of any firings of the retro-rocket. Consequently, the ship drifted off course and missed its target by some eight hundred miles, to join a growing ring of man-made space debris in perpetual solar orbit. Seventy-five percent of the mission was a near bust. Their final chance lay only three tense days down the calendar.

Deaf and mute nearly the entire way, *Mars 6* nevertheless completed two course corrections, determined its exact location in space, and automatically dropped its lander right on schedule. Three hours later the fat egg barreled through Mars's atmosphere. It popped a chute at sixty-six thousand feet and began transmitting local conditions on its own separate radio—one that Perminov had battled for the inclusion of and that to this point had survived any transistor failures. For nearly three minutes, the stoic holdout *Mars 6* swung under its parachute—describing thin air and calm winds and outstanding illumination and *kzzzz* . . . fading signals all of a sudden.

Sagdeev exhaled deeply. "Almost every piece of hardware and scientific instrumentation on board malfunctioned," he later recounted. On Lavochkin's worktables lay drawings and models of future Martian landers—with bigger rovers and even provisions for returning samples. However, *Mars 6* would end up being the last Soviet craft to ever visit the Red Planet's surface. Nobody ever figured out exactly what happened to it on the way in.

Quiet reflection on the experience would have to come later. In no time Sagdeev got thrust into a concluding press conference about the flights he'd literally walked into the middle of and was now strangely responsible for. It was his first really big face-off with reporters and the guy dripped nervousness.

To the sea of eager eyes before him, Sagdeev contended that the most substantial returns had undoubtedly come from *Mars 5*. During its abbreviated sojourn the craft had imaged large swaths of ground. It saw amazing detail: fault lines, craters, volcanoes, and plenty of evidence for water-esque processes like erosion channels and what appeared to be dried-up riverbeds. The ship had also measured atmospheric haze and humidity levels and appraised the amount of surface dust. During low passes, *Mars 5*'s hardware examined the chemical composition of various landforms. It pinpointed an ozone layer high above the planet. It characterized Martian cloud types. It recalculated surface pressures. It followed sandstorms. Sagdeev tried on a weak smile and adjusted his cuffs. Any questions?

Journalists let loose, badgering him with lethal volleys. Sagdeev answered freely. In fact, he could talk about anything he wished—so long as it didn't include a single word about the bad transistors. The crowd opened up again, questions machine-gunning forth in a hot spray: *What exactly malfunctioned on the ships? Were they lemons? Wired wrong?*

Finally the frazzled physicist cut everyone off. "Look. Don't ask me any more questions," he insisted. "Yes, I myself know the truth. And if it depended solely on me, I would tell you. However, I have to follow the rules that were established by our space community long before I joined it."

He wedged into the Volga and was driven home to emotionally confront the debacle on his own terms. A day or so later, Sagdeev heard from an American colleague. The *Mars* story, complete with final press conference, had made the front page of the *New York Times.* "How did you get there?" asked Sagdeev's friend. "Here in America, in order to get to the front page of the *New York Times,* you have to commit something—a very serious crime!"

If they'd somehow known the outcome in advance, would the people in that Kremlin meeting room have approved flying with bad transistors? "Absolutely not," professed Sagdeev, stifling a grimace. "*Four* Protons launched at the same time! Huge money! *Four* spacecraft! *No.*" Parted far to one side, Sagdeev's hair always had a way of slipping out of place and on down over his forehead. With a practiced sweep of the hand he shoved it back and adjusted his glasses.

"It was very painful," he remarked of the blatant *Mars* failures. "But somehow, what made my life a little easier? I was not responsible for that. *It was not my project.* And so it was easier to accept."

17. Downsurfing

It is certainly possible that our neighboring world possessed
liquid oceans for two billion years or more. This has interesting
implications for considerations of life elsewhere in our solar system.

—Mikhail Marov, scientific investigator on many Venera flights,
discussing the history of Venus

Mstislav Keldysh sat around the large meeting table with several other academy colleagues. Roald Sagdeev joined. Several months had elapsed since *Mars 6* piled it in, and the group had assembled to strategize their next leapfrogging move through space. Along with finding destinations that were scientifically relevant, each one also needed to be politically advantageous in some regard. Tough combo.

Absentmindedly as he listened, Sagdeev tore small pieces of paper from his notepad and folded them up into thin strips. In his younger days he'd been a monster chess player. The solar system was not exactly an eight-by-eight grid of black and white squares, but America owned the board. Roaming over it at will! Not long before this meeting, a white box called *Mariner 10* had made its second flyover of Mercury after an initial sweep past Venus. It went this way because a direct Mercurial commute required significantly more energy than reaching only as far as one planet over. So *Mariner 10* had not been targeted *to* Venus per se but *past* it in a judiciously planned maneuver that transferred some of the orb's rotational energy to the ship. It was like having a fresh set of boosters waiting out there, ready to put on. Such "gravity assist" maneuvers had been purely theoretical until *Mariner 10* proved them roadworthy. From Venus the lonely bugger sailed on to Mercury in a fashion that would loop it back around the innermost planet two more times. An impressed Sagdeev applauded the Americans. What a brilliant mission!

That wasn't even half of it. Something called *Pioneer 10* already had survived the asteroid belt past Mars and in just a few months' time would buzz Jupiter. Plucky America also had Viking launches coming up in less than eleven months and luxuriously discussed every mission detail openly, in the press. Then—in three years' time—another set of twins called *Voyager* would head out for Jupiter and Saturn flybys. Motivation, manpower, money: the hat trick of large technological projects, and America had scored every one.

Somebody asked for more tea. Cigarette smoke hung low. Keldysh moved paperwork around into different categories, options filling his meeting table. What about going to Phobos? It was more captured asteroid than moon of Mars and held great appeal. But nobody thought the idea to yet be viable. The French collaboration surfaced again: a (now larger) balloon on Venus. "Extremely sophisticated," remarked Sagdeev. It had potential, though they'd have to get creative on weight. "The science payload was very tiny. This huge balloon could carry only, I think, about no more than ten kilos of science. Yeah. So but okay, you know, we thought it's a good project."

Ballooning on Venus? Maybe that sounded featherbrained, but it actually made good sense. The planet offered a nice, dense atmosphere that moved rapidly over long distances. You could hang a balloon in there and learn gobs about the place in no time. Compare that with Mars. Its air is so thin that levitating anything of substance requires a mammoth envelope holding tons of gas. And due to the incoming supersonic descent, it would have to inflate almost immediately—generating large stresses on fragile materials that'd been folded up tight for nearly a year.

A groundbreaking idea for sure, but nobody at the meeting thought they'd get any traction on it. Recently the French president had died of cancer while in office and his replacement wasn't too wild about space. Venus balloons went to the back of the line and they moved on to other matters.

Next option: for half a decade, the Lavochkin wizards had been steadily massaging a longshot idea of bringing back Martian soil. Keldysh verbally reviewed the overall scheme. In order to deliver nineteen thousand pounds of spacecraft, this proposal advocated a launch of dual Proton rockets into Earth orbit. Combine their upper stages; depart. Months downstream the lander would grab samples, then shoot back up into Martian orbit and rendezvous with a *third* Proton magically waiting out there. Keldysh lifted his eyes from the pages. Did anyone else think this was overly complicated?

Returning to Earth orbit, that last Proton was supposed to dock with a manned station, where cosmonauts would transfer the diggings to their own ship and plunge back home. The whole initiative was so gargantuan that a scaled-back test-bed version had been envisioned to launch a year ahead of time and prove out various systems, as well as examine Mars with a new rover.

They talked dates. The next favorable launch period would occur in late summer of '75—almost perfectly matching the Viking blastoffs. Keldysh sighed; America's trump card. If Lavochkin's plan miraculously worked, its laudable success would still play out in the shadow of Viking. The sheer breadth of science on those flights—orbital mapping and life detection and ground photography, just for appetizers! *Much* better than anything even remotely possible from behind the Iron Curtain!

"In space research, very often important to be the first," Sagdeev pointed out. Whoever gets there before anyone else wins the big scoop. They publish first and become the de facto experts. Keldysh nodded his agreement. America was bleeding money into Viking. Why fly to Mars at all?

The longer the men talked the more dissonance crashed on through. From a political viewpoint it seemed obvious, but nobody fessed up until just the one option remained. "We made a conscious decision," indicated Sagdeev, summarizing their eventual conclusion. "It's like an international spontaneous division of labor: let Americans concentrate on Mars now. We will go to Venus." By early 1974 this became policy. "We chose Venus deliberately, to avoid duplication." And Lavochkin's Mars plan went back into filing cabinets.

The next mission's profile finally emerged: two ships would orbit the Goddess of Love—imaging her cloud strata while dispensing one lander apiece to run experiments and take photos. Surface heat? Conquered. Surface *pressure*? Vanquished. But as most airline pilots will say, the trickiest part of any flight is landing. What Lavochkin didn't have smoothly ironed out was an ideal method of descent through that wonky atmosphere. (Its staggering thickness actually rebuffs small meteorites.) Previous flights had used reefed parachutes that opened up more the lower they went and slowed things gradually. For Venus that now seemed backward. What they really needed to do was shed the approach speed early on, grab lots of measurements while still high up, and then accelerate through the lower, hotter, and more dangerous layers before finally setting down at parking-lot speeds. But what let you scoot fast through dense air?

All this time they'd been skydiving, and skydiving wasn't the answer at all. Better to *surf.*

The old *Venera 8* didn't get redesigned so much as it got accessorized. A thirty-one-inch titanium sphere received layers of insulation girdling its loins. In went batteries and electronics—plus generous measures of that heat-absorbing chemical salt to again bestow a cherished few extra minutes of protection. On opposing sides near the top, Lavochkin installed bulbous, half-inch-thick curving portholes made of pure quartz. One camera peeked out from each, periscope-style. A crushably hollow landing ring stood off from the globe's bottom via multiple paired shock absorbers. The shocks made great rigging points, and four halogen lights went on all around the perimeter.

Just above the portholed globe sat one of the more radical innovations to ever appear on a spacecraft. It resembled a gigantic metal snow saucer because it did pretty much the same thing: slid you down to the bottom. Six and one-half feet across, the saucer functioned in a way that Venus practically insisted upon. A design that could never have been arrived at by chance. Lavochkin built two total landers: *Venera 9* and *10.*

After two-plus years in his new corner of the world, Roald Sagdeev began devoting more and more waking hours to an upcoming *manned* space endeavor that had little to do with Venus or Mars or even his own institute. At long last the joint undertaking envisioned by the American Frank Borman was to be realized. Flying through low Earth orbit, an Apollo ship carrying three astronauts would dock with a Soviet two-man Soyuz. Among other complications, the flight required a custom-built docking collar to link two ships that obviously had never been designed to do so. Such villainously intricate technical hurdles were nothing compared to all the politics. Virtually all aspects of Soviet spaceflight were controlled by the military—and therefore classified—so a hand had been placed on the head of the Space Research Institute. It'd function as artful cover, a façade to mask who really pulled the spacey strings inside Russia.

"Oh, you cooperate," Sagdeev remembered people instructing him.

27. This Venera has not yet been fitted with its external insulation. Twin cooling tubes at far right port cold gas throughout the innards until just before descent. Spiraling on top is the radio antenna. This machine sits atop a work stand; its landing ring is at the waist level of the leftmost technician. Author's collection.

"Because you are less burdened with the secrets. Cooperate on science and so on." All the meetings inside Russia were held at Sagdeev's, and what better option existed? As it was, the institute already hosted infrequent visits by local schools and other groups. Sagdeev's own children came through a few times. He took pride in running the kind of place that kept its window shades up and the doors open. So when things like the docking collar needed international review, techs would ferry the equipment from its real place of assembly to a surplus workroom inside the Space Institute.

Sagdeev enjoyed hosting the Americans and practiced his improving English. Then, after every foreigner left, the equipment would be hauled back to its real facility for whatever needed doing.

As part of these endless Apollo-Soyuz preparations, a workman visited Sagdeev's office one morning and installed a nondescript light-beige telephone next to the burgeoning litter already crowding the desk's upper-right-hand corner. Each had a different look. This new phone featured pillars of socialist wheat in the center of the rotary dialer and was utterly useless in the absence of a certain thin and very classified little book. Roald Sagdeev had been slated for access to the *kremlovka*. This system of private telephones facilitated instant, direct communication between ministers, party bosses, factory heads, and other members of the *nomenklatura*. Keldysh had one. So did Kryukov at Lavochkin. Many of Sagdeev's contemporaries at design bureaus and manufacturing plants downright expected him to already be in the loop.

"What is the phone number of your *kremlovka*?" they'd been asking. "I couldn't find it in the directory."

Sagdeev always had to shrug and shake his head. "Sorry, I don't have a *kremlovka*."

"This is impossible!" would come the response. "It is so important for you to have it. Why didn't you ask for it?" Round and round. But with the approaching handshake in space, Sagdeev needed real-time communication with top bosses at any given ministry or factory or institute. He got approved. Coordinating the actual hookup took weeks of patient diplomacy.

Reclined in his enormous leather chair with a high back, Sagdeev flipped through the little classified book. It had a nondescript, darkly red cover made of fake leather and was never to be left out. "I had to keep it in a closed space," he remembered. "Not on the desk." Inside, a series of typed pages listed out a Who's Who of high-level contacts at various institutions.

The phone itself wasn't anything to write home about. No caller ID lit up its face. It offered zero voice mail. But using one was almost like teleporting. The plump cube of beige plastic rang directly to Sagdeev and only from other phones on the network. There was never an unimportant call. Altogether it made for a thoroughly indispensable back door to skirt the layered bureaucracy typically preventing what, for any other country, would've been an ordinary person-to-person conversation.

By this point Sagdeev was trying to make the best of his undesirable environment. Though it offered little scenery beyond a gray concrete court-yard, the empty deck adjacent to his office served as a pleasing escape and Sagdeev occasionally sat out there to ruminate over the day's headaches. Lately he'd struggled with making copies. Friendly requests for a Xerox machine had recently earned him a public rebuke before the entire military-industrial commission assembled at the Kremlin. All he'd wanted to do was provide for visiting Americans—who more than likely would need to copy various papers. And, heavens above, did the government have a thing about photocopiers. The very technology of them instilled paranoia into career bureaucrats. Just imagine: What if someone reproduced a secret document? What if subversive pamphleteers leveraged such equipment to spread lies and disinformation? Accordingly, the machines had to be reg-istered and blank paper inventoried. Their use was rigorously controlled, to the point where some institutions actually stationed magisterial goons before the machines to ensure that unauthorized copies were not generated.

Even so, it was still very easy to make copies. Just bring chocolate. Or cigarettes. No kidding.

Some really bad news came through: a malfunctioning Soviet launch had prematurely brought the new Venus lander down in, of all places, Wyo-ming. The lander contained exotic instruments—not to mention proprietary metallic alloys—and as such the Reds were quite desirous of retrieving it.

With only twenty minutes' notice, the spacecraft designer Irina Leonova raced to gather equipment and hop a plane all the way to Wyoming. She loaded a yellow Jeep with her gear and struck out. Armed with the probe's rough position, Leonova intermittently sent radio commands to neutralize the ship. Nothing worked, and—wait! There it was! Zigzagging undam-aged through the remote scrub, reconnoitering the landscape exactly as intended! They'd built a rover after all.

But why wouldn't it shut down? With some horror she remembered hear-ing of the probe's initial hours after landing: a terrified farmer had shot his gun into the air—likely fooling the craft's sophisticated computing logic into thinking it'd already landed on Venus.

"If that happened, the probe would put itself on override," she informed KGB major Popov. As with many scientists, Leonova was not permitted to roam about freely and Popov functioned as her handler. Even from a distance the guy looked KGB, wearing a laughably out-of-date fedora. Though intelligent and seasoned, he didn't seem tuned in to how the ship had been designed for extremes of most every environmental variable. It now drove on autopilot using preprogrammed instructions. Every deactivation attempt would be fruitless. It'd roll through whatever stood in its way.

To Popov she cried, "There's nothing on Earth that can stop it now!"

Utterly unsympathetic, he lit her up. "What I *do* know is that you failed!" Popov now disclosed the truth behind a mysterious something he'd lugged along in a giant padlocked box. It was a missile—with enough destructive force to obliterate the ship.

Leonova was aghast. "We were ordered to dismantle the probe and take its circuits back to Russia!" she argued. "Not destroy it!"

"Our main job is to keep the secrets of the probe from getting into the hands of the Americans!"

"You can't go *near* that probe," forbade Leonova. "It's operating as though it were on Venus. All its defense modes are on automatic." Popov regarded her with a mix of respect and frustration and didn't seem to find it odd that she talked in miles per hour and degrees Fahrenheit. Her accent wasn't holding up too well, either.

Popov cradled his missile box. He didn't like this situation one bit. After the snoopy Americans found out, they'd have no choice but to send in . . . a bionic man.

In the late 1970s American television viewers got a real treat that didn't bother with a whole lot of pesky realities. The core premise of *The Six Million Dollar Man* began with ex-astronaut Steve Austin losing limbs and nearly dying while on a test flight. Instead of fitting him with inert wooden prosthetics, deep-pocketed black op string pullers chose to install nuclear-powered legs, a right arm, and one eye.

Just go with it. After his recovery, "bionic" Steve could run sixty miles an hour and see things miles away and rip fenceposts out of the ground with one hand. It was totally bitchin'. He went to work for a shadowy arm of the U.S. government as a one-man operative engaged in everything from criminal apprehension to international intrigue to Bigfoot sightings without ever once letting his shirt come untucked. So when an errant Soviet spacecraft downed itself in Wyoming, America's first call naturally went to Steve.

Irina Leonova and Major Popov and the "Venus Death Probe" represented classically overblown American TV Cheez Whiz. Show creators played on the innocent ignorance of those watching. At the time of the *Venera 9* and *10* launches, in June '75, Soviet news agencies released pitifully few mission details. They even kept vague about the inclusion of landers. Who knew— maybe that eerily shrieking rover that bionic Steve fought *really was* what the Russkies had built? It made for perfect entertainment that would air just over a year after the real events played out in ways that were infinitely more beguiling than any fiction dreamed up by Hollywood.

When Keldysh started going downhill, the government wouldn't let him exit the country for treatment because so much of what he did was classified. The man needed heart surgery. Bureaucrats went so far as to bring in a prominent surgeon—of all people, an American from Texas—who flew to Moscow and operated. The results failed to bring about any miraculous turnarounds and the Academy of Sciences director slid further into depression. Here was an otherwise solid man who rarely lost his temper, whose chief means of recreation was enjoying his collection of Impressionist art prints. But no longer could he stand his own being.

Even considering the nation's space accomplishments, Roald Sagdeev felt the unfortunate events had everything to do with Keldysh's perception of himself as a failure. They'd lost the moon race. Both *Lunokhod*s died. Two Vikings had practically co-opted all their Martian glory, without having even landed yet. Keldysh's attempted revamping of the academy always encountered obstructionist legislative meddling. His recommendations for steering the nation's computer industry fell upon deaf ears. But— never did he show up to anything with so much as a single bellyache. "His character was to keep all the emotions inside," offered Sagdeev about his friend. That same year a moderately disabled Keldysh resigned his post and the academy set about finding a replacement for this irreplaceable man.

Outwardly pleased with the stability of *Venera 9* and *10* as they flew to Venus, Roald Sagdeev nonetheless wanted to quit his job. Again. "When I became the director," he lamented, "I was barely forty years old. And from that age was taken out of the creative life of a scientist. That was very tough." Sagdeev reported to the academy's head of physics—at the time a dark-haired, friendly looking man named Prokhorov who'd hear nothing of it. Several attempts to bolt had all been stonewalled. "It was very difficult, you know. I even was joking that to leave it, it's like to leave the Mafia."

Tema worked to be supportive—but nobody could deny the hazards of dealing with a husband who spent in excess of twelve hours every day churning through turmoil he hadn't created and didn't enjoy. They talked about it at home. They talked about it when Sagdeev made pilaf Tatar—a native rice dish traditionally cooked by men. Driving in the family's orange Lada also offered chances to discuss the jump. It wasn't as easy as just typing up a half-page letter and dropping it at Prokhorov's desk on the way out. "Very un-Soviet!" announced Sagdeev. "Your *bosses* would tell you when you have to step down! Or go up! It was not your decision."

The bedrock of physics is rules: action/reaction; cause and effect. Occasionally—like with controlled fusion—the rules are elusive. Someday they'll be deciphered and will no doubt make perfect sense in context. You know the rules are out there. But quitting the Space Institute? Unwritten cultural norms demanded that an employee wanting to leave first engage in conversation with his superior—but only during what amounted to utterly indefinable conditions. "I *had* to talk first," he reiterated. "And if I will find understanding, then the rest would be formality. *Then* you can send a letter."

An exasperated Sagdeev had once lectured his wife all about it. "Look, I am always trying to find a situation in which I can ask!" he bellowed. She told him she understood—but she truly couldn't have, because she never saw the goings-on through her husband's eyes. Often Prokhorov came through the Space Institute and well knew that Sagdeev wanted to get the heck out of there. He was even sympathetic about it. But such conversations were *not* to be conducted on these visits.

Sagdeev made random attempts during his own odd trips through Prokhorov's office at the academy. The latter man never once tried to talk his director out of quitting—instead thanking him in every direction for his wonderful efforts, claiming repeatedly that he understood Sagdeev's position and backed it 100 percent. *Ah . . . so sorry though,* a resignation could not be tendered at this point in time.

"It would be very difficult to get understanding and approval at higher and higher levels," Prokhorov once told Sagdeev—who apparently still hadn't lucked across that elusive "best time."

Well, gee. Some jobs are really that tough to quit?

Sagdeev propped both elbows on the table and let his fingers slowly col-lapse together. He stared away, out the window.

"You know, some jobs, yes. Some jobs."

On October 20, 1975, the U.S. Supreme Court ruled that teachers could, after a warning, spank their students. Millions of miles away from red bot-toms and nearly to Venus, the unspanked brown globe containing *Venera 9*'s lander separated from its mother ship and began a two-day solo plunge. It came in shallow, at twenty-four thousand miles an hour, experiencing fewer G-forces than any predecessor. After re-entry the brown cocoon split in half and fell away. Four distinct parachute stages began pop-popping at just over 213,000 feet—pop-pop, handing the baton off from one group to the next, greatly slowing the craft from its transit speed. Experiments alive: chemical detector, pressure, temperature. Down, down it came, the last round of metallic chutes letting go at 164,000 feet after twenty min-utes in suspension. A terse plunge followed. Then *Venera 9* caught the thickening air and undeniably began to surf. Glissading but not sailing, it approached hardpack like nothing else ever had—bearing mute witness to the ingenuity of kindred souls who would never see their beloved cre-ation again. Wind whistled; drifting . . . pressure increasing, hues growing more and more orange in the controlled plunge. Light and wispy clouds . . . ones that went on forever . . . the reason that ground features could never be seen from orbit. Rich, darkened orange now surrounded the lander. A heavy bromine color. Fifty-five minutes later it plunked onto Venus at six-teen miles an hour. Down and upright on a heavily sloped ridge within the petrous area known as Beta Regio. (People who study Venus have divvied it up into named regions they call provinces.)

The machine had to hurry because even though it'd been chilled to well below freezing, internal temperatures were already on their way up and the orbiting mother ship would stay in range for only about an hour. Twenty-five degrees Fahrenheit. One camera cover popped off no problem, but its idiot twin on the other side failed to budge. Sixty degrees. To understand the camera configuration and field of view, bend forward at the waist until your head is about three feet off the ground. Use both hands to block your peripheral vision and lightly swivel your head from shoulder to shoulder, keeping your neck rigid. With *Venera*, this returned a forced-perspective image covering 40 degrees up and down by 180 sideways: distant features to the extreme left, transitioning to close-ups in the middle, with the terrain receding once again on the right. Temp check: ninety degrees inside. Had both lens covers dropped, two panoramas could've been combined to produce a complete "walk-around." One hundred twenty degrees. But what they got was still pretty cool. Some of the landing ring was visible, along with a surface-density instrument laying politely on the fractured ground that looked for all the world like an oversized paint roller. A hundred and forty degrees Fahrenheit and still running.

Fifty-three minutes after landing, *Venera 9* had obediently completed one panoramic shot and was most of the way through a second: bursts of data wafting up from the dozen-odd instruments it carried to sniff air and lick the ground. Pastoral winds flitted through. It wasn't so dark down there after all; no flood-lamps necessary. Then *Venera 9*'s orbiter drifted out of range, severing communication. The abandoned probe did not know this. It kept recording nuggets of data one after another, splicing them into lines of picture, eagerly singing forth these bundles of grace and majesty up to something that was no longer there.

Three days after *Venera 9* made port, its sibling completed an encore descent and landed some 1,400 miles away. One lens cap again failed to dislodge, marking the start of a disturbing trend in Venusian surface photography. *Venera 10*'s other mechanicals worked flawlessly to return gobs of data and one full panoramic image. The ship had come to rest upon a wide, flat plain indicative of basalt and more basalt with plenty of basalt thrown in for good measure. Not a great place to lounge in the nude. *Venera 10*'s mother ship predictably flew out of range after an hour and five minutes, leaving the ground craft to persevere with its own declining defenses— obediently radioing pictures and factoids to a listening ear that had long since departed. Two vessels alone in hell. Their batteries withered and their core temperatures increased until the globes could resist no more.

Even considering the failed lens caps, both landers had knocked it out of the park. Bowled perfect games. Less glamorous but just as sophisticated, the two orbiting ships would persevere for months—repeatedly circling the planet, gathering images that offered an unparalleled study of just how Venusian clouds move about. Excitement over the nation's space exploits amplified and dilated. Paradoxically, then, trouble came blowing through Roald Sagdeev's office only days after the landings. The director hadn't embezzled anything or abused some privilege or, God forbid, used a copier without permission. It came down to politics and a buddy of his.

The friend was Andrei Sakharov, who'd risen to prominence as a key figure behind the Soviet hydrogen bomb. After figuring out how to make it, he became disillusioned with the very concept of nuclear weapons and gradually turned his energies to peace. The next big thing in weapons technology after nukes was that of antimissile missiles—shooting down the other guy's incoming warheads. Publicly Sakharov campaigned against this insane proliferation and also began muscling for human-rights reform. The latter activity is really what got his butt in a sling. Before year's end Sakharov won the Nobel Peace Prize, which grated on the Politburo like a carrot scraper in the nostrils. Nobody let him out of the country to collect. Before long, select academicians were summoned to ink their names at the bottom of a letter condemning Sakharov and his sophomorically subversive rants.

Sagdeev's turn came. He sat there for a time, staring at the page before him. It didn't read like anything that would've come from the academy outright—sounded more like rhetoric from the Central Committee.

Fingering the pen, Sagdeev—at this exact moment—blew a real chance to flee the institute forever. To the academy he could have denounced these proceedings, flatly refused to sign, and stomped the heck out. Rather, as delicately as was feasible, Sagdeev recommended that as an alternative to signing the letter he draft up some finger-wagging language of his own and submit that instead. The grumpy academy guy wasn't real happy with the plan but Sagdeev managed to convince him and get out of there. Three hours later he was back at his T-shaped desk and the phone rang. Had he completed that letter? Not yet? Then he needed to get back down here and sign like everybody else. From his typewriter Sagdeev wrung out a few anemic sentences and told his secretary to keep the whole thing under wraps.

That approach did not go over particularly well and not long afterward a whole bunch of dominoes began tumbling. First, Sagdeev lost out on an all-but-assured Lenin Prize, which could be considered the Soviet Union's own version of the Nobel Prize. Then he received a summons to appear before the Central Committee of the Communist Party.

One of the men asked Sagdeev, "Do you enjoy being director of an institute, or not?"

"I haven't yet made up my mind on that issue."

They almost booted him. "After I did not sign letter condemning Sakharov, I was considered as a kind of outcast." In Russian culture it's known as being a "white crow." "There was some discussion at the top to replace me," he went on. "And I personally think to this day that for my egotistic goals it would have been the best solution at that time." But nobody could locate a fitting replacement and Sagdeev got banished to his office just in time to see the *kremlovka* disappear—yanked out as punishment.

"Hard to get and easy to lose," he bemoaned after the lines were cut.

18. Gulliver's Travels

Honest to God, I never expected it to work.

—Patricia Straat, describing her expectations of
the Biology Instrument

Mars's Viking 1 *Lander* resembled no craft that had ever before visited another world. Although something on the moon came close. Ten years prior, NASA had dispatched a number of wiry, three-legged bumpkins called *Surveyor* to our nearest celestial neighbor. They prospected in the gray dirt and sent home gobs of imagery as preparatory steps before the manned Apollo landings. "Close" is relative. Outside of an extraterrestrial presence, the biggest things the *Surveyor* craft had in common with the Viking 1 *Lander* were stubby tripod legs.

Surveyor's institutionally white, skeletal frame lacked a central structure per se; things just sort of hung anywhere on its steel tubing. But *Lander* possessed a true body that assumed the form of a low, irregular hexagon—containing rechargeable batteries, two computers, data storage, and a radio system, plus oodles of brightly colored wire bundles linking everything together. *Surveyor* ran off solar panels, while *Lander* sported dual nuclear generators. They transformed radioactive heat into electricity and hung side-saddle off opposite ends of the hex frame, underneath white fabric covers. *Surveyor* wielded a camera, which in and of itself was a nice thing, but its monochrome output paled in comparison to *Lander*'s dual stereoscopic color cameras.

That wasn't everything. On the Mars ship's top deck, a modest antenna dish sprouted up for direct earthly communications. Nearby perched a thin, elbowed arm with a hand extended almost as if it were trying to thumb an

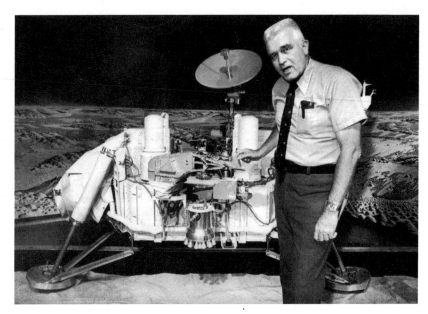

28. Jim Martin poses before the spare Viking *Lander*, arranged for display in JPL's von Karman Auditorium. His right index finger hovers directly over the retracted scoop head. Peeking from behind his shoulder are fingers of the weather station. Courtesy NASA/JPL-Caltech.

imaginary ride home. The sensors adorning its pseudo fingers made up a mini weather station.

A total of seven gleaming *Surveyors* landed on the moon. Later iterations carried a modest scoop, which could lengthen out scissor-style to nudge, dig, or trowel up a dirt sample. Beyond measuring the sample's basic properties, the craft could do nothing else except dump it all out. But each *Lander* possessed the ability to do a great many things with the soil gathered in its own extendable scoop, mounted right out in front.

For years already, project scientists had embroiled themselves in marathon arguments over where on Mars to park these things. Dropping in on any old spot was like asking for a nice crash landing on boulders or mountain ridges. As Jim Martin commented to the press, "If one sets off as Columbus did to find a new world, he would not apologize for looking for a safe harbor."

They'd been at it for years; the formal process of identifying sites reached all the way back to September '70—just before *Luna 16* flew. And from the get-go, nobody agreed. Engineers wanted flat and open. Biologists wanted low and warmer. It ping-ponged back and forth; the weather guys *also* wanted flat and open. A pecking order did not exist because no experiment was supposed to be more important than the next.

Constraints on top of constraints. They had to drop from an existing orbit. They had to land in the daytime. They had to enter the Martian atmosphere at a precisely calculated slant—attenuating heat buildup while taking full advantage of a slowing effect. This narrowed candidate sites to an equatorial band ranging thirty degrees north or south. Target regions also had to sit low enough to allow maximal fill of a parachute canopy. Maybe "land low" doesn't sound all bad, yet that single requirement banished roughly 75 percent of the planet from consideration.

Wow, could it get any more restrictive? Sure. Favored regions had to contain large enough target zones—wide, squashed ellipses measuring 248 by 522 miles. They had to occur in pairs: one super-safe option, coupled with another weighted for scientific potential. Remarkably, these specifications left a lot of Mars to contemplate. Safety always ranked supreme. In a memo, the Cornell astronomer Carl Sagan pressed engineering to "back off from this requirement a little bit." A member of Viking's imaging team, he wanted to land in the most biologically promising areas and started making a nuisance of himself about it. A fellow scientist responded with no punches pulled: "The engineering criteria must reign," he judged. "It hardly need be mentioned that a crashed lander is not very useful, even if it did crash in the most interesting part of the planet."

They drained every last usable clue from Mariner imagery. They scoured reports from the doomed *Mars* quartet. Viking's site group took everything in—mimeographing results, handing stacks around the bland meeting tables for discussion. Some constraints were relaxed; locales above thirty degrees north latitude were now permissible, a decision that endured vigorous debate because liquid water was thought to be more promising up there. Like sands through the hourglass, *Orbiter 1* held tightly onto its descent vehicle while the linked pair coasted along through space, halfway to Mars, beginning to relay its own pictures from up on high. The touchdown club welcomingly added them to a burgeoning trove already thick with material, rabidly weeding out undesirable swaths of ground. Mercifully, a short list of finalists bubbled to the surface.

Then the Viking stack dropped into orbit and continued snapping. Holy terror: from this vantage point, the favorites looked awful. Searches began anew. On one pass, *Orbiter* flew over a region termed Cydonia and grabbed a shot of what looked to be a human face carved into the surface. Oftentimes updated imaging arrived in the middle of a meeting, prompting everyone to suspend the current deliberations and undertake on-the-spot analyses of the fresh details before them. Contenders drifted in and out and new favorites emerged. People got antsy. Every change to a "final" landing site—or date—forced over sixty people to rework the overall mission plan.

A verdict finally materialized. Engineers locked the program and uploaded a complete ninety-day mission into *Lander 1*. If its radio link cracked after touchdown, the ship could still run solo.

Nobody reckoned that the task of choosing locations would be so prolonged, but by the same token nobody wanted to miss the big dismount— originally set for July 4. So by late June, the spacecraft's imminent arrival had beckoned eighty-plus visiting scientists to Pasadena, where they filled local hotels and apartments and diner booths and watering holes. The inflated number of attendees irritated Jim Martin, as his budget didn't account for so many.

Into preassigned JPL buildings and rooms these people seeded themselves: geology, seismology, weather. Up on the third floor of Building 264, the Biology Team's setup looked mostly like everyone else's. They got their own conference room—thirty feet on a side, maybe, with half a dozen modest workrooms branching off it. A detachment of secretaries perched just around the corner handling mail, memos, meetings. Pat Straat flicked on the lights in the room designated for Labeled Release. It wasn't much, ten by ten, but it held desks, telephones, and shelving for all the materials they'd undoubtedly pile up. "It was a nice, cozy little place," she said. Norm Horowitz commandeered his own room, Vance Oyama a third. TRW and Martin Marietta got another.

Quickly the participants fell into a regular routine. "I was usually there by seven and doing whatever I had to do," explained Straat. Everyone working the Biology Instrument gathered at nine, crowding into their main conference area. Someone had already pushed half a dozen white tables into the center, effectively creating one large one. Quickly it filled with binders, telephones, coffee mugs, ashtrays, and one of those quiescently formidable overhead projectors. A chalkboard adorned one wall. "And there were a couple people there from TRW, and we had the engineers that remained and worked with us on the experiment," Straat continued. "But mostly it was the Biology Team." Harold Klein drifted through; he liked the occasional cigar and wore two watches on his left wrist to help him track multiple time zones. They'd discuss the tasks of the day and plan operational sequences for the experiments. Straat always took a lot of notes. "I did whatever I needed to do for the rest of the day and usually I'd get home by ten, ten-thirty at night and try to get some sleep."

Despite his overarchingly pessimistic outlook on Martian life, Norm Horowitz had decided to follow through with searching for it after all. Whether or not Mars was legitimately inhabited seemed to hinge on the presence of moisture—another divisive topic. "There were enough theoretical mechanisms for getting some water on the surface," he granted, "to maintain the remote possibility—although by the time we launched Viking it was *very* remote—that there were either pools of brine, or, after snow or frost there might be enough meltwater at sunrise to sustain a population of microorganisms." Even so, conventional wisdom held the planet to be almost certainly a dry one. Consequently, Horowitz had evolved his machine to run without the need for moisture of any kind. Too much water—or too rich of nutrients—had, in his opinion, the potential to kill uniquely adapted organisms and plague his results with false negatives. He could add water or water vapor if desired, but it wasn't essential, like with the others.

Horowitz fronted a core team of three. One was a JPL man named George Hobby, who'd headed some of the Lab's original spacecraft sterility programs. "I came to JPL in 1959 and became associated with Norm after a month or two," he said. The men had been working directly together ever since '65. Hobby rose to be an essential collaborator on Horowitz's experiment and helped flesh out its design details.

And then the newest addition was a young Oklahoma native named Jerry Hubbard, on leave from the School of Biology at Georgia Tech. "A very well-trained laboratory microbiologist," embellished Horowitz, describing this fellow who'd been recommended to him by a colleague.

Lean and stylishly dressed, Hubbard wore dark, thick-rimmed glasses and droopy sideburns and torched a pack of Pall Malls a day. He kept his moustache on the bushy side, like a long-haul truck driver's. "We met in Washington in 1966 when he interviewed me over dinner," recollected

Hubbard of his first encounter with Horowitz. At the time, a taxing post-doc position at the National Institutes of Health had him scouting for new directions to head in. "After seeing Norm's sincerity and passion for Mars exploration, I stopped considering other options." But Viking wouldn't be green-lit for three more years; no payloads had been chosen and nobody was officially aboard. Joining up in '66 was one of those risk/reward deals where Hubbard had as much of a chance of becoming world famous as he did, well, of falling into a crevasse (indeed, it was on Hubbard's birthday that Wolf Vishniac had tumbled to his death).

Uninspired by more-sensible job prospects, Hubbard opted for Mars. Nimbly he dropped into the serrated quagmire of day-to-day experiment development—spending the first two years at JPL piecing together a lab mockup of Norm's vision, right alongside George Hobby.

And then prospects for flight funding improved. NASA short-listed the carbon device and all three men hustled to promote it before Viking selection committees. When they got picked, Hobby (like Straat) took point on TRW's interplay to ensure that hardware changes wouldn't compromise the experiment objectives. Hubbard ran lab tests on every little biological uncertainty raised by contractors and project officials. "I wound up with an ulcer because, hell, I couldn't delegate any authority to anybody. I did everything myself," he said. Once the dander began settling on the Biology Instrument, Hubbard temporarily berthed at Georgia Tech. Throughout all the stomach-churning turmoil he continually praised his superior. "Norm had a genius for steering us in the right direction without micromanaging. Our ideas and contributions were always noted."

The Carbon Assimilation Team. Three musketeers. Call them "H-cubed," which is what many others did.

The exhausted site group finally decided to shoot for an equatorial region known as Chryse Planitia, and *Lander 1* rewarded them with a perfect touchdown, only twenty miles from its aim point. Nineteen minutes later, Jim Martin and the thousand-odd souls who had labored on the project found out. In Pasadena it was just after 5:00 a.m. on Tuesday morning, July 20, 1976.

Sitting just off to the side of Martin's chair, fingering his goatee, Don Hearth couldn't help but feel warm satisfaction. He'd left NASA HQ in 1970 to join the Goddard Center as its assistant director. The residency lasted but three years, until Hearth managed to bounce into the director's chair at Langley. "I arrived in time for all the glory!" he smirked, from behind ever-present eyeglasses. "In a sense the circle was complete. And I had the joy of not having to go through all the development problems that Cortright had to go through!"

Twenty-five seconds after putting down, *Lander* began automatically relaying a first picture. It had to hurry; in fifteen minutes Mars's rotation would interrupt the link to its new campground for nineteen full hours. Despite his position atop the Viking pyramid, Jim Martin's glass-walled office measured as small as anyone's. Somehow he managed to fit two desks in there. One bisected the room's width, leaving just enough space to squeeze past a set of filing cabinets on the left and over to a corner desk loaded with three phones and just as many TV screens. With any luck, one of them would soon display Mars from the ground. Martin sipped coffee from a white mug with nautical flags on it. Hearth leaned in over his shoulder.

The composition of this first image had been subject to as much debate and infighting as the cogitations over where to land. Making the decision stretched back over a year and featured one snippy taunt after another. Like, "If you were transported to an unknown terrain, would you first look down at your *feet*?" So went the argument against what ended up being the inaugural Martian surface picture: close-up on *Lander 1's* footpad, in the dirt. Black and white. That's correct. No purple mountain's majesty, nor fruited plains, nor ribbon of highway below an endless skyway. Instead, the world got to see a riveted disk that had been made in Colorado. Windblown dust already covered part of it.

But the queer decision made sense from a variety of angles. If the ship did a *Mars 3* and conked out shortly after touchdown, the cameras worked so slowly that JPL might only receive one picture. If that happened, the shot ought to be of something never before seen. Like Martian soil, close-up. The goal, therefore, was to image what that riveted disk *sat on top of.* Black-and-white shots transmitted much faster than color. And there it was, flickering on heavy tube screens all over JPL. Hearth and Martin stared at it. Geologists inhaled the succulent, narrowly framed shot, resolving appreciable features down to a very fine two or three millimeters.

Three minutes later the footpad disappeared as JPL monitors refreshed and ponderously began displaying *Lander 1*'s encore—a monochromatic, three-hundred-degree panorama of the neighborhood. This one served as the explorer-contemplating-horizon shot and had been designed, once again, to quickly send home a maximal amount of information should the craft suddenly keel over and eat it. Color photography was on the schedule but still days away, and the Imaging Team had spent endless hours worrying about how to accurately reproduce whatever palette lay out there. As *Lander*'s camera panned, it caught a small grid of tinted swatches mounted prominently on the top deck. This five-by-seven card would serve as a reference for properly dialing in surface colors—whenever they finally started coming.

"Oh, isn't that sensational!" purred a cheery Tom Mutch as the panorama gradually revealed itself. He led the Imaging Team. "That's fantastic. That's just lovely." As soon as Mutch glimpsed the properly deployed meteorology arm coming into view, he heard the weather guys down the hall, cheering. Everyone stayed glued to monitors as the image built up. One large boulder after another sat in the immediate vicinity. Mutch shook his head; how easily could *Lander* have impaled itself on any one of them?

Carl Sagan lamented the absence of Viking mobility: "I keep having this fantasy that there, twenty feet away, will be this tree or something, and we can't get to it." Sagan had lots of worries. Another one involved seeing footprints all around Viking made by some nocturnal beast that never showed itself during the day. "I wanted a flashlight on Viking, but I didn't get it," he said. Tom Mutch went so far as to try and line up some kind of illumination, but the lander design couldn't handle any additional power loads.

"I don't really feel too cut up about it," explained Mutch. "Carl, by the way, also talked about putting out bait."

Viking's first complete panorama revealed a barren, windblown landscape filled with rocks and dirt. Unfortunately, that was about it. No trees, shrubbery, tennis courts, lawn ornaments, or formerly alive things laying dead on the ground. Not a one. No "squamous purple ovoids," as Sagan had once humorously postulated. And *no* canals. The place was as barren as a rock quarry and dusty as a ghost town.

It *did* appeal to some. "Rocks! That's beautiful!" crooned the emotional Thomas Mutch, who, like many, felt stunned to be upright on Mars and receiving pictures. "There's nothing like working eight years on something and then have it come across!"

Shortly after touchdown, JPL held a press conference. "This is the happiest day of my life," began Jim Martin, in a genuine moment of exultation. He wore a dark short-sleeve shirt, a string tie, and a decorative, clip-on Viking button. To his immediate right sat Don Hearth in a more businesslike coat and tie. "I've lived a long time for this," Martin rhapsodized. "And I want to thank all the people who made it possible. There must be ten thousand people in this country that deserve a part of the credit."

But souls like Jim Martin couldn't feel 100 percent happy until the machinery in their charge output more than two pictures. So now, with both "safety" photos in the bag, *Lander 1* proceeded with the shucking of its packing peanuts. In order to protect delicate spacecraft parts from the violence of earthly blastoff and Martian landing, a variety of locks, pins, and other restraints had been installed. After these fell out or released or otherwise undid, the remaining hardware could fire up. And thus came everyone's first instance of bad news: *Lander 1*'s seismometer—a highly sensitive device measuring planetary tremors—had not unlocked and never would. Tucked into their own little JPL office, an entire team of seismologists abruptly had nothing to do except hope the same tragedy would not befall *Lander 2* when it arrived a month downstream.

As promised, Mars's unstoppable rotation dutifully severed ties with *Lander 1*—affording scientists an opportunity to begin processing the reams of tractor-fed printouts already spilling over their desks and conference tables. While descending, *Lander* had sampled the air and reported back in a lengthy stream of coded digits. All that had to be translated and interpreted. Mars appeared to contain only traces of nitrogen—maybe 3 percent in total—which had never been previously detected. Argon levels measured around 2 percent, nearly mimicking earthly amounts. The most abundant material came as no surprise: carbon dioxide, at 94 percent the definitive big dog on the block of Martian atmospheric gases.

And everyone kept staring at those breathtaking pictures, continually spooling in. In them people like Tom Mutch found stateliness; Carl Sagan kept going on about what wasn't there. "There was not a hint of life—no bushes, no trees, no cactus, no giraffes, antelopes, or rabbits," mulled the Cornell astronomer. "Not a single recognizable funny-looking thing." He sounded defeated even though the pictures in question covered only one-twenty-millionth of the planet.

One day after landing, a forecast. "This is the first weather report from Mars in the history of mankind," began the chippy leader of Viking's Meteorology Team. "Light winds from the east in the late afternoon, changing to light winds from the southwest after midnight. Maximum wind was fifteen miles per hour." The guy could hardly contain his excitement. "Pressure is steady, at seven-point-seven-zero millibars!"

A day beyond that: jammed sampler arm. It couldn't move. No arm meant no dirt, which meant no testing for life. A protective cover encased the scoop itself, and that tumbled off just fine. But after the arm's initial extension, it wouldn't retract. In a glass-walled room adjacent to the press auditorium sat the single extra *Lander*, fully functioning and never to see Mars. Techs had been crawling over it all day and into the evening—running the arm back and forth, up and down, hunting for inspiration. After many hours of this their attention focused on a locking pin that was supposed to drop out during the arm's extensions and maybe didn't. By 10:00 p.m. engineers publicly fingered their leading suspect. "It has been a very busy day," commented a weary Jim Martin to reporters that night, while explaining the troubleshoot. Subsequent photography depicted a new bit of trash on the Martian surface: a certain noncompliant pin, having finally been liberated from its moorings.

Although the photographs were indeed quite remarkable, and the weather station worked like a dream, true victory would not be savored until the craft actually did something with all that dirt laying before it. This began to happen on what they termed sol 8. The Martian day times out as 2.7 percent longer than Earth's—as in, 24 hours plus 39.5 minutes. These are known as *sols*, which is the convention for metering time on the God of War. Special clocks went into use, employing traditional hours and minutes and seconds . . . only they all ran 2.7 percent more slowly.

At one o'clock in the morning (JPL time) on Wednesday, July 28, *Lander 1*'s scoop hauled back its first sample and beelined for a row of three openings situated between the cameras. This initial load went into the middle one, a large soup-can shape, which ground up the dirt and began rationing bite-size nibbles out into various chambers of the Biology Instrument. The scoop twice returned for a thermos-shaped hopper. Then a fourth trip around and into a modest funnel that led down into a gizmo for examining the dirt's chemical structure.

Below that second, thermos-shaped hopper sat a separate appliance. It was there to determine whether or not Mars contained organic compounds. That is to say, ones that are carbon-based. Now, this may come across as a pretty ho-hum, obtuse thing to study; people today are more concerned about organic broccoli than organic compounds. But the NASA bean counters would never have endured a 250 percent cost increase on a piece of equipment for mere esoterica. Like they did here.

"*I* wasn't the one who made it more expensive," piped up Klaus Biemann, principal investigator of the device. It has a long, tongue-jumbling name that requires a good deep breath prior to attempting. For everyday use the abbreviation GCMS is commonly employed—and over the course of its formative years the original $16.6 million budget had outgassed into more than $41 million. "I should say that I had nothing to do with those numbers," Biemann expanded. "And secondly, everybody agreed that the GCMS experiment is, to certain extents, the most important one."

Whoa, whoa, hang on—weren't the biology tests more significant than anything? Wasn't Viking all about detecting squiggly little microbes? Yes . . . but life on Earth is unquestionably intertwined with the presence of carbon-based organic compounds. We're loaded with them. Atoms of carbon are the most versatile, owing to their ease of bonding with other atoms. Carbon's nearest rival, silicon, is generally not considered robust enough to contain all the intricately complicated details of something like our genetic code. A philosophical Carl Sagan agreed. "We are, of course, biased toward what we're made of," he suggested at the time of Viking. "But when I try to think of other elements as a basis for life, I always wind up being what I call a 'carbon chauvinist.'"

Life as we know it requires organic substances. If they weren't on Mars, then Mars probably didn't have life, and this tangled relationship confused many. Declared Klaus Biemann, "While GCMS was not a life-detection instrument, it was very crucial for deciding whether or not the environment on Mars would be supportive of life."

Even Norm Horowitz agreed, once referring to this device as "probably the most important single instrument on the lander."

Viking's GCMS achieved results over the course of several convoluted steps. Delivered by scoop to the thermos-shaped hopper, dirt would be shredded in a glorified blender at its base. Underneath sat a funnel, leading directly into a holding cell that cached far more than the hundred milligrams destined for each test. On command, a sample would be ported into a tiny oven whose temperature could rise into the many hundreds of degrees. Heat like that essentially vaporizes organic compounds, releasing them from the soil to flow through a coiled metal pipe known as a gas chromatograph. This long spiral of thin, straw-like tubing separates molecules by type: dinky ones flow through more easily, while the chubbies get bogged down negotiating inert material filling the tube. (Think atherosclerosis, but with a purpose.) Upon exit they've been separated *and* lined up by size, making them easier to analyze.

Molecules would then reach their second waypoint on the trip—a mass spectrometer. After receiving a slight electrical charge, each molecule enjoys an arcing carnival ride through a curved chamber, while simultaneously being torn apart from whomping into each other. The resulting constituents get deflected at varying angles based on weight, and the amount of deflection is a sort of fingerprint, betraying the mass (and therefore the identity) of which one just flew by. Then, at long last, the waiting scientist becomes privy to what-all that dirt had buckled up inside it. "You can figure out what a compound is without ever having seen it before," lauded Biemann. Collectively, this piece of equipment is known as a gas chromatograph–mass spectrometer, or GCMS. They're commonplace in many vocations. Commercially produced GCMS devices are used to analyze urine and determine if the latest Ironman triathlon champ is truly gifted or whacked out on drugs. One comes in handy when testing air samples for carcinogens. And if the airport fuzz ever confiscated Grandma Fran's powder-blue Samsonite rollaway because they thought it was packed with heroin, odds are that samples from it went through a GCMS.

Today most of these instruments are the size of gas grills. Back in the early Seventies, Klaus Biemann had one in his MIT laboratory that filled a whole room. Never could Viking have lugged one of these berthas all the way to Mars; a completely new version had to be specially crafted to fit restrictive size, power, and weight specs. But oh so worth the effort because it perfectly applied to a complete unknown like Martian dirt. "It's so universal," claimed Biemann of the GCMS technique. And of course, the major problem involved not knowing what chemicals Mars had on it. "We had to expect *anything*," he stressed. "We had to expect *lots* of organics, and traces of organics, and anything in between." Biemann was quick to mention the so-called Wave of Darkening on Mars—a visual phenomenon commonly interpreted as seasonal changes across the planet's surface. Even though every probe that went by saw only mountains and craters, nobody knew for sure what might be down there.

"One had to expect that we could land in a cornfield," he hypothesized, with nary a hint of satire.

Filling *Lander 1*'s individual soil hoppers took hours. Via a series of meticulously written commands, its sampling arm had to swing about, drop down, extend, scoop, retract, rise, twist back, and dump its winnings into the different receptacles. After hitting the biology one, particles of dirt sifted through a fine colander. Then the hopper gently rotated on a small track and distributed three helpings into miniature containers that acted as measuring cups. After each one filled, a small plate closed above it. Another opened underneath, and dirt fell through tubes into each of the experiments.

Some eleven hours after the cumbersome process was initiated, word came back that at least one of the biology trials had commenced. It was Vance Oyama's. Standing by Jim Martin with hands on hips, a lanky Biemann—resplendent in a striped sport coat with a string tie—watched patiently through tortoiseshell glasses for one small number to appear on a telemetry screen and confirm that his own baby had a meal coming. He tried to keep his mind open for whatever the GCMS might tell them about Martian soil. "I shouldn't say that we didn't expect anything, because that means we expected nothing," he said. "What we *expected* to find is the organic stuff that comes in through meteorites, which are known to come on the surface of Mars all the time." Meteorites on Earth contain varying amounts of organics, which infuse the surrounding soil. Everyone figured the same of Mars.

The number on his screen didn't light up. Forty-one million bucks in, and no dirt.

This part was supposed to be about the easiest in the whole process. The scoop had scooped and most certainly had pivoted around and at least stopped above Biemann's hopper. If not, the lander would've thrown a No-Go error back at ground control. But everything seemed to be chugging along just fine. The chemical-analysis experiment had gotten its own sample; no problem there. One photo came back showing what appeared to be spilled dirt around the base of the GCMS hopper. Or had it gusted in from the wind? Hoppers one and three got fed, but not the second? An important aspect of future Mars machines would no doubt be the ability to *take pictures of the dirt going in.*

Biemann's team stood down. "And so we didn't do the grinding and filling in the oven because we thought, next time around we'll get a sample." *Lander's* programming meant the opportunity wouldn't come for days.

Although many categorized his machine as part of the biology gear, Klaus Biemann pointed out a fundamental difference between the two. "The data it produces had to be the same thing on Mars as on Earth," he said of a GCMS. "Because it's just physics. But biology is something completely different. You could not assume that biology on Mars is the same as on Earth." Obviously, no one knew what Martian biology consisted of, if it even existed at all. This put Levin and Horowitz and Oyama into the odd position of looking for something that might not exist in the first place.

"That's what the biologists of course realized," noted Biemann of the conundrum. "They can only test terrestrial biology on Mars—not *Martian* biology."

Labeled Release was now underway too, and Levin thought he had his bases covered. Well, what if something on Mars exhaled carbon monoxide, or methane, or even poisonous hydrogen cyanide? "It doesn't matter," he asserted. "*Any* carbon gas produced from the culture is going to use some of the radioactive carbon, and it will be radioactive."

To the cause of locating active Martian life, Vance Oyama had contributed a broad-ranging investigation predicated on the fact that organisms are constantly modifying the gaseous environment around them. For example, human breathing alters the relative amounts of oxygen, carbon dioxide, and other gases—and in a closed space this can be analyzed for signs of metabolic activity. Oyama called his experiment Gas Exchange, or GEX, and the cubic centimeter of dirt falling into its single test chamber didn't hit bottom; a perforated stainless-steel tray held it in suspension. Once the chamber sealed, a largely inert mix of prepared gases flowed in to create a known and controlled atmosphere. Oyama's next move depended on how he wished to run the trial. Things could be left totally as-is to simply monitor what happened. He could soak the dirt with measured amounts of his

29. Opinions varied on Vance Oyama—pictured here at Ames Lab. Offered GEX teammate Fritz Woeller: "Because of his warm personality and his cheerful ways, his group really was very loyal to him." Compare with Josh Lederberg: "We have really felt sometimes that we should just grab him by the coattails and make him sit down." Courtesy NASA/Ames.

own special nutrient. Or a teensy valve could be opened just a hair, allowing nutrient to flow in underneath the sample without actually touching it. On this first go-round Oyama chose the latter, knowing that over time the womblike warmth of *Lander*'s belly would lead to wispy swirls of water vapor humidifying his chamber. Every Viking biologist crafted his own nutrient, and Oyama's team called theirs M4. It contained water, plus a tour de force of organic compounds and other pepperings.

GEX's lengthy incubations sought to differentiate between chemical and biological reactions. During a solid twenty-day fermentation, the chamber's entire headspace would periodically be swept through a gas chromatograph to hunt for twelve specific culprits, like nitrogen or methane or even inert neon, which wasn't expected to be present on Mars at all. (M4 contained neon as a kind of marker to confirm the nutrient's presence in the sampling chamber.)

If their results formed any kind of pattern, explained Fritz Woeller, "one would have tried to match that fingerprint with terrestrial specimens" garnered from their own painstakingly assembled reference catalog of bacteria and fungi and algae and protozoa and what have you. Afterward, pumped-in helium would clear out any last remnants of the original environment. Then a new bath of gas and liquid could flow in to commune with the *existing* dirt sample. And this is where things would really get interesting. Over subsequent cycles, how might the levels of those twelve gases fluctuate? If they changed significantly or eventually increased—well then, Oyama's thinking held that microbes had taken a liking to the nutrient and begun using it. But if the activity folded, dollars to doughnuts it was chemistry.

One key word here is *eventually*. Compared to Levin's Geiger counter, Oyama's detection method was approximately one thousand times less sensitive. The gas changes needed time to passively amass at high enough levels for his gadgetry to detect. Useable results weren't expected for at least seventy-two numbing hours after start-up. It could turn into a marathon; some Antarctic soils contained such low microbial populations that two hundred days flew past before the gases rose to measurable amounts. "Bacteria cultures develop on their own schedules," reminded Woeller. A tranquil Vance Oyama had arrived in Pasadena with sufficient mental resilience to hang on for weeks or even months to see what his crystal ball ultimately whispered.

He didn't have to wait long. Less than three hours into the first run, Oyama's special buddy reported 130 times as much oxygen filing through, compared to initial levels. And the Biology Instrument appeared to be working great.

"That was kind of funny," noted Klaus Biemann of the initial results. "Such a large amount of oxygen being evolved. It really looked like, certainly *not* like terrestrial biology." One day later, oxygen levels in the chamber had risen by only 30 percent. The reaction—or whatever term made sense—had clearly leveled off, with most of the hoopla occurring almost immediately after the soil was humidified with Oyama's M4-flavored soup. He left it there, simmering. Next door, the Labeled Release equipment qui-

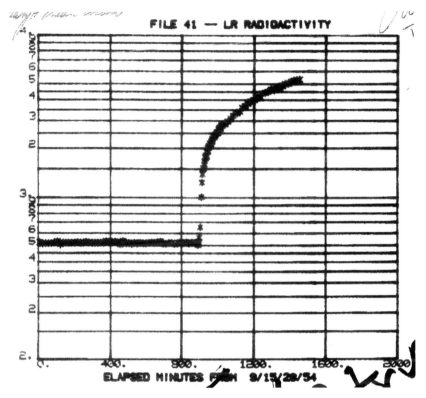

FILE 41 — LR RADIOACTIVITY

ELAPSED MINUTES FROM 9/15/22/54

30. LR's first report takes on a distinctly Alpinian shape. Courtesy Gil Levin.

etly carried on—its own sample moist with Straat's recipe of seven simple sugars and amino acids. The apparatus collected readings every four minutes for the first two hours. After that, the interval dropped to sixteen minutes per. LR relayed its data to *Lander 1*'s computer, which assembled the first nine hours of results and beamed them up to *Orbiter 1* when it came over the horizon. Everything then streamed home.

The signals hit a giant radio dish on Earth and whizzed quickly into JPL over dedicated trunk lines. As late afternoon changed to early evening, word came that the jumble of data was ready for access on the computer network. "We hadn't even thought of eating," remembered Levin of their vigil. "We were watching like a hawk."

After a quarter century of development stretching back to that red-letter day on the beach, Gulliver was finally producing.

Straat narrated what happened next. "I sat down at the console and manipulated the program and the printout came." It depicted a simple graph, with cumulative minutes extending along the bottom from left to right. Units up the vertical axis indicated a "counting rate"—basically, the amount of activity sensed by LR's Geiger counter. Owing to natural background radiation, plus *Lander*'s own power generators, a baseline signal measured about five hundred counts per minute.

Straat looked across the page. A stream of blips defined a curve extending rapidly past one thousand, then two, on up through three-four-five thousand counts per minute. Something up there inside that dinky sampling chamber was going to town on her recipe.

The rate kept climbing. Straat hit the PRINT button.

Levin sent someone for champagne.

Straat hit the PRINT button *again.*

19. Too Much Too Soon

It looks more like chemistry than biology. Because it would have
to be a large number of microorganisms that right away jumped on
that nutrient and immediately got wild about it.

—Klaus Biemann, putting forth a chemist's
perspective on the LR result

"I couldn't believe it when I saw that. I just couldn't believe it," remembered Straat of the ascending results. "It was *very* typical of a terrestrial life response."

She turned to Levin and declared, "This is life!"

"We'd better wait for the control."

"I *know* life when I see it," she sassed back. "I've done it thousands of times!"

Levin, the would-be sanitation engineer, stared at his colleague as implications began splashing on his brain like giant raindrops. Then—for reasons he still cannot fully explain—Gil Levin at that moment began mentally replaying the balcony scene from *West Side Story* in his head. *It all began tonight*, he mused, as Bernstein's rangy melodies wafted over him from an orchestra that seemed about eight inches off the tips of his shoes. *The world is wild and bright . . . going mad . . . shooting sparks into space.*

Levin grabbed the printout. In half-cursive script he penned "Tonight!" across the top, adding the date and time: "July 30, 1976 7:30 p.m. PDT SOL 10." Then it went around the room for everyone to sign. "When we saw that curve go up, we all flipped," he continued. "We knew we had a sample. We knew we had a nutrient injection. And we knew something was happening there."

What Straat and Levin really wanted to do next was run the control: blast a dirt sample with scorching temperatures, then douse it in nutrient. High heat would kill microbes and therefore the reaction. But it couldn't happen for over two weeks. This first gestation had long been preprogrammed to run automatically in case the radio link died after landing. For another thirteen agonizing days, it would fly on autopilot. All right, *then* the control? No—housekeeping. "You gotta clean up the instrument," Straat indicated regarding the regimen between cycles. Heat would circulate through all of LR's pipes and valves, followed by a purging of any built-up gases. "Then you've got to wait till everybody's ready to go again, and distribute the soil samples into the next test cell."

The following day Gil Levin planned to join a few others onstage in JPL's von Karman Auditorium for yet another press conference. Throughout Viking's launch, cruise, and landing, the Lab held them with clockwork regularity. But today's represented the first since any biology results had come down—the one where Harold Klein promised to describe "important, unique, and exciting things" transpiring on the surface of Mars.

One hour before the start time, nobody had fully agreed on what the hell they were going to say to the damn reporters. GEX activity had belly flopped. The LR graph looked downright phallic. Klaus Biemann and a few GCMS people joined a last-minute improvised gathering of the biologists. Biemann's colleague John Oro also sensed chemistry behind Oyama's blistering oxygen production. It was just too quick, he argued. Oro instead proposed to lay blame on a family of compounds known as peroxides. They carry surplus oxygen atoms, promiscuously giving them up at any opportunity. Falling into this category is the household cleaning agent hydrogen peroxide. It's based on normal water, but every molecule of H_2O contains one extra O—making the stuff unstable and reactive, like Dennis Rodman. Here Oro theorized that a peroxide blend in the bone-dry Martian soil had reacted with GEX's water vapor to produce what they'd all seen. Oyama agreed; no Earth soil had ever given off oxygen like that.

John Oro then took an eyebrow-raising step. "He made each of us sign a written agreement that it was his idea," claimed Levin of the peroxide business. "And that we would not publish it before him." Everyone raced over to von Karman.

Flanked by Jim Martin, the presenters took their chairs up front, Levin flaunting a silken disco shirt with his ID badge clipped just below the collar. He looked entirely at ease. Approaching the podium, a slightly disheveled Harold Klein donned half-moon reading glasses that sat high on his nose. "We believe there is something in the surface," he soberly began. "Some chemical or physical entity, which is affording the surface material a great deal of activity and may in fact mimic—let me emphasize that, *mimic*—in some respects, biological activity."

What happened next, Levin swore up and down, is that Jim Martin elbowed him and said in a low, guarded voice, "God dammit Gil, tell them you discovered life."

Klein now gestured at the large projection screen to his left. On it, a handwritten black-and-white graph depicted various peaks rising like impossibly tall inverted *V*s. Each had a caption: KRYPTON, OXYGEN, CARBON DIOXIDE. Oxygen towered like Everest. "In one of our experiments, the Gas Exchange," he elaborated, with measured prudence, "we believe that we have at least preliminary evidence for a very active surface material." One reporter wanted to know if that indicated photosynthesis. Klein told him no; photosynthesis requires light and GEX didn't have any. Horowitz's experiment did use light, but it was still running.

Next Klein turned his attention to Labeled Release. Oyama's graph disappeared from the projection screen, replaced with a new one depicting the steep uphill grade reported by LR's Geiger counter. "In the Labeled Release experiment, the preliminary data indicate that we are evolving a fairly high level of radioactivity." With the suggestion that things looked "very much like a biological signal," Klein cautioned that these results "must be viewed very, very carefully." Patience, people. They were less than twenty-four hours into the machine's very first cycle. It still needed many more days to complete. All-important control tests wouldn't run until mid-August.

"I know it's impossible not to ask," surmised the Biology Team leader as he perused the jungle of faces and lenses pointed at him. Film whirred through cameras. "At present, there's no way you can rule out the data as being due to biology." Klein leaned his jowly face in toward the microphone; a large ring on his right pinky knocked against the podium. "However, let me say: if it IS a biological response, IF it is, then it's a stronger response than we have seen with fairly rich terrestrial soils." Microbes typically begin in low gear, he emphasized. Only after they've gotten used to new food and then multiplied would the rate of response increase like it had on Mars.

Others took their turns to offer a word or two and field questions. Now Gil Levin approached the dark, wood-grained podium; he spoke last. "They told me to be very brief and not say anything," he later recalled about his preconference directives. To the reporters and assembled crowd Levin flatly asserted that chemistry failed to explain his results. If the activity inside LR was chemical, then why were they even getting a *curve*? Wouldn't the response just catapult straight up in the air and then die abruptly when all the nutrient was gone?

Levin squared himself. "The data we have are consistent with the possibility of life. But it is not assured."

Naturally, these were profound things for learned, scholarly professionals to be stating in public—not to mention on the record. Reporters blitzed Klein as soon as the press conference ended. If Oyama's imposing oxygen peak wasn't plant-like, then maybe it resembled something in the animal kingdom? Klein shook his head. Animals don't release oxygen. Even so, he ventured, the levels rose too quickly. What happened inside GEX really struck the group as chemistry: after starting with a bang, it promptly waned.

The ensuing meetings precipitated unavoidably copious speculation and inferences about their results to date: rehashing possibilities, gamely ferreting out potential weak spots in any argument. JPL meeting rooms commonly had a U-shaped table arrangement bracketing a central speaker's table, which itself was accessorized with two side-by-side overhead projectors. People would take turns jabbering away, flipping through reams of overheads thick with shmeer from index-finger erasures and revisions and heat—advancing hypotheses, filling chalkboards with notes about chemical reactions and possible hardware flaws. What was the data *not* telling them?

Many felt that oxidants, as with GEX, also resided at the core of Levin's results. Vance Oyama himself certainly leaned that way. Levin disagreed. Throughout subsequent gatherings, he continually pointed to stacks of just-received *Lander 1* printouts. After two days LR had eclipsed 8,500 counts a minute. Maybe it was slowing. Its activity leveled off a day later, around 10,000. But it did continue. Why, Levin argued, would chemistry slow down midreaction? Wouldn't this hypothetical oxidation continue unabated until every last atom of radioactive carbon had been spent? He and Straat calcu-

31. Jerry Hubbard (left) votes on a point of order by holding the "V" sign above his head. To the right of him are Pat Straat, Gil Levin, and Harold Klein (with his back to the camera). Past Klein is Norm Horowitz with upturned binder, clearly enjoying this lighter moment. Photo by and courtesy of Hans-Peter Biemann.

lated that if this happened, the total would hit 257,000 counts. Their low value, contended Levin, implied that Martian entities had chosen to gobble just *part* of LR's nutrient recipe. It made logical sense, as microbes are far more selective on any given day than plain old chemicals. Chemistry didn't care. That idea resonated with Carl Sagan, who followed the biology proceedings with great interest. "Could it instead be a finicky organism?" he speculated of LR's mystery curve, all kidding aside. "One that is fussy about its food?"

Harold Klein finally brought the exchange to a close by reminding everyone of what they'd all previously agreed on: before unconditionally notifying the world that life existed on Mars, the group needed to eliminate every single other possibility from the running. They still didn't have results from Horowitz. Or the GCMS. Nobody had run any controls. It was prehistorically early to be forming these all-or-nothing conclusions.

Everyone got back to work; *Lander 1* expelling fountains of data about everything from magnetic properties to weather. Roomfuls of people were studying how radio waves changed when traveling through Mars's atmosphere. Entire walls were filling with picture mosaics assembled from *Orbiter 1*. And Viking 2? Weeks out, still.

Straat and Oyama parsed through options for varying their upcoming experiment protocols. A few days remained until LR's first trial ended. The still-waiting Horowitz never received in-progress results of any sort from Carbon Assimilation. A single run generated two numerical values, not graphs, and that was it. As dirt rested in the first of his three sample chambers, a preparation of radioactive carbon gases drifted in through a tiny valve. His lamp switched on. If any sort of plant-like activity was occurring in the soil, it'd theoretically soak up the new gases and use them to flourish.

Following this otherwise idle period of days—"the incubation"—heating elements warmed the chamber to nearly 250 degrees Fahrenheit, driving out any surplus gas. Next, the bake cycle: 1,175 degrees, enough to break down most of the soil. Vaporized material drifted along a curving gold pipe, which, similar to Biemann's chromatograph tube, held back certain substances while allowing others through. A filter of sorts. Here, plump organics caught in the pipe and couldn't move, while unimpeded compounds flitted on past into a detector—which in turn coughed out a number. Horowitz named this value Peak One. The figure had nothing to do with the ultimate question of life, though it did speak to the soil's propensity to incorporate carbon gases.

After five total days of percolation, the lander sent home its Peak One and Horowitz noted a value of some sixty-seven thousand—employing a curious unit of measure known as disintegrations per minute that was completely different from the units on LR. Reporters yawned. Right then and there, all that number told anyone was that the thing seemed to be working. Horowitz got some food and cleaned his glasses. In three days he'd get the second value and definitively (in his mind, anyway) answer everyone's Big Question.

It was all going so fast—already they'd been on Mars for over a week. Horowitz had a beach condo not too far away in Orange County. He spent the weekends there with his wife, Pearl, in a relief-valve ritual that would persist through most of the mission. Jerry Hubbard got in lots of tennis with a guy from the surface sampling team. Everyone had their own ways of briefly disengaging, which helped to mitigate the close-quarters, horn-locking atmosphere of increasingly slanted rhetoric and hairsplitting.

"Vance and I argued like cats and dogs, but it was a good scientific argument," remembered Jerry Hubbard. "He would do some calculations, you know, and come up with something brilliant, and then the next day he would get stuck on some idea." One common dispute centered on how much water to use during their tests. Norm Horowitz recurrently advocated that any present-day Martian life must undoubtedly favor icy-dry conditions. Those marsh-like tropics Oyama had inside GEX? Wrong approach, he insisted.

"A man doesn't respire much in bed, and Martian microbes won't respire much either, unless we perturb them." So countered the biochemist from Ames Lab. "The more they get of what they want, the more there will be to measure." Horowitz mocked the high nutrient levels in GEX. "Oyama's Pharmacy," he called them. Hubbard thought similarly of the brew, saying, "I didn't agree with the idea of having so many rich goodies in there." And without prompting, Pat Straat joined in: "*So many* compounds in his nutrient. How do you interpret anything?" Now here came Fritz Woeller to prop up the defensive backfield: "I do not see why one would question the complexity of nutrients, as long as the situation was entirely speculative." Then someone would realize Levin hadn't been targeted for a while, and he'd come under attack about peroxides, or counting rates, or the warmth of his test cells. "Gil doused the soil with liquid," alleged Hubbard, "which Norm would say, If there were organisms there, they would'a died from shock." *Wasn't the simplest explanation*, Levin fought back, *that of biology?* Such was the air above the meeting tables in JPL Building 264.

For certain, it wasn't because Gerry Soffen hadn't been trying like crazy. "Gerry was perhaps the most sociable person I have known," related Gil Levin of the man who—despite overseeing the dozens of Viking scientists and coordinating their every activity, labored extra hard to forge just his biologists into a cohesive and merry ol' troupe. "He tried his best to make a team out of it. He would wine us and dine us and have us to his house and visit us late at night and just, everything possible to weld us together. Never worked."

Come August 4 they tried filling the GCMS hopper once more and *Lander 1* kicked back a No-Go. "So we were stuck again," mused Klaus Biemann. Something had bobbled with the sampler arm. It retracted from the ground with dirt in hand, rose as expected, but halted before executing its final moves. Metal-on-metal binding? Stage fright? Jim Martin dispatched fifty drones to scour the problem raw.

"I'm on the non-receiving end of the system," Biemann said at the time.

As any good scientist would, he started thinking about the process—breaking it down into quantifiable steps. The hopper's official capacity was 1.5 grams. Viking's "level-full" indicator came on only when at least that much soil resided in it.

"But we *need* only a hundred milligrams," contended Biemann to his group. So even if the hopper filled just halfway, they'd *still* have three-quarters of a gram in there. Right? "Plenty," he announced. "So let's just take the chance, and go through the process." To some his idea seemed irresponsible because the GCMS had but three single-use ovens in total, and the number-three one didn't heat (a routine test during the outbound trip discovered this).

Over the next two days, Biemann reevaluated his level of confidence. He gave the nod. One sol after that the arm ran again, though with a modified protocol intended to minimize strain on the hardware. Finally, Klaus Biemann was on the field and moving.

It wouldn't be the last morsel of drama in a process that was superficially mundane, and it certainly hadn't been the first. Ten dreadfully short months before launch, Biemann's assistant had been roosting at Martin Marietta with a flight-spec GCMS. Every trial output its results in the same way: graphs. The first is called a gas chromatogram, depicting increasing molecular weight along the bottom, with relative abundance up the vertical axis. The molecular weight of something is the weight of one of its molecules, and pros like Biemann can rattle the figures off even under duress: ammonia is seventeen grams per mole, for example. Natural gas? That's sixteen. In this fashion, the plot of some complex substance resembles a hill workout on one of those fitness-center treadmills: rollercoastering up and down in irregular Grand Teton peaks. And then the second graph, a mass spectrum, was actually hundreds of individual graphs—each a frozen-in-time snapshot taken every few moments, displaying in-depth characteristics of whichever molecule happened to be emerging from the gas chromatograph at that particular instant.

One day Biemann was auditing graphs from a recent trial and noticed something out of place. "There were some additional peaks which didn't belong to the test mixture." Peaks calling out specific organic compounds that Biemann knew his sample didn't contain. For some reason his supposedly infallible contraption was reporting phantoms that weren't there. Or were they?

A GCMS tells you exactly what's inside it . . .

The befuddling anomaly might have thrown a junior man, but dispersing the question marks came down to a simple matter of analyzing what those extra humps consisted of—and then drawing logical conclusions. "It didn't take long," claimed Biemann, "because that's what we always do every day. Figure out what we are looking at!"

Here, what they were looking at was something called a hydrocarbon. Viking's GCMS used a bottle of pressurized hydrogen to "push" hot vapors from each oven into the separation tube of the gas chromatograph. And their testing sample had reacted with that hydrogen to produce what showed up on the graph. But nothing in *that* sample . . . would react with hydrogen like *that . . . unless.* Biemann snapped his fingers: unless in the presence of a *catalyst.* He got in touch with the manufacturer, Litton, and recommended they have a close look at the working parts.

See, Biemann's device needed to macerate samples, coffee-grinder style, so they'd fit in the ovens. The equipment was made of top-quality carbon steel, hard and strong. When the grinder went to work, gnashing teeth chipped off microscopic crumbs of the grinder's own self, which fell into the test soil. This prompted a love connection between the soil and the already-present hydrogen. Chemistry took over and *alakazam*—a reaction that wouldn't have happened without carbon steel flakes.

Lamented one GCMS teammate, "What screws us up isn't the complex scientific problems, but the high-school problems like the grinder."

Alternatively, Klaus Biemann celebrated the objectivity of his equipment. "A mass spectrometer detects anything that is there, regardless!"

Everyone scrambled to upgrade. Litton further hardened the steel in the grinding mechanism, while Biemann isolated hydrogen from the ovens—electing to use carbon dioxide instead. He specified a "marked" version of it, carbon-13, which has an extra neutron. This way, even if something reacted with his new push gas, it would leap out at him on the final graphs. That meant two flavors of push: carbon-13 dioxide to move compounds through the oven, until hydrogen could take over and drive his vaporized material through the gas chromatograph. All of a sudden they needed lots of carbon-13 dioxide, which isn't exactly sitting on the shelf at Walgreens. Only about 1 percent of all carbon is like this in nature. With rapidity Biemann directed his assistants to purchase every molecule they could find.

"In fact," he laughed, "we had to buy the world's supply of carbon-13 dioxide. Fully!"

Resolution in hand, the change propagated through two flight GCMS units and a spare at Litton in Woodland Hills, California. Everything arrived in Florida less than three months before launch.

The GCMS fulfilled all of Biemann's expectations. It worked as advertised. "I was completely satisfied," he said.

Sol 16 commenced with a generous chicken soup breakfast for Gas Exchange. Mild-mannered Vance Oyama took a lot of ribbing about his experiment, along with outright denunciations and lampooning ("chicken soup" was one of the typical derogations of his nutrient mix). But GEX had been created with the best of intentions and within the most professionally academic of environments. Up in the penthouse of its Life Sciences Building, Ames Lab maintained an entire Life Detection Systems Branch—created by Oyama himself, replete with staff and budget and neoretro letterhead. Its ten rooms supported a robust habitat dedicated solely to the question that Viking sought to resolve.

Speaking directly about Vance Oyama, Josh Lederberg counterweighted the occasional upbraidings with solid praise: "He has been very dogged about his instrument. The way he has pursued the working of his instrument is really admirable."

During GEX's evolution, the team had gone full bore. "Weekends did not matter, and overtime pay was an unknown concept," related Fritz Woeller. One of his dicier jobs had been to evaluate any impact of the landers' exhaust gases on their results. "The work had typical microbiological and chemical character, and it was an attempt to simulate the possible conditions on Mars."

Since Viking's most recent press conference, nary a whiff of oxygen had come from GEX. Oyama retained his original sample and this time enough nutrient mix went in to drench the soil. Any oxygen? None. If germy Martian bugs filled his little chamber, reasoned Oyama, they would've leaped

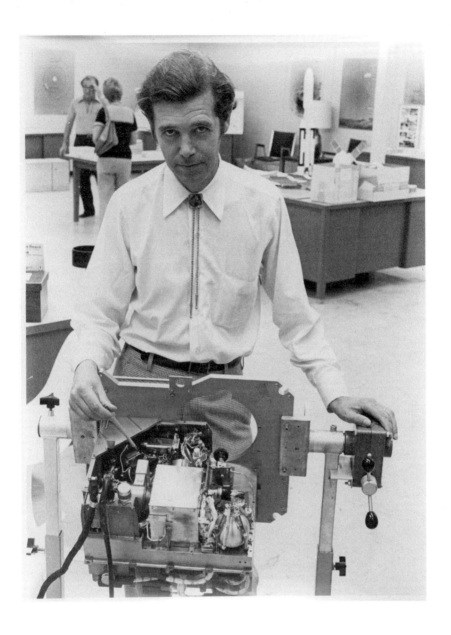

32. Klaus Biemann gestures to a component on the flight-spare GCMS, bolted to a mobile cart. "The GCMSs were mounted this way so that they could be moved around safely, rather than being carried by people and perhaps dropped." Photo by and courtesy of Hans-Peter Biemann.

all over the goods and created a new mountain range on the graphs. But he wasn't getting much of anything, and that suggested chemistry.

On the same day that GEX got its new breakfast, what remained in Horowitz's golden filter-pipe endured a second baking. Twelve hundred vicious degrees worth of indifferent heat liberated any radioactive carbon from the organic material trapped therein. The freed carbon merged with a preexisting mix of two simple compounds in the pipe. This generated carbon dioxide, which drifted through another detector and thereby gave Horowitz Peak Two—the number everyone cared about. The number that would or would not indicate a lifelike presence.

Far ahead of time, JPL had notified Horowitz's team of the need to wait approximately three sols between the determinations of Peak One and Two. The interval would factor out stray radiation from the lander's power source, they said. In the interim, H-cubed caught up on paperwork and attended more meetings. Something somewhere was always going on. For George Hobby, the Viking atmosphere amounted to a surreal experience. "When I was twelve years old I was a science fiction buff and I wished that I would live long enough to see a picture of the Martian surface. I got my wish at the age of fifty-seven," he cooed, over three and a half decades after Viking landed. "Fulfillment of that wish was my life's miracle. I never expected to be part of the program that took the picture!"

Peak Two wasn't a totally clean measurement because the value inevitably contained a fractional presence of the original carbon-based gases—which hadn't ever managed to combine with anything at all. "It was not a perfect separation," acknowledged Jerry Hubbard. "This carryover from a large Peak One makes it hard to interpret the results. But anyway, we did the best we could." They applied a lot of math to compensate.

Many lab trials over the years had established a value of one hundred disintegrations per minute as the Peak Two threshold. Above it, the carbon assimilators likely had something. *Well above* one hundred indicated a strong positive. And below? Practically no chance of any little critters scurrying around.

Since Norm Horowitz had pooh-poohed the likelihood of Martian life, he certainly didn't expect much of a Peak Two as his attention focused on a TRW runner bringing over tall stacks of paper, fresh off the printer. The guy dropped his bundle and left.

Hubbard crowded in as licked fingers turned pages. *No . . . no . . . wait—there it is*: 842, plus or minus 29.

Within the intracranial recesses of Norman Horowitz's noggin the mental tumblers slowly ticked into place, as a volley of imaginary alarm bells klanged in deafening succession. He dropped into a chair as his jaw fell.

20. Scientific Charity

I accepted these conditions, but I resent them. If there was a Viking
3, I wouldn't agree to go again under these circumstances.

—Norm Horowitz, discussing interdependencies between the
three biology experiments (and experimenters)

If anyone didn't appreciate the position he'd been shoved into, it had to be
sixty-one-year-old Norman Harold Horowitz, Pittsburgh native, husband
and father, one of three scientist brothers. Incessantly he'd espoused the
idea that any species of any kind had a ridiculously, we're talkin' *insanely*
low chance of existing on Mars. Now he occupied an uncomfortably ugly,
government-contracted JPL chair. An untold number of asses had sat in
it before his—none of which had likely been facing a turning point in its
career, like Norm's. Oh, to be home with his record collection, spinning
Bach inventions and Mozart sonatas and then sitting down at the family piano to bang them out himself. Or to be once again hiking Yosemite with the kiddos—right after checking on his prized rose bushes. Today
there would be none of that. Gradually, internally, Horowitz began coming to terms with the results of an experiment that he had essentially contended was not necessary.

"There's a possibility that it is biological," spilled Harold Klein at the latest press conference, about Carbon Assimilation's humdinger.

Paralleling Straat and Levin, Horowitz's three-man band had long ago
processed a wide variety of terra firma in order to build up their own reference library. By these calculations, a mere thousand cells would generate
values on par with what they'd just seen. Most samples gave considerably
higher responses than 842. Even one of those lightly inhabited Antarctic

soils tested stronger—though not by much, and this resemblance tended to underscore the instrument's accuracy. Everyone said the dry Antarctic valleys most resembled Mars, and now here came Norm Horowitz with his magic number to prove them right. In some ways he felt devastated.

"I want to emphasize that we have not discovered life on Mars—*not*. However, the data point we have is conceivably of biological origin." Lightly sweaty, Norm Horowitz stood behind von Karman's podium in a short-sleeved button-down with no undershirt, at a press conference the very same day his number came up. Glasses? Clean. Hair? Gray and receding. His weight shifted between tumbledown loafers. "But . . . the biological explanation is only one of a number of alternative explanations that have to be excluded. We hope by the end of this mission to have excluded all but one."

He was hedging. Behold the power of a single three-digit integer: with it alone, one man had been rudely displaced from his personal comfort bubble. Overhead studio lights blared down on him, the exposed Broadway performer, winging it live without a net. In times like these Horowitz took direction from a favorite saying of his: Be sincere, be brief, and be seated. But this was unlike any situation he'd ever encountered. Horowitz stared out over the crowd and as he spoke time itself seemed to gear down into a smeary, slow-motion blur. He saw the people and the reporters and the events before him, he saw them all: photons of light transporting his gesticulating image at 50 percent speed into an undulating sea of heavy glass camera lenses. Flashbulbs bobbing and popping; film gates opening, untold silver particles industriously exciting, burning themselves into plastic rectangles of emulsion. People languidly nodding as spinning spools of tape laid down his every extemporaneous word.

Finally Horowitz shook it off like a dog and regained his sense of real time. "If this were normal science we wouldn't even *be* here," he barked. "You wouldn't even know what was going on, and at the end of that time we would come out and tell you the answer. Having to work in a fishbowl like this is an experience that none of us is used to."

After the press conference ended, Horowitz cloomped off to his isolate workroom and pondered the upcoming GCMS procedure. Distracted and puttering, he browsed the increasing mounds of paper and reports and memos. Jerry Hubbard stood over him like divine counsel. The corner man.

33. Norm Horowitz combs through data with Jerry Hubbard, who stands at left in his groovy white belt. The chalkboard depicts a statistical analysis of Peak Two data. "We need to repeat the runs with fresh samples!" Horowitz was saying. Photo by Ron Gilje, courtesy of Jerry Hubbard.

Once Horowitz had opined to a reporter that Klaus Biemann's instrument and his own were the only ones necessary to settle the question of life on Mars. At that exact moment it was 50 percent assured.

Harold Klein focused the next Biology Team meeting on potential interpretations of the unexpected high score. What all could it be? What makes sense and what doesn't? Collectively the group tallied a dozen prospects that merited further consideration—from plugged valves to a busted radiation detector. A faulty lightbulb filter topped the list. Without it, the instrument could well be generating its own positive results.

Viking engineers tackled every conceivable equipment anomaly and found not a single thing wrong with Horowitz's machine. The lightbulb filter wasn't broken after all. No pipes had clogged. The radiation sensor appeared to be working normally. But several entries on the list had to do with oxides, and chasing down the intricate mechanics of a faraway chemical reaction would not be as simple as running hardware checks. For certain, hydrogen peroxide remained a viable culprit. So did iron oxide—the chief reason Mars looked red. Grouchily, Horowitz downed another cup of coffee. So much for easy troubleshooting!

Still on the first cycle, LR now automatically received a second helping of its own nutrient. Straat and Levin reacted with mute surprise when the counting rate, which had been hovering around ten thousand, briefly increased—then fell to a steady eight thousand. The anomalous rise proved to be a short-lived jump in the test chamber's pressure. All right, but what about that drop to a lower plateau?

Again: meetings. Perhaps Martian bacteria weren't multiplying, but the number of Viking gatherings, assemblies, talks, conferences, and symposia certainly had. Days that'd been clocking fourteen and sixteen hours went up to twenty, and the lack of sleep didn't help anyone's mood. Horowitz came at Levin with resounding theories of how oxidants neatly explained LR's recent behavior. If microbes dwelled inside that chamber, he maintained, the activity curve should have *resumed* after the second injection. Countered Levin, *Maybe everything in there is dead?*

Patricia Straat had invested a good chunk of a week in hovering over LR's counting rate. But after thirteen sols the programming automatically terminated her first at-bat and the cleaning cycle followed. While waiting, she and Levin contemplated what they'd been itching to do ever since that first arching climb.

"In order to confirm the positive response, that it *wasn't* a false positive," she laid out, "we had to run the heat control. And demonstrate that heat destroyed the positive response." They'd get to it—just as soon as LR came out of the wash.

Viking's heralded GCMS finally got down to business. Its sampling "ovens" were nothing more than miniature ceramic kilns, just over three-quarters of an inch long by less than eight-hundredths of an inch in diameter. And people thought the Easy-Bake Oven was dinky. A heating wire spiraled around the exterior of each. In one second an oven could hit 122 degrees Fahrenheit. From there the options rose to 392, then 662—finally topping out at 932, which needed only eight seconds. These values may sound random but the device had been created in a metric world and nominally used Celsius.

For his opening move Biemann kindled the oven to 392, figuring he'd baby-walk through the process and examine what happened after just that little first step. Depending on which way he wanted to run it, a complete trial took between forty and sixty minutes from start to finish. Except . . . no results would be in transit until the next time *Orbiter 1* crossed over to begin a forty-five-minute minute chitchat period. Media raced up while new commands fell. Now laden with data and telemetry and weather reports and even more pictures, *Orbiter 1* itself waited until the Earth rotated one of NASA's larger antenna dishes into alignment. Then a vomitous belch sent everything on a nineteen-minute ride at the pace of light, splashing down in the dish for relay into JPL and a summary parceling out. Meteorology got temperature and wind; engineering got valve positions. The world saw more photos. And Biemann got all his raw numbers. "We could print the numerical data on a line printer," he described, "but that of course was only for some very, very rudimentary look." To really be useful, the information needed specialized decoding and processing. The custom program for that ran flawlessly on his MIT mainframe sitting three thousand miles back east. Somewhere along the way, people had been hired to rewrite the code so it'd also run on JPL's computers. "But they never got that done right," criticized Biemann.

What happened next might be lampooned in today's near-instant world of high-speed web traffic. Inside JPL, the received data spooled onto a new reel of magnetic tape that someone drove out to the Los Angeles Airport and, by prearrangement, personally handed to a pilot on the next commercial flight to Boston. As the plane approached its destination, Biemann would grab one of the phones near his loaner desk and call MIT: "Send somebody in my lab to go out to the airport." And a guy on campus would race down Ames Street, pick up Memorial Drive, then scream east all the way to Logan Airport and grab the tape directly from the pilot. From there it was hightailin' back to the Chemistry Department and sessions on their mainframe to generate useable figures. The results were then scanned out to sixteen-millimeter microfilm—one frame apiece for each of the 210 chromatograms and five-hundred-odd mass spectra gathered during a GCMS run. "Because of the volume of such data, paper printouts could not be used," Biemann indicated. The complete, developed spool went into a cartridge, eight-track style, and then off to the airport. "Fly it back to Los Angeles, where we picked it up and got it back. So that took twenty-four hours." A whole extra day seems long. Biemann, however, had gone through every option with a number of experts who unanimously agreed that America's flimsy computer network simply wasn't dependable enough. Biemann dealt with the hindrance. "It was just another twenty-four hours," he shrugged.

Two dozen sols after *Lander 1* first alighted, Klaus Biemann handed the cartridge to a technician who looked like he'd just come from seeing Kiss on the Destroyer Tour. The tech loaded it into a microfilm reader the size of a console TV. Onlookers crowded in as the tech rotated a large knob, slowly advancing frames. Each one took the form of a line graph, depicting molecular weight versus abundance. If the GCMS found something, it would appear on the graph as a spike not unlike one of Oyama's.

Reviewing the film, they saw two spikes: Freon, and a substance called methyl chloride. Biemann pursed his lips. "Those two things wouldn't be on Mars," he recalled of his first impression. "Because methyl chloride is too volatile. And of course, Freon . . . the Martians haven't invented yet."

Actually, the synthetic Freon wasn't much of a surprise. Commonly thought of as a refrigerant, it'd been used to clean the instrument before launch. Then, during Viking 2's outbound flight, engineers had kick-started the GCMS for routine testing, whereupon it'd staunchly pronounced a variety of unanticipated toots and flatus to be coursing through its innards. They turned out to be residual cleaning solvents. One of them was Freon. Biemann now dismissed its presence: "The Freon already had been found in the cruise test, so we knew that there's some Freon contamination," he said. And then the presence of gaseous methyl chloride was undoubtedly a result of two other leftover cleaning agents having combined together during the oven's heat cycle. Overall, no big deal. This made for a small lump of comfort in that his machinery seemed to be working right. But strictly speaking, nobody yet knew whether the oven veritably had dirt in it or not.

A few days later Biemann decided to crank up his roaster to full potential. The oven held there for half a minute, as directed. Then came another time-consuming wait for the data return, MIT processing, and cross-country schlep. Yet when Biemann finally perused his new batch of film, shuttling through one frame after another, he concluded that something grand had transpired way up there inside his machine. As the oven hit 932, "suddenly lots of water and carbon dioxide came off. So that could only be from a sample in the oven." Those two things sure didn't come from nothing! "So we *knew* that there was a sample in."

But to their great surprise, the fancy contraption had traced flat lines throughout the remaining graphs. On those frames, the scientists stared down a complete lack of organic material. Unlike Oyama's oxygen level or Levin's counting rate or Horowitz's Peak Two, the GCMS data wasn't open to speculative interpretation. Everything was plotted right there on graph after graph. It found *nothing?* Biemann was perplexed. "There *should* be organic compounds, that one finds in meteorites," he commented. "We didn't even find *those.*"

When Gerry Soffen heard the news, he threw up his hands. "Well, there goes the ball game," he mourned.

Like him, Patricia Straat savored no excitement. "That was the first really tough problem to cope with," she grimaced. If no organic compounds existed on Mars, LR might not have discovered life after all. Or at least it made an interpretation of life rather difficult.

Everybody talked at once. *It didn't find organics because . . . they really and truly don't exist? Or maybe because . . . they actually do exist, but the soil didn't have any in the spot where they dug?*

In true scientific spirit, Biemann did not consider the absence of organics to be mutually exclusive with a positive outcome on any or all of the biology tests. He tried a hypothetical. What if organisms on hostile Mars had evolved to become uber-efficient at eating their dead? Biology could then still register inside LR, or Carbon Assimilation, without peppering enough detritus throughout the soil for his box to find.

Persnickety Horowitz loathed the idea and didn't hesitate to say so with great malice. Carl Sagan didn't like it, either. At one of the follow-up meetings, Biemann delved into more aspects of his scavenger hypothesis. "There is nothing on Mars that says this is the case!" shot back Horowitz, hot and lathered. "You have to endow your bugs with special qualities to fit the facts!"

"You're dealing with another planet," quibbled Pat Straat. Anything was possible.

But Horowitz saw Biemann's graphs as absolute. "The major fact that prevents us from offering a biological explanation on any of these instruments, is that there are *no* organics down to the part-per-billion level. And to maintain that there *are* organics, you have to invent a special model." Once again he chided the idea of scavenger bugs on Mars—so perfectly evolved that they consumed every trace of their dearly departed. "It's totally ad-hoc!"

One person not getting all worked up about things was Klaus Biemann. He listened quietly to the proceedings, always took notes, and spoke if appropriate. Why so impassive? Well, back home in Massachusetts, Biemann had his own completely separate line of research going that was totally unrelated to the pursuit of life on other planets. It didn't have a half cent to do with planetary sciences, or really any flavor of extraterrestrial research at all. His Big Thing was none of the above—just analytical and organic chemistry. "I often call my involvement in the space program 'scientific charity,'" he related, decades after the end of Viking. "It had nothing to do with my professional career." And in this way the guy could maintain a sort of cognitive distance.

Klaus Biemann made for an interesting study of where the family business can send a man. With the Biemanns it was a pharmacy near Vienna, Austria. In the late Forties, young Klaus chose to study pharmaceuticals at the University of Innsbruck. There he cultivated a fascination with organic chemistry and became, at the time, the university's only graduate student in that narrow field. His efforts led to a summer fellowship at the Massachusetts Institute of Technology. It was 1954 and Biemann liked what he saw. MIT seemed to hold more promise than anything Europe had on offer, so he returned in '55 as a postdoc and soon got appointed to the faculty in analytical chemistry. People working this field study the types and amounts of all the little compounds making up a particular something. The idea of determining what, exactly, the world was made of—and in what amounts—struck him as enthralling path through life.

Defying conventional methods of the time, he used a mass spectrometer to examine the structures of natural products like alkaloids and peptides. But in nature these exist only as highly complex mixtures. The situation led him to combine the mass spectrometer with a technique of separation—as was found in the gas chromatograph. Behold, a new way of doing things.

In one of his early victories, he determined a major component in the scent of a rose. He unearthed the structure of a crucial vision-related protein. Throughout his career to date, Klaus Biemann had studied endless compounds, taught hundreds of students, and in general worked very hard at all aspects of his job—none of which involved exploring other planets.

But when the opportunity came up, that unquenchable wonder present within him just couldn't resist. "To look for organic chemistry on Mars was an interesting problem. It was a challenge," he said. The GCMS seemed an ideal tool to send out there.

"If it should be done, I might as well do it."

On August 10 a core group convened in von Karman for an internal round-table discussion among the Biology Team members. It'd still be open, with reporters in attendance, but promised little of the back-and-forth characterizing true press conferences.

The scientists took their chairs in a kind of daze. "We are all terribly conscious of the fact that we might well be wrong in anything we say," voiced Norm Horowitz. "And nobody wants to be wrong, in public, on a question as important as that of life on Mars." He didn't want to get stuck, as they say, with his cheese flapping in the wind.

Advisor Josh Lederberg wondered aloud just what kind of indication would have to come from the Biology Instrument in order for everyone to be totally convinced of Martian life. The money in Harold Klein's pocket went to ongoing GEX peaks. Lederberg calmly supposed that nobody could *ever* unequivocally prove the existence of life on Mars using only what Viking carried. "We have to *see* growth; we have to *see* reproduction," he upheld. "We have to *see* the possibility of evolution and diversification." The meeting broke with little to show. Thirteen years prior, Lederberg's own microscopy experiment had not made the cut for Voyager Mars.

With Viking 2 still a few weeks out, Straat and Levin—plus Horowitz—began their second runs. The control cycles. Deep inside *Lander 1*'s Biology Instrument, two small carousels each rotated a fresh, triple-A-battery-sized testing chamber into place. Gradually the tiny vials filled with soil that'd been loitering in the hopper ever since the delivery on sol 8—material that had already tested positive. That was intentional; using the same source helped eliminate variables. After filling, the chambers rotated to a secondary location where each received a tortuous three-and-a-half-hour sterility bake. In Horowitz's case, the needle reached 347 degrees Fahrenheit. If any activity inside their two previous experiments came from a living process, this would kill it dead.

Once the heating finished, tiny openings vented both chambers directly to the Martian atmosphere. Again they sealed. The vials rotated back to locations where, just as before, nutrients and gases tenderly flowed in. Lamp on. Wait. A few sols later LR began flashing results back to JPL while Horowitz's experiment chugged through its separations and extractions. Almost from the gate, Levin's count surged up near eighteen hundred before immediately dropping back to about eight hundred. Engineers pored over the flood of telemetry, concluding that as testing got underway some radioactive gas had lingered at the Geiger counter. So, considering that, the true count ended up fluctuating right around the lower value. Basically, no activity. Days later, Horowitz's Peak Two came in: 105 disintegrations per minute. Both experiments had just validated their initial tests, and the case for life took a bold step up.

Horowitz felt himself being slowly edged into a biological corner. To the next gawking flock of reporters he offered, "This eliminates many of the instrument failures we had thought might be causing the positive results of the first cycle."

He yielded the podium to an animated Gil Levin, who demonstrated a gathering confidence. "Had we seen these two curves on Earth," he exhorted of his own results, "if we had run this experiment in the parking lot at JPL, we would have concluded that life is present in the sample." Levin spoke with dollops of Christmas-morning excitement. "We wish that Dr. Biemann would find a little bit of organics in his next test!"

If Levin—or even Horowitz—had been the sole experimenter, the issue might have rapidly drawn to a conclusion. "Don't get hung up on an absolute value of Peak Two," cautioned Jerry Hubbard. "There is always a carryover from Peak One." Regarding that 105, its "unmassaged value," as he put it, was plus or minus 29.5. "Clearly, a small positive response." As such, the entirety of H-cubed remained in the peroxide camp. This despite their gadget's supposed insensitivity to peroxides. Also, if the lamp filter was broken after all and stimulated the creation of organics, how could Peak Two have come back so low? Maybe one hundred disintegrations was not actually an indicator of absent metabolism? Horowitz had artificially pumped up that number, as kind of a hedge against the very sort of trouble they were now experiencing. Should it have been lower?

Within the meeting rooms postconference, an emotive tangle. Levin and Straat clung to their belief in the presence of life—after all, they'd just satisfied every prelaunch requirement for it. But Viking's Biology Team numbered several, and leader Harold Klein gathered all the brains in the center of the table to discuss what'd just come in. The guy preached objectivity and patience. *Don't mindlessly jump on something, people.* A very good case remained for chemistry. Heating a substance the way both machines did—at a certain temperature for a specific length of time—may well have eradicated any peroxides contained within it. This would slay the processes observed in the active cycles, and subsequent testing would indeed show no activity. Chemistry fit very well with what they were experiencing.

Martian soil wasn't soil anymore. It was a jigsaw puzzle—one of those annoying party-gag varieties where any piece fits with any other, but even so there's still only one solution. And some of the pieces are missing. Levin anticipated that sooner or later the scoop would haul in those missing chunks.

Two weeks in, he repacked his overused suitcase and headed for the airport. It marked kind of an odd time to leave, considering Viking 2's imminent arrival in Martian orbit. But work often intrudes: "He had to go back and run the company," explained Pat Straat, knowing her boss would return in due time. "I kept him informed by calling him every day and letting him know what was going on."

Others also took microsabbaticals. When Jerry Hubbard's family visited, he snuck off with them for a day to see the Los Angeles Zoo, having worked the preceding fifty-five days straight through. Vance Oyama sojourned to his roots in a prewar LA neighborhood. "He gave a somber account of his parents' grocery store being 'bought' by the U.S. government for forty dollars and the family being transported to an internment camp," remembered Hubbard. "When I talked about my day at the zoo, I said that I too had gone back to my roots. It was in poor taste but was recognized as just another salvo in my battles with Vance."

A new sample reached the GCMS on August 21. One day later Biemann started working the pinch of dirt—first at midrange temperatures, with full heat coming almost a week later in the form of two successive 932-degree, thirty-second cycles. He didn't get methyl chloride or Freon, which was to be expected, as the first run should've cleared them. What Biemann ultimately had to report wasn't much. "We found, as last time, copious amounts of water and little or no organic material. Organically speaking, both samples were very clean material." Not long after its second trial ended the GCMS went dark forever, as both good ovens had been used. Soon *Lander 2* would hopefully set down to begin making its own contribution.

Round three began at the very end of August, over thirty-five sols into *Lander 1*'s operation. The craft was in good shape. Daily weather reports streamed in. Levin returned. Photographs made for a continuingly popular attraction—JPL using them to create an accurate landscape of Styrofoam rocks around the flight-spare lander on display and testing scoop movements in advance to verify safe passage through the terrain.

And then, over in the Biology Team's roost, Horowitz and Levin had collectively knotted themselves into another conundrum. They both wanted new dirt. Already the hopper's current load had been imprisoned for over a month, and concern now widened that anything alive in it might've died. Fresh soil wasn't an inappropriate request, but the men were simply petrified by Biemann's sampling ordeal. They didn't want to chuck the old stuff until the last possible moment—after the scoop had ladled up a new round and stood there hovering directly over the inlet. But *Lander 1* didn't have any kind of garbage chute for the old soil to be dumped out. And its programming contained a simple maxim: no new soil until the old went into a testing chamber.

Miraculously, engineering stitched together a workaround. Part of it mandated a shutdown and reboot of the entire Biology Instrument—representing more of a near-death experience than not getting samples at all. Everything came back well enough, except for one small issue that would further coerce H-cubed into a biological corner.

Three sols between sampling and first injection. Then wait, wait . . . Levin and Straat biding time as their offspring stewed and simmered. Like always, the single drop of Instant Breakfast was just enough to create a moisture gradient on the soil—from wet, where the drop had hit, progressing all the way down to bone-dry at the chamber's bottom. A few days later, results began their long-distance trip and Straat parked before her computer terminal, Levin hovering. With a mixture of emotions the duo followed LR's activity curve as it surged past ten thousand over the course of two days, holding its own, climbing very slowly up near fifteen thousand. The partners looked at one other. This third go-round had handily eclipsed the first one.

Unlike in their initial preprogrammed trial, Team LR now relished the luxury of modifying test protocols—and decided to hold off ending this current one. They'd let it ferment, monitoring how the curve behaved during a long run. Might it slowly taper off as nutrients were consumed? "This would be convincing evidence for the existence of a living process," advocated Gil Levin. But the protracted run time would relegate Norm Horowitz to an involuntary holding pattern. Due to limitations in the Biology Instrument's design, he couldn't begin a new trial until LR's finished—though each of his three chambers could be reused one time apiece, for a total of six rounds.

In the interim, Straat ruminated on LR's near-constant feed of vital signs. Like junk mail, they kept arriving: voltages, chamber temperatures, nutrient levels, valve positions, detector temperatures, counting rates, elapsed time. Every sixteen minutes the Geiger counter took another reading. "I would get on the computer every day and work the data," offered Straat. When her blood sugar levels dropped too low, she'd begrudgingly peel away to the JPL cafeteria. "I'd go down there and get a sandwich to go and take it up to my office and keep going. We didn't take breaks. I didn't have time to take breaks!"

Her (new) respite always came at the day's beginning. Every morning from seven to eight, she joined others at the Flintridge Riding Club, which by the greatest of coincidences happened to sit directly on the other side of Oak Grove Drive from JPL. Since the age of nineteen Straat had owned at least one horse and rode quite often, but by mid-August 1976 she'd finally had it with months of all Viking and no equestrianism. She went over to Flintridge in a dress and heels and talked with the stable manager. He suggested she write the club's board of directors, asking for reciprocal privileges from her own riding club back east.

Straat got in and was on a rental one day when she hit it off with an elderly couple. At one point they happened to mention how hard it was for the two of them to keep *three* horses fit. Convenient! She got invited to ride their animal the very next morning. And soon a regular gig settled in. "We had a wonderful instructor who coached us four days a week, including Sunday, and I did jump four feet six inches a few times. Which was quite a thrill." After an hour she'd hop off and get cleaned up and hit the Biology Team rooms for another thirteen- or fourteen-hour day.

"Riding kept me sane during the mission." She paused, as if savoring the fondest of memories. "It cleared my mind. When you're galloping towards a four-foot jump you better not be thinking about anything else!"

During this long LR trial Gil Levin intermittently went and came, and then went again. The sols pressed on. Straat let sixteen of them pass before requesting a second injection; the count seemed to have stalled out around fifteen thousand. A spritz of new juice hit its target—prompting the response to falter somewhat before gradually picking up steam again. With interest she noted how that exact behavior had already happened once before, with the initial sample.

If results weren't coming in for your own experiment, they were probably coming for somebody else's. And if that wasn't happening, there was always some meeting to attend, or new pictures to look at from the now-orbiting Viking 2, or an interview request to comply with, or maybe a press conference to join. "It wasn't boring at all," remembered Klaus Biemann of the downtime between his own experiments. "I was not just sitting there, only contemplating my navel and the GCMS data." Once, during an abnormally slow period, he snuck away to attend a nearby auction. "Bought twenty-five volumes of an original edition of Mark Twain's books." The purchase mostly sat in his lonely hotel room, ignored. "I probably read the first few pages," he laughed. "But not twenty-five volumes!"

21. Last Man Home

The *Luna 24* sample is unique in two ways. First, it comes from
a region of the moon from which we have never obtained samples.
Even more important is the fact that *Luna 24* obtained a
complete core down to a depth of two meters.

—Noel Hinners, NASA associate administrator for space science,
to a newspaper reporter

Soviet moon operations finally closed down after *Luna 24* returned home in
August '76. "The spacecraft was already done," noted Alexander Basilevsky,
"so it will be stupid not to fly it." Up at administrative levels, Mstislav Keldysh and Roald Sagdeev had long been advocating the program's termination. "I think it was already clear that scientists had more than enough to
digest," upheld Sagdeev, referencing their existing piles of lunar data. "To
keep multiplying did not give a new quality."

His country sure needed another win. Late the previous year, *Luna 22*
had wrapped up sixteen months on-orbit. That outing went off essentially
without a hitch, as the ship completed two multiday photography sessions,
fired laser altimeters at big swaths of ground, and for months upon end sur-
veyed the moon's crazy gravitational field. Good science, but offering little
of the in-your-face attitude commensurate with retrieving new lunar samples. It eventually ran out of maneuvering fuel and dropped all contact.

Midway through that flight *Luna 23* had blasted off to augment the Soviet
sample inventory. But a catawampus landing knocked the entire rig clean
over—drill unused, return stage face-planted in endless gray chalk without any means of standing back up. At the time, nobody understood why
the contraption could maintain radio dialogue but fail to gather its sam-

ple and come on home. Another attempt went up nearly a year later. The stack didn't even reach Earth orbit: faulty Proton.

But success rewards the patient, and ten months downstream *Luna 24* arrived as intended, less than a mile and a half from *Luna 23*—right in the undulating Sea of Crises (which was also *Luna 15*'s lost harbor).

The machine represented an answer to one of the wants of researchers like Basilevsky. And this want had nothing to do with quantity, with great scoopfuls of dirt, but with a core drill. That is, a thin yet long vertical cross-section, taken from the ground in a way that preserved every fold and layer. Think of jabbing a giant beverage straw down through the surface and collecting what's inside. Scientists wanted to see exactly how material piled up and formed the moon. They wanted a *deep* core. How did eight feet sound?

We all have our wants. Main problem: the size of Luna's sample-holding return ball remained fixed almost to the hundredth of an inch. In seven years the thing had scarcely changed. But on August 18, 1976, when *Luna 24* finally mated its drill with the monochromatic landscape, eight feet of dirt were about to be perfectly preserved within twenty inches of return capsule. Just like the guys requested.

As *Luna 24*'s drill pushed deeper, its hollow bit passed the soil up into a length of flexible plastic tubing that was just over a third of an inch in diameter. Slowly the tube contorted into a compact, spiraling coil that scarcely fit the return sphere. But it fit. The way the dirt came up is the way it flew to Earth. The geologists got their core drill with all its layers (including crazy bits of brown glass thought to be sprayed-up volcanic liquid), and for reasons of politics and funding and sanity, no other Luna ever flew again.

"We knew that we will be back," declared Sagdeev—not knowing how empty that statement really was.

22. Bonneville, Notch Rock, Double Squirt, Sudden Death

NASA just seems to take a very negative view of the life hypothesis,
and in a way I can understand it. It would be an *astounding*
discovery to find out that there was life there, and that it had
evolved separately. I mean, it has all *sorts* of implications.

—Pat Straat

Both of the original Viking landing sites had been chosen after analyzing photos from the orbiting *Mariner 9*. It'd arrived in mid-November '71 and imaged great swaths of ground during its tenure. But Mariner's camera system, though accomplished, lacked the quality and refinement of that created for Viking. Via the latter's advanced imagers, a meticulously chosen *Lander 2* site revealed itself to be a minefield of craters and boulders and enormous cracks. Instructions went up to modify *Orbiter 2*'s flight path so that at the low point of its orbit it slowly walked around the entire planet— affording the site selection team an opportunity to closely appraise every sensible expanse of territory.

The quest led them north, to a region called Utopia. It lay twenty-five degrees higher up and nearly halfway round the globe from *Lander 1*. Poster-sized mosaics once again filled JPL meeting tables, intermingled with crappy box lunches that had been started, abandoned, resumed, then discarded but not thrown away. Wrappers and chip bags and pop cans. Every room buzzed slightly from cheap ballasts powering overhead fluorescent light fixtures. On the mosaics, geologists slid around cut-out ellipses, trying to find good locations in a bizarre half game known as "cosmic ice hockey."

The exhaustive certification process deemed a Utopia site acceptable, and *Lander 2* set down there in late afternoon on September 3. Part of it

34. *Lander's* grandeur: a view from the top deck of the Viking *Lander 2*. At left is a fuel tank cover. Checkerboard-patterned swatches are color-calibration targets. Courtesy NASA/JPL-Caltech.

smacked a rock, denting the lander. One footpad came down on a small boulder. For its entire working life the ship would operate at an eight-degree tilt, but it was down and in one piece.

Only a day later, Straat and Levin ended their third stint aboard *Lander 1*. From underneath a blaze of podium lights, "the experiment repeated completely," glowed Levin—having nattily duplicated the original trial, in tandem with gathering data over a much longer period. "We got the same vigorous response that we received the first time, and the shape of that response is essentially the same." So far, Labeled Release had performed consistently and without fail. "The experiments that are being played out now have been sixteen years in planning," he continued. "If we were getting these results anyplace on Earth, we'd say there's life there. And we would be certain of it."

When Horowitz's third *Lander 1* result finally popped back, it said 214.5—weakly positive. The value came with an asterisk. Normally, Carbon Assimilation's testing chamber maintained about a sixty-three-degree environment. But after that reboot of the Biology Instrument, Horowitz's soil had accidentally brewed at seventy-nine degrees Fahrenheit for almost three days until somebody noticed and corrected it. The question came up immediately: did hypothetical microbes behave less actively due to heat? Yeah, sixteen degrees wasn't much, but think about the summertime difference between seventy-four degrees and ninety. The calling card of any organism is behavioral changes over minute temperature differentials.

The microbes inside Norm Horowitz next reacted in a very terrestrial way: they gave him a cold, leaving Jerry Hubbard to weather the ensuing press conference. Although he tried to stay noncommittal, "some members of the press wanted a more declarative statement," he remembered.

ABC correspondent Jules Bergman leapt to his feet. "Dr. Hubbard," he charged, "when are you going to say whether there is or is not life on Mars?" Nervously massaging the podium sides, Hubbard grappled with internal voices reminding him that the outcome of his own control run should really count as positive. To the journalist he verbalized a strong inclination to try and repeat the results and then look at them in context.

Another reporter brusquely accused the scientist of being ambivalent. "I'm only trying to be 'polyvalent,'" cracked Hubbard, twisting a biology term to suit his needs. People carped about the jibe. "All possible interpretations need to be considered," he kept on. After the press conference broke he joined a private team discussion to rehash their new data. Deliberating on the 214.5, Hubbard flagged a point for life and Harold Klein agreed. So did Horowitz.

"It is difficult to do science in a fishbowl," Hubbard later complained of the reporters. "They rake you over the coals."

The number-one oven on *Lander 2*'s GCMS didn't heat, reducing Klaus Biemann's potential to only two Utopia samples. And he felt decidedly unenthusiastic about the planned locale for his first quarrying. It looked too much like Chryse. Why not process something distinctly dissimilar? In photographs, over to the right, he noticed another patch o' scratch christened Bonneville, as it resembled Utah's famously barren salt flats. *Let's dig there.* Result? In four heatings of the sample over thirteen sols, nada. No organics. Again.

Pat Straat's recipe hit its first smidgen of Utopia dirt, and the counting rate began a now-familiar ritual of quick ascension. Two sols on it cleared twelve thousand. Levin shook his head in adulation. "The odds were overwhelming that nothing would happen at all," he ventured, upbeat. After five more sols the black line on their fresh printout stopped climbing around fourteen thousand. Then it dropped slightly. Utopia's curve, when superimposed on the Chryse ones, proved to be even steeper. And once again the total amount of released carbon dioxide suggested that only part of the nutrient had been consumed. Many had their eyes on formate, one of the simplest organic acids and one that is commonly devoured by microbes.

After his Utopia GEX received *its* own sample, Vance Oyama . . . did nothing. He didn't add water, he didn't touch jack. The biochemist wanted to tiptoe. For an entire day he sat on it without injecting a blasted thing and, dispersed throughout that time, Oyama requested three sniffs of the chamber headspace. *Lander 2* reported no oxygen—or any other gas—coming off the dirt. This told him that when things just sat there idle, *nothing* happened inside that experiment. No spontaneous activity whatsoever. Now solidly convinced that his babe in arms worked properly, Oyama proceeded one day later to add his soup. He did so the same way as with his initial *Lander 1* trial—letting it dribble in from below so that only water vapor contacted the soil. And within hours, there it was again: a bursting oxygen peak, like somebody had outright pumped the stuff into GEX. It measured about 15 percent of what'd materialized at Chryse and fit with the going theory that more water existed at Utopia—which should therefore spawn a much more mellow reaction. Oxygen production hit a plateau by sol 12. Then came the "wet" cycle, beginning on sol 16, with nutrient directly molesting the soil. Oxygen levels took a serious nosedive.

At another of the ubiquitous press conferences, Oyama confidently surmised that his oxygen mountains resulted from chemical reactions—the likes of which were definitely capable of destroying "organic species," as he put it. "This may account for the GCMS lack of organic detection." But GEX used so much water, countered Norm Horowitz, so as to make the experiment almost laughable. Not to mention all those nutrients and gases! GEX didn't come *close* to simulating the actual Martian environment. Why make grand assumptions based on this white elephant?

These latest results filled Gil Levin with twinges of victory. "As a result of the fresh data at Utopia," he announced to reporters in mid-September, "we now find that a new constraint has been imposed on the chemical theory." Unlike in that very first brush with the media, Levin now spoke much more freely. He talked about the presumed abundance of water at the new site—something like ten times more than Chryse. On Mars, he pointed out, they now knew from Oyama that dirt plus water vapor equals oxygen. But with so much Utopia water supposedly present, "we might have expected to see *less* of a positive response in our experiment. Instead, we see a response that's about 25 percent *higher* than the response at the first site." It didn't jive—unless Martian bugs flocked to water-heavy areas? Levin wrapped up his talk with the assertion that if oxidants were at work here, an improbably disparate combination of them would be necessary in order to reproduce the Biology Team's collective results.

Questions flew through the air, many striking Harold Klein right in his jowly kisser.

Chances for life are on the rise, aren't they?

Klein said no. "I don't think we're that much further along."

Levin objected. "None of these steps has eliminated or diminished the possibility of a biological response."

The idea that Viking's tardy, imperfect, and discombobulated Biology Instrument would produce such useable and consistent results made for a fairly unexpected situation. "Everything worked like a charm and it was the biggest surprise of my life," tittered Pat Straat. Based on history, she figured the whole thing would either not work to begin with—or operate just long enough to give them hope before conking out forever. Straat hadn't even planned on being in Pasadena long: "I'd considered making flight reservations back to Maryland two weeks after the landers set down!" But the rigs were behaving as intended.

Except, that is, for Carbon Assimilation on *Lander 2*. It had sprung a leak in between its U-shaped organics filter and the radiation detector. A nonfatal problem. But while the experiment ran, a good 30 percent of its special radioactive gas would escape the test chamber. Horowitz parked Hobby and Hubbard and mulled over ways to "normalize" a Peak Two value by taking the leak into account.

His first Utopia cycle would run without any introduced water vapor— drier than a Mormon wedding. Horowitz also decided to keep the lamp off because *Lander 2*'s northerly location was actually warmer than Chryse, and he preferred to remain as close to Martian norms as manageable. Also, with the light off there'd be no possibility of it manufacturing organics—serving as one check on whether or not the filter worked. Part of his rationale went back to a decade-old theory that some life on Mars might have developed a light-free way of turning carbon monoxide into carbon dioxide. A bizarre process, but one that does occur on Earth. Maybe it was also happening on the next planet out?

Horowitz did the run and got a shock: 178, or weakly weakly positive. One toe across the line. Possibly, Martians were capable of some weird hybrid photosynthesis that omitted the photo part yet still did the synthesizing. But—how much of that number had to do with the leak?

His result could also be explained by the combo of water and hydrogen peroxide. For Horowitz to start with only carbon dioxide yet end up with organics required the carbon to mingle with hydrogen. And the only place that said hydrogen could come from was Martian soil. Ergo, hydrogen peroxide. Again.

Up on the von Karman podium, Gentry Lee spoke. "I think it is fair to say that the preponderance of scientific opinion is that most of what we have seen can be more easily explained by chemistry. However, it is by no means that clean-cut." Balding on top but with neck-length hair, the colorfully animated Lee served as Viking's director of science analysis—on a rung above Harold Klein and parallel to Gerry Soffen.

Others took turns—conveying alternate interpretations of the biology results, or the fact that the only baseline anyone ever had up to now came from tests done on Earth. A reporter wondered if Viking scientists might not be ready to concede that Mars contained no life after all. For Gerry Soffen, this remained something of a touchy point. "Dr. Biemann's experiment has examined two samples that are less than a thimble-full of soil from Mars," he quipped. "And we're going to make deductions as broad as whether life has ever evolved on that planet, based upon *that* amount of soil?"

"There *does* exist a plausible hypothesis," reminded Lee, "that says there cannot be enough organics for Klaus to detect them, and still be biology of the quantitative nature that Norm saw."

"I don't think the data fully support either biology *or* chemistry," ventured one of the later speakers.

This flavor of controversy was not new. It harkened back to a time over one hundred years before when the Frenchman Louis Pasteur brooded over the process of fermentation. Was it—as the locals maintained—one of chemistry, or did the miracle of sugar becoming alcohol result from a biological process? As with his Viking compatriots of the future, Pasteur's task remained complicated by the fact that biology *is* chemistry.

Straat and Horowitz wanted to get on with their next *Lander 2* cycle. Horowitz fancied the distinct Bonneville soil that had so enraptured Klaus Biemann and suggested they get some. But Straat preferred more diggings from the existing site—they'd registered positive, after all, and her upcoming control run really necessitated the use of identical samples. At one of the increasingly afflictive team gatherings, most favored advancing to Bonneville. Yet a motion to go there failed when Straat successfully counterclaimed that duplicate control soil took priority.

"We're in lockstep," growled Norm Horowitz about the interconnectedness. All these crazy restrictions on his work. Horowitz tired of it all; so many variations he wanted to pursue and just plain couldn't. How he ached to run a dry trial at very low temperatures in order to closely simulate Mars. Turn off all the Biology Instrument heaters. But that couldn't happen without freezing the liquids in the other two gadgets and maybe destroying them. And then he had to deal with Levin's constant maneuvering for every possible advantage. "If I want to start a new experiment next week," whined Horowitz, "I can't—because he is in the middle of a long incubation." Scientific test equipment had never resembled Siamese triplets—hitched at the hip and sharing one brain among three!

Desired sample in hand, Straat and Levin still weren't totally comfortable with kicking off their first Utopia control. It felt like a wasted chamber; the flat-line result could almost be predicted. What might be done differently? To convincingly swing the needle toward chemistry *or* biology? They got to discussing variables in the control protocol—like, for example, not heating it up so much. A chemical reaction shouldn't vary with relatively small temperature changes . . . but microbes were a whole different story. This led the pair to embrace an approach they termed "cold sterilization." Instead of roasting the next sample at 320 degrees, they'd take it up to just 125. If the curve still tacked high and long, the sensible reason would be chemistry. But if they got a *subdued* version of their previous activity levels, it'd finger biology.

On October 1 the duo gave it a whirl. "And we *still* got a response, which was greatly reduced," recalled Pat Straat. "And that's exactly what you'd expect if it was biology." The graph before her told all: after injecting the nutrient, LR's activity quickly rose to just over one thousand counts a minute. Then over the next three sols it progressively sank back, to less than half of that.

Elated, Straat and Levin thought they had life sewn up in a bag and postmarked. Several members of the team, however, pointed out how the activity didn't form a smooth, curved line like before. Instead, it traced a number of angling, shark-fin peaks, bobbing up and down in regular pulses. Oh geez. Did they also have a leak, like Horowitz?

Engineers hauled bunches of lander telemetry up to Straat and Levin, who rumpused through it and saw nothing amiss. But this wavy-line issue had doused the entire test with cold water. Until a solid determination could be made about what was happening up there, nobody accepted the new results at face value.

A focused Straat pondered how the hardware actually went together. Inside LR, the Geiger counter didn't sit directly atop a test chamber; they were linked by a thirteen-inch tube. And the chambers had a little heater right on top to keep any nutrient from freezing—too far away from the Geiger counter to have much of an influence. Ultimately Straat theorized that their mysterious waving graph came down to an innocent matter of heat transfer. Warmth drove carbon dioxide up the pipe to the Geiger counter, where it cooled and drifted back into the testing chamber. Repeat and voilà: shark fins. This had actually happened on every run but was just much more pronounced during cold sterilization. Years later, Straat's opinion remained largely unchanged. "I still believe that it's a result of heat fluctuations," she maintained, upholding LR's Utopia anomaly. "Nonetheless, it was a greatly reduced positive. It indicated biology."

The peroxide charge came up again and Levin went on the offensive. *The stuff couldn't well last long on Mars*, he intoned. It would rapidly decompose because of ultraviolet light stabbing through the planet's thin atmosphere.

Maybe that applied to pure *hydrogen peroxide*, responded some, *but not when mixed up with whatever else dwelled in Martian soil.*

As if the pondwater wasn't murky enough, Utopia's second Peak Two shuffled in. For this round, Horowitz had opted to cook with the lamp on, while introducing a miniscule amount of water vapor. In return his group received a minus seven. Nobody knew what to make of that. If anything, the test as structured should've given them a positive result. That leak in the instrument's pipework seemed to be worsening. H-cubed had jiggered up a mathematical offset to account for it, but . . . maybe they overcompensated?

Everyone's scores and stats went before the world at the next press conference. No yearlong periods of reflection, or retesting, or insightful peer review, or mild-mannered discussions at low-key symposia. Instead: a hot box called von Karman Auditorium, with heavy, bright lights and heavier TV cameras and miles of cable littering the floor. Heat visibly blurred the ceiling. Reporters—who generally lacked PhDs or science backgrounds and were decidedly prone to large hand gestures—lurked with steno pads and disheveled tie knots and kinetically waved sweaty ballpoints at the scientists, who sat uncomfortably arranged before them like suspects in a carjacking lineup. The researchers took their measured turns at the podium, splashing through overheads, offering claims or refutations or tentative hypotheses and doing their absolute darndest to field the rampantly diverse queries that some thought might never ever end.

Without question, the one thing most conspicuously absent from the entire proceeding was consensus.

Attention now returned to *Lander 1* and the evolving activity of LR's third (and protracted) incubation at that site. Forty-one sols into this round, Straat gamely prescribed a third infusion of nutrient. In return she got the same behavioral pattern as with the second injections on her other trials: the quick drop back, followed by another slow climb. The rate never pushed beyond twelve thousand—typical, once again, of partial nutrient consumption. She more or less expected to witness a steadily increasing curve as the hypothetical microbes grew and reproduced. Didn't seem to be happening. Straat called it after fifty sols and that's where Horowitz made his plea.

Don't forget, he started, *in a few weeks Mars will go behind the sun.* That'd break radio contact with all four ships and end what was termed "the primary mission." Conceivably both landers might not rouse afterward, which had everyone contemplating their Viking last wills and testaments. Horowitz certainly knew his and laid it on the table: *I want to do that extremely cold test. Please?* It meant shutting down part of the Biology Instrument, prompting Oyama and Levin to veto the idea. More sooty disagreement swirled through the corridors of Building 264. And realistically, the Biology Team should have taken a hiatus right then and there. Forget this impending break, no matter how close it loomed. They were disagreeable siblings on a long-ass car trip. Everybody had been spending way too much time in close quarters at high levels of concentration with tons of reporters staring over them and noting down every word. Both Josh Lederberg and Alex Rich had outright stopped coming to team gatherings because neither wanted to experience any more naked bickering. Harold Klein was enjoying his role less and less; he'd completed a slow transformation from team leader into playground monitor. Though not an official member, Carl Sagan often loitered in Biology Team meetings to suggest his own take on the latest happenings. And Norm Horowitz had long grown sick as all get-out of Sagan's preposterous theories about life on Mars. *Maybe he should permanently emigrate there!*

The ice run voted down, Horowitz now set out with his last sterile *Lander 1* chamber to try and duplicate Carbon Assimilation's very first result. Only a third of its radioactive gas remained—the handicap skewing any face-value results, forcing the trio to compensate with a fair amount of estimation. The test yielded a Peak Two of 289. Feebly positive, it nonetheless marked Horowitz's second-strongest response—and on a full gas bottle likely would've scored higher. Maybe a 289 at 33 percent gas equaled 842 on a full charge?

Over at Utopia, things had swung in interesting directions. Around its twenty-ninth or thirtieth sol, *Lander 2*'s mechanical arm had been working away when the scoop head accidentally bumped a small rock that obligingly shifted. Everyone froze, wide-eyed—and not because they thought the arm had been damaged. The unforeseen ability to *move rocks* opened the possibility of gathering samples from underneath them. That is to say, dirt that had *not* spent the last hundred-million-odd years basking in the destructive glow of ultraviolet light. Virgin soil: the crack cocaine of Mars exploration. Everybody wanted dirt from under a rock. But—which one? Many lay within the scoop's reach.

A horde of Viking geologists dropped what they were doing and embraced the situation, ranking every candidate rock using a not-uncomplicated set of elaborately itemized criteria more kooky than that used to pick Miss America. Once their decision came down, instructions went up command-

35. Jerry Hubbard, on right, also served as Biology Team rep to the Surface-Sampling Team. Here he stands before the spare *Lander* in JPL's von Karman Auditorium, pondering which rock they should try to move. To Hubbard's side is project scientist Don Flory. Photo by William Ashley, courtesy of Jerry Hubbard.

ing *Lander 2* to reach out and move *that* rock. The craft obeyed, shoving its scoop against the one in question . . . which stayed firmly rooted in place and slightly dislodged the spacecraft from its original position.

The geologists' cumbersome judging process went in the garbage can, and many sols later a completely different rock was finally coerced to move. Its shape inspired the moniker Badger Rock. Dirt from underneath it went into the GCMS hopper; Biemann exhaled. Fourteen draggy sols later, samples from below a different one, Notch Rock, at last reached the Biology Instrument. Unlike its brethren, the GEX design had but a lone sampling chamber—with no way to empty it. After the previous run had ended, the chamber drained of nutrients and gases and vented directly to the Martian atmosphere for a period of days. Notch Rock dirt then went in on top of the old. (Straat and Horowitz used entirely new chambers.) As with the GCMS sample, Viking controllers worked from the first crack of dawn to gather material as quickly as possible—the goal being to limit its exposure to ultraviolet light.

Well, how'd they do?

No hint of organics, declared Biemann. Vance Oyama braved his lowest oxygen peak yet. A curve developed on Pat Straat's printout that nicely complemented her others. Point blank: if something *besides* life was causing her LR activity, then it should be more closely paralleling Oyama's stunted harvest. After seven sols she ordered up a second injection and vowed to let it steep for a mighty long time.

Norm Horowitz then announced his Peak Two value for Notch Rock—whipped up in the dark and sans water. It was thirty-six: resoundingly negative. Jerry Hubbard marked the occasion by swearing off cigarettes.

At another press conference on November 8, Carl Sagan bundled up some pro-life energy and came out swingin'. Two-thirds of the experiments, he insinuated, had already met all the premission criteria for active Martian biology. He wasn't bothered in the slightest that every GCMS run had failed to uncloak any organics. *They've gotta be there*, testified the Cornell astronomer. *Just in levels too small to detect.* He even reoriented Oyama's flaccid oxygen peak into an asset. Before the reporters, Sagan charged that it nicely demonstrated an absence of stowaway earthborn organisms inside *Lander 2*.

Having laid waste to nonbiological arguments—at least, in his own mind—Sagan now publicly proposed a species he himself had dreamed up to handsomely unify all the disjointed results everyone had been getting. Pencils ready? Sagan's line of best fit utilized bugs that sported dense yet breathable turtle-like shells made of iron and silicon. "Say some of these bugs get shoveled into Biemann's GCMS," he put forward. "The heat can't break the silicate bonds. Biemann's instrument is full of bugs, and he's not registering any!"

To explain the GEX response, Sagan's micro-pseudo-wonder turtles soaked up water until they burst like popcorn, creating oxygen peaks. *Voilà!* When it came to Horowitz's test, the armored critters easily accounted for every high Peak Two. And those varying negatives during control runs could be explained by the bugs' ability to endure high temps and still generate a semblance of results. *There you go!* And what about Labeled Release? *Well, yeah, hmm . . .* Sagan ventured that LR used too much water or simply hadn't been designed to detect what he proposed.

"I don't buy it," Gil Levin told him at a side meeting, after the press conference.

Levin had kept his cool. Horowitz, on the other hand, went off like a bomb. "It's terrible!" he exploded. "It's totally uncompelling and ad-hoc! It's simply to preserve the notion that life might exist on Mars."

Shortly after this tense exchange, celestial mechanics twisted the sun in between Earth and Mars and communication with all four ships effectively ceased. Both scoop arms retracted into their housings; the Utopia GCMS shut down. Every camera went dark. Along with a smattering of other experiments, both GEX and *Lander 2*'s LR continued their long gestations. Many at JPL took a much-needed furlough.

His one-time ovens used, his tanks of gas nearly spent, Klaus Biemann and his string tie and his briefcase full of Mars returned to MIT, where he began drafting up the voluminously anhydrous scientific papers that one has to create when doing things like this. The "most important" device aboard Viking had evidently found the least.

"The reason that we didn't find anything," clarified Biemann of the AWOL organics, "is because there *isn't* anything—at least, not in the first ten centimeters of the regolith."

Pat Straat got in one last ride at Flintridge on November 23 and then headed out that same day. Jerry Hubbard needed time to line up his January course schedule at Georgia Tech. "And there was nothing I could accomplish at JPL between the restart on December fifteenth and January." So he packed his things and swiped his nameplate off the door and went and got in the car.

Lonely curiosity is what had rousted him onto this cluttery path in the first place. "Growing up in poverty during the Depression and Dust Bowl, with no playmates, taught me to entertain myself by exploring things." Hubbard had an introverted and noticeably gradual way of revealing details about his life. "For me, eighth grade general science was the *one* challenging course in my school." And from then on his mind was all about discoveries. The GI Bill provided a means to get into college. The Russkies freed up American research dollars, inadvertently, by launching their first satellite in 1957. And with this winning combination he settled into a rich academic life.

Hubbard's car ambled south down Oak Grove Drive, away from JPL. Between it and his next waypoint lay eighteen hours and 1,243 miles of freeways. TRW had given everyone little gold-foil matchboxes that inquired "LIFE ON MARS?" along with the company's logo and a caricature of a Viking warrior. Hubbard stuffed one into his ashtray and resisted the urge to light up. "Driving cross-country while quitting smoking was the ultimate test of my resolve," he granted.

Hubbard used this long interval to contemplate the mazelike string linking his time on Viking to those early days outside with an uncluttered mind, pawing in the dirt, not a care in the universe. He pitted in Tipton, Oklahoma, to visit his recently widowed mother. "It was our first one-on-one in twenty-plus years," he offered. "Sadly, it was our last."

Come mid-December, as each radio locked back on Earth, at least two things were known to live on Mars: the Viking *Lander*s. Both had survived.

The only one in position to start a fresh test, Norm Horowitz rolled out a variation for Chryse he called Sudden Death. This gambit of extremes aimed to once and for all time immortal determine whether his group's results hailed from chemistry or biology. Inside *Lander 1* he'd tsunami some soil with water vapor and let it wallow. Four hours later he planned to, as it were, open the windows—vent every molecule of leftover vapor to Mars's bitterly dry outdoors. The flue would then close, as a sterilization-grade cremation ensued: two minutes of 248 bug-dusting degrees, dropping to 194 for nearly two hours. By then every rascally varmint inside that chamber should've rightfully bought the farm. Encore: an everyday lamp-on incubation. "Any positive response," surmised Horowitz, "would be bound to be chemical." At Chryse he and George Hobby only had about 10 percent of their special carbon gas left. Three times the normal amount went in, and both men settled down to wait.

Five days later, Peak Two came back and said 275—a startling parallel of the 289, nailed with steady illumination and zero water at the same site. To Horowitz, Sudden Death pointed squarely at chemical reactions, no question. But he kept staring at its low Peak One. If that figure was indeed correct, only a very small amount of water vapor had actually made it into the chamber. Their water-delivery unit might not be working properly; engineering would have to sort through a bunch of things.

Pat Straat's lengthy Notch Rock gestation aboard *Lander 2* had reached eighty sols and counting. Following her second injection in early November, the rate had briefly spiked—after which point the count increased bit by bit at a gradually diminishing pace. *Well, well, exactly what happened on the other second injections.* Were her microbes dead, or just never there in the first place? She and Levin had left it to simmer like that during their time off but terminated the proceedings after returning to JPL in late January. They moved on to Utopia round four—where a pleased Horowitz simultaneously began his own test there. Each used new soil, with Horowitz unaware of his machine's looming break point.

Levin and Straat went for another cold sterilization. Their fresh dirt received just over three and a half hours of bake time at a relatively mundane 115 degrees Fahrenheit. Bathwater. Twenty-six hours later the recipe went on top and Straat got what she expected: a very slow rise and quick plateau that never went above six thousand—about an 80 percent reduction from the active cycles. It marked another big plus for biology. Few chemicals are destroyed by such low amounts of heat, while 115 degrees would definitely inhibit—but not destroy—the carousing of little critter guys.

Horowitz and Hobby ran out of luck. Before Peak Two could be measured, a valve deep inside their box let go and all the vapors dispersed. For them it was the end of the line at Utopia.

The powerfully familiar sense of vindication once more encircled Pat Straat and Gil Levin. At even lower temperatures than before, the response had been stifled. Straat beamed; only living things were that sensitive to change. But further Biology Team meetings saw the likes of Harold Klein reanimating the worn-out peroxide issue. Someone brought up how Sudden Death more or less eliminated peroxides. *Well, results could still be explained by that stuff,* parried Klein. It hadn't been excluded.

Nothing moved Gil Levin like the sense of injustice. In a chemistry textbook he found some esoteric yet highly relevant details about the properties of hydrogen peroxide. According to his source, the compound did indeed begin to disperse at 122, Fahrenheit, but only by 1 percent an hour. LR cooked its sample for three hours, meaning that if hydrogen peroxide were inside the little chamber, the end response should've dropped by only 3 percent or so—not the 70 percent they'd all just witnessed.

By now the soil inside *Lander 1*'s biology hopper had been sitting there well in excess of half a year. Straat and Horowitz both wanted fresh samples, as well as underground ones—devoid of any ultraviolet exposure and

36. Gil Levin defends his findings at a Biology Team meeting. What's with the bow tie? "I used to wear them very often, inspired by my mentor, Abel Wolman, who always wore them." Photo by and courtesy of Hans-Peter Biemann.

more likely to house moisture. Controllers obligingly prepared to mine a foot-deep hole.

But the hopper was full. It'd never been designed with a straightforward way to dump soil already in it. The trappings had to first move into at least one of the three instruments. The others approached Vance Oyama with the selfish idea of piling all the old soil into GEX, which would savagely end its usefulness. Remarkably, Oyama did not object—though he needed a couple more weeks until the end of his grand mal two-hundred-day incubation.

The deep-core dig took about a month. Right before it finished, *Lander 1* hit some problems with its radio link that spooked the crap out of Horowitz and Straat. Was the ship about to breathe its last? Rather than wait any longer, the dysfunctional duo ran their final Chryse cycles immediately and in tandem, with the old soil. Horowitz prescribed a Sudden Death double-check. Every radio glitch abated shortly after the tests were underway.

After 197 sols, Oyama called a halt to his inaugural Chryse run. Nothing had ever vibrantly leaped out screaming *life*. He noticed some minor chemical variations, surges of this and that and whatnot, but little else. The Ames man now decided to run a different kind of trial—one that would hopefully unmask something called superoxides and demonstrate a non-biological origin for his now-famous peaks.

GEX underwent the cleansing process. Within it a small door flipped open that vented the test cell directly to Mars's atmosphere. After three house-clearing days of purge, everything closed up tight for Oyama to begin anew. This would be a chemistry experiment, not life detection. He went with the same old dirt that Straat and Horowitz had used because damp samples from underground might attack the very substances he was trying to identify.

Now came time to warm his dirt. The temperature had to be very carefully controlled—peroxides begin coming apart around 212 degrees, while supers hold on well up to 392. Oyama needed to eliminate the former and preserve the latter, so he split the difference—leaving GEX's heater at 293 for nearly four hours in order to bust up the conjectural peroxide. Then, in went just enough nutrient to humidify the soil. Two and a half hours later, bingo: glorious oxygen, the timing and amount of which suggested that he'd successfully thrown back the curtain on superoxides. The cause and effect of this little exchange—water vapor becomes oxygen—clinched it for Oyama, that all along he'd been witnessing chemistry.

Like chess openings, various experiment protocols had taken on names and meanings of their own. Horowitz already had Sudden Death. Aboard *Lander 1*, Pat Straat executed her and Levin's much-anticipated Double Squirt. The variation aimed to look at what an *early* second helping of nutrient did to the curve. It would occur only three hours after the first, compared to the multi-sol delay used on previous trials.

When the early second spritz went in, LR's counting rate loitered near the four hundred or so it'd been charting. Over several sols the response gradually picked up steam—but failed to manage anything much beyond two thousand. What *was* that . . . maybe an 80 or even 90 percent reduction from the active cycles? It felt like a control run but hadn't been structured as such. Monkishly Straat combed through the spacecraft's vitals, trying to lay a finger on some anomalous prime suspect.

In time her pupils drifted across a thermometer readout for the biology hopper: fifty-nine degrees, it said. Her eyebrows went up. Considering how the dirt had been maintained at or near that temperature for over six months, they'd essentially performed another cold sterilization! Whatever active agents lurked in that soil did not remain stable for long periods; LR activity fluctuated to a great degree with the most inconsequential of temperature changes. Straat declared another thick point for biology. Then Horowitz got his Chryse figure: a 255, very close to Sudden Death—which, unlike this recent one, had included heating. But a number of creeping variables mottled its believability. Owing to the leak in his plumbing, Horowitz had been forced to pump many times more gas than normal into the testing chamber.

This marked Horowitz's swan song. Further leaks debilitated the working parts inside *Lander 2* and his group abandoned it. They were done. Every LR chamber had also been exhausted. *Lander 1*'s GEX supposedly had some miles left in the tires, so Vance Oyama loaded up on new soil from deep inside that excavated hole. But GEX's testing chamber failed to close, and no workaround ever materialized. Oyama too gave up and the polite, round-faced researcher adjourned to pack his things.

Norm Horowitz walked away from it all convinced that his experiment had proved one fundamental something: whatever was occurring on the Martian surface, it went by the name of chemistry. Jerry Hubbard quickly agreed, laying praise at the feet of Vance Oyama: "God knows what kind of a misinterpretation we would have made had he not seen that oxygen evolution. You know, when he humidified his soil?" Hubbard insisted that the original idea to do that came from Alexander Rich and was not well received by team GEX. "Vance went kicking and screaming, he didn't wanna do it, but that turned out to be the most important part of the whole gommish." Without that clue, nobody would've thought to consider oxidants in the soil.

H-cubed had thrown a ton of variables at their dirt—modifying the amounts of water or heat or carbon gas. Lamp on or off. Yet all the results stayed within a comparatively narrow range. They still got positives from darkness. Heat didn't seem to make a difference—unless they thoroughly baked the dirt for hours upon end. And—relative to the catalog of earthly reference samples—every outcome had been low.

Horowitz and Hobby departed JPL—severing themselves from tense meetings, glaring TV lights, rubbernecking reporters, and the overall public hoopla of real-time life detection. How nice it would be to partake in a low-key family meal and not be asked a hundred questions for which easy answers didn't exist. Compared to the native habitat of research scientists, the preceding experience had been as alien as the microbes they were trying to find.

Even walking out the door, Norm Horowitz held fast to objectivity. "My feeling is that my instrument has not found a biological response," he declared. "But I still don't have a chemical proof. And as long as I don't have one, there will be a residue of doubt."

Pat Straat and Gil Levin bundled up their notebooks and graphs and skirts (just Straat) and bow ties (Levin only) and retreated home. Both resonated with the obviousness of what they'd discovered. But everyone else on the Biology Team considered LR's results only in context with the other two experiments *plus* the GCMS. When viewed as a whole, the verdict stood firmly in the world of chemical reactions.

"We were very upset at this," remarked Levin.

"The Viking response *was* a small response," conceded Straat of her low-level counting rates. "When we would test a terrestrial sample, we'd get a couple hundred thousand counts evolved. And on Mars we'd get ten to fifteen thousand." Levin planned to dig back into their data. He took faith in Louis Pasteur's own conundrum, because after decades of research, an answer did finally present itself to the French chemist. Mystical fermentation centered on the yeast microbe; it was biology after all.

Inside von Karman Auditorium, workmen removed the topographically correct fake rocks and flight-spare Viking *Lander* and prepared to install a different model that represented those crazy Voyager ships due to launch at Jupiter sometime in the next several months. Over at Building 264, custodians emptied trash cans full of abandoned box lunches, moved tables back into position, scrubbed the chalkboards. On the way out they hit the wall switches and the grating buzz of fluorescent lighting fell silent.

23. Postmortem

It is not correct to say that Mars has been shown to be lifeless. We
failed to demonstrate that life is there, but we didn't disprove it.

—Biology Team advisor Alexander Rich

Gil Levin was in a stew, insides roiling from all that godawful Pasadena
pressure to rapidly interpret his findings. *Answers! We want answers!!* Seems
like that's all he heard sometimes. A chemical response? A biological one?
Jeepers, couldn't anybody be patient? Anxious, he wanted to conduct a
methodical review of LR's behavior and results, establishing the direction
in which they leaned.

Levin exhaled heavily, like a man who'd spent all day cleaning up storm
damage. "Pat and I submitted such a proposal," he mentioned. "For analysis and interpretation of the Viking LR results, and to develop both biological and nonbiological explanations for the LR data." A NASA contract
came their way, specifying two years to get to the bottom of the muck.

In the lab, Straat and Levin platonically secluded themselves, decompil-
ing the reams of printouts generated by both *Lander*s and spreading everything out for mental magnifying glasses. Comparative testing needed to be
done on flight-spec LR hardware, and they threw every imaginable variation
at it. "Pat was ingenious at rigging-up experiments trying to make hydrogen peroxide work, other chemicals work," applauded Levin.

In contrast, Ames didn't pursue any follow-on GEX studies at all. "As
long as the return data were blank," confided Fritz Woeller, "there seemed
to be little incentive to continue." Anyway, he and the rest of Oyama's team
would soon have to transition to a separate mission called Pioneer Venus
and design a study of that planet's upper atmosphere.

Come late May '77, JPL completely powered down *Lander 2*'s Biology Instrument. Two days later its sibling at Chryse suffered the same indignity. The remaining equipment on the *Lander*s chugged away silently, more or less forgotten by the public at large, flinging home minutiae about the weather, or soil properties, and recording tons of pictures.

That same year Carl Sagan obtained a modest grant to study a potentially overlooked aspect of the Viking *Orbiter* photographs. He spent over two years perusing them in search of any traces of intelligent civilizations. He found zilch. No ruined cities, no aqueducts, no engineered canals that'd escaped earlier detection. What about the supposed Face on Mars? Nope— just another rock formation, its eerily humanoid features drawn by a trick of light and shadow.

Gil Levin and Pat Straat knocked themselves out trying to duplicate LR's outcomes using hypothesized substances like hydrogen peroxide. "But at the end of the two years, we had been unable to produce a physical or chemical reaction that would explain away the LR data on Mars," Levin testified. Which left them with only one real explanation.

Thirty-five years after the fact, Klaus Biemann recollected a prelaunch discussion that some had possibly forgotten during the mad stampede that was Viking: "The Biology Team had, before the mission, decided unanimously that even if their results are positive—if there are no organics, and if that is sort of rather certain, then their results must be anomalous."

"In that case," Norm Horowitz had added at the time, "I'd tend to put my faith in the organic chemistry experiment and wonder what went wrong with ours."

Looking back today, Jerry Hubbard has a fairly clear answer: Carbon Assimilation was too convoluted in design and beset with multiple weaknesses. "You cannot believe the number of commands and steps that were involved," he said of the experiment's operation. "You know, all those *multiple steps* of the columns and sweeping them and the gases, and, it just made it terribly complex." He singled out the organic vapor filter—that U-shaped golden tube. It didn't separate compounds nearly as well as they would've liked. And it was finicky; Viking's eleven-month outbound coast through space may have increased the pipe's affinity for amassing carbon dioxide. Not good! Hubbard also detested the heating of dirt samples: an inefficient way of releasing organics. The xenon lamp made a sorry substitute for sunlight. Hubbard flat-out declared that he'd never send the thing again. He, along with Horowitz, felt that the GCMS results should be held high above all others.

"Organic analysis is the best," he said.

Biemann continued with his point about a lack of organics negating any positive biology results. "And so those people were not just the three experimenters—Horowitz, Levin, and Oyama—but also the other members of the Biology Team: Joshua Lederberg at Stanford, Alex Rich at MIT—both eminent biologists—and Chuck Klein." (For reasons unknown, lots of people referred to Harold Klein as "Chuck.")

Nobody would ever have reckoned on three biological green lights and nary a carbon squawk from the GCMS. It was just so unfathomably improbable—more indicative of catastrophic system failure than pure, clean data. Obviously, no organics would mean no life as we know it—regardless of what *any* biology experiment reported. If the team saw eye-to-eye on only one single point, it was this.

"They all agreed," said Biemann, "without any input on my side, that that would be the case. And that's what turned out."

Viking's GCMS operated flawlessly *up to the limits of design*. Biemann never claimed his machine was perfect. Despite superior engineering and meticulous craftsmanship, room-sized high technology will always be compromised when reduced to the volume of a box of ice skates and forced to operate in a total hands-off environment.

Here's a whopper: the initial heating step, used to liberate compounds from soil. By Biemann's own estimate, heating releases only about 10 percent of any given material. "In the laboratory, you would *extract*," he explained. Instead of high temperatures, a liquid solvent uncouples the soil constituents for delivery into a GCMS. The solvent method is far preferable—a thousand times more efficient, in some cases—but involves a complicated, multistep process. "Very difficult to do on Mars," he stated, going on to explain how that was simply beyond Viking's capabilities. Along with Horowitz, he had no real choice except to use heat because it offered the simplest and most reliable approach to sample preparation.

Another charge was sensitivity; it varied based on the type of molecule. Many so-called aromatic molecules, like benzene, for example, could be detected down to the level of a tenth of a part per billion. But others, including very common substances like methane and ammonia, weren't detectable at all, as they'd get swamped by the large amounts of water and carbon dioxide simultaneously coming off—translating into ultimate stealth for flatulent, Windex-using Martians.

Most earthly organisms are composed of roughly 90 percent water—the remainder being dry mass. And of *that*, only a fraction consists of organic material. As Biemann clarified, "We would need one million microorganisms per gram of soil to be able to detect the organic material that they represent." Labeled Release, similarly using just one gram, would need only ten microorganisms.

If Gil Levin had a smoking gun, it would be something called Antarctic 726—one of the bonded soils originally used to augment his reference catalog. It came from Coalsack Bluff, a modest and snow-free ridge of shales and coals in the Central Transantarctic Mountains. In 1979 Levin noticed a disturbing aside in the PhD thesis from a Biemann student who'd worked on Viking's GCMS. Buried among its hundreds of pages was a note about how this particular sample, despite containing 0.03 percent carbon, produced no detectable organic molecules when processed in a flight-like GCMS. The term "Antarctic 726" rang a bell in Levin's head. He double-checked records and found that a pinch of it had failed to germinate any colonies of microbes in a traditional culture. But another pinch had gone into LR and immediately registered positive. His experiment never needed *growth* for results—only metabolism.

Levin didn't exactly scream it from the rooftops, but he did make something of a professional fuss about the situation. *Viking results were compatible after all*, he insisted. *Wasn't it time to reexamine?*

Biemann certainly didn't attempt to conceal or otherwise obfuscate these details; they were all right there in his scientific papers. And with deliberate carefulness, he had crafted their language to never specifically exclude the possibility of organics on the Red Planet. In one report he plainly stated, "If organic materials are present in the samples analyzed, they must be there at extremely low levels." At face value, that made for quite an admission. His gazillion-dollar baby could sniff out most organics way down deep at the level of just a few parts per billion. Even so, the MIT man was readily granting that microbes could exist in such fantastically low numbers that the device would never register organic material from just them alone. In another paper he said, "Nothing that has been learned about Mars at this point rules out the possibility that organic compounds have concentrated at favored sites on the surface of the planet."

Biemann never dismissed the existence of Martian life itself. "The demonstration," he wrote, "that very little, if any, organic material is present does not exclude the existence of living organisms in the samples analyzed, and certainly does not rule out the possibility of a rich biota out of range of the Viking landing sites."

Nor did he discount the potentiality of life itself in the samples he tested: "It is possible to have a small population of micro-organisms in a sample without being able to detect the organic compounds evolved from their biomass." And that was no retrospective from thirty years on; that particular comment went to press in September 1976—while both *Lander*s were still trundling along on the surface of Mars.

The man with the smallest professional and emotional investment in Viking's results was the same one holding the door open the widest.

24. Sons of a Bitch

The USSR and France have been cooperating, not too successfully,
in certain space ventures for a number of years.

—A (formerly) top-secret U.S. National
Intelligence Estimate, July 1971

All anyone knew for sure was this: Mstislav Keldysh entered his garage on June 24, 1978, and started up a car. But he left the garage door shut and never came back out. Official versions of this story claim his heart failed immediately after he keyed the ignition. This detail—oddly vague for a public figure of his stature—has never been resolved. Various close friends reckoned it was suicide. He was sixty-seven.

In that garage Keldysh left behind a widespread legacy on multiple levels. He ratcheted science up onto a pedestal and tirelessly evangelized its relevance. After noticing how the ranks of academicians seemed to be clogged with stodgy old fogies who cared more about social privileges than honest science, Keldysh advocated radical changes in the membership policies—bringing younger people aboard to invigorate the Academy of Sciences and spearhead critical innovation. For reasons like these had he tapped Roald Sagdeev to lead the Space Institute.

Keldysh opposed the practice of blindly copying American computer designs (not to mention their Space Shuttle), campaigning instead for good-ol' Soviet originality. Keldysh was insanely curious about *everything*—habitually spending ten or twelve hours on an otherwise routine walk-through of any given facility.

"Very difficult to accompany him in such tours!" announced Sagdeev, who, while in attendance, presumably had to cross his legs and hold it more than once.

A few years down the road they'd name a six-thousand-ton ocean research vessel after him: the *Academician Mstislav Keldysh*, which entered service in March '81. Sagdeev liked the ship and all; nice gesture. But he would've much preferred Keldysh back at his desk, as he was, slaving away in the name of good science. Even if that meant no potty breaks.

A funk settled in at the Space Institute. The dour mood failed to improve when two new Venera flights rudely broke Sagdeev's winning streak. The first to set down, in late December, *Venera 12* failed to eject the lens caps from both its cameras. Then, on Christmas Day no less, its twin *Venera 11* barreled into the same yucky problem. Zero-for-four, ouch—with cameras able to serve up double the resolution as beforehand! (A recent innovation has been the use of *clear lens caps*, in case of similar pitfalls.)

These next-gen machines also carried remarkable implements to bore holes in the surface rock and analyze fragments. But pressure seals ruptured on both and the drills never worked. Thwarted engineers argued that rough descents played a major role in the fiasco. Sagdeev rocked back in his chair. Having thumbed each report, he balanced them atop the clerical gridlock adorning his desk. Last time around everything had worked so painlessly.

The failures made for a double bummer because Sagdeev, almost from the week he took office, had been encouraging a dilation of the science aboard Venera ships—and he sought to capitalize on the resources of the Space Institute in building them. It formed part of a grander scheme to lessen dependence on what he often perceived as ridiculously unreliable outside contractors. Lately the institute's capabilities had grown— albeit on a sluggish timescale. Years of maturation would have to occur before they'd be able to chaperone something from scratch paper to flight-ready mission and do it all in-house. But he was working in that direction nonetheless.

After *Venera 11* and *12* shut down, Sagdeev had to once again present himself before an eager crowd at the Polytechnical Museum. This place can be thought of as a Russian counterpart to the Smithsonian and resides just a couple streets northeast of the Kremlin in downtown Moscow.

Speaking there had come to be a regular gig for Sagdeev after flights ended, and the usual questions came rolling forth from curious proletarians in their big fur hats: *What did the missions find? What were the highlights?* Sagdeev mentioned a possible presence of chlorine gas up in the clouds. The result came from sensors on *Venera 12*, but he cautioned that it'd have to be affirmed.

How come no pictures?

Admitting technical failures was a definite no-no in any public forum. Deftly Sagdeev side-stepped the inquiry and moved on.

Why are we always going just to Venus?

Ooh, truthfully? "The lifetime of the spacecraft was very short," he acknowledged, many years later. The nation had simply been unable to fabricate robust, long-lived electronics. "*Anything* beyond nearby planets— Mars and Venus—was unrealistic," griped Sagdeev. "The industry would be unable to guarantee survival of the spacecraft." As high-tech and advanced as they were, every surfing Venera made a fundamental bow to immaturity by safeguarding its computing brain deep inside a spherical core that had been pressurized to one Earth atmosphere. Early on the United States did this kind of thing, too. Then evolution happened. "Americans quickly stepped over this little barrier. And all the chief electronic components were made to be survivable in an open space vacuum environment." Sagdeev threw up his hands; they'd been outclassed. "It saved everything. Saved weight, mass, whatever." Soviet engineers never cleared the hurdle and General Secretary Brezhnev never seemed real interested in improving the funding of projects unless they had missiles attached.

"It created a lot of trouble; it limited the life of the spacecraft."

Up on stage, that "why nowhere else" question still hung in the air like a stale fart. Would Sagdeev level with his audience? Blab to everyone how the science payload on a Venera or Mars ship generally outlived the brain of the spacecraft itself? Ah, *nyet.* He went for the smoke screen—playing up the notion of Venus as Soviet turf, skirting reality largely because he wasn't in the mood to commit political suicide while standing defenseless behind a thin little podium.

The U.S. has put four ships through the asteroid belt. Why can the Americans fly anywhere they want?

"*Because they are sons of a bitch!*" he sputtered, utterly fed up with diplomacy. And everyone broke into raucous applause that lasted for several minutes.

A Los Angeles court ordered Clayton Moore to stop wearing his Lone Ranger mask because of trademark issues. CompuServe and ESPN began. "Message in a Bottle" hit number one on the British charts. Also in September '79, an exuberantly cocktailing Jacques Blamont hunted down Roald Sagdeev. Think *friendly* hunt. Both men were in Corsica, unwinding after an international symposium, and honestly, Blamont wasn't feeling real chipper that evening. Over the course of the multiday conference, Soviet and French delegations had explored a myriad of collaborative ventures in space. Days ran long; most everybody propelled themselves to extreme fatigue. Like Blamont. Armed with wavy white hair and long cheeks and shrubbery for eyebrows, he routinely advised the French national space agency from his vantage point as a physicist at Paris's Curie University.

A fractional percentage of Blamont's sourpuss attitude had to do with exhaustion. Most of it, however, stemmed from NASA's recent cancellation of any dedicated mission to Halley's comet during its 1986 fly-through of the inner solar system. French astronomers had been all giddy to partner up with America and study it—only to get weed-whacked at the ankles. *Sorry, too burdened*, claimed the Washington naysayers, *with getting our Space Shuttle off the ground.* The white-winged wonder was supposed to fly that year but languished far behind schedule and over budget. It had more foibles than the shah of Iran. France, it seemed, would not be visiting this comet.

Blamont hefted another libation and silently bemoaned his predicament. What was a planetary scientist to do? His nation couldn't go alone. The French possessed no Cape Canaveral or Titan rocket. Yeah, they had the wherewithal to make good instruments—heck, look at those sexy range finders on the *Lunokhod*s. But design and develop a whole mission?

At this point, Blamont innocently committed what he later referred to as "the most stupid thing of my life." After locating Sagdeev he offhandedly vocalized how America had bailed on the planned collaboration to visit Halley's comet. He then suggested that the institute might want to at least look into the possibility of going themselves. Have a couple meetings, you know? Give the idea a once-over? The Germans and the Japanese were going, but not the first nation in space?

A comet? *What* comet? Sagdeev wasn't at all familiar with the object, and a rapt discussion ensued. What could they do? How might they go about studying it? Ties and collars loosened, the men freely batted around ideas like cats on a moth, swirling half-melted ice in their highballs. Despite a general weariness from the preceding days' activities, chatting about blue-sky options somehow energized them both. Maybe a giant telescope in Earth orbit? Hmm, probably not. Unlike Halley's last fly-through, in 1910, our planet wouldn't enjoy front-row seats as the comet angled on through. Interestingly though . . . it would not be terribly far from the Goddess of Love.

A baggy-eyed Sagdeev jabbed the air with his index finger. "Look, Jacques, what about our own Venus balloon project?"

Once slated for *Venera 11* and *12*, the farsighted notion of launching French weather balloons into the atmosphere of Venus had unsurprisingly been pushed back. Again. Maybe someday it'd happen: a thirty-three-foot balloon portaging fifty-five pounds of science through the wacky clouds. In one breath Sagdeev reminded his friend of the special ultraviolet sensors also planned for the same flight. In orbit around Venus, they'd dangle off the mother ship. Perhaps this could also be used for cometary observations?

That was kind of reaching. Blamont morphed the paradigm: what about parking a regular optical telescope in Venusian orbit? Out there it'd be a superior vantage point, he reckoned.

Talk like this further cranked the gears. On bar napkins the rejuvenated pair doodled planets and comets and boxes and circles with lines connecting all of them and arrows pointing in various directions. Without context it looked like maniacal rugby strategy but definitely felt like the start of something. How about: Send balloon down from Venus orbit. Mother ship waits for comet. Deploy balloon. Study comet with telescopes. Um, from twenty-five million miles away? "Still was a very far distance," confessed Sagdeev. In order to even *fund* a beast like this the images would have to be dumbfounding—an order of magnitude superior to any from Earth. Maybe that could happen with Western optics . . . but . . . Sagdeev nixed any ridiculous fantasies of putting American experiments aboard.

Whirlpooling discussions and brainstorming and pencils-in-the-ceiling-type activities continued long after the conference broke and everyone had flown home to their respective daily grinds. "He got extremely excited about this when he came back to Moscow," claimed an individual in a position to watch Sagdeev ramble on about the comet as if he'd just met the love of his life. "For a few months he could not speak about anything else."

Mission possibilities grew like kudzu, but a realization had already dawned upon Roald Sagdeev: wasn't Halley's comet itself the real jewel, here? The once-in-a-lifetime thing? "Are we bound," Sagdeev and Blamont finally asked one another, "to staying in orbit around Venus? Could we possibly *move closer* to the comet?"

Why not? Indeed, why not pick up an energy boost at Venus and then gun straight for it? Fly out to where the comet *was*, instead of hanging back like some coy voyeur outside a peep show? Space Institute staff astronomer Vladimir Kurt recommended they multitask: Fly to Venus. Launch balloons. Retarget. Barrel *through* the comet. Yes, that was it! Sagdeev felt a rush of positive energy filling his soul.

But would it work? Space missions typically *avoid* hazardous activities. The closer something approached a boiling, hissing dust bomb of a cometary nucleus, the more risk it'd face. "There were completely new engineering technical issues," indicated Sagdeev. "How to protect spacecraft from micrometeorites. Dust particles emitted by Halley's comet." Problems trailed off the edge of the paper.

Zealous development spilled over into the offices of design bureaus and contractors who'd actually have to build hardware. One of Sagdeev's major subissues involved not cometary dust but a particular guy at Lavochkin who, coincidentally enough, shared the same first name. Assistant to the Chief Designer Roald Kremnev regarded himself as a by-the-book engineer who ran the plays tight and safe. "He was *very* cautious," remembered Sagdeev, and the idea of pushing the boundaries of spacecraft operations—so terribly far from home—did not excite Kremnev in the slightest. He "wanted to build something much more primitive."

That elemental conflict: scientists always favored uncharted lands. Go forth and tease out the secrets! But engineers? "They try to make everything safer for themselves, you know?" It frustrated Sagdeev to no end. "You cannot do a real great job without accepting some risk. That's a problem!" Often the two Roalds crossed swords—figuratively—while searching out common ground. Sagdeev tried everything he could dream up to bend the guy's opinions into more agreeable ones. "Look. We are now making this project in the eyes of the rest of the world," he preached during one meeting. "Let's try to do in such a way that we will show the best what we can do."

Nevertheless, Kremnev's approach did have some validity. Were they asking for failure? Was this a suicide job? The academy ran feasibility studies. "You know, we cannot come close to the comet," insisted one engineer. Like many, he balked at the idea of chasing down a wayward ice ball in the middle of space. "At most, we can predict the trajectory of Halley's comet with an accuracy of something like a hundred thousand kilometers."

Pressed Sagdeev, "How you make this prediction?"

"Oh-kayyy," said the guy. "We will take the old data of 1910, calculate how it would come back, and then the error box is that high."

Crickets.

Finally Sagdeev rolled his eyes. "It is that high if we would not *see* the comet!" What he meant was, precisely graphing Halley's course would indeed be difficult relying only on generations-old figures. But long before it approached Venus, years ahead of time, the thing would come into view of earthbound telescopes. Upon first sight, a comet is said to have been "recovered." And sakes alive, couldn't new measurements be taken after that happened? "Then we will drastically improve the coordinates of the comet!" lectured Sagdeev. He tried to cheerfully seal the deal. "Why don't we plan a *much closer* encounter."

Little victories. Big thinking. Sagdeev's own personal morale went through the ceiling. Venera and Mars—great projects, yeah, but ones already up to bat when he arrived. Even the two remaining half-assembled Veneras had already been in the works long before Keldysh made him change jobs. What Sagdeev mostly did with those things was administrate them.

Change now beckoned. This crazy comet combo, whatever form its wet clay hardened into, remained a purebred original. Optimistically he envisioned the project as a truly international one—comprising scientists from as many nations as could possibly be rounded up, all working toward a common goal. And before long the appellation "Vega" came into play, resulting from a contraction of "Venus" and the comet's name. Anyone with a Russian tongue said "Galley" because the language contains no sound for "H."

Even before that fateful discussion in Corsica, Blamont knew the Soviets would never be able to do any ballooning on their own. Specifically, he was thinking about their tracking network. The country did have several installations within its own borders that were basically similar in capability to Yevpatoria station. It also had a few oceangoing ships with giant dishes sitting precariously on their decks, looking like the whole deal might fall over any second.

But to track a balloon on Venus, in real time, called for exquisitely sensitive gear spread over the entirety of Earth. Blamont needed a bigger, better footprint. One that offered uninterrupted coverage. He needed America and its Deep Space Network—an internationally distributed array of antennas and tracking facilities.

And really, he was about the only guy in a position to ask. Roald Sagdeev—at that time, anyway—couldn't have rung up America for help. Like Chris Kraft, the Soviets *also* needed an intermediary. So, seeing as how he'd fully recognized this tracking deficiency well over a year prior, Blamont had had one of his assistants visit JPL, connecting there with a man named Bob Preston. To him, Blamont's assistant conveyed a proposal in two parts. First, could they please help track a balloon on Venus? And second, might America ever wish to contribute experiments to the balloon's payload?

Out of all the possibilities, Bob Preston certainly was not an arbitrary choice. At JPL he ran a research group dedicated to observing celestial objects. For that, they used a specialized technique employing several large radio telescopes all working together to observe the same feature. This resulted in measurements with extremely fine angular resolution—as if the many telescopes were actually one gigantic one, so big it could never be built. Preston described his group as "a hotbed of expertise in this particular discipline," talking with the calm precision and gravelly undertones that would also have made him an excellent radio DJ. "If you wanted to get angular measurements of what was going on, angular measurements of the balloon's motion, JPL was certainly the place to come. So the French realized that."

After reviewing the documents forwarded to him, Preston sent a memo to Blamont's assistant. JPL, he confided, was pretty underwhelmed. "The Soviet proposal is quite vague and details and concepts are unclear," went part of it. "The Soviets understood a number of key concepts about such an experiment, however the explanations are terribly muddied and the science goals are not discussed at all."

Preston offered perspective. "That's the way missions start," he said, excusing the inadvertent vagueness and lack of clarity. "You have things you'd like to do, but you haven't really put all the glue to it yet to really hold it together."

So the French and Soviets wanted the Americans to help out and provide experiments. For *something* involving balloons on Venus. (And, at least as far as the U.S. State Department was concerned, the arrangement would always be regarded as a French-American one.) This mystery venture now appeared to be plowing forward, although the Soviets hadn't yet fully decided on exactly what their special something would be. Documents from them had talked of flying both high- and low-altitude balloons. Did one approach make more sense than the other? Inside JPL, a modest group formed to start combing through ideas.

Behind the Iron Curtain, the spring of 1980 finally brought Sagdeev's Big Sell. With determination he marched into a churning tempest of misanthropic faces: the Commission on Military-Industrial Issues. Without them Vega wouldn't rise a foot; these humorless scabs lorded over every particle of range facilities and booster rockets and made for difficult customers indeed.

Purposefully, almost as if on trial, Sagdeev thumbed a projector to life and began clacking through reams of color slides. Each one gorgeously detailed a key Vega mission phase. Bearing hundreds of pounds of science, two mother ships would approach Venus and its crucial well of gravity. *Something must drop low enough to deploy each balloon*, explained Sagdeev. *We propose to do this with Venera-style landers, enabling truly saturated coverage of the planet*. Each lander would inhale cloud vapors on the way down and then drill the surface.

Provided by the French, Vega's massive balloons would ride the winds and shed light on the Venusian atmosphere—a bizarrely puzzling amalgam of layered chemicals. In simultaneity, the planet's gravity would slingshot Vega's mother ships out and away for unbridled intercourse with Halley's comet—ideally closing to within five thousand miles of its nucleus.

Let's talk audacious, goaded Sagdeev, working the room. *Breathtaking. A real package deal!* No cometary nucleus had ever, *ever* been seen by the eye of man and Vega would bravely plunge headfirst into this unknown to produce revealing photos and measurements. *Like a true Soviet pioneer! Absolutely unprecedented.*

Most every slide had been expended by the time one commissioner took the floor. "I am ready to agree," he mused. "It sounds extremely impressive. But have you prepared a soft bed to protect yourself from a rough landing?" He thought the plan too grandiose and turned to regard the audience, looking for supporters. Trepidation slowly crept through the room at knee height, like stage fog.

"I knew it was a moment of truth for the institute," Sagdeev later asserted. "I had never felt such a drive to succeed." But to line up his next trick shot the game had to be played on their level, under their terms.

He tried this: "What you see here is essentially a three-warhead rocket." Sagdeev inhaled deeply before continuing the rebuttal, gauging audience provocation. "Two deliveries to Venus—a balloon and a lander to the surface. And the third to encounter Halley's comet. What we are going to do is simply use the military technology that you developed." With that he stood aside. Waiting.

Came the eventual answer, *Stay tuned.*

Retrieve slides. Pack up. Smile like it matters. Sagdeev returned to the office and plunked down in his over-worn chair at the end of the table. He needed tea. His secretary brought phone messages. *Vega Vega Vega.* The slides went on a shelf. Biding his time, Sagdeev monitored the prep for *Venera 13* and *14*, attended conferences, and kept up on news—marking with some sadness the passing of Viking's *Lander 2*, after its batteries failed in mid-April.

25. The Sum of All Nations

It was the Cold War, and these were the bad guys. And we
learned they weren't bad guys; they were really good guys.

—JPL's Bob Preston, after collaborating with Soviet scientists

Halley's is one of the few comets with a small-enough circuit that a single
individual has a fighting chance of seeing it twice within his or her lifetime. A whole lap takes about seventy-six years. The thing's been around
virtually forever; even documented observations show it to have been coming and going for thousands of years. Sky-watching Chinese took notice
in 240 BC. Centuries later, Attila the Hun went down for the count in 452
AD—around the same time a certain celestial something flew overhead.
Totally coincidental, yet enough to get some wondering about what kind
of power that arcing light-ball might actually wield.

There are other records of the comet's passage. Within a dark room in
Normandy, France, sits a purpose-built clear enclosure that glows from indirect lighting. Inside rests a particularly intriguing example of early medi-
eval embroidery—depicting the Norman Conquest of England in 1066.
This is the Bayeux Tapestry, an utterly irreplaceable document portraying
its war story over the course of one uninterrupted 230-foot piece of cloth.

Midway through it, soldiers pause to gesture at the sky. An ornately
flaming sphere of energy above them represents a comet, and perhaps a
bad omen as well for King Harold II of England.

But for Sir Edmund Halley it was altogether quite different. An eighteenth-
century English astronomer, Halley convinced himself that the comet that
appeared in 1066, at least two others charted later on by different people,
and the one seen by the Chinese were really all one and the same. Halley

was buddies with Isaac Newton and applied some of his good friend's new-fangled formulae to predict the comet's recurrence in the later months of 1758. Halley didn't live to verify this prediction . . . but he sure nailed the date. On Christmas of that year it neatly bisected the heavens to demonstrate that more than just planets orbited the sun. One year later a French astronomer proposed that the object be known by the name of the man who predicted Earth's first regularly scheduled cometary event.

The light-ball came streaking back through in 1835 and again returned as expected in 1910. At that time, it passed within fifteen million miles of our planet and actually washed its tail over us for about six hours. Months beforehand, the Yerkes Observatory in Chicago had erroneously reported lethal cyanogen gas as having been detected inside the comet's tail. Some newspapers ran articles instructing housewives to close all their doors and windows, while many New York City churches held all-night services for the devoutly fearful.

With the news that August to go ahead and do Vega, only one small catch remained. Probably could get handled with a phone call.

"I was in vacation in my country home, and then telephone rings and it's Sagdeev." Blamont described the call as if it had brought news of a loved one's car crash. But the first sentences he heard indicated nothing of the sort—merely a proposal coming from left field. "A fantastic plan. Very surprising," reacted Blamont. "They would be devoted to a mission both to 'aleey and to Venus," using two identical spacecraft flying the same profile. What a ballsy move. He'd guessed the Soviets would probably try *something*—but not nearly as much as what flowed into his ear. "It looked crazy. Absolutely crazy. And it was!"

A buoyant Sagdeev continued jabbering away through the scratchy line, and this is where things got dicey. "He explained me that everything is changed," Blamont professed—starting to feel less excited about the mission. "Big balloon is out, that we have back to small balloon."

Wha—? See, as with many space missions, Vega's planned objectives had quickly outgrown reality. Even after lengthening the mother ships to carry additional fuel and electronics, there was no way each of these spacecraft could leave the ground fully provisioned for a Venus landing, the balloon, *and* Halley. The trifecta would exhaust their abilities. Something had to give.

Let's see . . . the chief goal remained Halley's virginal nucleus. That meant the mother ships couldn't be shrunken down or otherwise suffer any reductions in capability. And the lander configs were already a known good—no real way to change things there, either. As such, France's balloons were going to have to shed a few pant sizes. Naturally Sagdeev got stuck with breaking the news. To Blamont he explained that they were now looking at two airships, each just eleven feet crosswise and buttressing a flyweight gondola holding less than ten pounds of goodies. The reimagined balloons would still be large enough to return good science, although a chunk of that weight would have to go toward batteries and radio transmitters strong enough to fling the signals home.

"The Soviets went berserk with comet 'aleey!" decried Jacques Blamont, so upset he almost lapsed back into French. "It destroyed everything!" He almost couldn't comprehend what they were now supposed to do: "Remove the big balloon which *they* had imposed to us, and we had developed with great difficulty." Was all that previous work really bound for the sewer? "Everything was shipshape!" he proclaimed of France's large balloon design. "It was ready! And suddenly they said, 'No no no no, this is not good, we go back to your early proposal of a series of small balloon.'"

The men restated their positions to one another, grumbling (all in English). Blamont denounced the institute's kowtowing. Sagdeev pleaded that this final configuration simply couldn't be modified. They were locked in. French authorities would just have to be talked into submissive compliance.

As Blamont later hotly summarized the quandary, "I am in charge for convincing CNES to abandon all what they had been doing, which was a *very large* amount of money, and I was supposed to convince them to accept this complete change!" (CNES, or Centre National d'Études Spatiales, is the French national space agency.)

Imperceptibly, Blamont's new ulcer germinated. He heaved his gut and said, *Okay, I'll try.*

As might have been expected, the attempted convincing did not go over well. CNES didn't want anything to do with the new arrangement. Puny balloons? Honestly! They'd been the unwitting victims of involuntary genitalia-reduction surgery, a doggone underhanded bait and switch by a load of two-faced, swindling commie carpetbaggers. "I tried but I could not do it," sighed Blamont. "CNES decided that they had been fooled by the Soviets and they got out of it, which was a disaster for everybody."

"The whole engineering team which was working on designing the French balloon refused to work," is how Sagdeev recollected the fallout.

Commitments flew off the table and in the blink of an eye Vega no longer had any balloons. The topic was a dead carp in toxic water. Bob Preston got notified that both the French *and* the Soviets were declaring Venus balloons a dead issue. He grimaced and shelved all his own work. JPL moved on.

Eventually, startlingly, CNES relented (slightly) by pledging assistance on various minor aspects of the Vega mission. But that was it; no balloons would be coming from them. *Fin de la discussion.* Sagdeev tried adding perspective to the wilted relationship: "It was very painful for someone who invested so much, not necessarily even financially, but emotionally. It was their deal," he said. "They had a large team to design and to build that balloon. And then suddenly, some other group would come and say, 'Look. We have a better project.'" How would that make *anybody* feel?

Even so, Sagdeev gasped at the sheer breadth of French-fried outrage. "Maybe some of them thought that since Russians had no experience in this type of ballooning, maybe we will drop this new project." He tried to appear upbeat, but it looked forced and altogether unnatural. *"Maybe."* The prospect of trolling Moscow to find some half-asleep condom manufacturer and imploring him to create otherworldly balloons, well . . . it gave him night tremors. It chapped his lips. The calendar stared him down: forty-eight months until launch day. Far beyond Moscow and Sagdeev's unrecoverably overchoked office, an indifferent comet that had unknowingly marked eons of death and defeat and harried housewives mindlessly traced a broad arc that would eventually draw it through our inner solar system and within spittin' distance of Venus. It could've cared less about one guy's problems.

"How we can start from the scratch?" protested Roald Sagdeev, to his own reflection in the mirror. "From the *very scratch*?"

He asked staff scientist Slava Linkin to please find out what their options might be. Linkin gave a nod, then zealously disappeared into the subterranean catacombs of politics and Soviet contractors. Lurking out there was the Stradivari of ballooning.

A contender soon appeared in Moscow's north central outskirts; the decades-old facility specialized in dirigibles of all kinds for everything from transporting goods to espionage. One time these hotshots built an airship holding 106 million cubic feet of gas. They made another that could carry six and a half tons of cargo. Yet another happily endured altitudes up to 150,000 feet. Despite these masterpieces, very little time passed before the team of wizened virtuosos got bogged down in creating a teensy-weensy balloon that only had to survive a couple days in the Venusian sky. They couldn't get a handle on its quirky deployment, or the corrosive atmosphere, and they bailed.

For the umpteenth time, the floor had dropped out from under Sagdeev—and now Linkin. The latter man went shopping anew and ultimately hooked a solution inside the well-traveled hallways of the Lavochkin Bureau. For them it was (yawn) kind of the same old build-the-unbuildable they'd been doing for years. What else was new? Lavochkin went at it piecemeal, breaking down the problem into bite-size chunks. Already they knew the weight budget: 250 pounds for airship and gondola, plus experiments. From there they could interpolate various individual size limits. And the whole contraption could realistically survive for only a limited amount of time, which did much to contain the scope.

Of all things, the balloon itself—outwardly the most unsophisticated, simplest part of the whole conglomeration—needed the most ground-floor bootstrapping. It couldn't be some off-the-shelf gunny sack. Pancake-flat and tightly folded, the material had to endure months of travel in frigid space only to inflate perfectly on cue in the midst of a full frontal assault by thick clouds of sulfuric acid vapor. They needed fearless fabric that was everything-proof. Or darn near.

Inside their own country, Lavochkin gumshoes stumbled upon a weird relative of Teflon called Ftorlon. It'd been around since the end of the Great Patriotic War and was used for things like filtering highly caustic liquids. This stuff is impervious to many acids. Doesn't burn. If something would work better on Venus, it hadn't been invented yet. Assemblers carefully stitched together pie-shaped wedges of Ftorlon while layering the seams with a custom paint mix that further resisted corrosive substances. One inflation test after another demonstrated that helium leaked out slowly enough to give them roughly five days of flight time. The complete articles were also radio transparent—meaning that precious communication signals from the gondola wouldn't bounce off the fabric and miss Earth. Assemblers lovingly wiped them down with soft cloths, preparing good-byes to their handiwork.

Although this nation suffered from gutterball electronics and laughably out-of-date computing technology, Soviet ingenuity had formulated balloons for another world and now moved on to matters of delivering them. In order to properly rendezvous with the elusive comet Halley, both Vega mother ships would have to shed their payload on the nighttime side of Venus. Cameras disappeared from the lander drawings, freeing up trunk space for other equipment. A slight redesign also emerged. Venera's evolution meant that more and more experiments could be installed on the sides of them. So many, in fact, that the accouterments were generating more turbulence than anyone felt comfortable with. Stability must reign. Thick aerodynamic vanes now filled the landing hoop, forming a five-spoke pattern radiating out from a hub that lay just below the squat central globe. To further aid in control, a stubby skirt of thin metal went underneath the circumference of the main surfboard. To cradle the balloon and gondola, white-jacketed clean-room installers dropped a hollow, lifebuoy-style hard shell ring over top of the roof-mounted antenna. And then Vega's lander was basically there.

The 1985 Soviet-French Venus balloon mission lives!
According to Jacques Blamont, the French government must make a final decision on the joint mission in two weeks.
He estimates 95% chance of approval.
This is quite a surprising development.

Memo from Bob Preston to several JPL colleagues, 1982

Late in 1981, two Proton rockets finally headed for Venus—carrying not Vega spacecraft but reworked Veneras, that they might avenge broken drills and stuck-on lens caps. Enhanced with additional experiments and longer run times—yet lacking the stability changes mandated for Vega—Lavochkin's mature gizmos failed to disappoint. During the first week of March, four days apart, each cleanly plummeted through the dense high-altitude haze, which resembles a mix of Beijing smog and aerosolized cat pee. Microphones powered up on each one, recording wind and impact sounds. They hit at seventeen miles an hour, bounced one time off the scraggy terrain, then settled for good and forever.

Radio transmitters chirped the arrival, sending but unable to receive. Controllers heard the sounds of all four lens caps popping off and tumbling onto the ground. They heard whispery-faint winds dancing along. Had Soviet bureaucrats ever released these audio recordings to the world at large, they could've reaped a public-relations windfall. Now the color-chip charts sprang out, two on each lander. These strips with red, green, blue, and gray squares resembled the sample cards people get when shopping for paint. Extreme heat and pressure affect how colors look, so these aided in interpreting the true surface hues.

They were underway. Inside Moscow's "state-of-the-art" control center, Roald Sagdeev watched as a top official spun on the balls of his feet and strode over to the center's *kremlovka* phone. This particular guy had been waiting hours upon end doing absolutely nothing and now his golden moment had finally arrived. After punching some numbers the official was connected with General Secretary Brezhnev himself.

"Leonid Ilyich, we have a success." Task perfectly executed, the man hung up and left. That was it—the sole reason he'd come.

Each lander pressed ahead with its automated agenda. Charges now freed a spring-loaded arm that snap-unfolded from *Venera 13* and set its nose down on the turf. Underneath, a smallish knuckle began twisting in order to measure ground hardness. During *Venera 14*'s own turn four days later, the mechanism deployed exactly as intended. Then it swung down—right onto the discarded lens cap.

Reaching the control center from Sagdeev's office consumed nearly an hour's worth of travel over a northeasterly transection of greater Moscow. He wouldn't have had to make the trip up—a television was right there in his office, along with other monitors where graphs and data got piped in. But all the action was up here and besides, the TV screens were better quality. He adjusted his glasses and leaned in close to the flickering frame. No humans had ever seen this terrain before now. Facts crawled through his noggin: this hellish world existed underneath acid clouds at nearly a thousand degrees Fahrenheit and ninety atmospheres of pressure and yet it was right here in front of his nose. A landscape that wouldn't be visible

37. The view from *Venera 13*, as its soil-probing arm extends at left. The discarded camera cover sits on the ground at center. "We knew that this is our little beloved part of space," offered Roald Sagdeev. "Nobody else is touching it right now." Courtesy Don P. Mitchell.

from even a couple of miles off the ground. Only single-digit percentages of sunlight ever reach it. Within moments the entire periphery of the universe faded away, and for Roald Sagdeev nothing else existed except the blistery Venusian surface glaring back at him. *Venera 14* had come down on slabby volcanic rocks. About six hundred miles away, *Venera 13* sent its own imagery from a crust of hardpack. Evidence of flowing lava shimmered everywhere in the dense inferno.

Of Muslim heritage, Sagdeev might have at that moment been inspired to recollect Qu'ran 5:37: "They will long to leave the Fire, but never will they leave there from; and theirs will be a lasting torment."

While the cameras scanned away, technicians listened as the percussive drills whirred up to speed. Nestled deep among circuit boards and batteries and insulation, each pressurized *Venera* belly held equipment to analyze surface samples. But no technique had ever materialized with which to poke a drill bit out through any kind of air lock.

Undaunted engineers mounted the drills right on the landing rings. Next, they simply pioneered innovative, high-temperature metal alloys and built a new species of drill whose innards didn't begin working until heated to well above nine hundred degrees. The final, as-built apparatus could ream down through an inch of solid rock without so much as blinking, and it could do so only on Venus. The drill wouldn't have worked on the crumbly sidewalk behind Lavochkin.

Both *Venera* augers bored for two solid minutes, whereupon a tiny valve in the drill heads flipped open and ambient pressure alone shoved the flakes up a tube. A gauntlet of valves cracked open in series, pressure gradually stepping down as the sample traveled deeper inside. Presently a small hatch opened and the diggings fell into a tray, which moved through another airlock before finally reaching an inner sanctum where a chemical analysis awaited. All told, only a few minutes had elapsed. *Otleechna!* Excellent!

The cameras finished an entire panorama, reversed themselves, and kept going. Like this they'd continue in perpetuity until the batteries ran out or contact broke. Despite having a design life of thirty minutes, *Venera 14* survived for nearly a full hour, while *Venera 13* operated well beyond two . . . until the Goddess of Love unforgivingly consumed her latest suitors. Both mother ships, however, would last months—firing their engines to simulate the exact about-face that a Vega would have to make after dropping its own cargo. The move worked, boosting spirits, and Sagdeev climbed into his Volga for the homeward commute.

I have rewarded them this Day for their patient endurance; they are indeed the ones who are successful.

Qu'ran 23:111

They had Vega's basic configuration nailed down. First came two landers. Blind. Lavochkin also had the airship payloads coming together, under the tutelage of Slava Linkin. People like Bob Preston held out hope that even a small piece of those payloads might conceivably be American—if everyone could agree. Scientists from the two nations had finally connected in early September '83. They met on neutral ground, at the French space agency in Paris, and a palpable tension clouded the occasion because Soviet fighter jets had just shot down a Korean airliner on September 1. As soon as Preston got in he was accosted by men from the U.S. State Department who told him, "Don't meet the Soviets." Accordingly, the Yanks took one floor of offices and conference rooms, while the Reds had another.

"Jacques was shuttling in between," explained Preston of Blamont's mediation. The arrangement was impractical. Inefficient. But if this venture was to work, the two sides needed to cooperatively address a great breadth of topics—starting with how to keep tabs on the mission's space-borne operations. Reminded Preston, "For radio tracking, the U.S. and the Soviets were the real experts," not the French. During such early meetings as this one, procedures for accurate shadowing of the balloons dominated all conversation. Getting in even an edgewise word about more payload seemed, for the time being, near impossible.

Participant Andy Ingersoll of Caltech, at that time one of the top planetary atmosphere scientists in the world, kept a journal of these exchanges. At one point he wrote, "The meetings were like arm control negotiations. Tough, with people being evasive and argumentative and not supplying critical information." Preston did not disagree. "We locked horns on several things," he said, and proffered a vivid example relating to balloon tracking. Preston categorized this topic not as a task so much as "an experiment" because it went hand-in-hand with charting Venusian winds.

"To do the tracking experiment you need to know where the tracking stations *are*. Precisely. Like, to inside of a meter or something. And the Soviets didn't want to give us the locations to inside of 500 meters." No matter how hard they were pressed, nobody seemed willing to be the guy who turned over the exact coordinates of Mother Russia's antenna dishes. Summarized Preston, "It was Andy's speculation that that was the target accuracy of an ICBM!"

Back and forth, up and down, Blamont wearing out shoe leather as he conveyed messages from one side to another, endeavoring to end this stalemate. A sense of mute relief washed over Preston when Blamont came to their floor announcing that the major stumbling blocks—at least for the time being—had been resolved. Dish coordinates would be forthcoming.

If the meeting accomplished one thing, it was proving to each side that the other guy only wanted to do good science on Venus. Things started getting easier. The Americans received an invitation to Moscow, where they finally savored full-on direct interaction with their Soviet counterparts. Only a few had any kind of basic handle on English, "so there was always constant translation," Preston continued. "Which slows things down to a snail's pace. But you could be extremely eloquent because you could always be thinking about your next sentence!"

Via many interpreters, Preston's team now suggested that they provide a device on the balloon payloads to measure cloud density. It seemed perfectly applicable to something like an airship and met with rapturous support. Instead of just helping to track balloons, the United States was now *going to* Venus.

Over the course of several Moscow trips, Preston noted how the same thing happened every time he returned to work. "There were these people in dark suits that would arrive. And you could pick them out a mile away here at JPL, which is a very casual place," he pointed out. It was true; anyone wearing a tie likely had some high-level off-campus conference to attend. Or maybe a court date. "So they would come and interview me after every trip to the Soviet Union, to figure out what I could tell 'em. Probably to make sure I was behaving myself as well!" Years later Preston would also learn that his long lunches in Moscow were deliberately long, so that security agents could come rifle the briefcases of JPL people.

With America on board, the balloon payload seemed fairly rounded out. Some good science there. But the Halley fly-by module didn't yet have all of its own space filled. Less than two years remained before launch, a dreadfully short amount of time.

Sagdeev went fishing in international waters to try and harpoon more scientists. It became a habit upon arriving at his office each morning: tear through the incoming mail and see if anyone sent a proposal. For a while, zippo. Were they going to Halley's comet with half-empty pockets? Two nations responded. Then five. Altogether Sagdeev got proposals from nine different countries. Some of them ended up working among themselves: a Hungarian-made camera would ride atop a Czechoslovak gimbal mount, for example. On occasion the Soviet government mailed out airline tickets so that foreign contributors could attend meetings at the Space Institute. Without explanation people always got one-way tickets, collecting the return paperwork only after arriving in Moscow. But doing it this way halved the expenditure of "hard," or non-Soviet, currency. The ticket home was paid for in rubles.

By this time, Vega had become an unavoidably high-profile venture. If the

38. Three horsemen of the Vega project gather during one of many international meetings. From left are Bob Preston, Slava Linkin, and Jacques Blamont. Courtesy Robert Preston.

Soviet Union missed their launch window or sent a wad of crap that broke down, the consequences would be far worse than having no balloons over Venus or no pictures of Halley's comet. In front of the entire world would they look like a bunch of dipshits. As such, the impending mission found an unlikely ally in "Big Hammer" Sergei Afanasyev. As Sagdeev extolled, "I don't think we would be able to succeed with Vega project without his very firm support." He paused for a moment to contemplate his departed associate, who had habitually clocked fourteen-hour days. "Can you imagine, you know, when this huge collaboration with many enterprises, companies, having their own subcontracts. Everything had to be synchronous. If someone would be delaying delivery of something, it would stop the whole conveyor belt."

So Afanasyev began sitting everyone down once a month, every single month, to comb through the entire state of preparations. "Okay, what is your problem?" he'd challenge a contractor. "Where do you stand today? Okay, you have a delay. What is the reason? Do you need additional help?" For a guy who had once literally threatened Sagdeev's own testicles, this consultative approach made for quite a refreshing change in attitude.

His mailbox nicely filled as of late, Roald Sagdeev was just starting to lament the dearth of further American involvement when he got a fax from West Germany. Over in the land of beer and the Bundestag, a cadre of scientists at the European Space Agency were applying the finishing touches to their own Halley mission. They'd named it Giotto, after the Italian Renaissance painter Giotto di Bondone. Supposedly, di Bondone saw the comèt in 1301 and worked it into his *Adoration of the Magi*. Respectful Germans were now paying homage.

To Sagdeev, the Giotto folks delivered a message all the way from Illinois. At the University of Chicago, a physics professor named John Simpson had a comet experiment he wanted to run involving dust particles. Now, dust may not seem like the kind of thing to fuss about, but Simpson held a different perspective. "This is the stuff from which our solar system was born," he once said. "It's like looking for the Holy Grail. We're going after the essence."

Already Simpson had approached the Giotto team about finding a spot for his little dust devil. But he was late and Giotto, being much smaller than Vega, had no room at the inn. The West German fax asked if the Soviets might be interested in Simpson's offering. Wow, Sagdeev hadn't seen that one coming. Having the obvious place in his heart for physics—not to mention a secret wish to get America more involved—he gave the issue his close attention. "We looked at it, and thought very interesting. It actually was very tiny," he remembered of the instrument. Simpson wanted to measure the pattern and intensity of cometary dust using a thin plastic sheet that had an electrical charge on it. When dust particles hit, they'd send a voltage spike directionally through the sheet—bigger particles registering as bigger spikes.

An addition like that could be huge. If it rode on *Vega 1*, the institute would benefit from high-quality dust readings that could potentially be used to adjust *Vega 2*'s flight path. Simpson's gadget could mitigate risk and allow them to get as close as possible to the nucleus of the comet—while *knowing* they'd done so.

However advantageous it seemed, Sagdeev well appreciated the intimidating politics of slapping this gizmo on Vega without buffering it through France, like all of JPL's dealings. "If we would have gone by official channels, it would take *ages* to get approvals," he groused. The government seemed to be reaching a pinnacle of stagnation; even less was getting done than was the norm. Sagdeev got a message over to Simpson: Let's meet on neutral territory.

"I was totally surprised," offered the Chicago physicist. "I never proposed the detector to them."

They chose Budapest. Simpson flew over and connected with guys from the institute. Sagdeev remained in Moscow, issuing clear directions to gather every speck of detail in order to resolve whether the dust box could be added to a spacecraft the engineers were now trying to call finished. "Industry considered that everything already was done, fixed, we cannot change the design," he moaned. A potentially tense Budapest meeting was quickly defused with Simpson's laid-back attitude. He started off by tattling on his own government. Before the trip, he explained, U.S. officials had more or less asked him, *Won't the Soviets attempt to hijack your secrets?*

In response, Simpson had guffawed. "We at the University of Chicago intentionally built our instrument only from components purchased at the Radio Shack store on the next corner." Would-be reverse engineers certainly wouldn't find any revelations under *that* hood. "It would set them back ten years!" he boomed. Such a cavalier attitude had evolved from experience. The holder of multiple patents, John Simpson had been doing this since 1965. He had boxes on the Pioneer flights to Jupiter and Saturn and wasn't about to miss a shot at Halley's comet. "The opportunity seemed important not only for its scientific value," he noted, "but also as a demonstration of the cooperative, peaceful space exploration which can be achieved between our two countries."

Once his guys reported back, Sagdeev's enchantment broadened. Simpson looked to have a solid piece of gear. It aligned well with Vega's overall objectives. "We probably could find the room for it," hinted Sagdeev to his colleagues, with an influential tone of voice.

But Lavochkin kept whining about how finished the spacecraft was. Nothing else could fit, don't reinvent the wheel, leave well enough alone, we need to prep, roll up the windows and lock the doors; stop messing with Vega.

Recounted Sagdeev, "It was a serious argument."

But the device got installed anyway. With a cheat. Instead of occupying its own distinct slot, Simpson's experiment "came as an appendix," chortled Sagdeev, his eyes twinkling. "Little addendum to existing Hungarian instrument." Remember that the Space Institute ran Vega—not Lavoch-kin or any other design bureau. So the institute simply instructed Lavoch-kin assemblers to wire up Simpson's box *through* another instrument from Hungary.

"It was little cheating," Sagdeev coolly shrugged. "Whatever helps science was great!"

And he didn't even stop there. Less than a year before launch—an impossibly short period of time when spacecraft are unquestionably locked down and all but launched, Bob Preston got word that the balloons could accommodate just one more experiment. They weren't kidding; there was still time. U.S. scientists hurriedly suggested that an optical lightning detector might make for a nice inclusion. Astonishingly, the device was approved almost immediately and got built and went aboard. "You know, the contrasts were just a never-ending source of interest to us," offered Preston of the differences between American and Soviet space operations. "One was, how easily—especially in a country that's filled with red tape—the Soviets were able to deal with design changes. Nowhere near the level of bureaucracy that NASA had for its missions!"

Astronomers at California's Mount Palomar Observatory spotted Halley's comet in October 1982, just over a billion miles away from the sun. To find it they'd been going through stacks of pictures generated by the facility's two-hundred-inch mirror. Nobody would actually *see* the comet directly—with their own eyes, peering through a telescope in real time—for another two years. But it was out there all the same. It was coming. Just like with Attila the Hun or British defenders, Halley's comet could've once again been thought of as a harbinger of bad news: contact with Viking's *Lander 1* broke down only one month later.

After *Vega 1* and *2* launched in December '84, the stubby little director of the Soviet Space Institute enjoyed a brief respite to catch up on secret activities. On rare occasions—no more than once a week for extremely short periods of time—he gathered a select group of theoretical physicists in his office to talk shop. Never were they able to get into as much detail as he wanted; it was always watercooler stuff. But it nevertheless kept the flickering flame alive, burning lightly in the deepest recesses of Roald Sagdeev's mind.

26. Hang Time

In the end, you are left with a few people who are good because
they are driven to be good—inside themselves. I am stuck with
some people on my staff who are openly hostile toward me, who
are what I call my "dedicated enemies." I can't get rid of them, no
matter how much they poison the work of the institute.

—Roald Sagdeev to a colleague, in the early 1980s

The days fell into a cadence. Regularly, Sagdeev sieged the office well before
nine in the morning and never clocked out until at least nine or ten at night.
He had a couch brought in for his escalating number of overnight stays.
First thing every morning his core team would gather in Sagdeev's office
at his giant T-shaped table. The Operative Meeting, he called it. "Twenty
minutes, half an hour, quickly going through what the current urgent problems are. What we have to do today. What are the assignments." Staffers
would wheel in carts of tea glasses and coffee urns, lubing the proceedings along. It also gave them an opportunity to check in on their director.
*How does he look today? Is he getting enough sleep? Can we bring him any-
thing else?* Unbeknownst to Sagdeev, many of the institute's support workers had been increasingly fawning over him behind his back, making him
an object of concern and worry. They did it because Sagdeev was different.
Worth it. At no time before had someone in his position worked so hard
to promote *their* institute, *their* cause, and the greater patronage of exploration in general. He evangelized science to anybody and everybody—even
the surprised Western press, to whom Sagdeev had been giving a lot of pre-
Vega interviews about the institute's plans and intentions. One writer for
Time labeled him "too good to be true."

After the Operative Meeting concluded and everyone had scurried away to their respective to-do lists, Sagdeev generally had to face down the heap of telephone messages and correspondence from other institutions, contractors, or individuals who felt it necessary to contact the director of the Space Research Institute. "*Huge* spectrum of requests," he intoned, exhibiting a wide-eyed, you-wouldn't-believe-it look. "Some will come, wanted simply to report about what they have done. But mostly they will come to ask for something."

Whenever matters took him off-site, which was often, Ivan would spirit him to the day's appointment. The luxury of having a driver enabled Sagdeev to attack his pile while on the go and minimize down time. Countless solicitations involved employment at the institute, which was an entirely reasonable thing to inquire about. It could be tricky if the individual didn't live in Moscow, as Sagdeev would have to secure permission for him or her to relocate—as well as find the individual an apartment.

It also could be tricky for other reasons. Established policy forced Sagdeev to reluctantly detour employment requests through his old pal Georgy the KGB guy, who'd spend days backgrounding someone. Usually the applications sailed through with no problem. On occasion, though, Georgy would ring into Sagdeev's office, calling one of the ever-present phones adorning his desk. Even without the *kremlovka*, he still maintained quite a collection. Each looked nothing like the others and they all had wildly varying functions. Georgy always used the interfacility phone; it was only for when both parties were inside the institute. Next to that sat a high-frequency, secure phone for long-distance chats with remote facilities like Yevpatoria station or the Kazakhstan launch site. They lived alongside a pair of standard telephones. On Sagdeev's desk entropy reigned: owing to his anaerobic movements, all four phones were in constant danger of getting nudged off the edge.

One time when Georgy called about the latest candidate, Sagdeev took the handset with lassitude. He knew exactly what was coming because it'd happened so very many times before.

"So, what is the prognosis?"

Beat. Beat. "Well, I was unable to find any contradictions in the applicant's pedigree," volunteered Georgy. "But there are some nuances around Article Five."

Wordlessly Sagdeev leaned his head to one side, stretching the neck muscles. This kind of crap really wore him down sometimes. Article Five meant *Jewish*. After a brief silence, he rose from his chair to go down the hall and face Georgy in person. "What's wrong with that?" Sagdeev insisted, storming the room. "Don't you think we should care, above all else, about getting the best brains here?"

Georgy wasn't your average knuckle-dragging KGB thug without any furniture upstairs. He had skills. He'd risen to this prestigious posting due to a carefully cultivated diplomatic talent. "Unofficially, I completely agree with you," he finally offered. "However, I had a hint from one of my bosses that the institute has already exceeded its unwritten quota of such employees."

A frank and categorically off-the-record debate ensued. Both men argued the same things they always did when this came up . . . after which Georgy agreed to yet another exception for the sake of the institute. And science.

"I think he actually turned into a fan," Sagdeev later ventured of the not-so-hard-boiled Georgy. "He had a soul, and we kind of found a way to kind of cooperate."

Looking out over the exterior courtyard one day, Roald Sagdeev got a snap idea to transform his deck. It was nice enough, a good conversation piece he supposed, but definitely underutilized. "You know: in summer, too hot. In winter, it was usually covered by the snow." Sagdeev brought in workmen to encase the deck with large glass panels, like a greenhouse. He paraded around the new enclosure, stepping high, all smiles. *Warm and dry!* Staffers caught wind of his improvements and filled the deck with miscellaneous plants and flowers and even palm trees and *tah-dah* . . . a Winter Garden. Instant hit. Conversation piece. Bargaining chip. Normally tough-to-reach Kremlin ministers could now be more easily lured over by dropping reference to a nice chat in the Winter Garden. For particularly stubborn cases, Sagdeev would obliquely mention "a cup of tea"—shorthand for liquor. "Every foreign guest would bring some souvenir. What is the simplest souvenir?" he asked rhetorically. "A bottle of scotch or French cognac. And we never consumed it; it was there for when we had important guests from government. We could use it for good purpose!"

Two weeks before *Vega 1*'s arrival at Venus, the train leaving Moscow got Viktor Kerzhanovich as far as Simferopol. From there he hopped a west-going bus that rumbled across narrow roads all the way to Yevpatoria's own

39. Designed by Stalin's personal architect, this is the iconic Simferopol train station in the early 1980s. It is Crimea's main transit hub. Author's collection.

train station. But reaching his final destination meant transferring to a separate, military-only bus that went another twelve miles west to the actual control buildings. This transfer always had to be precisely timed because the military bus ran only twice a day. As it groaned along through two miniscule towns rung by swaths of empty fields, views out the right-side bus windows offered little. But careful observers on the left could spot a panorama of antennae slowly growing from the distant horizon.

At the gate Kerzhanovich received a badge with a stamp on it indicating which areas he could venture through. The guards smiled at him: repeat visitor. He made his way into the small cluster of low buildings to reunite with other colleagues who'd already been on-site for varying lengths of time. They were happy to see each other. What revelations might *Vega* have to offer—ones that nobody knew were coming? It formed the station's undercurrent of discourse. An upbeat, sociable man, Kerzhanovich enjoyed a solid reputation and was regarded as something of an old-timer in this youngish field. He had a playful, innovative mind that never failed to think in unforeseen directions.

His early stages, though, were entirely run of the mill. Born in March 1938, Viktor V. Kerzhanovich grew up just inside "The Boulevard," which is Moscow's innermost ring road. The dark-haired young Viktor could look out his family's apartment window and across the street to the apartment of a Stalin-appointed state security minister. That such a high-ranking fellow lived in the same neighborhood as a couple of academics like Viktor's parents clearly illustrated the superior horizontality of socialism. As a teenager, Viktor didn't seem terribly affected when, in the summer of '51, the minister was taken away and shot.

In 1961 Kerzhanovich graduated from Moscow University with a physics degree but encountered roadblocks while attempting to land a job. "When we graduated, there was no vacancies in this area and you take what's available," he said matter-of-factly. "You don't know exactly where you're going, and what you will go to do!"

The energetic upstart managed to worm into a place called Research Institute Number 648; they produced the master command-and-control apparatus for all types of satellites. "It was *very* intense," he reported, with a lightheartedness that comes from not being there anymore. "Not twenty-four-seven, but sometimes it was twenty-four, several days a week." Kerzhanovich spent his many hours there collaborating over system designs, coding, and innumerable flight tests with a group of seven or eight peers.

After three years of toil came a migration over to Institute 885. It also worked on command systems, but for spacecraft of another breed. Why jump ship? "I progressed very fast on the career scale, but after that it was just engineering," he yawned, referring to 648. "Routine-style engineering job, that's quite boring. And I don't like." At the time Kerzhanovich joined, Institute 885 was just gearing up to commence work on the control system for a bizarre machine called *Venera 4*. Of all things, it was supposed to land on Venus! "*There* was some more color!" he inflected.

A month after the ship launched, Kerzhanovich got to daydreaming about what it might be like to sit on top of the craft's parachute while it descended into hazy oblivion. And that offbeat hypothetical eventually formed an idea in his head that nobody else seemed to have. During *Venera 4*'s plummet, it would transmit the customary stats on temperature and pressure and the like. Great stuff, but certainly not the whole picture. Kerzhanovich's eureka moment was appreciating what would be revealed by measuring Doppler changes to the incoming radio signal.

We experience the Doppler effect most every day. When something is moving toward or away from you and making noise at the same time, the pitch of that noise will change. Imagine you're standing motionless in the office hallway. A pithy coworker in low-budget business casual is dashing toward you, screaming bloody murder because some meathead brewed the darkest of French roasts and what the screamer really wanted was a nice light Guatemalan.

As this crazed, caffeine-dependent nutjob approaches, the pitch of his screaming will increase—making it sound like he's upscaling from tenor to alto. This is because new sound waves from his mouth essentially back up against your ears as he comes closer. And with no time to spread out, the waves sound higher in pitch.

Once the maniac passes and begins to recede from your immobile self, the pitch begins dropping as new sound waves now have farther to travel in order to reach you. If he then were to inadvertently trip into an abandoned elevator shaft and plummet many stories, the sound waves would grow very long and low indeed.

Apply this same principle to radio signals from Venus. If Kerzhanovich measured their Doppler changes over time, he'd learn how the spacecraft moved vertically up and down during its plunge. And *that* would reveal how the wind itself moved on Venus.

"It was extremely exciting," he suggested—half aware that this kind of thing is not exactly everyone's cup of custard.

Now, his brainchild may sound like it's plagued with contradictions. If something is going down, how can it also be going up? Directions of travel are not absolute. Hanging underneath a parachute, with no independent means of propulsion, a descending object is subject to the forces of the surrounding atmosphere. It moves with them. Gusts of wind, turbulence, weather fronts—all would buffet a craft. Nobody had ever recognized a way to measure these movements, and certainly no one had ever had the foresight to associate them with a planet's weather system. Until now. Track the wind on another world! With old-fashioned *radio*! Viktor Kerzhanovich had figured out how to put a completely new experiment on Venera using no additional hardware, and he unknowingly had begun his evolution from frontline engineer to renowned scientist.

In short order he was able to secure backing for his idea precisely because of Soviet work culture—the kind that wouldn't gel in today's feely good PC milieu. "People are more emotional. They can talk, can yell on each other and this is normal. Even threats sometimes," contended Kerzhanovich of the Soviet "way" that he experienced. "They will not be fired for that." People like Big Hammer Afanasyev were known far and wide for dressing down their subordinates with barnyard vulgarities and rampantly juvenile dramatics. But the outbursts and sporadic fisticuffs (which also happened sometimes) were not why Kerzhanovich's pet project ended up a reality.

Back then, the heads of technical institutes had much less to deal with in terms of general managerial responsibility. Human resources departments? Acronym-laced team-building retreats? Six Sigma? Uh, no. The lack of such workweek filler left great amounts of time to actually *work*—for these technical heads to delve into the tiniest of minutiae occurring under their roofs. "The leadership was involved in the details," Kerzhanovich summarized. In his experience it was entirely common for a director to have at least a basic grasp of the responsibilities and status of *every* person in his employ.

Directors walked their shop floors, talking openly with line workers about unsticking the current poltergeist or vexation or other technical issue. They understood and were easily approachable and consistently open to ideas and suggestions. "Okay," said Kerzhanovich, beginning an imaginary example of someone with a great new initiative. "I'm going to my director who *knew* me, and director has about five thousand people like myself!" If your boss liked the suggestion, he'd facilitate your pursuit of it.

Soon Kerzhanovich was clocking 60 or 70 percent of each workday on the Doppler scheme. It needed lots of fleshing out, refining of the protocols and procedures. And Institute 885 gladly permitted such extracurriculars, despite their having nothing to do with the production of space science experiments. It was just good for the country!

Wind measurements couldn't be derived from *Venera 4* because, at that

40. Viktor Kerzhanovich works with a frequency meter during *Venera 5* and *6*. Unfortunately, on these flights the crafts weren't properly lined up with Earth, so their output was not of much value to him. Courtesy Viktor Kerzhanovich.

time, Yevpatoria's equipment allowed for only the most elemental of Doppler readings. Later it got upgraded. Then came a couple of follow-ons, *Venera 5* and *6*.

Kerzhanovich got his first real break on *Venera 7*. "Only my Doppler data could clarify what happened with the probe and its parachute." Today his technique is a canonical element of many robotic space missions.

Despite support from his bosses, the man yearned to relocate. "Several reasons," he volunteered. "I had some strange relations with my director. I want to make my doctorate, and he did not permit it." Hmm, what about the Space Research Institute? His old classmate Slava Linkin was already over there and in 1981 extended a well-timed invitation to come aboard for Vega. The opportunity thrilled Kerzhanovich: reap a couple *days* of balloon-borne wind readings, versus less than one hour's worth during a lander's descent. And Vega planners wanted nothing less than a full, three-dimensional representation of the balloon paths as they drifted! He was in.

At Yevpatoria station the reddish-colored hotel, if it could even be called that, would've struggled to qualify as one-star. "Primitive," remembered

Kerzhanovich. "It's not hotel in common understanding. More like a dorm." He described its white-walled rooms as "small, like prison cells inside," with a shared bathroom on each of the three floors to accommodate the dozen-odd Space Institute guests—plus another forty or so in the Lavochkin contingent. Despite the swelling census, "I never remember any big arguments there." No snoring issues, dueling elbows, or jostling for bathroom time. People had different expectations from those of recreational travelers. What about the breakfast buffet? Donuts and coffee? Questions like that only get Kerzhanovich laughing again. "But at least this is more convenient than stay in Yevpatoria," owing to unpredictable work hours and the hassle of commuting.

Kerzhanovich dropped his stuff on one of his room's two beds and hung several garments in a freestanding wardrobe. Back outside again, he began walking south along a chalky white footpath. To his immediate left stood the meager dining facility. Along with the hotel, it joined a sparse grid of buildings huddled at the complex's northwest end. No high concrete walls or intentional slopes of land concealed them because Yevpatoria station, unlike Shkolnoye, was not at all secret. Civilian and foreign scientists routinely visited to conduct astronomical observations and talk about the latest findings.

Kerzhanovich cut left past the dining hall, then jogged right onto what passed for a narrow street. This took him due south and a couple of walking minutes later revealed the business end of the complex. Its buildings numbered about half a dozen and were arranged in a left-leaning L shape with banks of antenna dishes on the two outer sides. Field grass and random shrubbery dominated any unclaimed space.

One constantly amusing aspect of Yevpatoria station remained the glut of young soldiers milling around the entire complex. "There was not much work for them," remembered Kerzhanovich, who described a total labor surplus. "Mostly it's cleaning." During the brief intervals when every window ledge and urinal and floor tile was theoretically spic-and-span, the conscripts performed routine equipment maintenance and even had a little down time. But planetary encounters typically equaled more labor, so the men greeted their temporary houseguests with somewhat mixed feelings. Kerzhanovich got along quite well with the troops and even succeeded at getting to know a few.

41. Looking northwest, this is only part of Yevpatoria station. It's more campus-like than Shkolnoye, with many dishes and dish arrays spread among three distinct sites. Photo by and courtesy of Alexander Dzhuly.

Taking a page from the Space Institute, Yevpatoria's operational staff convened every morning to discuss issues of the day and whatever scheduled events would be happening. Beyond that, Kerzhanovich enjoyed the dual freedom/responsibility of being his own boss and wasn't specifically under instructions to report to or otherwise check in with anyone. "Essentially you know what is your duty," he conveyed. "I know what activities are, when should I show up, et cetera." Kerzhanovich bustled through the dim hallways of his long, white, double-decker building, which sat in the back of two stubby rows and had a four-pointed whatzit on its roof that looked more like a Buck Rogers ray gun than the radio antenna it really was.

He set up shop in a dreary side room filled with radio equipment. So much remained to be done before the grand moments of lander separation and balloon deployment. "My working place was always where the signal detection was." If either *Vega* behaved as expected and traced the secrets of Venus onto his bitty display screen, Kerzhanovich would hyperfocus right there in front of it to catch every last detail.

That is, if the gear was ready. "You have to be sure that everything is working," he cautioned—a fundamental concern when dealing with electronics that have been idle since the last planetary mission. *Soviet* electronics, no less. Did they limit the value of scientific returns from spacecraft? "Absolutely," said an unhesitant Kerzhanovich—who never felt terribly satisfied about the iffy gear he relied on. "The precision was very poor—precision, resolution, and lifetime."

Every piece needed exercise—to be calibrated and put through its paces, assuring operators like him that the signals would be properly received and recorded. People needed to drill on procedures. "Then all the planning of the transmissions, and planning of the, yeah . . ." Kerzhanovich caught himself, wobbling on the edge of a pit of detail he no longer had the energy to venture into. Finally: "There was a lot of work!" He hadn't even bothered to tote along a book. "Absolutely no time to read anything there." The now-international effort to track *Vega*'s balloons ultimately resulted in half a dozen participating Soviet sites like this one—along with fourteen others spread throughout ten separate countries. None were in France itself.

"Jacques could marshal troops like no one," saluted Bob Preston. "He got us involved at no cost to him!"

Equipment vetted, Kerzhanovich's remaining days leading up to *Vega*'s encounter went toward various fine-tunings of his environment. "Dealing with different logistical and the organizational things," he expounded, rattling off a never-ending set of tasks: "What should be turned on, when, how, when will transmission start, when it will finish, who will be reception, how will we communicate, what's going on." If some worry needed addressing, no matter how small—if it was too hot in the radio room or he didn't have enough pencils or the light glared slightly into his face at certain times of day, *now* was the time to lick that issue.

Outside his window, less than three miles of scraggly farmland separated him from tranquil Black Sea waters that lapped deliciously against a meandering expanse of faultless sandy beaches. It's precious ground; geographers call this plug of clay and limestone "the key to the Black Sea" due to its location and singular point of access. Even the name Crimea is thought to come from the Tatar word *kirim*, meaning "fortress with moat." Regardless of the name, it's a strategic jewel. Hitler sure knew.

For miles in either direction the beaches were choked with swimsuit-clad vacationers who waded and splashed and drank. They did not know what was going on at that nearby inland outpost with the mysteriously imposing antenna dishes. And Kerzhanovich did not come down to join them.

People began arriving in early June: representatives from the various industrial contractors, state commissioners, the French ambassador. All were welcomed with tremendous excitement as Roald Sagdeev crowded his institute with these hordes of well-wishing revelers who'd come to experience the Venus landing and balloon deployment—albeit on an eight-minute time delay.

Anyone watching Sagdeev—that is, anyone who'd been around long enough to experience the bulk of Soviet planetary exploration—regarded him with a mixture of admiration and disbelief. Foreigners entering the institute used to endure scathing interrogations by KGB personnel. "We were required to be accompanied everywhere. Even to the bathroom," noted Carl Sagan. But under Sagdeev, the last dozen years had seen the gradual development of a welcoming atmosphere of fellowship. Foreign guests at the institute were now greeted at a dedicated entrance, nothing was inspected, and they were told that they could go anywhere. During one visit Sagan got completely lost in a maze of hallways and wandered into the mainframe computing center. "No one stopped me!" he marveled about an act that might have previously severed diplomatic ties.

"It was just welcome," praised another man. "It was Sagdeev approach."

All doors were open to the Winter Garden. Its foliage looked awesome. Liquor flowed. Everyone was having a great time. About the only hitch was Venus herself. *Vega*'s first action rounds would occur while Moscow faced completely away from the planet. Turned like that, Asia as a whole lay out of range. Australia and America would therefore be the ones to initially know whether the parachute on the first lander had come out. Or if its balloon had deployed. "So we had a real-time connection to JPL," indicated Sagdeev. It came via a telephone hooked to a loudspeaker propped in the institute's modular conference room. Everyone in attendance could hear miscellaneous background chatter from the JPL guys—especially Jacques Blamont, who'd chosen to experience Venus from Pasadena. ("Well, we were in Moscow for the *launch!*" he defended.) Owing to the reliance on America's equipment, Blamont felt it more important to be where he was in case anyone needed answers from a high-level Vega coordinator. Sagdeev took advantage of the open line to chat up the JPL director, Lew Allen.

"They exchanged a number of views," said Blamont, clearly pleased with the interaction.

By then *Vega 1*'s lander should've been entering the uppermost fringes of the Venusian atmosphere. "We were waiting for the moment when the balloon would be injected and start sending signals," recalled Sagdeev. He was insanely nervous. *Anytime now.* In a room full of terribly important people, Sagdeev made sure he was standing near his inner circle of assistants who'd worked so hard for this moment. He had to believe that Blamont was also insanely nervous.

What's important to understand about Jacques Blamont is that he had this *thing* for balloons stretching back almost thirty years before the time of Vega. In 1959, as a research fellow at the University of Minnesota, Blamont intermingled with a group of physicists engaged in studying the atmosphere by way of high-altitude balloons. "I was very impressed by what they were doing." It was a fantastic idea, really, quite cheap compared to sounding rockets, with lots of hang time up at the edge of space. "And I decided to introduce balloons in the French program," he resolved. "In 1966, our president General de Gaulle decided that we had to have a space program in collaboration with the Soviets. So I was sent by him with my boss, chief of the French space agency, to Moscow and we established a long-standing relationship." Cultivating this involved one yearly meeting between representatives of the two space agencies. As Blamont continued, "At those meeting we would essentially elaborate and decide about the program. And then every time we had decided that it would be in a different place. So every two years it would be in Soviet Union, and then in France, and it would always be in a different place. So we could know each other."

Months later, Blamont was in the middle of a satellite project. On one otherwise unremarkable night, the biggest cliché in the world occurred: he had a dream. "This dream was that I could see a balloon in the Venus atmosphere. And I had never worked on Venus, so I don't know why. But anyway, I got very impressed by this dream, so I wrote a proposal immediately," involving very small experiments carried on a handful of modestly sized balloons. He hand delivered the paperwork to Mstislav Keldysh late in '67 during a Paris luncheon. Blamont already knew Keldysh well—in part due to the latter man's excellent knowledge of French. Keldysh loved the balloon idea and pledged to work it on through.

But then a wave of stagnation hit. "Nothing happened!" said a whimpery Blamont, sounding rather dejected. "We did not know at all what was happening inside the Soviet system, because they were extremely secretive.

And so it was very hard to guess what they wanted." According to him, the Reds basically sat on his idea for half a decade before coming back to France with a counterproposal. "They came up with the idea of very large balloon with a laboratory. Floating laboratory. And we had to accept it." That was a year before Sagdeev came aboard the institute; French engineers struggled to prototype the concept. Forward movement ground to a stop from '74 to '76 owing to budget cuts and the election of a new French president. "But in '76 we started moving again." They about had the finer kinks ironed out when Sagdeev made that phone call to Blamont with news that the balloon was a go—except at a much smaller scale. Their collaborative exploration had turned into a fiasco.

Great measures of diplomacy helped refurbish the partnership—though France categorically refused to supply the balloon almost as a matter of principle. At regular intervals Blamont continued his Sagdeev meetups; genuine face time was much more prevalent than today. Often Sagdeev traveled to Paris, where the country provided linguistic assistance. "We had a lot of interpreters. We had at least three or four French girls," chuckled Blamont. "They were aristocratic white Russians, all princesses and countesses, and so they were working for us." But the interpreters tended to get in the way and slow things down, so Blamont and Sagdeev progressively talked more and more between themselves in English. "It was too boring to have the interpreters."

Despite their intense working relationship, Blamont stressed that at no time did Sagdeev ever let his guard down about career dissatisfaction. "We never discussed that. He always looked very cheerful and satisfied with his job," indicated Blamont. "He did the job with great enthusiasm."

A couple of hours prior to encounter, Bob Preston gave a talk at JPL to a large audience gathered for the event. He spent the following hour or so waiting anxiously with Blamont in the mission's control building. "We knew for months ahead, *years* ahead, virtually to the second or two, when we should hear something from the balloons," commented Preston. That moment was supposed to occur just after 6:00 p.m. on the West Coast. "And it's like many of these planetary missions: you know when something has to happen; you just don't know if it's gonna work. It's a moment of terror." And Blamont definitely *was* nervous as hell, with the flight on autopilot and building to crescendo in real time. From here on in there was nothing else he could do.

Decelerating from twenty-five thousand miles an hour, *Vega 1*'s lander—still encased in a heat-shielding ball—endured hundreds of G-forces as it began losing speed and altitude. POP went the ball top, 210,000 feet up, one parachute out and a timer coming to life, slaughtering seconds until that precise moment to cue the balloon release. If *Vega*'s timer failed, a backup would fill in. If the backup died, a pressure sensor waited to take over. In a blink three thousand feet disappeared, first timer working, ball opening, passing 200,000 feet with glorified furniture gliders easing the lifeguard ring off the top of the lander in a game of reverse ring toss. Out it whistled, 180,000, a separate parachute taking the initial shock of atmospheric contact and the ring split open and the folded balloon caught its first whiffs of acid clouds. It dropped quickly; thin air up here still. 177,000. Helium slowly crept through folds of Ftorlon. 174,000 and going down, down, the parachute—*snip*—cut itself away and the freed balloon dropped like a safe to fight for its life.

Bob Preston: "We had had *terrible* problems at JPL with our tracking network, and getting it in shape. And we had worked just *all hours* for months ahead of time and we'd *just* finished getting the network ready for this experiment. So it really wasn't tested as well as it should be. But we hoped."

Straight down, straining, 170,000.

The trick is getting the darn balloon pumped up before it smacks the ground. But not so quickly that it bursts. Here, the thing could still fall for miles—but it'd been designed to operate only in the uppermost layer of clouds, where temperatures and pressures were much lower than near the ground. If the airship took too long to inflate, it'd get trapped in the heavy lower atmosphere and never be able to rise high enough to do any good.

"All we had in front of us was an oscilloscope that refreshed every second and showed us the spectrum of the receiver," continued Preston, coloring in the scene before him. "And we knew we should see the balloons at a particular time. The first balloon signal. We didn't see it."

Air thickening, 167,000. Balloon heating up and feeling the squeeze of rising pressure.

"Time kept marching by and seemed like an infinity and we didn't see anything refreshing second by second." Preston and Blamont stared dry-eyed at the display before them. It was indeed just after 6:00 p.m., Pasadena time. If it didn't come then, it wouldn't at all. "And finally, in one of the second refreshes, there was *just the hint* that there was a peak in the spectrum. And in the next second there it was, big and bold."

Sagdeev's phone erupted. "We heard a loud applause on the other end," he remembered—one of those moments that was instantly burned into his long-term memory. At 164,000 feet above Venus, the orb's inflation had arrested its own fall. JPL director Lew Allen got on the mike and congratulated everyone on the unqualified successes to that point.

Rotund and plump, the balloon slowly rose.

Preston couldn't take his gaze off the screen. The event momentarily disrupted his command of the English language. After some effort he finally managed, "Wow."

Earth rotated; as the signal "set" in the west, Venus was just rising in Spain and the Madrid dish grabbed it. Thousands of miles east of Blamont and nine hundred miles south of Sagdeev, *Vega* transmissions also hit Yevpatoria's big dishes and were funneled throughout the station. Different entities stripped off what they needed and ran decoding cycles to interpret. One group got lander health; another cared only about engineering data.

And then another part of the transmission flowed into the rear input panel of Viktor Kerzhanovich's spectrum analyzer. Its tiny screen displayed a graph of frequency versus signal strength and had been previously dialed in to match that of the balloon. "This was the first place where you *see* the signal; you see it from the spectrum analyzer and it's a spike," he described. But the analyzer was blank, blank, blank, blank; maybe there's trouble? Yevpatoria wasn't privy to the open phone line. Things suddenly lit up. "Then I see there's a signal!" Kerzhanovich yelled with joy. To use the slang of the station, they had a "strong horse"—the radio's carrier signal—along with a "good rider," or solid data.

The balloon rose, higher still, back past 170,000, climbing farther before leveling off at 177,000 feet, more or less exactly where envisioned. In stark contrast to the hellish ground conditions, "it's essentially at room temperatures," Kerzhanovich described this altitudinal zone. Pressures there approximate what's at the summit of an eighteen-thousand-foot mountain; humans could themselves balloon on Venus at that height, in an open gondola no less. We'd just have to don scuba tanks.

Rapunzeling down forty-three feet underneath the plump round orb, a gondola unfolded and came to life. "The balloon itself? It becomes a heat source, and it disturbs the air," lectured Kerzhanovich. "The further the balloon is from the gondola, the better off you are!" Closest to the balloon rode an upside-down ice-cream cone: the antenna, five and a half inches wide, broadcasting Radio Venus directly to Earth on a whopping five watts of power. Underneath it hung a pair of straps, which in turn supported the radio transmitter and mini electronic brain. Jutting out from the transmitter's base, right next to sensors for pressure and light levels, a nine-inch rod of carbon fiber held a toy-like plastic propeller spinning wildly in the bracing Venusian squalls. At the very bottom, separated by another length of straps, hung miniature packs of lithium batteries—along with the American-designed device to examine cloud density. Everything, top to bottom, had been slathered in weird paint to help guard against the fuming acidity of the atmosphere. A separate, expendable component to manage the balloon's inflation had been slung underneath them all. Presently it fell away, taking spare ballast along with.

It happened in a microsecond. Turbulence abruptly heaved the balloon askew, yanking the gondola with such force that ground antennas briefly lost their lock on its radio signal. The airship's inaugural broadcast came through as pure gibberish. But then the ride settled, their balloon shrugging off any malaise. Off it went, bobbing westward through the sky like nothing ever happened.

The lander continued its plummet. Forty-five minutes of surf and counting. But with only ninety-five thousand feet remaining, disaster spat once again. Call it a "shock layer," call it "lightning clouds": planetary scientists can't agree on a name but the effect is the same regardless. An incredible surge of energy buffeted the *Vega 1* lander, flinging it back upward at seventy miles an hour and fooling the urn into thinking it was already on the ground. With absolutely nothing at its feet the soil drill fired up, probing for scratchy rock that wasn't there. Methodically the craft proceeded through its automatic regimen: gathering sensor readings from what it assumed was zero altitude and processing nonexistent soil samples. Fifteen long minutes elapsed. Then it knocked against Venus's real surface to complete the trailing remainders of its post-touchdown sequence. Less than an hour later all transmissions blanked out, marking the end of contact with

42. Using a model, Slava Linkin explains various aspects of the Vega balloon payload during a meeting at the Space Institute. "He really knew how to make the Russian system work—getting things approved, getting things built," lauded Bob Preston. Courtesy RIA Novosti.

Vega 1's lander. They had spent so long to make it as perfect as they could and it was all over so very, very fast.

The balloon continued on its merry way. Whisking though alien clouds, the gondola computer took attendance every seventy-five seconds. *What are the wind speed and direction? The temperature? The pressure?* Every ten minutes a brightness reading joined the party. Findings piled on top of each other in a small onboard memory bank, bursting home at periodic radio intervals. Approximately sixty-seven million miles away, ground stations were able to resolve the speed of the balloon to within two miles an hour.

In the predawn blackness of the next morning, Bob Preston left the control building to head for another. Blamont tagged along. The Frenchman would end up staying awake for the balloon's entire lifetime. Preston sure needed his own respite but was too keyed up to sack out for very long. "I managed a couple of hours on a couch in a women's restroom," he later ventured.

Outside, they both glanced up at the night sky—and saw Venus.

"Wow," said Bob. The only word in his mind.

In Yevpatoria, Viktor Kerzhanovich sat mesmerized as wind-flavored riddles unspooled from the humming equipment before him. Nearly the planet's entire atmosphere—down to just a few miles above its surface—is caught in a burly super-rotation of winds gunning between 90 and 112 miles an hour with never a letup. "Unbelievable!" he crowed. Huge rolls of computer tape filled with all the signals. Venus was in line with central Asia only about half the day, but this crushing mountain of data meant that people like him worked largely round the clock to stay atop of as much as possible.

A day passed. With four thousand miles of travel under its belt, the jouncing gondola reported gradually increasing light levels. It was sunrise coming: a new dawn. Information drizzled on back to additional stations in Ulan-Ude, Russia; Canberra, Australia; Penticton, Canada. Twenty in all. Signals hit North Liberty, Iowa—the second-smallest dish, and one that had been practically willed into being by a local university professor named James Van Allen. Each site joined a gallant enterprise where simultaneous observations from multiple ground stations were accurately tracking the wind on Venus. Hundreds of people had glued themselves to events they could not see, hear, or touch. But by the grace of radio could they be experienced. Six thousand miles covered at a leisurely 150 miles per hour, egged on by the planet's backward rotation. More turbulence bustled through. The batteries waned, pushing what they could. Penultimate squeezes in a toothpaste tube. Another, weakened burst: wind speed and direction. Pressure, temperature.

Hours later, no juice at all remained in the batteries and everything shut down.

One of the world's simplest machines, light gas in a bag, had just traveled a full third of the way around the foreign lands of Venus without so much as batting an eye—lasting fifty times longer than the heavier and more complex lander.

As epic as the experience was, Viktor Kerzhanovich barely had time to grab a snack as *Vega 2* repeated the same whole pattern only two days later. Near déjà vu: another chest-grabbing entry, a successful balloon inflation, followed by an unintelligible first transmission owing to extreme bounce and sway as the varying parts unfolded and calmed themselves. This time the lander put down on an ancient mountain flank with no trouble at all, only eight hundred miles from its comrade.

A day and a half after it started out, *Vega 2*'s balloon floated into daylight and strong, thrashing one hundred mile an hour gusts that lasted hours— nearly exceeding the instruments' ability to measure them. The defenseless contraption plummeted almost two whole miles.

Just above the lowest altitude it could tolerate before succumbing, all turbulence mercifully dissipated and the balloon clawed upward once again. It drifted about a third of the way around the entire planet, until weakened batteries ceased their transfer of usable data and purposefully nipped the radio link. *Vega*'s still-floating gondola went quiet. Ninety-five percent of raw balloon data made it home and was accurately decoded.

Several days after the operations completed, Yevpatoria station drained out. Viktor Kerzhanovich stole a moment to call his wife. He said he'd be leaving soon. Said he missed her terribly. "Very happy but quite tired. It was almost four days continuous," he mentioned. Then Kerzhanovich cleared his things from the dismal hotel, shuttled on the military bus back to town, then took a second bus to Simferopol and clambered aboard a waiting train.

The Crimean Peninsula is revered as a superb vacation site; back then it was the Soviet Union's Venice Beach. Yet Kerzhanovich had spent the entirety of his time there either hunkered in an overcrowded room staring

43. An artist's rendering of *Vega 2* as it fights to survive the downdraft. The cone-shaped antenna uses no more power than what's in an alarm clock. © Michael Carroll, http://stock-space-images.com.

at electronic pulses or fetal in a creaky-cramped hotel bed, trying to grab some frantic winks. The long days? Crappy accommodations? They began to recede as the green-colored train hissed, picking up speed. Late summer is a busy time for Simferopol train traffic, with upwards of fifty thousand people a day passing through. Locals call it "velvet season," as the rails carry twenty to thirty cars at a time—versus six or ten from October through spring. Kerzhanovich stuffed the light-blue rail ticket in his pants. Long trip back, and it would not be his last.

He settled back into a worn seat and reflected on the balloon's unequivocal success. Even in this modern space age, something uncomplicated and straightforward and so amazingly modest like *ballooning* still had a place. "It's one of the reasons why it worked so well," Kerzhanovich remarked. "Because it was pretty simple, and we tested it A LOT here on Earth." Nothing else, frankly, would've given him two contiguous days of wind measurements at a shot.

Head back on the seat, Kerzhanovich let the train motions rock him gently from side to side: infant in a cradle. It made him drowsy. How he looked forward to reuniting with his precious Svetlana and their young Dmitri and having a bit of a rest. Sometime during his trip—no one can be sure exactly when—each *Vega* balloon met its fate in one of two ways: a sufficient amount of helium leaked or hot sunlight burst their envelopes. Either way, they fluttered down into the pressure cooker and became debris— the remnants of meticulous planning, of clever engineering, of plain old human curiosity.

And the remnants of one Frenchman's dream.

But Viktor Kerzhanovich did not think of the *Vega* balloons, or of France or the missed beach outings, for he was already fast asleep.

Nine months till Halley's comet.

27. The Rules of Resigning

It is a paradox that we can successfully launch Vega spacecraft to
encounter Halley's comet, but we are unable to produce
decent washing machines or vacuum cleaners.

—Soviet premier Mikhail Gorbachev

After returning home, smoochin' up Svetlana, catching some winks, and
then processing his abundant reams of data, Viktor Kerzhanovich still
couldn't get a handle on the mechanism of Venusian winds. At 215,000
feet above the planet they blow gale-force at 230 miles an hour. No sus-
tained wind speed on Earth has ever come close. As altitude declines the
speeds gradually lessen but are still well above the hundred-mile-an-hour
range at the heights where both *Vega* airships operated. Yet below a hundred thousand feet, the tempest effectively stalls out. Winds hit seventy
miles an hour, tops. What gives?

"There was no model for that," Kerzhanovich quizzically admitted. "So this
for me, it was the greatest mystery." Venus's overall composition remained a
question mark as well—not to mention the grain and character of its inner
layers. "Is it a dead planet or is it alive?" he queried. "In terms of the geology.
Is there any active volcanism there?" For as much as had been learned about
this bizarre planet, well, really, inquiring minds were only getting started.

"The more you know, the more you don't know."

Quality time still needed to be spent on results from the previous missions, too. In 1983, after *Venera 13* and *14* but before either *Vega* set out,
two orbiters had scoured the planet with mapping radar. Twins *Venera 15*
and *16* revealed a host of lip-licking ground detail, including idle volcanoes and static lava fields and scads of wrinkly terrain—without unleash-

ing any balloons or secondary landing vessels. These tandem flyers could never have analyzed wind dynamics from such high orbital positions and didn't have near-enough resolution to image other Veneras on the surface. But their unqualified cartographical successes added another voluminous installment to the general knowledge base.

Sagdeev was right; it's a drug. As with fresh-ground coffee or deep-green pine trees, planetary scientists all longed to inhale the delectable scent: *Mmmm . . . data.* An eager Kerzhanovich looked forward to revisiting the clouds of Venus for an extended period of days—to bob once again through the planet's atmosphere and find the unfound. Sense the unsensed. They just needed better batteries. Larger balloons. With benevolent international support, anything was possible. Blamont would make it happen. Kerzhanovich rubbed his hands in anticipation of their next steps. But first: to the comet! Only a few dwindling months remained until both *Vega* mother ships encountered Halley.

If you had gone to Viktor Kerzhanovich right then and told him that in less than ten years he'd be living large in Southern California, he would've laughed in your face. Little did the man know that the Soviet Union would never again go back to Venus. There would be no Venera follow-ons, ever. He also did not know that a clock loudly ticked on the very fabric of his nation and that Roald Sagdeev—escape artist that he aspired to be—had been timing its moving hands for his final jump from administration.

Comets are intriguing remnants of solar system formation. They're gargantuan daubs of rock-encrusted ice that have never bumped bellies with an accreting planet (or moon) and instead arc through space in long, slow orbits without end. That is, unless they fall into the sun. Or eventually hit something. They are runaway commuter trains, interstellar hamsters on cosmic exercise wheels. Basal and biotic, yet eye-catching all the same, they carry water and organic compounds and may quite possibly have delivered one or both to Earth many eons ago.

"When we study the comets, we are studying our own origins," Carl Sagan once said.

Any comet really gets to strut its stuff when it flies close to a star. Frenetic solar energy ravages away the comet's surface dust to expose an icy nucleus, or core. Immediately the ice froths away into water vapor that blooms around the nucleus, joining with dust to create a monstrous "coma" that trails off behind and makes the whole comet appear exponentially larger than it really is—sort of like a frightened cat doing poof-tail. After racking up large numbers of close stellar encounters, nearly all a comet's ice has been exhausted. At that point it turns into more of a humdrum asteroid that nobody pays attention to.

Nearly a thousand comets have been tracked and cataloged, although the orbits of fewer than two hundred are known with certainty. Undoubtedly more have regular circuits, or "periods," but their exact rounds through space haven't yet been determined. Many have come by only once, waved a quick hello, and aren't expected to return for thousands of years.

Until Halley's 1986 fly-through, no piece of astronomical equipment save the telescope and human eyes had ever studied any comet. And neither one of those could penetrate a visually opaque, bright-glowing coma from millions of miles away. Therefore, a comet's nucleus remained the exotic, intoxicatingly veiled treasure room that everyone wanted to frolic in. But never had. It was the big brass ring, the Lamborghini, the gorgeous redhead in the coffee shop . . . always out of reach.

By now, each *Vega* had only a few weeks left to go. Flying *near* a comet was one thing, but—locating its *nucleus*? Tracking it, locking on, homing in? "Since initially we wouldn't know where the nucleus *is*, how we will navigate spacecraft, which would enter inside coma to find this nucleus?" The multifaceted conundrum troubled Roald Sagdeev even decades afterward. "Biggest concern throughout the whole mission. Number-one concern," he stressed. "Tiny body inside huge, bright coma with all the dust particles, you know, scattering sunlight."

Years of preparation followed by many many months of flight would all be for naught unless navigational perfection was achieved during those final, crucial minutes of terminal approach—when each *Vega* would have to acquire the nucleus completely by itself. And once identified, keep it in the crosshairs. Reminded Sagdeev, "We had to know *always* where it is while we are passing, so we would be able to turn the instrument and the cameras and everything *toward* the nucleus." During these moments, no help could come from Earth. Things would be happening too quickly, the probe on the end of a nine- to nine-and-a-half-minute radio delay. Well, gee. An automatic nucleus finder. How to skin *that* cat?

Until a year before launch, Sagdeev had been halfway content with the original plan: as each *Vega* entered Halley's coma, a computer attached to the Hungarian camera would process images as fast as it could and order the instruments to point in the direction where the nucleus was thought to be. If that computer failed, a backup solution from Czechoslovakia waited in the wings. This Czech backup depended on a unique sensor and microchip, already in widespread use by the missile industry, that detected bright areas and steered toward them. "Very popular. All the military guys were using it at that time," recalled Sagdeev. And for a self-targeting missile, it worked great.

"What was my problem?"

Sagdeev stood there with arms out, palms up, demanding to know how the rubber hit the road on this one. Plainly he was not missileering; he needed to kiss a comet. What was being overlooked here? (Unsurprisingly, Sagdeev always assumed that things were being overlooked.) Where was the point of failure, the lethal supposition, the hole in the plan?

Gas jets. Missiles *don't* have to deal with gas jets. Surface ice abrades away from cometary nuclei in the form of large and extremely bright jets of gas. Their blinding flashes could and would easily overwhelm whatever light was coming from the nucleus itself.

"We knew it. All the mathematical models."

But Sagdeev was nothing if not a theorist, so he theorized a special microchip of his own design that worked in stages. As *Vega* dipped inside Halley's coma a large, sensitive zone on this hypothetical new chip would detect the brightest of the bright and head straight for it. Progressively smaller and less sensitive stages of the chip would then sequentially come into play as *Vega* closed on the nucleus. In this fashion, bothersome gas jets would essentially be factored out. Sagdeev reckoned on needing three stages, although "you can have as many as you wish," he explained. The new arrangement might sound complex but Sagdeev dismissed that notion out of hand. "It was not technically complicated chip. Was actually very simple design."

In Moscow he convened with a super-secret enterprise that made targeting chips for intercept missiles. Without much hesitation they threw cold water on his idea. "We didn't reach an agreement," the gloomy Sagdeev related. "We were very disappointed." On the way out, though, he got ambushed by one of the low-level engineers who'd attended the meeting. The guy pulled Sagdeev off to one side.

"Professor. I can do it," he pleaded, with a fistful of upbeat attitude. "I can do it with our workshop, within couple of weeks. If you are able to pay privately to the workmen?" The topography of his face indicated sheer resolve. He wanted this like little else.

How much?

"Ten thousand rubles."

Sagdeev choked back laughter. "Such a ridiculously small amount of money!" He waved his arm; make it happen. Within the deadline the moonlighting crew delivered. Out came the Czech chip and into *Vega* went Sagdeev's unique staging version. It was only a backup, but it would wait there patiently just in case.

Explaining the switch to the Czech team was excruciating by comparison. "I think they took it as an insult somehow, as an offense. Just like French took the balloon." But nuzzling the nucleus was more important than pride on any day of the week. Sagdeev hated waiting, but the ongoing day-to-day workload kept him occupied as the comet and both hearty *Vega*s rapidly converged. Sagdeev told himself that they'd been well designed. They were in good shape.

They could do it.

John Simpson's experiment started picking up dust while they were still almost four hundred thousand miles out. Rapidly the dust crescendoed into a veritable hailstorm—washing filth and debris over *Vega 1* in all manner of sizes and weights and hazards, right down to the detection limits of his equipment. *Vega* hung on, power levels dipping as the gutsy flyer's solar panels endured cascading swarms of dense rubble. *Clack-clack-clack* went the Hungarian camera, firing data to its computer, seeking, twisting, tweaking, twanging the punch-drunk chassis. And then suddenly—on Thursday, March 6, 1986—Roald Sagdeev involuntarily broke into a smile. The flickery TV monitor before him had finally begun to outline Halley's nucleus—from its south pole, no less. Whether an Amundsen or a Sagdeev, the legacy of the name had been fulfilled. Visitors surged in to gape at the screen. Many of these early images were coming through blurry and indistinct, but they went out live to any TV outlet in the world that wanted them.

44. "All the answers to all the questions you want to know are inside that light. And when you walk to it, you become a part of it forever." Here, *Vega 1* enters the coma of Halley's comet in this artist's interpretation. © Michael Carroll, http://stock-space-images.com.

Final approach for *Vega 1*, roaring through suffocating dust only thirty-one thousand miles from the jeweled target. Closing. An instrument died. The electrics on another misperformed. Yet another gagged on bad commands and thought it was supposed to recalibrate itself. Just before the money shot! Sagdeev's TV refreshed to show him an improved view. Why—the nucleus wasn't rotund at all. Almost looked like two balls sewn together. Or maybe a potato? None of the images were as clear as he wished.

Tag: closest approach, 5,500 miles from ground zero, a hundred hits a second on Simpson leapt to four thousand, another instrument went out, dust now stifling more than 55 percent of regular solar power as the nucleus of Halley's comet whipped by at a relative speed of 177,000 miles an hour. Less than ten hours later *Vega 1* emerged from the other side of the coma and promptly lost its orientation in space.

"The first time we have ever seen the nucleus of a comet, as anything other than a point of light!" So celebrated one astronomer.

Press images went out in false color. This a common technique, used to emphasize detail and render the imagery somewhat more comprehensible—

especially for those who aren't sure what to look at. Subtle features are much more apparent in false color. The darkest parts of a shot are commonly assigned black, while the next lightest are colored blue, and so on up to the absolute brightest sections—often depicted as white. When a false-color interpretation was applied to Halley's nucleus, the image showed an oblong and lumpy crimson blob among bluish surroundings, with intermittent spears of yellow darting away.

"The Soviet press was very happy of the fact that comet 'aleey was red!" laughed Jacques Blamont. "They had a lot of fun with this story." In America, ABC's *Nightline* ran a special overnight episode to carry the imagery as it arrived, even lassoing Sagdeev for a quick sit-down.

The Space Institute had packed them in to an unprecedented degree, putting foreigners up at the academy's own nearby hotel. A dozen U.S. observers attended—only one contingent of nearly a hundred visiting scientists, including Blamont, who'd come to witness the final act of his generation-old dream. Sagdeev himself had been practically living there. The institute's cafeteria stayed open round-the-clock throughout the encounter period—enabling him to creep down in those lean moments when he had time to pounce on a soup and salad. The place carried pretty much everything, minus beer. Usually Sagdeev lateraled into a private seating area to serenely masticate while rapping with key individuals, cheeks distended with massive helpings of chow. If the group was in a huge hurry, aides took orders and hand-delivered the food.

Only three days after *Vega 1*'s encounter, with one instrument already leaking, *Vega 2* bulldozed through the dust gauntlet for its Sunday assault. A hundred quick pictures aided in more tightly defining the location of Halley's nucleus. Unlike its twin, the ship didn't notice a surge in dust levels until it closed to within ninety-three thousand miles of the comet's epicenter—and greatly reduced dust levels at that.

But twenty minutes before closest approach one of Sagdeev's engineers grabbed him and said, "Director, we have a problem. It looks like the onboard computer is malfunctioning."

On *Vega 1*, the approach computer and Hungarian camera had made for a reliable combo. "It was at larger distance from nucleus, and also that side was smeared by lot of dust," reported Sagdeev. Altogether, their equipment had been *good enough*. "With *Vega 2*, we knew we were coming little closer. We hoped to get something better."

Again he looked at his man, who was in the middle of saying, "We need your permission to switch to the backup option." He wanted to use Sagdeev's brainchild—that little staging sensor that'd been slapped together in the dwindling months prior to launch. Immediately Sagdeev okayed the change. And froze—no *kremlovka*! With a nine-minute radio delay! Over a regular phone the urgent call went out to Moscow control, and at great speed the instructions left Earth on a radio beam, whizzing out, seeking a mate in deep space that took nine tense minutes to reach. Oh, hello, here it was, new directive. Caught by antenna, shoved to computer. Voltages flying. New commands pushing through wires. Relays. Servos. Motors. *Twist-twist* went the chassis in space. Locking . . .

. . . Locked. *Vega 2* whipped past Halley's nucleus five hundred miles closer than its twin, forfeiting 80 percent of total power this deep in the coma, sipping emergency batteries, shotgunning hundreds of pictures earthward, surfacing hours later with five whole equipment pieces damaged or failed. But in the ancient spray from Halley's nucleus, millions of miles from the surface of any planet, *Vega 2* found something that the Viking program never did: organic compounds, the very building blocks of life.

What a heavy weekend. That very same day, NASA announced their discovery of the *Challenger* crew's remains.

Many Halley images were overexposed. Even so, the nucleus ones tantalized like celebrity nudes. Comet Halley's richly black epicenter was peanut-shaped, of all things, measuring roughly nine by five miles, with material pouring from at least five primary jets on its backside.

Astronomers had long theorized comets to be fat, dirty snowballs, and they were more or less correct. The overall density of Halley's nucleus turned out to be quite low; it was nearly porous and crying forty tons of water a second, with a temperature ranging between 80 and 260 degrees Fahrenheit. Such warmth suggested that the nucleus might be covered by a thin crust of debris-like insulation that protects a subterranean ice core.

While inside the coma, *Vega* had measured copious amounts of water and ammonia, plus carbon dioxide. And dust: holy housecleaning, Batman, lots and lots of dust—tens of tons per second shedding off. Coma particles fell into three categories. There were plain-Jane kinds, made of carbon and nitrogen. There were metallic ones, which on Earth would constitute iron-rich meteorites. And the third? Ice—formed of either water or carbon

45. The nucleus of Halley's comet reveals itself in this picture taken from only 370 miles away by the *Giotto* spacecraft. Courtesy European Space Agency.

dioxide. United, the materials formed a hundred-thousand-mile cocoon around the nucleus, tapering into a gauzy tail that stretched back thirty to fifty *million* miles. All born of that gigantic peanut hiding deep inside.

Felicitations abounded. "It's the first time in history we have had this sort of imaging system this close to a comet," lauded one American scientist. "It is truly a triumph."

"We've never seen the nucleus of a comet before!" celebrated another.

John Simpson referred to his experiment as "a total success" and couldn't help but feel a heaping measure of paternal pride. "Worked beautifully!" he sang. "Our instruments have touched for the first time on matter from the beginning of the solar system."

In a manner of speaking, Roald Sagdeev and Jacques Blamont had galloped through the most intimate bedchambers of a comet, thrown back the covers for all of mankind to behold its forbidden physique, and lived to tell about it.

After the excitement of the encounters died down, both ships provided an additional surprise in that they were still working. *Vega 1* even regained its orientation. Something of a scramble ensued, to press them into further service. Every bright idea that came up—like flying by certain asteroids— proved unworkable for various big-picture reasons. They'd be too far away from the target for quality readings or for the pictures to have any merit, or a *Vega* just wouldn't have enough fuel to get there in the first place. Come early '87, both craft were directed through the stream of dust left by an obscure, second-tier comet. The anticlimactic blind date happened not a moment too soon, as *Vega 1* ran out of fuel near the end of January. *Vega 2* depleted itself in late March, and the game clock went dark.

Halley's comet, blissfully ignorant of the last-minute dramatics and boisterous celebrations on that third dot over, continued its long, slow exit from the visible recesses of our solar system. Not to return until 2061.

The departure of Halley's comet coincided with the departure of Roald Sagdeev from his marriage. He basically saw it coming. Who'd really want to put up with the stifling secrecy, long days, endless nights away, and ulcerous traumatics of an always-on job like that of Space Institute director? His family cracked. Tema and the kids remained in their Moscow apartment, while Sagdeev emigrated into a pathetic one of his own. For a hundred rubles a month, the most powerful man in Soviet planetary exploration got a combo sitting-dining-bedroom, single bath, and miniature kitchen featuring peeled-up wallpaper and buckling linoleum floors. All linked by a narrow passageway.

Sagdeev tried to keep his mind on work. Undertakings like Vega don't just "end" when the ships run out of fuel. Unprocessed data remnants had to finish trickling through the institute's mainframe computers. Wrap-up meetings required scheduling, paperwork needed closing out, hallways had to be vacuumed. The plants in the Winter Garden craved attention. And of course, a private nation of Vega scientists had generated dozens of papers— most of which required Sagdeev's obliging review and input.

The piles occluding his desk increased to precipitous altitudes. He daydreamed of somehow resigning from the institute once and for all and transitioning back into his darling physics. Wouldn't it be just perfect timing? To go out on the high trilling notes of Vega? *With music*, as it were? But ooh, what a struggle. Unlocking that door would require a magic combination of emotional appeal, logical counterarguments, and timing. Each day was going to be another pull at the slot machine until Sagdeev caught those three cherries on the payline. He promised himself to remain vigilant for the next opportunity, and in the meantime supposed that their new Phobos venture offered a worthy follow-on to the comet hullabaloo.

Unusually dark, the severely cratered Phobos resembles a giant potato more than your average roundish moon. It is Mars's largest satellite, measures about seven miles across, and orbits so low that from the Red Planet's surface you'd have to be near the equator to see Phobos at all. It'd whip clear across the sky in a morning—quickly enough to circle back again once more before day's end, while imperceptibly dropping just a bit closer on every lap. Someday Phobos will lose this fight against Martian gravity and shatter into black gravel (but, please, give it a few million years).

Having languished in the conceptual stages for over a decade, the oft-discussed, far-flung, and superficially absurd plan for actually *landing* on this hideous purgatory had finally crossed two important thresholds. First, the *Vegas* had demonstrated a genuinely uplifting new plateau of maturity for Soviet electronics. They'd survived the months-long trip to Venus, plus two-thirds of a year to the comet, and still worked as expected. Fantastic.

Second, the Phobos idea enjoyed wide popular support. "The interest in choosing Phobos as a target," justified Sagdeev, "was based on its analogy with asteroids. And the idea of astronomers that Phobos might be a captured asteroid." Since asteroids comprise some of the oldest material in the solar system, they remained universally attractive targets. Um, as well as pretty darn hard to get to. Almost incredibly, here was a probable asteroid orbiting Mars?

Easy sell.

Following the Vega model, Sagdeev recruited more than a dozen countries to provide experiments and instrumentation and got to work kicking around different scenarios. Already-squeamish Lavochkin engineers waved off any landing attempts as too risky. Phobos's orbit varied; they could pin it down only to within ninety miles or so. And its gravity was unbelievably weak and not well understood. To counter, engineers proposed wading through some sketchy middle ground that was altogether unheard of in solar system exploration. First, a close rendezvous between ship and moon. A low, tight orbit. Two partners on the dance floor but no touching, like middle school. Once in formation, at a dangerously proximal sixty-five feet off the surface, Lavochkin wished to fire harpoons into Phobos and reel back samples. Analyze them in the spacecraft's belly. On paper it worked like a charm, and this operative scheme started appearing on meeting agendas. But when the time came to commit, Lavochkin got cold feet and backed away from supporting it.

Eventually all parties agreed on a feasible, if unproven, method of attack. The spacecraft would still approach Phobos at very close range—to less than a hundred feet away. Then, during a brief and particularly low pass of some twenty minutes' duration, lasers would vaporize minute patches of the surface while other instruments analyzed what came off. A bevy of close-up pictures would also be taken.

If laser beams didn't take it to the next level, dual minilanders sure would. The first was envisioned to anchor itself into Phobos and unfold solar panels—remaining on the scene for two months while radioing back data on surface conditions. The other lander, unlike any in existence, resembled a sphere with one flat side. It *hopped* by means of a large coil spring that could send the twenty-inch ball of instruments 65 feet in the air and 130 feet away, down to a new spot. The hopper was coming together nicely under the tutelage of wise old Alexander Kemurdzhian, still up at the former tank plant in Leningrad. His men had been throwing mock-ups out of helicopters for over three years already and testing their operation by means of low-gravity parabolic flights. Built conservatively, the lander could make about ten jumps over a four-hour life span. And if the first of the two mother ships fulfilled its original intentions, the other could potentially be retargeted at Mars's second moon, Deimos.

They called the mission Phobos. Two ships and three landers. The hopping thingamajig would only go on *Phobos 2*.

Roald Sagdeev got so busy with the 272-million-ruble project that he didn't notice how Big Hammer Afanasyev's recent departure had precipitated a string of underappraised managerial tweaks. On Vega things had worked beautifully because Sagdeev and his colleagues hovered over every element and implement and instrument. *They* ran the mission. "We had an international scientific and technical committee," explained Sagdeev, speaking of the formalized oversight process. "I chaired it, and we had representatives of *every* participating country. And we were in position to ask *every* enterprise in Russia: What's happening? What stage of the work, stage of preparedness? *Regularly.*" If snags arose, he could tattle to Momma Hammer. The combination bully, babysitter, and playground monitor that was Afanasyev had been a mighty lynchpin giving institute scientists their teeth.

"That was very efficient," praised Sagdeev. "I was very thankful for him doing so."

But Afanasyev's replacement wasn't so keen on preserving what worked. In the Soviet Union's thickening environment of stagnation, the new guy performed a top-level regime change. Apathetically he disbanded the institute's scientific committees and allowed all that oversight to wilt like old plants. Lamented Sagdeev, "So we didn't have much control, much influence."

Why on earth would anyone deviate from such a slick-running arrangement? Apparently because of politics. Many Soviet contractors, asserted Sagdeev, had grown weary of the endless meddling and backseat driving. How dare these packs of undisciplined scientists roam unfettered over their turf. Calling the shots! The audaciousness! Oh, the inhumanity! And to boot—so little praise being directed at their own design bureaus, without which the scientists would have been nothing but helpless pimples! Sagdeev let free a knowing eye roll and launched into his impersonation of the chief designers: "Look—Vega. So successful!" He could imagine them saying every word of it. "And this bastard Sagdeev got all the credits! We have to limit their intervention in the process!" Managerial responsibility for Phobos went instead to Lavochkin, which—although full of talent—was of course not in the business of administrating entire space missions.

"So essentially, we didn't have much help in running the whole preparatory stage for Phobos. We knew that everything was done at the last moment and so on." Fettered by the hands of authority, a beaten-back Roald Sagdeev shuddered to think what was coming.

Both *Phobos* spacecraft left the ground in early July '88 and coasted along without incident until just over seven weeks later. A Lavochkin man then unexpectedly rang up Sagdeev with abominable news. "I think we have lost *Phobos 1*," he said, in rather a blank fashion. The ship had, ah, just been inadvertently told to switch off all its maneuvering thrusters. Forever.

Sagdeev inhaled sharply. Nobody had a precaution against that?

It took awhile to untangle the wretched sequence of events. When the Phobos computer programs had first been written, they contained a number of instruction sets for testing various components aboard the ship. One set in particular dealt with vetting the network of twenty-eight microthrusters used to adjust its orientation in space. And the last line was something like, "Now that you are done working, shut down for good." Later on, when flight-prepped computer code was ready, engineers ran into a hitch, as many test codes were already burned into ROM chips and couldn't be expunged without disassembling the machinery. "We would have had to remove the computer from the spacecraft and take it to the people who could do it," explained Lavochkin point man Roald Kremnev. "We had *very* little time before the voyage."

Sagdeev echoed Kremnev's frustration with the subcontractor's just-in-time attitude. "They had huge delays until the very end. We were not sure that it would work properly." But programmers there glossed over the issues and waved it through, reasoning that no sane individual would ever transmit the command for *Phobos* to permanently disable its thrusters. Well, guess what.

Overnight, between August 29 and 30, a string of directives went up to *Phobos 1* that contained a typo. Instead of triggering an experiment check, the erroneous code exactly duplicated that forgotten test set instructing the ship to exercise its thrusters—and then fully shut them down. *Phobos 1* contained no provision for "undo" and, in a total miscarriage of engineering, was not equipped with enough smarts to reject an order like that in the first place. Every thruster winked off-line. Gradually the craft drifted until its solar panels no longer caught sunlight and its radio dish angled away from Earth. Nobody noticed the weakening signals for three solid days, until the next scheduled radio session came up and every onboard battery had drained. Game over for *Phobos 1*, its lander remaining solidly attached to the mother ship for all eternity.

"Soviets See Little Hope of Controlling Spacecraft" heckled the *New*

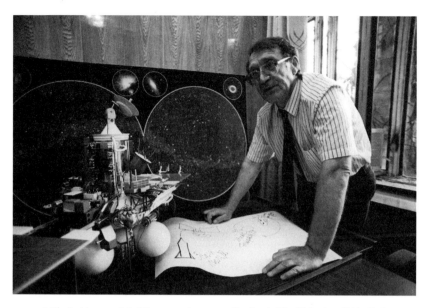

46. Flanked by a model of the namesake spacecraft, a harried Roald Sagdeev fields *Phobos* questions. "Nothing could be done. It's a dead body." Courtesy RIA Novosti.

York Times on September 10, in an article that conveyed an honest disclosure of the errant programming snafu. More vain attempts were made to contact the ship, with no happy outcomes, and in November they gave up.

A resentful Sagdeev chewed his tongue. A totally avoidable situation had nipped their butts on account of laziness. Nobody checked the instructions before they went up. Nothing in the computer code prevented blind obedience to ludicrous commands. One thing after another!

For the zillionth time Sagdeev met with his boss Prokhorov, and it wasn't about any upcoming Phobos fallout they both knew was rumbling to speed in the background. Rather, it was just Sagdeev trying to quit again. Timing factored in; soon a meeting would occur to procedurally renew the directorships of the various institutes contained within the academy. That had a way of putting a clock on things. Seated before Prokhorov, the bespectacled physicist felt nervous and tentative in the face of a thousand previous *nyets*. But he went for it anyway.

In another emotional, soul-baring affair, Roald Sagdeev conjured the fireworks of revolt. At length he recapped his dismal fifteen-year tenure— convulsing at the hands of shoestring budgets and unyielding bureaucratic hobgoblins. He yearned to abdicate, to vanish from this place. Adjourn home. "I told him how much I wanted to go back to science." Sagdeev also worked in mention of a recently introduced series of academy rules governing the reelection of institute directors. As well as their age limits. That part was a smokescreen ploy; he fit no criteria that would exclude him from continuing. But the remaining discussion involved legitimate grievances that couldn't be ignored any longer.

Prokhorov's long, lean face was accentuated by classically receding dark hair, from which dropped a steep forehead above tired eyes. Gently he appraised his subordinate, Prokhorov's ridged and rumply eyelids blinking turtle-like. Maybe it was the nation's emerging Perestroika, or his response to being worn down by these endless requests, or simply the men's advancing age. Basic human compassion might also have played a role. Nevertheless, something was different this time.

"I think he had a sympathy to this desire," offered the wanting man. "He understands, and he supported me." Magical phrases began audibly emanating from Prokhorov's mouth: a verbal lungful of opium smoke. "At that time, in 1988, he said *Okay*. He will help me; this is how." Sagdeev's request would mercifully push on through.

Now, not even Prokhorov's endorsement totally cleared the way. Final approval still had to come from the Central Committee. However, "At that time I think it was very clear that it's *going* to happen." Wasting no daylight, Sagdeev convened key members of his staff to brief them on the impending change.

"Now I will leave you," he told them after finishing. "You have to start discussing the potential candidates." Their beloved director walked out to address other matters.

Two hours later they called him back. Excitedly, Sagdeev rushed in to hear the decision. "Before we proceed, we would like to ask you a question," one of the people said. "Would you agree to stay for at least two more years? So we could prepare for a smooth transition?"

He was incredulous. "Democracy and freedom to choose should be extended also to the directors!"

The meeting broke and, following a long series of debates, eventually a new man was indeed chosen. "I don't think he was particularly happy with such a promotion," observed Sagdeev of the successful nominee. "He knew very well how much more his life would be burdened with all of the responsibilities and duties of such a post."

Everything ran fairly well with *Phobos 2* right up to when it closed on Martian orbit in late January '89. "Morale is high," reported one observer. "Everyone feels there's a chance that they'll still have a very successful project." Some random malfunctions blew on through, one camera died, and the ship's data-transmission system flipped to a low transfer rate. Overall, no showstoppers. Sagdeev got a phone update from Roald Kremnev saying, "We are in orbit."

But then Kremnev's tone changed drastically. "Roald," he warned, "we have a real problem with the computer. I'm afraid it hasn't enough resources to make its encounter with Phobos."

The computer on *Phobos* was actually a series of three. All worked together in a holy triumvirate of electronic checks and balances. Engineered in a communist state, they ran on principles of democracy: each got one vote. If a computer went bad—which was entirely possible—the others could outvote their sick friend and take over like nothing happened.

To Sagdeev, Roald Kremnev verified that one *Phobos 2* computer had died and another was malfunctioning. They were like this, it subsequently emerged, because of a known flaw whereby tiny silver "whiskers" grew on electronic components deep inside the computers' power supplies and created short circuits. Yet the gear was allowed to fly anyway because no time remained for completely reengineering and requalifying new power supplies.

"It would be possible to postpone, of course, the launch for two years." So commented a senior-level participant. "But ballistic conditions of 1990 would have demanded a full alteration of the hardware. As a result we counted on the Russian 'perhaps.'" To clarify his statement, try, "Perhaps these power supplies will work correctly anyway."

The flip side of that naturally becomes, "Perhaps they will *not* work correctly." Aaand they didn't. Instead: electronic delirium. This condition left the ship with only a single remaining operable computer, the potentiality of which had never been accounted for. No matter how healthy, one individual could not outvote two bad seeds. A February meeting of the mission's science group was postponed until March. Once March came, this meeting would be postponed indefinitely.

The lone computer hung on. *Phobos 2* looped Mars, fired up several instruments, and began adjusting course to gradually shift into high orbit over the next couple of months. One day the radio dropped out, but it came back. Data flowed—albeit at low speeds. The ship nailed a close fly-by of Phobos itself and more precisely detailed the moon's orbit. Pictures began streaming back at the end of February, from between five hundred and seven hundred miles out. TASS issued a weird facsimile of success. "That's terrific news," crowed one American researcher, freshly back from Moscow. "When I was over there, just about all of the instruments were working. They now have a completely operating science payload. It's just great."

Almost there. Hanging tough. *Phobos 2* made a low swoop of its namesake, down below two hundred miles, calculating the moon's true orbit to within sixteen thousand feet of uncertainty. The science instruments ran another full suite in mid-March. The ship caught a second low pass, down to 119 miles, scouting landing spots. More than 80 percent of the moon had now been imaged. Things were looking nifty. April 9 seemed realistic for deploying landers. Buckle up—here comes the gold.

On the last day of March another imaging session went off with no trouble, and a follow-on was set to happen three hours downstream. In order to shoot pictures, *Phobos 2* had to rotate its entire self around—which also turned the antenna dish away from Earth and severed contact. More sophisticated ships mounted cameras and other instruments on articulating boom arms; they could be pointed in most any direction without having to move the fixed antenna away from home base. *Phobos* accounted for its rotation scenario with timers. After a preset interval had elapsed, the craft would swivel back and reestablish communication. During any picture taking its radio transmitter was also turned off, helping to conserve energy.

After that second session, the ship didn't report in. Controllers jousted with the situation for four hours and during that time managed to catch only thirteen minutes of extremely weak gibberish. *Phobos 2*, like its sibling, had undoubtedly lost orientation and now drifted in an uncontrolled state. In time the onboard batteries, starved of power by darkened solar panels, would be unable to recharge themselves.

Sagdeev learned about it while on his way to a scientific gathering in Stockholm. He thought about canceling. The incoming director ordered him to make the trip regardless and keep his head high; returning to Moscow wouldn't help any. April 9 came and went. One week later, the deteriorating nation begrudgingly announced a wholesale loss of *Phobos 2*. They kept the language pretty sparse, leaving out what actually happened up there.

Director Roald Sagdeev, full academician of the Soviet Academy of Sciences, celebrated plasma physicist, and 1986 Hero of Socialist Labor, would not be leaving the Space Research Institute with music. He would instead be leaving in shame. Quietly, Sagdeev finished packing his office and took one last stroll through the Winter Garden before abandoning it forever.

28. Wonders Never Cease

We still do not have a proper balance between robotic and human
flights. And whatever ratio between these two areas we
have is driven *not* by interests of science.

—Roald Sagdeev

Her name was Susan Eisenhower. They'd originally met in late August '87, and one of the first things Roald Sagdeev said to her was that she looked like her grandfather—who happened to be former U.S. president Dwight Eisenhower. This is a comment that could have easily been interpreted in exactly the wrong fashion.

But Susan was no high-maintenance hothead and was of an ambassadorial mind-set. To clarify she lightly asked, "May I take that as a compliment?"

"Of course!"

Both were attending a conference in upstate New York on U.S.-Soviet relations. Nineteen years his junior, she presided over a firm aiming to expand dialogue on matters of global public policy, in part by organizing events like this one. The gathering had little to do with space, but it did involve topics like nuclear arms and the role of big business in military affairs. Right up Sagdeev's alley. He'd been wetting his feet in politics— having won election to the Congress of People's Deputies, a new Soviet legislative body. In one particularly memorable session, Sagdeev tendered the lone negative vote on a proposed law restricting public demonstrations. "No one seemed to know how to count a 'No,'" he sighed. "I had to keep my hand up for fifteen or twenty minutes."

Repeatedly they crossed paths in the world's major cities, Eisenhower conducting her business affairs while Sagdeev attended scientific forums.

Occasionally it was the same event—a conference on the future of international cooperation in space, for example.

"From the moment we started to talk, I felt that I could confide in her," he said.

Initially Eisenhower did not feel the same way. At all. "I was very suspicious of every open thing Roald said. I thought, 'This is some kind of setup.'"

Nevertheless, over dinners and marathon walks and labyrinthine discussions of Perestroika their cordial, professional association blossomed into a warm friendship. Shortly after the loss of *Phobos 1*, Sagdeev gave her two identical watches. "Just like *Phobos*," he smiled. "One can serve as a backup in case the other one no longer works." Endless letters went forth and back and forth again through the mail. Hours ticked by on teenage-style phone calls. And in due time both admitted that they cared about one another to a much greater degree than two ordinary colleagues in the platonic pursuit of détente. Sagdeev requested Eisenhower's hand in marriage.

Almost simultaneously, what remained of the Soviet Union disintegrated into more than a dozen variegated republics—all eager to scream independence. President Gorbachev resigned office early on Christmas Day in 1991 and that night the red hammer and sickle came down from Kremlin flagpoles for the very last time.

"What I really want more than anything else," Sagdeev had told Eisenhower a couple of years beforehand, "is to do my work as an international scientist and be a citizen of the world. I have never been a politician." Eisenhower's core career was focused in the Washington DC area, plus that's where her daughters lived. So the couple relocated there and Sagdeev took a job teaching physics at the University of Maryland. Both of his grown children also came to the States.

"I feel very comfortable here," he puts forward. "It's a nice place to work." His eyes reflect on his spacious corner office, his lips in a faint smile.

Today Roald Sagdeev has the hands of a livestock farmer. They are aged and well worked, with liver spots on crooked fingers. His English is fluent, although he humbly claims it isn't much better than it was during that awkward moment so many decades ago when he told a Boston barber to cut his hair "medium." Laughter pours forth. "You know, the funny thing is, I'm still doing the same, right now! So, *medium*! Yes!" He dabbles a little in space, researching topics like galactic explosions. The proper disposal of nuclear waste also commands a fair share of his attention. Gravely concerned over its untamed buildup, he's been exploring different ways of converting the sludge into material that's no longer hazardous.

The most enduring legacy of Sagdeev's tenure at the institute is undoubtedly that of Venus exploration. Despite the impressive roster of Venera outings, he feels that numerous important questions about the planet remain unanswered. "In the overall science of Venus, I think the real question is what happened with water," he suggests. Surface features indicate that it used to be everywhere on Venus—but then what? Evolving atmospheric forces broke it down into oxygen and hydrogen? The latter of which ascended into space and never came back? Second possibility: all the water's still there, but it's chemically locked up in rocks. The conundrum "would require much more detailed geochemical analysis." That means future landers, drills, sampling chambers. How will they have improved? What'll be different? Will the Russians go, or maybe the Chinese?

Sagdeev also remains intrigued by the planet's bizarre atmosphere. "I would like to learn much more about the sulfur acids. How it's distributed with altitude," he says. "At such quantity which is found in the atmosphere, one could think that there could be even something like sulfur acid lakes on the surface!"

Both *Vega* balloons directly confirmed that Venus's middle cloud layers travel completely around the planet in about six days, while the topmost ones do it in four. But a lingering question is: why? The mechanism that sustains such feloniously brisk rotation is still not understood. Sagdeev would love to see more ballooning on Venus, to help solve the riddle of what's happening oh so high up in her clouds.

Half the Venera flights occurred on his watch. An argument could be made that, in an environment of teensy budgets and red tape and slapdash quality, the Soviets should've launched fewer probes and endeavored to improve the caliber of each. Sagdeev dismisses the idea. "I don't think it would work this way," he responds. "It might have been even counterproductive because it would bring some kind of different attitudes to the industry: 'Oh, you don't need so much? Great!' And at the same time there was a huge pressure on the side of the scientific community—they wanted to fly more often. So I was joking. I said, 'You guys are like drug addicts. It's like injection!'"

Occasionally Sagdeev's travels return him to the well-worn hallways of the Space Research Institute. What became of his Winter Garden? "I think female staff of institute liked very much and they took care of it." Ivan, however, is no longer at hand. Sagdeev's enterprising driver ultimately surrendered his black Volga and went on to run a horse farm near Kiev.

Even so, many of Sagdeev's associates remain. "When I walk in the corridor," he says, "the old-timers you know, these staffers—not scientists—would stop me and say something nice." He glances away and briefly appears embarrassed.

"It's such a rewarding feeling."

Few missions since Vega have imaged cometary nuclei, and none have successfully replicated ballooning on any planet or moon. The ambitious European Rosetta mission did actually *land* on the surface of a comet's nucleus in late 2014; one onboard experiment even detected organic compounds flitting about in the surrounding atmosphere. A proud Roald Sagdeev notes that the release of gas and dust from that comet is about two orders of magnitude lower than what'd been faced by either *Vega* at Halley's. "*Ours* is genuinely older and pristine," he can't help pointing out.

Not long after the Halley encounters, Jacques Blamont sweet-talked his way onto a Soviet flight called *Mars-94*. Enormous watermelon-shaped balloons—138 feet tall by 43 feet across—would float only a couple of miles off the Martian scrag, assessing dust and wind and shooting what promised to be mesmerizing TV footage of whatever rolled on below. At night, colder temperatures would force each balloon low enough to drag an articulated "snake" of sensors across the ground. They complemented a twin flight called *Mars-96* that aimed to deliver orbiters and rovers.

The colossal Phobos mistakes led to a solemn slashing of budgets. The payloads were traded around, with the now-single balloon being shifted over to *Mars-96*. General financial distress related to the Soviet Union's breakup then pushed the 1994 blastoff to at least 1996 and the '96 flight to '98. The project hung on the edge of total damnation. France had already kicked in over $100 million, and in America an advocacy group called the Planetary Society independently kept the snake on fiscal life support. Russia could no longer afford a Proton rocket, and switching boosters put the whole payload on a crash diet. By late '95 a bevy of enduring money problems forced Russia to drop the '98 launch altogether and just send up *Mars-*

96. At that point, Blamont ran out of second chances. No balloon of his ever went to Mars.

From his long-standing post at Curie University in Paris, Jacques Blamont maintains a rigorous involvement in many of the world's space programs. "He's more active than ever before," emphasizes Viktor Kerzhanovich of his friend. And that's for a man pushing ninety. Blamont's been a visiting scientist at JPL and an ongoing advisor to the French space agency CNES. He's also influenced every breed of mission, from lunar-mapping flights to the *Cassini* Saturn orbiter—while managing to write at least five books during his time in between, some of which aren't related to space at all.

A few years after Sagdeev's wedding, during the whole *Mars-96* episode, Viktor and Svetlana Kerzhanovich prudently concluded that Mother Russia's space program was indeed circling the drain of bankruptcy. They fled to California, with their son Dmitri following some years later. In no time Kerzhanovich got recruited to be a walk-on at JPL—working with the likes of Bob Preston, who couldn't believe that an old Vega teammate from the Iron Curtain now lived inside of a mile from his own abode.

Kerzhanovich spent his next fifteen years developing mission scenarios under NASA's Discovery program, which aimed to fly lower-cost spacecraft in pursuit of highly specialized objectives. It seemed an ideal avenue for continued ballooning. On the cheap you could do practically anything with them, practically anywhere: Venus, Mars, the moons of Saturn; big payloads or small, blimps or spheres or ones shaped like monkeys with jet packs (contact the Macy's Thanksgiving Day parade for that last one).

But Discovery proved to be a crippling slog; Kerzhanovich sounded weary even talking about it decades later. "*Every* Discovery opportunity, we submitted proposal for the balloon. One way or another. But okay it's America; there is big competition here." Kerzhanovich then alluded to the cultural differences inherent in his previous life. "In Soviet Union, it could be much easier if you *excite* with your idea," he advised. Remember Vladimir Chelomey? He knew the trick: catch your boss's interest with some newfangled angle like pop-out wings, and you're on the roster. "Here, it is not like that. There is another thirty guys who are doing the same thing." Landing a slot on the next bus out means crafting a proposal that's not only relevant but technically and intellectually superior. It's got to consume less power and fit into a smaller space. And of course, it must return the greatest amount of science—as if science itself were a raw material like iron or silver that could somehow be mined from the destination world and trucked home in a boxcar.

"We made probably about six or eight proposals for different Discovery mission, for European mission, for *everything*. All was not selected." No balloon of *his* ever went to Mars either—or anywhere else. The process utterly fatigued him. "And I don't like this feeling." It wasn't the newer technology or even the dissimilar work environment. He was just sick of killing himself on paper projects that never went anywhere. The Lab suffered rounds of budget cuts and by 2011 Kerzhanovich assumed that none of those proposals would fly in his lifetime.

"So that's why I decided to retire."

Altogether disinterested in his own retirement, Bob Preston still attacks the job each day. "JPL is like a Disneyland for scientists and engineers," he touts. "I'm still thrilled at all the amazing things that go on here, and hope I still add my share of creative energy."

A strong emotional link exists between him and a certain nearby planet. In reference to this he confesses, "I can't look at Venus at night without thinking, *There are two balloons on the surface that I once flew there.*

"And that's pretty special."

"I'm not the youngest guy anymore."

Klaus Biemann also hung up the lab coat. "I officially retired in 1996 and I closed my laboratory in 1999." He continues to have a shadow of a presence at MIT, stores all his records there, and occasionally surfaces to rebut charges that his Viking GCMs failed to find organics because of poor design or construction.

"I would take Biemann's side that his instrument did what it was asked to do," asserts Robert Cotter of the Johns Hopkins School of Medicine. He's a professor of pharmacology and molecular sciences there. "The instrument had a lot of fine engineering."

"Worked beautifully," echoes astrobiologist David Des Marais of Ames Lab. "Anyone claiming that the instrument didn't work as planned is wrong—that's not an accurate recapitulation."

If he could somehow rewind time, Klaus Biemann would've preferred a greater assortment of Viking destinations. "I would have liked that the second site would be near the polar cap," he says of his dream spot up north. In that region (which is lower in altitude than the Martian south pole, not to mention warmer), atmospheric carbon dioxide freezes out during wintertime—amassing thick layers of dry ice. As summer comes this sublimates to gas, whereupon the cycle repeats. An identical process happens at the Martian south pole.

Biemann's position is that when this carbon dioxide freezes, it'd capture any airborne organic material and imprison it in dry ice to collect on the ground. "So this kind of a precipitation process *could* enrich organics around the polar cap. But we couldn't go there because there was no radar information about the surface conditions." It always comes back to that delicate dilemma of finding Viking the *safest* landing sites versus ones with the *most potential for life*. In 2008 a NASA machine called *Phoenix* came down right atop plains of water ice in Mars's high north latitudes. Despite this, and decades of instrument maturity, it too failed to find any organic material—though it *did* unmask a substance called perchlorate, which sheds oxygen in the presence of heat. Hey—is that Oyama's oxidant? Well, perchlorate needs a good 650 degrees F to even begin releasing oxygen. So, no, it can't be. But researchers will keep looking.

And discovering. In 2013 a study fronted by Ames Lab suggested that the irradiation of these perchlorates, as would occur in a Martian environment, well explained both the LR and GEX results—without a hint of organics or life being necessary. JPL's car-sized *Curiosity* rover also found perchlorate on Mars, implying its broad distribution across the planet's surface.

Curiosity's find made for an intriguing reinforcement of the "it's just chemistry" hypothesis . . . until the rover hit genuine pay dirt. Its own GCMS, an eighty-eight-pound gold-colored box the size of a microwave oven, boasts seventy-four individual sample cups and can optionally perform the wet, solvent-based preparations that'd been denied to Klaus Biemann on Viking. This advanced and rather sensitive GCMS can also analyze what's in the air. From one of *Curiosity*'s drilled rock samples has come news of several organic compounds—first mined in 2013 and decisively confirmed just over a year later. On the heels of that arrived word of organic methane wafting through the atmosphere. At fluctuating levels, no less.

Airborne methane doesn't mean that *Curiosity* found life on Mars. Nobody yet knows whether the stuff originates from chemical processes or little stealthy critters that haven't been fingered yet. But methane doesn't last long, by its very nature, and must be replenished. What's producing this methane is a hot new question.

Glancing back, how does Jerry Hubbard rate his own time on Viking? "The most enjoyable and productive period of my life," he says—utterly without hesitation. "Lookin' for life on Mars is like winning Miss America when you're eighteen years old. What do you do for the rest of your life? What's gonna excite you?" Once his NASA commitments finished in '79, Hubbard stayed in close contact with Norm Horowitz even though the two men lived on opposite sides of the country. "We remained friends and I sought his counsel. I tried to mentor my students à la Norm and I was very pleased with the successes." Interleaved with his microbiology lectures, Hubbard researched the practicality of differing experimental biofuels—along with "green" remedies for cleaning up environmental waste. An unofficial retirement came in 1995. Then, after two supplemental years of part-time lecturing, he hung it up for good.

These days Hubbard relaxes with his wife in Florida, southeast of Orlando. He's remained smoke-free and regards his 1970s attire with amusement: "I wonder what happened to my white belt?" He stays abreast of what's happening in the world of microbiology. And Mars. One of Hubbard's recent manuscripts forecast that future Mars experiments will indeed find low levels of solar-generated organics—much the same as Carbon Assimilation seems to have done. He does not think life was found on Mars in 1976. "As one who was there as the Viking data unfolded, I've always felt the kinetic data did not support a biological explanation." But he's also quick to blurt out a mantra that is common among all real scientists: "We need more data!"

Saddening to Hubbard is the dwindling of Viking's personnel. "It's a nightmare the number of people that have died. Gosh almighty," he says. Jim Martin and Gerry Soffen are gone. Vance Oyama. Harold Klein has also left the building. When Norm Horowitz passed in 2005, less than three months after turning ninety, Hubbard couldn't attend the memorial service. But George Hobby did.

"I went to Norm's ninetieth birthday party," offered a mellow Hobby to the assembled mourners, speaking of what'd happened only a couple months beforehand. "And I congratulated him and told him that I would call him in a week or two and I didn't. And now I'm sorry," he divulged.

"But I gave him a birthday card and on it I wrote, *Norm, I've lived a wonderful life and you contributed to the most important part of it.*"

Hobby steadied himself. "Those days were some of the most rewarding days of my life," he went on. "And working with Norm was a reward in itself."

Horowitz's son Joel also took a turn at the microphone that day. "He was a convinced, a very firm atheist," Joel said of his father. "And believed that was the only way one should think." Joel's wife, a practicing Catholic, would occasionally tease her father-in-law by offering to pray for him. It was all accepted as lighthearted ribbing. "He was very proud of his roses," the younger Horowitz added, in a moment of paternal admiration. "The roses that he—so to speak—*still has* look far better than any roses I have."

Gil Levin once described Patricia Straat as feisty—a label she does not try to refute. "I never was a yes-man." Straat corrects herself. "A yes-*woman.* If I didn't like what he said, I told him so. So maybe that's where that comes from."

Independently, Straat and Levin speak of one another not just with admiration but in notably reverential tones. They were ideal complements. Yin and yang; each others' sidekick. "She perfectly implemented my concepts and made the instrument work," celebrates Levin. In his eyes, nobody else this side of Mars could've pulled that off.

Realize also that the Viking effort was not regarded positively by everyone who knew Straat. "You're killing yourself career-wise," implored her Johns Hopkins colleagues, back when she started with Levin. "It's a dead end." And yeah, outwardly it contained all the trappings of a bad Lifetime Original Movie: smart girl abandons stable university gig for unrepentant mad scientist hell-bent on finding little green men. But the overall experience was a defining moment in her career.

She remains puzzled by the absence of life-detection experiments aboard JPL's *Curiosity* rover. It landed in August 2012 with the express purpose of determining whether Mars ever had the capacity to support living organisms. *Curiosity* seeks worthy habitats—not life itself. "I don't really understand why they don't want to go back and test for it again," Straat posits of the apparently gun-shy NASA. "The only reasons that I can think of are to make such a pronouncement has so many ramifications." Plausible enough. You think you found life on another planet? Cue the naysayers, the blog posters, the conservatives on congressional budgetary committees, the Vatican.

Not to gang up, but Gil Levin heaps on a little unfiltered criticism of his own: "NASA has grossly mishandled this prime scientific effort, spending billions of dollars in dallying pursuits, with fail-safe missions that provided little scientific return beyond what Viking had already found."

What does he mean by "fail-safe"? NASA's contemporary Mars approach is called Follow the Water. It aims to reconnoiter locales such as polar caps and dried-up riverbeds in search of true liquid water, subsurface ice, hydrothermal vents, or other sources of moisture. The goal is to identify "hospitable" areas—ones that could've harbored life in the distant past or maybe have it there right now, today. In support of this JPL has, to date, put one additional lander and four rovers on Mars, none of which carried any carbon assimilators, gas exchangers, or labeled releasers. Two orbiting ships have also helped to characterize the planet's climate and map its surface.

Wait, wait. Follow the Water? That's it? Almost two decades into the twenty-first century, the best they've got is "follow the water"? Why does this sound conspicuously vague? Why is Mars exploration heading in an apparently backward direction from Viking? Are NASA stooges conspiring to duck the issue, employing cutesy catchphrases to placate us and throw us off the scent?

No, they aren't. There is no controlled demolition here, no shooters on the grassy knoll. What came first wasn't necessarily the best way to start. During a public forum in 2011 a Curiosity mission director acknowledged 1976's giant overstep. "With Viking we went for the home run," he volunteered, almost apologetically. "But at the time we really didn't know *where the best places were* to look for life. And we still don't know. That's why we keep looking, with tools like our new rover." If life exists out there among all those reddish rocks, it'll probably need at least trace amounts of water in order to thrive. So before another biology package is sent—ideally with much less in the way of potentially ambiguous interpretations—the most likely habitats will need to be identified. That's why the Americans are, as they say, following the water.

Of course, that strategy accounts for only one variety of organism—the obvious one. Nobody's going to land on Mars with the idea of seeking out, say, big worms that live on poison gas. "Life evolved millions and millions of years ago," Straat continues, "and it has managed to survive and adapt to every known type of environment. And some of them are *extreme* environments." Only a year after both Vikings touched down, a manned submersible probing the eight-thousand-foot ocean depths west of Ecuador ran across what never could've been foretold. Suddenly appearing in the hazy glare of floodlights were giant tube worms, one end firmly rooted to the ocean floor.

Marine biologists went jelly-kneed. Only microbes were thought to be capable of surviving without oxygen or sunlight, yet here before them stood vast communities of these things. Six feet tall or better, they swayed gently in the near-freezing ocean current—happily at home under 236 atmospheres of squeezing pressure against their milk-white bodies with feathery red plumes on the free end. They had blood and exoskeletons and laid eggs. They slurped up nourishment from scalding-hot hydrogen sulfide gas billowing from nearby vent cracks in the ocean floor. A perfect adaptation.

Tube worms don't talk, but they make a point. No longer can life be thought of as merely something like us. Even so, our next steps in the pursuit of alien beings will logically follow the water.

Straat fulfilled her NASA obligations in 1980 and went on to roost at one of America's premier medical research agencies: the National Institutes of Health in Bethesda, Maryland. Over the course of twenty-one subsequent years she cycled through various disciplines—toxicology, biophysics— and finished out the remainder of her time evaluating grant applications. A 2001 retirement saw Straat retreat to her ten-acre farm to enjoy a menagerie of animals. And of course, horse riding—from which she dismounted for good in 2007 at age seventy-one. The horses are still around, though.

Most people have an opinion about whether or not life exists on Mars. But Straat is in the unique position of being able to render a verdict based on direct investigation.

"We think that it *is* life on Mars," she says plainly, citing her Himalayan LR curves. "And I get more and more convinced as time goes on."

Straat pauses.

"It took me a lot longer to come to that conclusion than it took Gil. 'Course I think Gil . . . Gil wants to go down in history as the man who discovered life on Mars."

Hey, who wouldn't? Gil Levin, as may be predicted, has little need for retirement in his minimally downtimed universe of entrepreneurship and innovation. To date he's collected a hat trick of degrees from Johns Hopkins and spent three years on its board of trustees. Levin's newest company,

47a & b. Pat Straat and Gil Levin have time to smile, now that Viking has ended.
Courtesy Patricia Ann Straat and Gil Levin, respectively.

Spherix, created an organic process that removes chemicals from wastewater. For livestock farms, they put out a natural, citric acid–based compound that dramatically reduces fly populations by preventing larvae from maturing into adults. They also patented a sugar substitute called tagatose that's derived from whey. However, bringing a sweetener to market takes peer review, FDA approval, taste testing, field testing, package design, retesting. People have to get comfortable with it. Spherix began the journey in 1988 but, so far, tagatose-containing products have only appeared in a smattering of European stores.

"It takes persistence," notes Levin with a calming, professorial tone of voice that bears no hint of the glacial pace at which these things move. He's got all the time in the world to see it through. Another month or year—whatever. If Straat is feisty, the word to describe Levin is *stubborn*. Beyond killing flies and inventing sweetness, he's continued a virtually uninterrupted stream of paper writing and public speaking about his Mars findings—lest anyone forget. "The Viking LR tests indicated life," he reminds, "and the controls confirmed the positive signals to be of biological origin. The data were very similar in magnitude and kinetics to those obtained from tests on many terrestrial soils—falling well within the range of the thousands of tests performed before and after Viking." Over time, he's quick to note, no new barriers to his results have ever come up. They've only been falling.

"In view of all these post-Viking developments," he insists of LR's results, "it's time for an objective review!"

And last but certainly not least, there is the matter of his experiment's original name. Levin guffaws. "I named it Gulliver because it was going to look for Lilliputians on a strange, faraway place." He sounds like an unremorseful adolescent who's been caught violating curfew. Just a little fun 'n' games; that's all. "And NASA thought that was too cute, I guess, and the public wouldn't understand that. And they thought it should be a more scientific name, and somehow they thought 'Labeled Release' was that."

He sighs. "I still like 'Gulliver.'"

Lunokhod's undeniable success bestowed upon Izrail Rozentsveyg the requisite medals and special privileges. He also received a cash award equating to two months' salary.

Helpful gestures. But for Rozentsveyg a certain invisible scar cannot be sanded away with mere medals and moolah. He's looking for some group honesty, on account of so many of his countrymen having never publicly come clean about their abysmal working conditions. It seems downright backward: the completely unprecedented technological achievement of Lunokhod's chassis occurred in a dungeon of poverty and self-sacrifice. "While living in Russia, it was somehow immoral to talk about the shortcomings," he puts forward of the culture. "Perhaps another reason that I left."

Yup, him too. After retiring in 1987, Rozentsveyg emigrated from the Soviet Union and put down roots in, of all places, Northern California. The contrast in lifestyles was altogether unimaginable. "We lived in a different world," he says of Leningrad—now called St. Petersburg. "And felt it was the norm."

If, throughout the entirety of Lunokhod, a singular name must be held highest—if only one chest can wear a medal—then Izrail Rozentsveyg would pin it on his forward-thinking supervisor at TransMash. "Kemurdzhian was a great diplomat," he praises. "Able to communicate with the right people. Was quite cunning and clever. He knew how not to annoy the authorities." In Alexander Kemurdzhian, Rozentsveyg had a friend for life.

Appearing at a Lunokhod fortieth anniversary gala in 2010, Vyacheslav Dovgan looked trim and athletic and needed eyeglasses only when reading small print. Out of uniform he's probably mistaken more for a master's-level marathon runner than a sitting cosmonaut. If Dovgan's grateful for anything, it's not fitness or good eyesight but how the dark curtain of Soviet-era secrecy has finally been torn asunder from the Lunokhod drivers. Rightfully. "Our names were called just after twenty-three years," he mourns of pointless setbacks in recognizing the team.

He reserves overwhelmingly positive comments for the crew selection and training process. "Before us," he remarks, "they had tried to use aviators, tractor drivers, car drivers, and even cyclists." In sum, *wheelmen* were thought ideal for this job.

"Not good enough!"

He's right; nobody clicked. What killed every one of these drivers was the time delay between seeing an image and having to irrevocably execute a decision based on it. "None of them could pass the test," snickers Dovgan, recollecting the invalidated contenders.

The other infraction that torpedoed anyone's chances was freaking out when bad things happened unexpectedly. One early evaluation placed candidates behind the wheel of a Moskvitch sedan rolling down the street at

48. A group of Lunokhod participants and spouses convene in 2001 to socialize. From left, Rozentsveyg's wife, Galina; engineer Mikhail Malenkov; Alexander Kemurdzhian; Malenkov's wife, Svetlana; and Izrail Rozentsveyg himself. Courtesy Mikhail Malenkov.

ten miles an hour. All of a sudden guys would leap out and throw a blanket over the windshield. Those who screamed, swore, let go of the wheel, covered their eyes, and/or frantically pumped the brakes got handed a summary dismissal.

But the solution, as everyone finally realized, was to stop thinking about *drivers* of some kind being the real answer. Instead, as Dovgan observes, "They selected men who knew how to assess a situation rapidly, and who could memorize and reproduce the situation immediately." That made all the difference. Result: success.

Out of all those months of shepherding the only two Soviet lunar rovers, ever, what is his fondest memory?

The answer takes nary a second. "One of the brightest and perhaps most beautiful scenes," he lilts, "was the sunrise on the moon."

Odd, perhaps, that his own personal "magnificent desolation" was borne from unvarnished international rivalry and surplus gear. Once, long ago, in a faraway time and political climate, two countries raced to the moon. And in every race there is someone who must lose. "We had good chances to bring samples from the moon before, or at least simultaneously *with*, the Apollo mission." That's Alexander Basilevsky talking. He's not ashamed in the slightest that his nation abandoned their original bleeding-edge fandango in favor of round-tripping excavation and unmanned rovers. "Sample returns were very competitive," he goes on. "And if we would continue after *Luna 24* with *25, 26, 27*, it was quite cheap. We could do this. It was political decision to change."

A trace of regret creeps into his voice. "For me, I still think it was a mistake."

These days, Basilevsky betrays no sign of retarding his pace. Russia is planning at least two innovative lunar missions for the near future—one of which will examine its poles for water ice thought to dwell beneath the surface. He's a core person winnowing out prime landing sites. He's also analyzing images from a sexy European number called *Venus Express*, which orbited the Goddess of Love from April 1, 2006, until December 2014.

The nearly complete *Lunokhod 3* occupies a hallowed section of Lavochkin's in-house museum. The rover's got a power feed so visitors can marvel at its nodding front camera, rotating antenna, and high-pitched whine of eight spinny wheels.

But the thing shouldn't even *be* there. Detailed museum models are cool to walk around and educationally illustrative. Fully operational, unflown spacecraft are tragedies of budgets, politics, or whatever else conspired to keep them on the ground. The difference is because it's genuine flight hardware. Wouldn't it be great to stage an intervention—to rip *Lunokhod 3* from its current moorings and shoot 'er off on a voyage of lunar discovery? Plant Dovgan and Basilevsky back in their spots! Fancifully encouraging, yes, but impractical if not already impossible, and technologically pointless. Today's cell phone cameras offer better resolution than Lunokhod's own. Its electronics are not only archaic but dried up and fracturing. Everybody's forgotten the procedures, which are just as outdated as the machine itself. If *Lunokhod 3* goes up, you might as well put a floppy drive in the IBM Sequoia.

And the control facility is literally gone. When Soviet society fragmented, Ukraine reverted to its original borders—appropriating Yevpatoria and Shkolnoye and all of Crimea in one fell swoop. As a bonus the new (old) country also inherited a landing strip for the Buran space shuttle, which had previously necessitated the unceremonious bulldozing of an entire town.

Ukraine had little use for multiple spacecraft control campuses. Yevpa-

49. Hard at work in 2004, Alexander Basilevsky would love nothing more than to finally realize the "Sparka" initiative of uniting Lunokhod variants with a sample-returning Luna. "We are still thinking about this and pressing now to our engineers to return to these plans." Photo by Mikhail Ivanov, courtesy of Alexander Basilevsky.

toria station was the largest and most capable, which led to the 1998 closing and abandonment of the Shkolnoye Technical Zone. Today it's in ruins, the Lunadrome grown over. Visitors approaching the site can duck between saggy lines of barbed-wire and roam at will. The giant hundred-foot dish still stands, yet it is frozen in time, as nothing remains with which to maneuver it.

Go wherever you like; rubbish litters the mildly undulating grounds. Enter dilapidated buildings that used to be the province of armed guards and state secrets. Tour empty rooms with missing windows, missing people, missing history. Everything's been stripped to the skivvies: power modules, radios, amplifiers, signal distribution, and every last piece of equipment all ripped out. Over there's the derelict meeting room, bare and blank and library quiet with no indication of what transpired in it so very long ago. A rusty wrecking crane takes periodic swipes at the half-demolished Lunokhod control building. Most of its roof is down; mismatched rubble trails on out over the worn steps that Basilevsky, Dovgan, and others used to climb

50. This trash heap was all that remained of Lunokhod's control center in 2009. The drive team's room is gone. Like, completely. Photo by and courtesy of Alexander Dzhuly.

each day for weeks at a time. Magnetic tape hangs in the overgrown scrub brush like Christmas tinsel.

Why knock down such a historic building? Concrete. "It's a very good road construction material," explained one Simferopol native who married a woman from Shkolnoye. "That sells well."

Eastern Shkolnoye, on the other hand, remains vibrantly alive. Apartments and schools and playgrounds dot the area, lighting up with children and conversation and laughter and life in general. The hotel everyone used to stay at during Lunokhod sessions has been transformed into an additional apartment block. Despite the forsaking of that which defined it in the first place, this town and its people have resolutely persevered. Today Shkolnoye is regarded as a suburb of Simferopol; many residents work in the latter yet return to the former each night—to enjoy a slower pace, quieter streets, and an unmolested landscape.

The old Federal Office Building 6 still exists in Washington DC but is no longer called FOB 6 and no longer houses NASA headquarters. In 1992 employees adjusted their commutes to end two blocks farther south at a brand-new edifice purpose-built to serve as the unified headquarters. Within its 1.4 miles of hallways, one wall is smooth while the opposite is textured. For those who are visually impaired—or in case of smoky emergencies—this provides a tactile guide for safely navigating out. The place also has two saunas, a TV studio, and some really huge-ass copy machines.

With abundant pleasantries Don Hearth recalls his time in the saddle at FOB 6 and NASA HQ. "It's a period of my life and my professional career that I take the greatest pride in, very frankly. And include in that statement my ten years as director of Langley." For many an aerospace engineer, *director of Langley* is sort of up there with the papacy. So, life at NASA was better than running one of the world's foremost aeronautics research facilities?

"I think it was in a way more professionally rewarding, because of what I basically inherited, and what was in place when I left the job."

When Hearth came aboard, NASA's number-one goal was putting a man on the moon. JPL flew their Rangers and Mariners with no sensible plan for leveling up. Unfocused and lackluster, planetary exploration was more of a side project: crack filler to round out the NASA mission statement. Voyager Mars? One name on a sheet of paper.

So Hearth escalated things, kick-starting Martian orbiters and a flyby of Mercury. His hands were all over *Pioneer 10* and *11*, which went from spoken idea to the asteroid belt and then to Jupiter and Saturn. He expedited collaboration between America and West Germany that begat twin solar-orbiting labs called *Helios*. After leaving HQ, he was instrumental in green-lighting childcare facilities at both Langley and Goddard—long before such facilities were in vogue. "The day care centers were the right thing to do and helpful in hiring women professions as well. I wasn't a hero."

Of his more recent activities he insists, "I am very busy right now. How can that be, since I'm retired?" His darling companion, wife Joan, is no longer with him. "We were ten weeks from our fifty-fifth anniversary when she died in 2005." He speaks in a muted tone that suggests reluctant acceptance. But the familial verve generated by four children and multiple grandchildren keeps him hopping. Life presses forward.

Regardless of what your average five-year-old might have to say about it, nobody needs a red cape to fly to other worlds. All that's necessary is dedi-

51. Don Hearth kickin' it in 2008. "I've been gone from the system a long time," he said of NASA. "When I left it was a great place." Courtesy Don Hearth.

cation and resolve and—yes—plenty of curiosity. This last trait is not typically inaccessible because humans are fundamentally born to explore. And the human spirit cannot sit idle. Even shortly after birth we're taking in the sights, reaching for anything within our grasp—and many things that aren't. Time gives us mobility. We delight in stomping down that unwalked park path or that previously unseen aisle in the bookstore, riding around that unridden curve in the road, or dog-paddling beyond the weathered buoys cordoning off a beachfront swim area. We just *have* to go and see what's out there, don't we?

At heart it is mankind's insatiable curiosity that propels the continued reconnaissance of our solar system. It's not just some force-fed lesson plan from elementary school. Yeah, sure, we all had to study the planets; it was that one-week unit in science class where so-so movies were shown of bright blobby balls hanging in space, elucidated by disembodied narrators rattling off uninspiring trivia that many seemed determined to ignore. Then, agony: "Break up into small groups," the teacher would command, excruciatingly, and everyone had to spend an afternoon perusing encyclopedias. Venus, Mars, the moon: find pictures and facts and write four coherent paragraphs in your wide-ruled spiral notebooks, due tomorrow. Part of the grind, right?

But a select few—unconsciously responding to the soft patter of a rhythm they couldn't quite place—seemed more engaged, more responsive. They wrote nineteen paragraphs instead of four, troweling up deep layers of facts nobody else heard of. They got branded Teacher's Pet or kooky, or both. Really, they just *had* to know more. Even after the unit ended they got an extra book about planets from the library. They asked to look through a telescope. They wanted to go to a planetarium or to a geology exhibit and touch a meteorite. They sketched hypothetical spacecraft of their own. They asked *how* do we know, *when* did we learn, *why* is it like that? Maybe one of these people was you.

If so, rejoice—for the exploration of our solar system will never end. It hasn't even ended with the planet we live on. How many new species of insect, of flora, were documented this past year? What's going to be the next big unknown, tomorrow's giant tube worm? An ongoing continuum of launches fills the calendar, from nations all around the globe. More craft are set to go up, will go up, have gone up. The probes will keep coming: missions not yet dreamed up, by people who haven't been born, constructed with hardware that doesn't exist. Yet. Exploration is nothing less than a wondrous gift—a simple offering from generations who lived in the past to citizenry who are yet to come.

For those—those followers of the beat, those students who cared, who wondered how they brought dirt from the moon, or what really happened when they sought out life on Mars; for those who stared at a picture from the surface of Venus or the middle of a comet and wondered *when* they got there, *how* they nailed that shot, *what* they found? Well, now the answers are known.

Along with who *they* really were.

Sources

Books

Andersen, David P. *At the Field: Offbeat Stories about R/C Model Airplanes and the People Who Fly Them*. Burnsville MN: Scale Flyers of Minnesota, 2004. No-cost ebook at http://www.mnbigbirds.com.

Ball, Andrew J., James R. C. Garry, Ralph Lorenz, and Viktor V. Kerzhanovich. *Planetary Landers and Entry Probes*. Cambridge: Cambridge University Press, 2007.

Bar-Cohen, Yoseph, and Kris Zacny. *Drilling in Extreme Environments*. Hoboken NJ: John Wiley and Sons, 2009.

Berlin, Peter, trans., and John Rhea, ed. *Roads to Space: An Oral History of the Soviet Space Program*. New York: Aviation Week Group / McGraw-Hill, 1995.

Biemann, Hans-Peter. *The Vikings of '76*. Cambridge: Hans-Peter Biemann, 1977.

Borman, Frank, with Robert J. Serling. *Countdown: An Autobiography*. New York: Silver Arrow Books / William Morrow, 1988.

Burgess, Colin, and Chris Dubbs. *Animals in Space: From Research Rockets to the Space Shuttle*. Chichester, UK: Springer-Praxis, 2007.

Burgess, Eric. *To the Red Planet*. New York: Columbia University Press, 1978.

Burrows, William E. *Exploring Space: Voyages in the Solar System and Beyond*. New York: Random House, 1990.

Chaikin, Andrew. *A Man on the Moon: The Voyages of the Apollo Astronauts*. New York: Penguin Books, 1994.

Chertok, Boris. *Rockets and People*. Vol. 1. NASA History Series. Washington DC: NASA History Office, 2005.

———. *Rockets and People*. Vol. 2, *Creating a Rocket Industry*. NASA History Series. Washington DC: NASA History Office, 2006.

DiGregorio, Barry. *Mars: The Living Planet*. Berkeley CA: Frog, 1997.

Dumnov, Dmitry Fakeevich, and Svyatoslav Kazimirovich Sosnowsky. *Simferopol Guide* [in Russian]. Simferopol, USSR: Tavria, 1973.

Eisenhower, Susan. *Breaking Free: A Memoir of Love and Revolution*. New York: Farrar, Straus, Giroux, 1995.

Ezell, Edward Clinton, and Linda Neuman Ezell. *On Mars: Exploration of the Red Planet, 1958–1978*. Mineola NY: Dover, 2009.

Farmer, Gene, and Dora Jane Hamblin. *First on the Moon: A Voyage with Neil Armstrong, Michael Collins, and Edwin E. Aldrin Jr*. Boston: Little, Brown, 1970.

Gatland, Kenneth. *Robot Explorers*. London: Blandford Press, 1972.

Gordon, Yefim. *Lavochkin's Last Jets*. Hinckley, UK: Midland, 2007.

———. *Soviet/Russian Unmanned Aerial Vehicles*. Hinckley, UK: Midland, 2005.

Griffin, Michael D., and James R. French. *Space Vehicle Design*. 2nd ed. Reston VA: American Institute of Aeronautics and Astronautics, 2004.

Harford, James. *Korolev: How One Man Masterminded the Soviet Drive to Beat America to the Moon*. New York: John Wiley and Sons, 1997.

Harland, David M., and Ralph D. Lorenz. *Space Systems Failures: Disasters and Rescues of Satellites, Rockets and Space Probes*. Chichester, UK: Springer-Praxis, 2005.

Harvey, Brian. *The New Russian Space Program: From Competition to Collaboration*. Chichester, UK: Springer-Praxis, 1996.

———. *Russia in Space: The Failed Frontier*. Chichester, UK: Springer-Praxis, 2001.

———. *Soviet and Russian Lunar Exploration*. Chichester, UK: Springer-Praxis, 2007.

History of Strategic Air and Ballistic Missile Defense. Vol. 1, *1945–1955*. Vol. 2, *1956–1972*. Washington DC: U.S. Army Center of Military History, 2009.

Horowitz, Norman H. *To Utopia and Back: The Search for Life in the Solar System*. New York: W. H. Freeman, 1986.

Koltovaya, B., G. N. Ostrumov, B. Konovalov, S. Vernov, N. Kantor, A. Selivanov, A. Vinogradov, S. Sokolov, N. D. Shumilov, and L. N. Tolkunov. *Bridge into Space* [in Russian]. Moscow: Izvestia, 1976.

Koppes, Clayton R. *JPL and the American Space Program*. New Haven CT: Yale University Press, 1982.

Krieger, F. J. *Behind the Sputniks: A Survey of Soviet Space Science*. Washington DC: Public Affairs Press, 1958.

Marov, Mikhail. "The Discovered Space." In *Space: The First Step*, edited by Alexander Zakharov, O. Zakutnyaya, and V. Kornilenko, 249. Moscow: Space Research Institute of Russian Academy of Sciences, 2007.

Marov, Mikhail, with David H. Grinspoon. *The Planet Venus*. New Haven CT: Yale University Press, 1998.

McNab, David, and James Younger. *The Planets.* New Haven CT: Yale University Press, 1999.

Meltzer, Michael. *Mission to Jupiter: A History of the Galileo Project.* NASA SP-2007-4231. Washington DC: NASA History Division, 2007.

Perminov, Vladimir. *The Difficult Road to Mars: A Brief History of Mars Exploration in the Soviet Union.* NASA Monographs in American History, no. 15. Washington DC: NASA History Division, 1999.

Podgorodetsky, P. D., gen. ed. *Guidebook Crimea* [in Russian]. Simferopol, USSR: Tavria, 1972.

Sagdeev, Roald Z. *The Making of a Soviet Scientist: My Adventures in Nuclear Fusion and Space from Stalin to Star Wars.* New York: John Wiley and Sons, 1994.

Siddiqi, Asif. *The Soviet Space Race with Apollo.* Gainesville: University Press of Florida, 2003.

———. *Sputnik and the Soviet Space Challenge.* Gainesville: University Press of Florida, 2000.

Soviet Space Programs, 1966–1970: Goals and Purposes, Organization, Resources, Facilities and Hardware, Manned and Unmanned Flight Programs, Bioastronautics, Civil and Military Applications, Projections of Future Plans, Attitudes toward International Cooperation and Space Law. Doc. 92-51. Washington DC: U.S. Government Printing Office, 1971.

Soviet Space Programs, 1976–1980: Supporting Vehicles and Launch Vehicles, Political Goals and Purposes, International Cooperation in Space, Administration, Resource Burden, Future Outlook. Washington DC: U.S. Government Printing Office, 1982.

Ulivi, Paolo, with David M. Harland. *Lunar Exploration: Human Pioneers and Robotic Surveyors.* Chichester, UK: Springer-Praxis, 2004.

———. *Robotic Exploration of the Solar System.* Pt. 1, *The Golden Age, 1957–1982.* Chichester, UK: Springer-Praxis, 2007.

———. *Robotic Exploration of the Solar System.* Pt. 2, *Hiatus and Renewal.* Chichester, UK: Springer-Praxis, 2009.

Vorontsova, S. V., and E. A. Vorontsov. *Great Yalta.* Simferopol, USSR, 1968.

Periodicals and Online Articles

Afanasyev, I. "Without the Secret Stamp: Halt the Work, Destroy All Materials." *Aviatsiya i Kosmonavtika,* no. 6 (June 1993): 42–44.

Associated Press. "*Luna 15* Orbits Moon, Russia Remains Silent." *Pittsburgh Post-Gazette,* July 18, 1969, 1.

———. "Soviet Probe to Approach Comet Today." *Houston Chronicle*, March 6, 1986, sec. 1, 13.

———. "Soviets Remain Mum on *Luna 15* Purpose." *Owosso (MI) Argus-Press*, July 15, 1969, 2.

Bada, Jeffrey L. "State-of-the-Art Instruments for Detecting Extraterrestrial Life." *Proceedings of the National Academy of Sciences of the United States of America*, January 30, 2001, 797–800.

Barringer, Felicity. "Soviets See Little Hope of Controlling Spacecraft." *New York Times*, September 10, 1988.

Basilevsky, A. T., C. P. Florensky, and L. B. Ronca. "A Possible Lunar Outcrop: A Study of *Lunokhod 2* Data." *Moon* 17 (1977): 19–28.

Biemann, K., J. Oro, P. Toulmin III, L. E. Orgel, A. O Nier, D. M. Anderson, et al. "Search for Organic and Volatile Inorganic Compounds in Two Surface Samples from the Chryse Planitia Region of Mars." *Science*, n.s., 194, no. 4260 (October 1, 1976): 72–76.

———. "The Search for Organic Substances and Inorganic Volatile Compounds in the Surface of Mars." *Journal of Geophysical Research* 82, no. 28 (September 30, 1977): 4641–58.

Biemann, K., and John M. Lavoie Jr. "Some Final Conclusions and Supporting Experiments Related to the Search for Organic Compounds on the Surface of Mars." *Journal of Geophysical Research* 84, no. B14 (December 30, 1979): 8385–90.

"Biography of Semyon Lavochkin." Russia InfoCenter. http://www.russia-ic.com/people /education_science/374/.

Borisov, V. "Lunokhodchik Slept for Three Hours a Day and Time to Play Volleyball" [in Russian]. RIA Novosti. http://www.rian.ru/science/20101117/297239297 .html.

Brown, Jonathan. "Recording Tracks Russia's Moon Gatecrash Attempt." *London Independent*, July 3, 2009. http://www.independent.co.uk/news/science /recording-tracks-russias-moon-gatecrash-attempt-1730851.html.

Chaikin, Andrew. "The Other Moon Landings." *Air & Space Smithsonian*, March 1, 2004, 30–37.

Chandler, David L. "Is There Life on Mars? Scientists Renew Debate." *Montreal Gazette*, August 6, 1983, 1-5.

Chang, Kenneth. "No Methane, Low Methane, High Methane—Mars Has It All." *Minneapolis Star Tribune*, January 4, 2015, SH1.

Clarity, James F. "Top Soviet Aides Observe the 4th." *New York Times*, July 5, 1969, 36.

"Comet's Poisonous Tail: Yerkes Observatory Finds Cyanogen in Spectrum of Halley's Comet." *New York Times*, February 8, 1010, 1.

Corneille, Philip. "Half a Century of Venus Exploration." *BIS Spaceflight Magazine* 47 (December 2005): 454.

Dovgan, Vyacheslav. "'Lunar Wanderer' Left a Tracke." *Military Parade*, no. 2 (2010): 54–56.

———. "Patriotic Lunar Odyssey" [in Russian]. *Physics*, no. 2 (2010). http://fiz.1september.ru/articles/2010/12/11.

———. "Remote Control of Moon Rovers and Planet Research Vehicles" [in Russian]. *Earth and Universe*, no. 2 (2005): 76–81.

Dye, Lee. "Soviet Mission to Photograph Comet Called 'a Triumph.'" *Los Angeles Times*, March 7, 1986.

———. "Spacecraft Zeros In on Little Moon." *Anchorage Daily News*, February 23, 1989, A1.

Eaton, William J. "Soviet Probe of Halley's Comet Called a Success." *Los Angeles Times*, March 10, 1986.

Florensky, C. P., A. T. Basilevsky, N. N. Bobina, G. A. Burba, N. N. Grebennik, R. O. Kuzmin, B. P. Polosukhin, V. D. Popovich, and A. A. Pronin. "The Floor of Crater Le Monnier: A Study of *Lunokhod 2* Data." *Proceedings of the Ninth Lunar and Planetary Scientific Conference*, 1978, 1449–58.

Gascon, Louis. "Piloto de Lunakhod." http://www.espacial.org/astronautica/sondas_robots/piloto_lunakhod2.htm.

"Georgi Babakin." *Flight International*, August 19, 1971.

"Giant Step for Lunokhod." *Time*, November 30, 1970.

Gracieux, Serge. "*Luna 15*, le joker Soviétique" [*Luna 15*, the Soviet joker]. *Espace*, May–June 2005, 36–41. (Translated by Philip Corneille.)

Horowitz, N. H., G. L. Hobby, and Jerry S. Hubbard. "The Viking Carbon Assimilation Experiments: Interim Report." *Science* 194 (December 17, 1976): 1321–22.

———. "Viking on Mars: The Carbon Assimilation Experiments." *Journal of Geophysical Research* 82, no. 28 (September 30, 1977): 4659–62.

Hubbard, Jerry S., James P. Hardy, and N. H. Horowitz. "Photocatalytic Production of Organic Compounds from CO and H_2O in a Simulated Martian Atmosphere." *Proceedings of the National Academy of Sciences* 68, no. 3 (March 1971): 574–78.

Klein, Harold, Norman H. Horowitz, Gilbert V. Levin, Vance I. Oyama, Joshua Lederberg, Alexander Rich, et al. "The Viking Biological Investigation: Preliminary Results." *Science*, n.s., 194, no. 4260 (October 1, 1976): 99–105.

Kostyrchenko, Gennadii. "The Abakumov-Shvartsman Case." *Russian Studies in History* 43, no. 2 (Fall 2004): 85–94.

Kotulak, Ronald. "Hitching a Ride Fulfills Dream for a Comet Watcher." *Chicago Tribune*, March 2, 1986.

Kremnev, Roald S., A. S. Selivanov, V. M. Linkin, A. N. Lipatov, I. Ia. Tranoruder, V. I. Puchkov, V. D. Kustodiev, A. A. Shurupov, B. Ragent, and R. A. Preston. "The Vega Balloons: A Tool for Studying Atmosphere Dynamics on Venus." *Soviet Astronomy Letters* 12, no. 1 (January–February 1986): 7–9.

Krulwich, Robert. "Neil Armstrong Talks about the First Moon Walk." *Krulwich Wonders* (blog). December 8, 2010. NPR.org. http://www.npr.org/blogs/krulwich/2010/12/08/131910930/neil-armstrong-talks-about-the-first-moon-walk?sc=emaf.

Lambert, Pam. "Warming Trend." *People*, September 11, 1995, 79.

Lauterbach, Richard E. "Stalin at 65." *Life*, January 1, 1945, 64.

Levin, Gilbert V., and Patricia Ann Straat. "Antarctic Soil No. 726 and Implications for the Viking Labeled Release Experiment." *Journal of Theoretical Biology* 91, no. 1 (July 7, 1981): 41–45

———. "Recent Results from the Viking Labeled Release Experiment on Mars." *Journal of Geophysical Research* 82, no. 28 (September 30, 1977): 4663–67.

Lewis, Tom. "'A Godlike Presence': The Impact of Radio on the 1920s and 1930s." "Communication in History: The Key to Understanding," special issue, OAH *Magazine of History* (Organization of American Historians) 6, no. 4 (Spring 1992): 26–33.

Luckett, Don. "CSR's Patricia Straat Retires." *NIH Record*, March 6, 2001. http://nihrecord.od.nih.gov/newsletters/03_06_2001/retirees.htm.

"*Luna 15* Is No Threat to Apollo, Soviets Say." *St. Petersburg (FL) Times*, July 19, 1969, 1.

"*Luna 18* Landing Attempt 'Unlucky.'" *Sarasota (FL) Herald-Tribune*, September 12, 1971, 8A.

"*Luna 20* Returns with Moon Soil." *Bowling Green (OH) Daily News*, February 27, 1972, 5.

"*Luna 20* Samples the Oldest Yet?" *Deseret News* (Salt Lake City UT), February 26, 1972, 1.

"*Luna 20* Sends Back Samples." *Bowling Green (OH) Daily News*, February 20, 1972, 10.

Markov, Yuri. "Chief Designer of Interplanetary Stations." *Science in Russia*, 2004-12-31SIR-No. 006 (2004): 70–76.

"Mission of *Luna 15* Remains a Mystery." *Pennsylvania Reading Eagle*, July 22, 1969, 6.

Molodtsov, Vladimir A. "About the Death of Automatic Station Phobos" [in Russian]. *Novosti Kosmonavtiki* 254, no. 3 (2004): 36–38.

"The Moon: Scoopy, Snoopy or Sour Grapes?" *Time*, July 25, 1969.

Mukhopadhyay, Rajendrani. "The Viking GC/MS and the Search for Organics on Mars." *Analytical Chemistry* 79, no. 19 (October 1, 2007): 7249–56.

"One of Four Soviet Mars Shots Will Attempt Landing." *St. Joseph (MO) Gazette*, September 24, 1973, 6A.

Oyama, Vance I., and Bonnie J. Berdahl. "The Viking Gas Exchange Experiment Results from Chryse and Utopia Surface Samples." *Journal of Geophysical Research* 82, no. 28 (September 30, 1977): 4669–76.

Parker, Eugene N. "John Alexander Simpson, 3 November 1916–31 August 2000." *Proceedings of the American Philosophical Society* 150, no. 3 (September 2006): 500–503.

"People." *Time*, July 11, 1969.

Quinn, Richard C., et al. "Perchlorate Radiolysis on Mars and the Origin of Martian Solar Reactivity." *Astrobiology* 13 (2013): 515–20.

Ratmansky, Vladimir. "Lunar Motion" [in Russian]. *Evening Moscow*. http://www.vm .ru/news/2007/04/12/lunnij-hod-32451.html.

"Red Claims Hard Mass Covers Moon." *Spokane (WA) Spokesman-Review*, December 17, 1961, 8.

"Reds Disclose That *Luna 15* No Threat to U.S. Astronauts." *Bend (OR) Bulletin*, July 18, 1969, 1.

Safire, William. "Nixon Prepared for an Apollo Disaster." *Minneapolis Star Tribune*, July 13, 1999, A11.

Samodelova, Svetlana. "Little-Known Facts about Georgiy Babakin" [in Russian]. *Evening Moscow*, May 7, 2008. http://www.vm.ru/news/2008/05/07/maloizvestnie -fakti-biografii-georgiya-babakina-56557.html.

"Sends Signals to Earth." *Daytona Beach (FL) Morning Journal*, December 8, 1971.

Shanker, Tom. "A Glimpse of the Beginning." *Chicago Tribune*, March 7, 1986.

———. "Scientists Put Heads Together in Unraveling Comet Mystery." *Chicago Tribune*, March 11, 1986.

Shevalev, I. L. "Six Years and the Whole Life of Designer G. N. Babakin" [in Russian]. *Moscow Oblast* (Khimki), 2004.

Siegel, Lee. "American TV Audience Watches Soviet Spacecraft Pictures of Halley's Comet." Associated Press. http://www.apnewsarchive.com/1986/URGENT -American-TV-Audience-Watches-Soviet-Spacecraft-Pictures-Of-Halley-s -Comet/id-9c94667e49d212ca0323a12ec9e3c315.

Skelley, Alison, James R. Scherer, Andrew D. Aubrey, William H. Grover, Robin H. C. Ivester, Pascale Ehrenfreund, Frank J. Grunthaner, Jeffrey L. Bada, and Richard A. Mathies. "Development and Evaluation of a Microdevice for Amino Acid Biomarker Detection and Analysis on Mars." *Proceedings of the National Academy of Sciences of the United States of America* 102, no. 4 (2005): 1041–46.

Smollar, David. "Astronomers Getting Set for the Event of a Lifetime." *Los Angeles Times*, March 11, 1985.

"Soviet-Launched Space Probe to Slide by Venus." *Schenectady (NY) Gazette*, December 22, 1984, 1.

"Soviet *Luna 20* to Orbit Moon." *Bonham (TX) Daily Favorite*, February 14, 1972, 2.

"Soviets on the Moon 40th Anniversary." Ekaterinburg.com. November 17, 2010. http://www.ekaterinburg.com/news/spool/news_id-338917-section_id-102 .html.

Stelzried, C. T., R. A. Preston, C. E. Hildebrand, J. H. Wilcher, and J. Ellis. "The Venus Balloon Project." *TDA Progress Report* 42, no. 85 (January–March 1986): 191–98.

Stockton, Bill. "Soviet Mars Missions Puzzle Scientists." *Free Lance-Star* (Fredericksburg VA), December 1, 1971, 23.

Trivedi, Bijal. "Giant Tubeworms Probed for Clues to Survival." National Geographic Today. October 28, 2002. http://news.nationalgeographic.com/news/2002 /10/1028_021028_TVtubeworm.html.

"Vegas at Venus—I." *Sky & Telescope*, September 1986, 231–32.

Wagner, Erica. "How US Was Nearly Pipped to First Moon Rock Samples." *London Times*, July 3, 2009. http://www.thetimes.co.uk/tto/science/space/article 1967374.ece.

Waldrop, M. Mitchell. "Phobos at Mars: A Dramatic View—And Then Failure." *Science* 245 (September 8, 1989): 1044–45.

Zaloga, Steven J. "Defending the Capitals: The First Generation of Soviet Strategic Air Defense Systems, 1950–1960." *Journal of Slavic Military Studies* 10 (December 1997): 30–43.

Interviews and Personal Communications

Babakin, Nikolay. Interview by the author, February 20, 2011, and related correspondence regarding the Lavochkin Design Bureau along with the life and work of his father, Georgiy Babakin.

Basilevsky, Alexander. Interview by the author, September 16, 2010, and related correspondence.

Biemann, Klaus. Interviews by the author, October 18 and November 22, 2011, and related correspondence.

Blamont, Jacques. Interview by the author, June 24, 2012, and related correspondence.

Borman, Frank. Interview by the author, October 7, 2009, and related correspondence.

Brooks, Michael. Emails beginning December 10, 2012, regarding Gil Levin's comments during Viking press conferences.

Casani, John. Interview by the author, April 24, 2007.

Dovgan, Vyacheslav. Emails and letters beginning December 21, 2010, regarding his experiences on Lunokhod.

Dzhuly, Alexander. Numerous emails beginning January 14, 2011, regarding the geography, culture, and history of the Crimean Peninsula, including details of Simferopol and Shkolnoye.

Friedman, Louis. Email dated December 9, 2011, regarding particulars of the proposed Mars balloon "snake."

Hearth, Donald P. Interviews by the author, June 14 and September 14, 2011, and related correspondence.

Hobby, George. Email dated October 26, 2012, regarding Viking recollections.

Horowitz, Elizabeth. Emails dated February 12–28, 2013, regarding the life and work of her father, Norman H. Horowitz.

Horowitz, Joel L. Emails beginning February 26, 2013, regarding the life and work of his father, Norman H. Horowitz.

Horowitz, Norman H. Interviews by Rachel Prud'homme, July 9 and 10, 1984. Copy in author's possession.

Hubbard, Jerry. Interview by the author, December 13, 2011, and related correspondence.

Kerzhanovich, Viktor. Interviews by the author, May 7 and 12, 2012, and related correspondence.

Khrushchev, Sergei. Telephone conversations with the author on January 17, January 18, and January 24, 2014, and related correspondence regarding Soviet postwar missile defense systems.

Kraft, Christopher C. Interview by the author, October 19, 2009, and related correspondence.

Kuzmin, Ruslan. Email on January 26, 2011, regarding miscellaneous details of the termination of *Lunokhod 2*'s mission.

Lederberg, Joshua. Interview by Edward Ezell, August 23, 1977, and by Steven J. Dick, November 12, 1992. Copies in author's possession.

Lee, Gentry B. Telephone calls and emails, March–July 2014, regarding the Viking Mars Project.

Levin, Gilbert V. Interview by the author, May 10, 2011, and related correspondence.

Mahaffy, Paul. Email exchange on March 22, 2015, regarding the discoveries of soil-based organic compounds, as well as airborne methane, by the Sample Analysis at Mars (SAM) instrument aboard the Mars Science Laboratory *Curiosity*.

Malenkov, Mikhail. Numerous emails between November 25, 2010, and February 11, 2011, regarding Institute 100 and particulars of Lunokhod chassis development (in Russian).

O'Hara, Bonnie Berdahl. Comments on chapter drafts dated January 29, 2013, regarding design and operation of the Viking Gas Exchange Experiment.

Peterson, Eric. Interview by the author, September 15, 2011, and related correspondence concerning organic chemistry and GCMS operation.

Preston, Robert. Interview by the author, June 10, 2013, and related correspondence.

Pryadchenko, Revmira. Interview by Alexander Dzhuly, April 4, 2011 (in Russian). Copy in author's possession.

Rozentsveyg, Izrail. Numerous letters and emails beginning February 11, 2011, regarding Institute 100 and particulars of Lunokhod chassis development (in Russian).

Sagdeev, Roald. Interviews by the author, May 24, 25, and 26, 2010.

Smith, Peter. Emails on October 15 and 16, 2012, regarding the Phoenix Mars mission and its testing for organic compounds.

Straat, Patricia Ann. Interviews by the author, September 5, 2011, July 14 and October 20, 2012, and related correspondence.

Woeller, Fritz. Numerous emails beginning October 19, 2012, regarding Ames Lab's Life Detection Systems Branch and the people involved with Viking's Gas Exchange Experiment.

Worden, Alfred. Interview by Francis French, September 2010. Copy in author's possession.

Other Sources

ALEXANDER BASILEVSKY, PRIVATE COLLECTION

Basilevsky, Alexander. "Diary L2." January–June 1973.

JERRY HUBBARD, PRIVATE COLLECTION

Horowitz, Norman. Letter to Edward C. Ezell, "Outrageous misrepresentation of work." February 28, 1986.

———. Letter to Jerry Hubbard, "Selection of Viking Biology Experiments." November 24, 1982.

Hubbard, Jerry. "Prediction for Curiosity Analysis of Soil Organics Based on Viking Biology Findings." Unpublished manuscript.

ROBERT PRESTON, PRIVATE COLLECTION

Ingersoll, Andrew. "Journal of Vega Trip to Moscow, February 7–18, 1985."
Preston, Robert. Internal JPL memo, "The balloon mission lives!" October 29, 1982.
———. Personal notes, "Comments on Soviet Delta-VLBI Proposal." September 28, 1979.
Preston, Robert, and D. Curkendall. Letter to Michel Lefebvre, "Design for international balloon tracking network." July 25, 1980.

Barton, Larry. "Luna 15 Salvage Ship." Editorial cartoon. *Toledo (OH) Blade*, July 23, 1969, 24.
Bogatchev, Alexei. "Soviet and Russian Planetary & Mobile Robots 1963–2007." Part of the guest lecture material from course AS.84-3144, Field and Service Robotics, Helsinki Automation Technology Laboratory.
Dologoprudny Design Bureau website. www.dkba.ru/. [In Russian.]
Grahn, Sven. Sven's Space Page. http://www.svengrahn.pp.se/.
Jet Propulsion Laboratory, California Institute of Technology. "How NASA Curiosity Instrument Made First Detection of Organic Matter on Mars." News release, December 16, 2014. http://www.jpl.nasa.gov/news/news.php?feature=4414.
———. "NASA Rover Finds Active and Ancient Organic Chemistry on Mars." News release, December 16, 2014. http://www.jpl.nasa.gov/news/news.php?feature=4413.
Kassel, Simon. *Lunokhod-1 Soviet Lunar Surface Vehicle*. Rand Corporation, report R-802-ARPA, prepared for the Advanced Research Projects Agency, September 1971.
Lavoie, John Milan, Jr. "Support Experiments to the Pyrolysis/Gas Chromatographic/Mass Spectrometric Analysis of the Surface of Mars." PhD thesis, Massachusetts Institute of Technology, 1979.
Meyer, Charles, comp. "*Luna 24* Drill Core." In *The Lunar Sample Compendium*. Prepared for Astromaterials Research and Exploration Science, Lyndon B. Johnson Space Center. Astromaterials Acquisition and Curation Office, NASA. http://curator.jsc.nasa.gov/lunar/lsc/Luna24Core.pdf.
Ming, D. W., H. V. Lauer Jr., P. D. Archer Jr., B. Sutter, D. C. Golden, R. V. Morris, P. B. Niles, and W. V. Boynton. "Combustion of Organic Molecules by the Thermal Decomposition of Perchlorate Salts: Implications

for Organics at the Mars Phoenix Scout Landing Site." Paper presented
at the Fortieth Lunar and Planetary Science Conference, Houston TX,
March 23–27, 2009. http://ntrs.nasa.gov/archive/nasa/casi.ntrs.nasa.gov
/20090010422_2009010505.pdf.

Mitchell, Don P. Mental Landscape (personal webpage). www.mentallandscape.com.

NASA. "Apollo 11 Technical Air-to-Ground Transcript." OCR HTML version courtesy Thomas Schwagmeier. Apollo 11 Lunar Surface Journal, Raw Voice
Transcripts, NASA. http://history.nasa.gov/alsj/a11/a11transcript_tec.html.

———. *Fourth Semiannual Report to Congress, April 1, 1960 through September
30, 1960.*

———. "National Aeronautics and Space Administration Organizational Chart."
November 1, 1961.

NASA, Life-Detection Experiments Team. *A Survey of Life-Detection Experiments.*
Moffet Field CA: National Aeronautics and Space Administration, Ames
Research Center, August 1963.

NASA, Office of Space Science and Applications. "Summary of the Voyager Program." January 1967.

"Norman Horowitz Memorial Service." Audio recording made at Dabney Lounge
and Gardens, Caltech. September 12, 2005.

The Planets. BBC Television/A&E Network. Executive Producer John Lynch, Series
Producer David McNab. 1999.

Rauschenbach, Boris V. "The Soviet Program of Moon Surface Research (1966–
1979)." Paper presented at the Twenty-Eighth History Symposium of the
International Academy of Astronautics, Jerusalem, Israel, 1994.

Sagan, Carl. "Wolf Vladimir Vishniac: An Obituary." Unpublished version with
handwritten corrections and comments.

Sokolov, Oleg A. "The Race to the Moon: A Look Back from Baikonour." Paper
presented at the Twenty-Eighth History Symposium of the International
Academy of Astronautics, Jerusalem, Israel, 1994.

"Soviets on the Moon: Secrets of 'Lunar Tanks.'" YouTube video. From a report
on Russia Today. Uploaded November 17, 2010. http://www.youtube.com
/watch?v=GFIFO8fVVWM.

S. P. Korolev Rocket and Space Corporation website. http://www.energia.ru/english/.

Suckow, Elizabeth. "Hidden Headquarters." PowerPoint presentation at brown
bag meeting, NASA headquarters, March 24, 2009.

"Tank on the Moon." Disclose.tv, from a Science Channel program. Uploaded
July 13, 2012. http://www.disclose.tv/action/viewvideo/108208/Science
_Channel_Tank_On_The_Moon_720p/.

U. S. National Photographic Interpretation Center. "SIMFEROPOL SPACE FLIGHT CENTER: DEPLOYED COMM/ELEC/RADAR FACILITIES USSR JUNE 1969." Declassified report. February 22, 2007. www.kik-sssr.ru/download /Otchet_NPIC_b.ym_1969.pdf.

Zak, Anatoly. Russian Space Web. www.russianspaceweb.com.

Index

Bold They Rise
David Hitt and Heather R. Smith
Foreword by Bob Crippen

Go, Flight! The Unsung Heroes of Mission Control, 1965–1992
Rick Houston and Milt Heflin
Foreword by John Aaron

*Infinity Beckoned: Adventuring Through the
Inner Solar System, 1969–1989*
Jay Gallentine
Foreword by Bobak Ferdowsi